ECONOMIC TRANSITION IN EASTERN EUROPE AND RUSSIA

Realities of Reform

Edited by
EDWARD P. LAZEAR

HOOVER INSTITUTION PRESS
Stanford University   Stanford, California

Hoover Institution Press Publication No. 425

Copyright © 1995 by the Board of Trustees of the
  Leland Stanford Junior University

First printing, 1995
01 00 99 98 97 96 95   9 8 7 6 5 4 3 2 1
First paperback printing, 1995
01 00 99 98 97 96 95   9 8 7 6 5 4 3 2 1

Manufactured in the United States of America

The paper used in this publication meets the minimum requirements
of American National Standard for Information Sciences—Permanence
of Paper for Printed Library Materials, ANSI Z39.48–1984. ∞

Library of Congress Cataloging-in-Publication Data

Economic transition in Eastern Europe and Russia :
realities of reform / edited by Edward P. Lazear.
        p.   cm.
    Includes bibliographical references and index.
    ISBN 0-8179-9331-2. — ISBN 0-8179-9332-0 (pbk.)
    1. Europe, Eastern—Economic conditions—1989–   2. Europe,
Eastern—Economic policy—1989–   3. Post-communism—
Economic aspects—Europe, Eastern.   4. Russia (Federation)—
Economic conditions—1991–   5. Russia (Federation)—Economic
policy—1991–   I. Lazear, Edward P.
HC244.E24474   1995
338.947—dc20
                                        94-42148
                                        CIP

Contents

Preface

It has now been almost a half-decade since the fall of communism in Eastern Europe. Enough information is now available to take stock. We can now begin to determine which policies are effective and which are counterproductive.

This book consists of thirteen self-contained essays on economic and political reform in Eastern Europe. The first essay is a general statement of the problem and assessment of the results. It is followed by more specific discussions of the most important issues that face transition economies. Essay topics cover political and economic freedom to monetary and fiscal control, privatization, labor markets and social safety nets, crime, and taxation. A discussion of China is also included for the purpose of comparison. Our goal is to present academically responsible work that is accessible to the interested layperson.

PART ONE
INTRODUCTION

1

Economic Reform: Appropriate Steps and Actual Policies

EDWARD P. LAZEAR

Successful market economies have a number of prevalent features, including generally free prices, a large amount of privately owned capital, and a stable monetary system. This introduction first details the key features of a market economy and discusses their role in creating a highly productive environment. Second, it examines and evaluates the courses followed by the transition economies of Eastern Europe. Countries have undertaken economic reform at various paces, with the Czech Republic and Poland seeming to have adopted the most dramatic steps. Third, it is argued that there is no evidence that rapid economic reform has led to short-term declines in output, as is sometimes alleged. Rather, output declines have come about because of the disruption in trade and requisite reorganization of the industrial structure caused by the dissolution of the Council of Mutual Economic Assistance.

IT HAS BEEN ALMOST HALF A DECADE since the communist governments of Eastern Europe crumbled under the pressure of demands for political and economic freedom. The disintegration of the Soviet Union, an event even more surprising than those that befell the former satellites, has brought opportunity and challenge to a region that was smothered by communism for half a century.

The destruction of communism in Eastern Europe was met with hopes of political self-determination and rapid economic progress. Free elections were held in virtually all previously totalitarian states, and for the most part, democracy, punctuated by some significant deviations, has been the rule. Economic progress has been somewhat slower in coming, with most countries suffering, at least initially, a decline in the average standard of living.

Even politics have not moved steadily in one direction. Poland, Lithuania, Russia, and, most recently, Hungary have experienced elections where discontent with current economic progress led the electorate to "throw the bums out." In Poland, Lithuania, and Hungary, this has meant a move back toward the left. In Russia, a strong nationalist group, led by Vladimir Zhirinovsky, surprised Boris Yeltsin and his liberal-minded followers.

Despite the inability of Warsaw to transform itself into Frankfurt overnight, or of Budapest to attain the wealth of Vienna in the five years since the fall of communism, the public's reaction against the policies of reform is based on poor public relations, rather than reality. In this book, we examine some of those policies and discuss their impacts on political and economic progress.

In particular, this introduction will attempt to do three things. First, it will discuss the basic ingredients of economic reform. Second, it will summarize critically some of the actions taken and consequences undergone by the transition economies in Eastern Europe and in China. Third, it will outline a case for the efficacy of such reform policies, ascribing the current failures to their proper causes. Additionally, because so much has happened since 1989, a chronicle of significant events in Eastern European economic reform is presented in the appendix to this chapter.

How to Create a Successful Market Economy

We know a great deal more about the necessary components of a successful market economy than we do about the steps to getting there. Clichés

Comments from Misha Klimenko are gratefully acknowledged. I would like to thank Muriel Karr for compiling the material in the appendix.

support both slow and rapid transitions. For example, proponents of rapid change state that "it is better to jump over a chasm with one large stride than with two short ones" and that "a dog prefers to have his tail cut off in one stroke rather than a little at a time." But "Rome wasn't built in a day," and "haste makes waste." None of these pieces of popular wisdom is particularly useful in guiding the speed of transition.[1]

Let us begin with the easier task of describing the factors that characterize a well-functioning market economy, most of which were absent before 1989 in the former satellites and before 1991 in the former USSR. Since then, a number of changes have moved the economies closer to a market structure, but none has been complete.

Economic Reform in Eastern Europe

One of the most important aspects of a market economy is the ability of prices of both goods and services to adjust to supply and demand. Any restriction on prices causes distortions, which then get amplified throughout the economy. In the former command economies prices were set by the centralized authority, rather than by market forces. Those prices, which, at least in theory, need bear no relation to true market prices, caused severe shortages of some goods and services.

As of 1994, much progress has been made in bringing prices to market levels. In Bulgaria, Czechoslovakia, Hungary, Poland, and Romania, prices have been liberalized. Russia, too, freed many of its prices in the early days after the August 1991 coup. It is important to free up prices for a number of reasons. First, as already mentioned, constraining prices results in distortions. When bread is cheap, people buy too much of it and waste it or feed it to their animals. When energy is cheap, industry engages in inefficient methods of production. For example, in Czechoslovakia, highly polluting brown coal was burned because it was available at relatively low prices. The harder, high-calorie black coal was reserved for more privileged cities such as Moscow. Were Czechoslovakians charged even low world prices, the highly polluting soft coal would have been too inefficient to use because its cost-to-output ratio would have then been too high.

Another example is housing, which was allocated, in large part, through queues based on seniority in the particular firm or the length of time that an individual's name was on a list at a municipality. Need or desire for a particular kind of house played only a minor role in allocating scarce housing resources, so that people were misassigned to various housing units. For example, an old person, by virtue of seniority, might have been assigned a relatively large, well-located apartment. At market prices, the old individual would be unwilling to live in that space, but he continued to hold onto the apartment because of seniority rights. In a market economy, even if the individual owned the space, she or he would have the right to sell it or to sublet it. In fact, activity of this sort now occurs even in the constrained housing market.

Housing and energy are mentioned as examples and because they are the two most important commodities that continue to have constrained prices in Eastern Europe. The production technologies used, and the distribution of individuals across housing, remain inefficient as a consequence.

Constrained prices not only create distortions but also cause corruption. When prices are set below their market levels, the ability to obtain a good can be a valuable asset. As a result, those in control of allocating scarce goods have power and the ability to extract money from an economy. For example, a store manager who is in charge of selling goods priced well below market level can sell places in the queue to individuals, sometimes for high prices.[2] Managers have an interest in maintaining the system of low prices because doing so provides them with power and brings about a transfer of wealth from the general society to the managerial group.[3] Additionally, those who are not directly involved in management but who can, through a variety of means, obtain goods illegally are then in a position to sell those goods for high prices. Thus, the distortion creates an incentive for individuals to engage in illegal or quasi-legal activity. In a market economy anyone who can steal a good and resell it at the market price can make money on the transaction but theft is unnecessary in an economy where prices are constrained. A black marketer profits by buying from individuals who wait in the queue for goods at state prices and then reselling to individuals who are unwilling to wait in the queue. Such activity is efficiency enhancing because it allocates goods to those individuals who are willing to pay the most for them; an adverse side effect is creating a class of individuals who are willing to break the law in order to profit.[4]

Allowing prices to go to market levels will impose severe hardships on certain segments of the population if not offset by other policies. For example, low-income individuals were implicitly receiving food and housing subsidies by being able to purchase those goods at low prices. When the prices of the goods on which they spend a large portion of their budget increase, those individuals become relatively worse off. Rather than constraining prices and creating distortions throughout the whole economy, however, it is better to allow prices to move to their market levels and subsidize low-income individuals to cover the increase in the prices of those necessities.

Most countries made the self-defeating mistake of attempting to increase all wages by a percentage that reflected the increase in price levels. The relevant subsidies should have covered subsistence levels of necessities only, making available a very small portion of total income to high-wage earners and a much larger portion of total income to low-wage earners. An even more directed policy would pass the subsidies on only to those individuals whose incomes were below a certain level; in this way, lower rates of overall inflation would be obtained without any significant redistribution.

ENCOURAGING PRIVATE CAPITAL

Virtually everyone who has thought about moving to a market economy realizes that its essential feature is that most industry is run privately, with ownership in private hands. Under communism, of course, most industry was state controlled, with various levels of government having claim to the implicit profits of the enterprise. There are two ways to move an economy from state to private ownership. The first, and the one most frequently discussed, is privatizing state enterprises. In fact, a great deal of progress has been made on privatization, primarily in small and middle-sized firms. Many large firms, and those that were involved in the defense industry, still remain under state control. The second way for firms to foster a private economy is to allow the spontaneous creation of new enterprises to compete with the state-controlled firms, which is how economies are likely to move ahead. Important here is eliminating state controls, which prevent firms from establishing competitive enterprises. Institutions such as licensure and permits or high levels of taxation (discussed later) can prevent what would otherwise be a thriving private sector from coming into existence.

The importance of privatizing existing state enterprises varies from country to country. In some countries, the state enterprises were so unproductive, and the capital so inefficient and out of date, that privatizing them would not do much to further the growth of the economy. But in other countries, most notably the Czech Republic, some high-quality state firms are producing goods that can be competitive even at world market prices. Privatizing these firms contributes to the growth of the Czech economy.

There are a number of reasons to privatize state firms. The first, and the one most frequently mentioned, has to do with incentives. It is often argued that state firms do not provide workers and managers with appropriate incentives, as private firms do. That argument is only partly correct. Private firms must produce efficiently or be driven out of business by the market. State firms can be protected through the use of licensure and other exclusionary devices. But not all private firms provide the appropriate incentives for their managers. Indeed, one criticism often leveled at large corporations is that their managers become entrenched and end up behaving like the managers of state-run enterprises. The difference, of course, is that in a private firm, managers who do not behave efficiently and in the interests of the shareholders can be removed. Although the same may be true for state-run enterprises, removing a manager depends on governmental politics, not on economics or industrial politics.

Second, incentives can be provided to managers of state-owned firms even without privatization. As McMillan (1994) points out, Chinese firms (which are collectively owned) and other state-run organizations provide their management with strong incentives to produce profitable products, not just high levels of unwanted output.

Still, aligning the incentives of managers with those of the economy is done almost automatically in a market with private firms. When state firms are involved, more conscious intervention is required, and there are fewer guarantees that the state firm will get it right, especially because such firms are often prevented from going out of business. Poor managers or inefficient management techniques can persist for long periods of time in state organizations. The solution to this problem is to allow competition. Competition can come from domestic firms created by individual entrepreneurs who see an opportunity to produce a product that is better or cheaper than that produced by the state or from foreign suppliers who can provide goods and services more efficiently than can be done internally. Both routes, if encouraged, are likely to lead to higher rates of growth for the transition economy.

Beyond incentives are other reasons privatization is an important feature of a growing economy. When capital is owned by the state, economic and political issues tend to be confounded through two primary avenues. First, the government tends to protect its own industries. This is true not only in Eastern European countries but also in Western ones. For example, in the United States it is illegal to compete with the U. S. Post Office for the delivery of first-class mail. The state may be no worse than private entities desiring to protect their businesses from competition; the difference is that the state has the authority to act on its desire.

The second way politics and economics get confused is that individuals use economic means to accomplish political ends when the state owns capital. For example, Romanian sailors demanded favorable treatment for the goods they brought into Romania from foreign lands. They did not want to pay the duty that was levied on other importers but wanted to sell their goods within Romania. When the government refused their demands, they went on strike, which was a reasonable strategy because the government owned the shipping company and a strike directly affected the state's revenues. A strike against a private enterprise might have indirect effects on government revenues, but the links are less close. When the state owns the capital, workers and consumers can influence the state by exerting economic pressure on industries in which the state is involved.

ESTABLISHING PRIVATE FARMS

The distribution of private plots across countries varies significantly. Poland, for example, has always had significant amounts of private agriculture. Ukraine, by contrast, has virtually no formal private agriculture, but individuals tend to have their own gardens (dachas) outside the cities, where they grow many of the fruits and vegetables that they eat during the year. Russia is in the middle: Although the ability to have private plots, the output of which belongs to the individual who works it, has been available for the past few years, private agriculture is still somewhat limited.

Limitations on private agriculture result, in part, from the inability to obtain the necessary complementary factors of production partly because of a lack of demand. For example, in Ukraine farms are very large and the equipment used to work them, extremely expensive. An individual farmer could not possibly afford to buy such equipment, and no private firms exist to rent it. But it is common in agriculture, when plots are small, to share equipment by having another firm supply tractors, combines, and other large equipment to the small farms for a fee. (The provision of such services is almost an automatic consequence of private-sector agriculture.) But some financial considerations may come into play. Because the large pieces of equipment are expensive, some individual or group of individuals must raise sufficient capital to purchase the equipment in the first place. In an economy where capital markets are still in their embryonic stages, raising the necessary capital may be difficult.

Another issue that comes up in agriculture privatization is not unique to agriculture but seems to carry particular force there. Local farm managers and bureaucrats may oppose any privatization of agriculture because it erodes their power. Indeed, privatization will significantly erode bureaucrats' power, but bureaucrats can be bribed to give up some of their power. The Chinese example is instructive. When the Chinese decided to allow individuals to farm their own plots of land, they allowed local party people to allocate the land to the villagers. In so doing, the party bureaucrats were able to extract rent but in an efficient manner. As a result, bureaucrats were essentially bought out of obstructing the movement to a freer economy, and all parties benefited. This may be viewed as offensive by some, but it is probably an important consideration in many countries currently involved in marketization; indeed, it is likely a small price to pay for sustained improvements in the long-run output of agriculture. The numerous examples from China provide overwhelming evidence to the efficacy of such a move.

CREATING COMPETITION AND DESTROYING MONOPOLY

Monopoly generally results in restricted output and higher prices. Many economies in Eastern Europe are characterized by one or two firms producing most of the output of a particular kind for the entire economy. For an economy to function efficiently, its monopolies must be broken up so that competition can prevail, ensuring lower prices and higher levels of output.

Creating competition is in part a result of the privatization process. When firms are privatized, the ways in which firms are broken up and distributed to new entities will affect competition. For example, if a large state-run factory is sold as a single unit, it is unlikely that its new owners will choose to break it into two units that compete with one another. By contrast, if two separate entities are created, competition between them is a natural consequence. Although nothing automatically prevents merging these two entities into one large monopolistic firm, implementing the merger may be difficult, particularly when capital markets do not function particularly well and when individuals who run the separate entities have vested interests in maintaining control over a large part of the organization.

Competition also is affected by the willingness of the state to allow domestic and foreign competition. As mentioned earlier, a program of strict licensure will tend to reduce the amount of competition in a society. An economy where firms are free to begin business without major restrictions and where foreign competition is permitted is likely to have a competitive environment, high levels of output, and low prices.

WELL-DEFINED PROPERTY RIGHTS

In going from a command economy, where almost all property is owned or controlled by the state, to a market economy, where individuals control their own property, an entire new set of rules must be established. The sanctity of private residual claims ensures a well-functioning capital market. Under communism, when the state owned all the capital, the state (or the collective population) was the residual claimant. If things went badly in a particular industry, the society as a whole bore the costs. If things went well in a particular industry, the society as a whole, at least in theory, reaped the value. With the move to private capital, *individuals* can now be big winners or big losers. That the private market eliminates the risk sharing and insurance function previously played by the state is sometimes difficult for a society to accept, especially when it involves large losses to particular individuals. When people who make bad decisions are significantly hurt by those decisions, it is often difficult or impossible for the rest of society to stand by and refuse to help those persons out. This happens not only in command economies but in market economies like the United States; individuals who buy property close to a river that floods find that the government will bail them out when their house and possessions are lost to heavy rains. But the tendency to bail out losers in the former communist countries may be greater because the history of communism has made bailouts an acceptable part of economic activity; indeed, the entire program of subsidies to state enterprises is, in part, a reflection of this tendency to bail out losers.

There is also an unwillingness to tolerate large winners. Individuals who invest in private activity and make large fortunes as a result of skill, hard work, and sometimes good luck are frequently subject to criticism from the rest of society. Their windfalls are not only looked at jealously but are thought to reflect antisocial behavior. This, too, is not surprising, given the historical context. Under the old system, the only way an individual could get rich was by opportunistically exploiting the system, gaming against the government to garner a larger part of society's resources for oneself. But private investment is an important component of a market economy, and individuals need to be able to reap most of the benefits that would accrue to those investments without having them taxed away or confiscated outright.

Concern by investors, both domestic and foreign, about the stability and sanctity of their investments is not without foundation. Society has already deemed certain activities to be beneficial, whereas others are not. Retail trade, for example, and arbitrage of any kind are viewed as socially unproductive. Even wholesaling is thought of, in large part, as taking a portion of the pie from those who produced it. This holdover from communist doctrine is absurd on the face of it. One need only look at food rotting in the fields because there are no distribution or transportation services available to get it to market to know that wholesaling, distribution, and transportation are indeed socially productive. A step that increases production by 10 percent is socially harmful if in the process it destroys 15 percent because goods are not distributed appropriately.

Focusing on certain industries and occupations as being good or bad is not limited to the former communist countries but is stronger in those contexts, partly from an unwillingness to accept property rights as important. Individuals who buy goods wholesale and sell them at retail bear risk and become residual claimants. Until society can accept that gains and losses are enjoyed or borne by the individual, there will be a concern about the sanctity of private property.

AN EFFICIENT TAX SYSTEM

As already mentioned, high taxes can be used to confiscate property by imposing them on those activities in which, say, foreigners have a great deal of investment. For example, if all banks are owned by foreigners, then a tax on banking profits will tend to hurt foreigners more than local citizens; thus the tax system can be used to target particular segments of the population and redistribute much of society's resources. But such redistribution and confiscation are not without costs, for taxes produce distortions in any system. When taxes are high, individuals reduce their consumption of the taxed commodity and substitute other goods for it. That substitution is generally inefficient. An efficient tax structure minimizes the distortions produced by taxes that are necessary to raise a certain amount of revenue. Extremely high income tax rates cause nonmarket labor to be substituted for market labor. At high enough rates, it does not pay for a spouse to go to work to earn the income necessary to buy market-produced foods. He or she is better off staying home to produce those goods, even if such production is relatively inefficient. An income tax system creates distortion by keeping people out of the labor market. Similarly, sales taxes, when levied on certain commodities, induce people to stop consuming those commodities.

The old system of taxation was implicit: the state kept the proceeds from sales and paid out wages; the difference between revenues and wage payments was the implicit tax collected by the government. As a result, tax rates could vary greatly. If the price were sufficiently high, or if wage payments were sufficiently low, the tax on that commodity could be extremely large. In a market economy, such differential tax rates would result in enormous distortions.

Taxes must be raised for a number of reasons, as will be discussed below, but without an effective tax system, it is impossible to achieve monetary stability and low inflation rates.

CURRENCY CONVERTIBILITY

Under the old communist system, monetary controls meant that communist currencies could not be freely exchanged with the hard currencies of the rest of the world. Exchange rates were inflated; at official exchange rates, there was excess demand for foreign currency. Indeed, in most of these countries, black markets existed for foreign currencies as well as for goods.

Without full currency convertibility, trade patterns are disrupted and investment by foreigners is reduced. Interestingly, the resistance to making currencies convertible in the transition economies has often been based on the fear of a balance-of-trade surplus. At current exchange rates, Eastern European goods appear cheap to the rest of the world; as a result, many Eastern European governments feared that freeing up the currency would imply large net exports. When a country is running a balance-of-trade surplus, it is necessarily importing financial claims. Poor countries in transition would be lending to the rest of the world, which is exactly the wrong thing to be doing at this point in the transition.

The fear was somewhat justified. Poland initially ran a trade surplus when it went to a convertible currency; this was quickly remedied. The argument against convertibility ignores that free exchange rates will adjust to supply and demand pressures. If Russia, say, were exporting too many of its natural resources to the rest of the world, then prices and wages within Russia would rise. Individuals would demand that some of their goods remain at home or would use the currency obtained from abroad to purchase foreign goods that substitute for local commodities. In either case, the exchange rates rise to equilibrate markets. In general, both countries are better off with open trade, which is extremely difficult to have without convertible currencies.

Convertibility is also important because access to foreign currency provides a mechanism through which the financial system can function in the presence of high inflation. In a highly inflationary economy, the most practical way to attract deposits and make loans with reasonable and predictable real rates of interest is to denominate those loans in foreign currency. For example, a Ukrainian who lends one million coupons to a bank in January 1996 would be credited with the U.S. dollar equivalent of one million coupons on that date. If the conversion rate were $1 per ten thousand coupons, his deposit of one million coupons would translate into an initial deposit equal to $100. Suppose that the market rate of interest on dollars is 5 percent. At the end of the year, he would be entitled to receive $105 back, which would be paid out to him in coupons. But the conversion rate used on December 31, 1996, would be the conversion rate on that date, say, $1 per fifty thousand coupons. The lender would then receive $105 times fifty thousand, or 5.25 million coupons.

Notice that neither the lender nor the borrower needs dollars to make this transaction work. Loans are denominated in dollars; but dollars are never exchanged, and the bank need not hold any dollars in its coffers. All that is needed for this system to work properly is a well-functioning foreign exchange market with high liquidity. Such a market will make domestic lenders confident that the rate at which they retrieve their assets will not be subject to arbitrary fluctuations in rates that have little to do with purchasing power. Thus, convertibility of the currency is necessary, not only to assist in trade and investment across international borders but also to allow financial and credit markets to operate in an economy that is characterized by high inflation.

MONETARY STABILITY

Most economists believe that it is difficult, though not impossible, to run an economy at high levels of growth during periods of hyperinflation. As such, a general principle of economic reform is that a monetary system should be responsible and produce relatively low rates of inflation, but this is a bit misleading. Monetary responsibility is closely tied to government expenditures; without control over government expenditures, it is necessary to raise revenue. There are three methods of raising revenue, one of which is expanding the money supply, which produces inflation and which is essentially an implicit tax on current currency holders. When individuals know that their currency may be taxed away through inflation, they are reluctant to hold it, creating frenetic buying patterns and distorted economic activity. As a result, monetary stability can eliminate some of these distortions but at a cost. When the money supply is constrained, then some other taxing method must be used, and those other taxing methods, as already mentioned, create their own distortions.

The issue of monetary responsibility, then, is one of fiscal control and restraint that cannot be accomplished without reducing government expenditures during periods when economies are in industrial reorganization. (More will be said on this below.)

DEVELOPING A COMMERCIAL BANKING SYSTEM

One major problem in command economies that are in the process of transiting to the market is the anemic flow of capital for new investment, partly stemming from the virtual nonexistence of a commercial banking system. Under communism, commercial bank functions and central bank functions were combined. As a result, individual commercial banks did not develop. Those that were present in the former Soviet Union were tied to large state enterprises and performed specific roles. To the extent that intermediaries are lacking in a growing economy, it will be difficult for capital to flow from potential lenders to potential borrowers. The nonexistence of capital markets has implications for monetary stability and fiscal policy as well.

Banks can be imported rapidly by setting up branches of foreign banks within the country to assist in the flow of capital. Foreign banks have the expertise to intermediate capital transactions and can provide human capital to those who, as a result of working under the communist system, do not have the necessary know-how to run banking operations. Indeed, it may be that human capital is the most important component of developing financial intermediaries.

Most view it as important that banks be private rather than government controlled. Even if the government were to set up its own commercial banks, the lack of an arm's length relationship between the bank and the government would put undue pressure on the government to make bad loans in the private sector. Even when banks are private, governments often cannot resist the temptation to bail out those that fail because of inappropriate policies. For example, in the United States, the savings and loan crisis that has plagued the country for the last few years resulted from changes in regulation that permitted banks to engage in risky lending behavior when their losses were covered by government insurance.

OPERATING STATE ENTERPRISES EFFICIENTLY

State enterprises are likely to be a significant feature of the economies of Eastern Europe, at least until the turn of the century. But some actions can be taken to improve the performance of those enterprises. Specifically, to the extent possible, compensation and incentives for managers in state enterprises should mimic, or go beyond, those in the private sector. For example, managerial compensation can be directly tied to the profitability of the enterprise before subsidy; similarly, the job security of managers and workers alike can depend, in large part, on the ability of a state enterprise to turn a profit at market prices.

Both of these require political fortitude. A failing enterprise will attempt to lobby politicians into subsidizing its firm, claiming special status or extraordinary circumstances. A government's willingness to stand firm will enhance both the short-run and the long-run productivity of the economy.

THE SOCIAL SAFETY NET

High levels of unemployment, and the resulting unrest, could threaten economic reform in a country. Furthermore, without reasonably generous unemployment benefits, it is difficult for a state enterprise to find the will to lay off its workers. In contrast, when unemployment compensation is too generous, unemployed individuals have little incentive to seek new jobs. One solution is to make unemployment compensation a lump-sum severance payment. In that way, individuals have the capital not only to care for themselves during periods of unemployment but also to start new businesses, if they are so inclined. Furthermore, that the unemployment compensation is a lump sum removes any incentives for individuals to remain out of work so that they can collect additional payments. Once the lump sum is received, individuals have every incentive to go back to work or to start their own businesses.

Coupled with a severance-pay program must be some subsistence-level welfare payments, which should be much less generous than the severance-pay program and there only as the absolute last resort.

Finally, Eastern European countries have eroded the real value of pension payments, placing extreme hardships on some pension recipients. One recommendation is that pensions be indexed just enough to cover the increase in the cost of a subsistence level of basic commodities. In this way, a minimum standard of living can be guaranteed to pension recipients without creating an unworkable burden for the central government.

The Correct Transition Strategy

There is much controversy over the appropriate path to a market economy. Some believe that the correct approach is a "big bang," or "shock therapy," whereby the economy is liberalized at once and a tight monetary policy is forcefully applied. Others argue for a slower, more deliberate method, whereby markets are introduced gradually and state control is allowed to coexist with market sectors. Up to now the evidence has been sketchy, but enough experience has been cited on which to base some statements.

Much of the controversy has revolved around ambiguity in the description of the process. For example, many point to Russia as evidence of the failure of rapid marketization policies and to China as evidence of the success of gradual transition.[5] Although the description fits on some counts, it fails on others.

We need a definition of speed, which can readily be provided by analyzing the previous section, where the premise was that a number of factors were necessary ingredients of a market economy. We can then evaluate various countries on the speed with which they have moved toward obtaining these conditions. Thus, a country that truly followed the rapid-change approach would satisfy most of the following conditions:

1. Prices were freed rapidly and pervasively.
2. Production moved rapidly from the state sector to the private sector.
3. Monetary stability and fiscal responsibility resulted in low inflation rates.
4. An efficient tax system replaced the inefficient and distortionary implicit taxation of command economies.
5. Well-functioning capital markets sprang up.
6. Agriculture moved from collectives to private plots.
7. Active competition replaced monopolistic supply of goods and services.
8. Investment was encouraged by establishing and enforcing a commercial code and protecting private property.
9. Full currency convertibility, without restrictions and controls, was established.
10. State enterprises were made more rational by providing managers and workers with appropriate incentives.
11. A social safety net was created with reasonable rules and conditions that provided for subsistence living but discouraged taking advantage of the system.

Although observers may differ on the weight to attach to each of these factors, most define shock therapy as including at least the first three on this list.

PRICES

Most transition economies have done well on the first criterion, with few exceptions. Prices were liberalized rapidly in most of Eastern Europe. Two examples of such liberalization are Poland and the Czech Republic. In Poland, which has had generally free prices since January 1, 1990, both private and state firms have the authority to set prices. Some limitations on price liberalization included the price paid by consumers of coal and electricity, which was below the market price because of government subsidy. State apartment rents were controlled. Similarly, transportation services are free, a below-market price because local authorities subsidize transportation. Subsidies for coal and electricity were reduced on July 1, 1991.[6]

Wage decontrol was less rapid and not universal. All private firms and 20 percent of state-owned firms are free to set wages. But the other 80 percent of the state-owned firms were initially required to pay a tax on wage increases as an anti-inflationary device. A tax of 100 percent was levied on wage increases that exceeded the norm, which was based on the previous month's data, up to an excess of 3 percent. If the norm was surpassed by 3 to 5 percent, the tax was 200 percent. If the excess was greater than 5 percent, a tax of 500 percent was levied on the incremental amount. The tax was not imposed on joint ventures.[7]

In the Czech Republic (at the time, part of Czechoslovakia), price liberalization also proceeded quickly and smoothly. During 1990, prices were increased on food and oil to prepare for the market prices that were allowed to take effect on January 1, 1991. On that date, the vast majority of goods had their prices decontrolled. There was an additional decontrol at the end of March 1991. By mid 1991, about 85 percent of goods turnover (at both wholesale and retail levels) took place at market prices. Shortly thereafter, the Czech koruna was devalued and international trade restrictions were liberalized. Some goods (e.g., sugar, potatoes, flour) were not decontrolled initially. Additionally, increases in the prices of other selected (nonfood) items were limited by increases in the costs of production of those goods. Energy (i.e., electricity, gas and oil), rent on state housing, public transportation, coal, and medicine remained controlled during the early phases of price liberalization.[8]

Russia freed its prices on January 1, 1992, but many prices remained controlled. As in Eastern Europe, these included energy and housing. One significant difference is that Russia began to charge other former Soviet republics, like Ukraine, market or near-market rates for oil and gas after prices were liberalized.

China, as McMillan points out, has followed a different strategy from that of Eastern Europe. The Chinese have allowed some quantity of a given good to trade at market prices, while constraining some quantity to be sold at the state-set price. In reality, this means that the marginal price is the market price as far as producers are concerned. As long as resale is possible, the marginal price is also the market price for all consumers, irrespective of the price at which they buy the good.

The rationale behind the Chinese system is a tax in kind, ensuring that enough of a particular good is available to the state or its users at a low price. To accomplish the same end, it is better to allow the firm to charge the market price, to subsidize consumers so that they can purchase those goods at the market price, and then to tax society efficiently to provide revenues for those subsidies. The tax in kind of the Chinese system is likely to deviate substantially from the tax that creates the least amount of economic distortion or social disruption.

Table 1.1   Number of Private Firms in Eastern Europe
                (in thousands)

	December 1989	December 1990	December 1991
Bulgaria	9.58	18.3	
Czechoslovakia	87.0	488.0	1338.
Hungary	368.0	478.0	
Poland	11.6	29.6	45.0
Romania	97.0	154.0	

SOURCE: *Employment Outlook*. Organization for Economic Cooperation and Development. Paris, 1993.

If judged by the free-price criteria, Russia and the former satellites have moved more rapidly toward the market than has China. In Eastern Europe, Poland and Czechoslovakia were more rapid price liberalizers than were Bulgaria, Romania, Hungary, and probably Russia.

PRIVATE CAPITAL

The comparisons are less clear for other criteria. Private enterprise is more important in China than it is in most of Eastern Europe. The enclaves of private or essentially private enterprise are booming in China. Eastern Europe, however, is not without its successes (see table 1.1). Hungarian officials estimate that about 40 percent of employment is now in private firms, accounting for about 55 percent of gross domestic product.[9]

The numbers in table 1.1 do not necessarily have the same meaning across countries. For example, the numbers for Czechoslovakia represent the number of individual owners of private firms. Thus, one partnership having three partners would count as three in the table. For Poland, the numbers reflect the actual number of private firms.

Despite these difficulties, we can see from the table that Hungary had a headstart on private markets by the time the iron curtain fell. But the big changes in private enterprise appear to have occurred in Czechoslovakia, where the number of private entrepreneurs increased by a factor of fifteen in two years. Admittedly, many of these private firms may consist of single individuals or small nuclear families that are engaged in trade, farming, or small manufacture. But the growth in the number of owners of these enterprises is indeed remarkable. The Czechoslovakian labor force during this period was about eight and one half million; thus, about 15 percent of the Czech labor force owned its own business by the end of 1991.

Poland's increase in private firms was also impressive, increasing more than fourfold over the two-year period. Thus, Poland and Czechoslovakia satisfy the private-enterprise criterion for rapid change. Russia, which has been praised for its moves toward privatization, has been primarily successful in privatizing small and medium-sized enterprises. Countries like Ukraine, which have made little progress on formal privatization, have set up the agencies to deal with the privatization process. Ukraine, however, is not committed to rapid movement toward a market economy; in fact, Ukraine wants a more balanced and gradual movement toward the market. Ukraine, however, does tolerate, even if somewhat informally, a burgeoning of small shops, stands, and self-employed individuals who offer goods and services privately in competition with the state enterprises. Indeed, the growth of the informal private sector in Ukraine probably accounts for the fact that the standard of living has not fallen by as much as official output figures would suggest.

Compared with China, Russia and the other former Soviet republics are far behind. China has a booming private sector, while Russia's is more limited and still in its initial phases. Under Anatoly Chubais, chairman of the State Committee on Property, Russia has engaged in significant privatization by distributing vouchers and auctioning off small enterprises. But at this point the Chinese have a much larger, relatively more productive, and more important private sector than does Russia.

FISCAL RESPONSIBILITY AND MONETARY STABILITY

Fiscal responsibility and monetary control have been exercised with a vengeance only by Czechoslovakia. Vaclav Klaus, initially as finance minister, kept inflation low through a policy of strict, some argued too strict, monetary control. Ukraine, at the other extreme, was printing coupons so fast that inflation rates were running at an estimated 2,000 percent a year. Ukraine's experience made Russia, with its rates in 1992–1993 of around 600 percent a year, look monetarily responsible. Most Russian spending took the form of explicit and implicit subsidies that could not be controlled administratively. The Russian government particularly became subject to blackmail by the managers and workers in the state enterprises spending money they did not have. The central government then had to play tough with the state enterprises or give in to demands for higher subsidies. If the government played tough, then the state firms would default on their obligations to other state firms, which then would be unable to pay their workers. In most circumstances, the central government gave into the blackmail, printed more money, and subsidized the state enterprises.

That state enterprises were able to induce the central bank to print more money has led to several suggestions of ways to control inflation. The first has been to explicitly limit the amount of subsidy that a firm or the state enterprise system as a whole could receive. Formulas have been suggested that prescribe specific limitations on the amount to be spent by state enterprises before some automatic tax on the rest of society would be levied.

This scheme may help, but it does not deal with the underlying problem. Especially in Russia, there appears to be no way for the central government to commit to a limit on spending. Because any one state enterprise is small relative to the system as a whole, it does not significantly affect the total level of expenditures. As a result, every single enterprise wants to spend more than its budget and is limited from doing so only to the extent that the state can make credible its promise to limit subsidies to a prescribed amount. But there is little reason to believe that the threat used in the past by the state enterprises to default on wage payments will not work in the future. If the central government does not provide the revenue, eventually workers are not paid, a reality that prevents any formula method from solving the problem. The key is committing to the subsidy formula, irrespective of the costs. Unfortunately, the inability to resist the temptation to subsidize translates into an inability to stick to a particular formula.

Ukraine proposed limiting state expenditures to a cash basis only: If an enterprise did not have the money to purchase resources, it could not place an order for supplies. This policy, while seemingly sound, eliminates any implicit credit market without providing any budgetary control. The state enterprise credit system was not merely a checking account; it was how commercial credit markets operated under the old system. Thus a policy that sought to eliminate the use of credit meant that investments could not be financed but had to be taken from cash on hand. Were a similar constraint against borrowing and lending placed on American firms, the repercussions on investment and output would be enormous.

Further, the policy of requiring cash is no guarantee of control on expenditures by state enterprises, for, rather than affecting the demands by state enterprises on the central authority, it primarily changes the timing of those demands. Under the cash-only policy, the firm would have to threaten the government with massive layoffs and wage payment default *before* placing its order for supplies (rather than after). But the flow of demands to the government from all firms would be the same over time as it was when the threats were made after the supplies had been delivered. The government's inability to hold firm against those threats implies that it is likely to be unable to hold firm against before-the-expenditure threats.

Hungary, Poland under Balcerowicz, and Romania under Stolojan did not reach Czech standards but were more effective than Russia in controlling government spending and inflation. Part of the difference might have been a result of the differential impact of International Monetary Fund (IMF) pressure; Russia seemed more inclined to buck the IMF or to pretend to comply with IMF guidelines than the former satellites.

China's economy is more difficult to evaluate on this score. Because many prices remain controlled and because most of the taxation takes the command economy/implicit tax form, standard measures of fiscal restraint, such as inflation rates and monetary growth, have neither the same meaning nor impact.

Let us take stock. On the basis of the first three criteria, the Czech Republic is the clear leader in terms of speed toward transition. Because of its significant amount of private enterprise, China in many ways has moved as rapidly toward a market economy as any of the Eastern European countries. Within Eastern Europe, the Czech Republic and Poland have taken the most dramatic steps toward a market economy. Hungary's transition has been much more gradual, but Hungary is further along than many other countries by virtue of its headstart on marketization. Romania and Russia follow those already mentioned in terms of speed of transition. Finally, Bulgaria and then Ukraine have taken the fewest steps toward moving to the market, at least as far as price liberalization, private capital, fiscal responsibility, and monetary stability are concerned.

TAXATION

Related to monetary stability and price decontrol is creating an efficient tax system.[10] Under command economies, taxation was implicit rather than explicit. The government supported its activity by collecting revenue from the sale of output; its costs were wages and payments to foreign suppliers. Thus, tax revenue was closely related to the difference between sales and wages. Under the old system, all price increases were implicit tax increases (as long as demand was inelastic) and all wage increases were tax decreases (as long as the labor supply was sufficiently inelastic).[11] The central governments were reluctant to delegate the power to reduce net revenues to the managers of enterprises. Finance ministers of Eastern European countries felt that they could not afford to allow wages to rise because the state pays those wages (freeing wages in those economies is akin to giving U.S. government workers a raise).

There are basically three methods by which a government finances itself: explicitly, by levying an income tax, profits tax, or a value-added tax; by borrowing and by issuing securities, like government treasury bills or bonds; or by simply printing money to finance its expenditures, causing inflation. Inflation transfers society's resources from those who hold currency to the government and works as an implicit tax. Thus, the absence of a well-functioning tax administration constrains the ways in which governments can finance their expenditures.

Most transition economies do not have a well-established taxing agency. In Russia, for example, the beginning of reforms brought the announcement of a 28 percent value-added tax. Initially, however, little revenue was generated by the tax because enterprises refused to turn the required revenue over to the state.

Because bookkeeping was poor, it was almost impossible to keep track of and punish tax violators.

In the absence of agencies to handle explicit taxation, the central government may turn to borrowing. But the ability to float bonds that the market will buy is also limited, in this case by the credibility of the central government. The poor reputation of a particular government for debt repayment reduces lenders' willingness to offer credit to that government by buying its debt. Raising the offered interest rate does not always help and may hurt. As the rate rises, the government's promise to repay the loan becomes less credible because it will be more difficult to repay a large amount of interest.[12] Indeed, the ability to finance current government expenditures by the new governments of Eastern Europe has been limited at best.

Given the ineffective tax agencies and the inability to finance current expenditures through borrowing, the governments were forced to use the third method of public finance: printing money at high rates that induced high levels of inflation. In an ideal world, it would be unwise to use inflation as the primary method of taxation. But the circumstances that faced the new economies were far from ideal. Under those circumstances, inflation was the only way available to finance expenditures.

The clear solution to the inflation problem is, therefore, reducing government expenditures. The problem is not unique to emerging economies. In the United States, much attention in recent years has been focused on the large deficit, with deficit defined as the difference between government expenditures and revenues. But the deficit itself is not the problem. Raising taxes to finance a deficit, even if it can be done, addresses the *way in which* expenditures are financed. It is not obvious that financing expenditures through current taxes, thereby reducing the deficit, is better than financing those expenditures through borrowing or inflation. The issue is not so much how expenditures are financed but rather whether the expenditures are worthwhile. When attention is focused on the deficit, the public tends to lose sight of the true problem, which is not that we are paying for public expenditures out of current revenues but that public expenditures are too high.

This demonstrates how monetary stability and fiscal responsibility are linked. Unless governments can control their expenditures, they will be forced to finance them through one of the three methods. With limited taxing and borrowing power, they are forced to monetize the debt, thereby causing inflation. But even if expenditures could be financed from borrowing or direct taxation, the situation would not be much improved. The key problem is that economies, emerging or established, must control their desire to use the state as a major redistributive device and must reduce their expenditures.[13]

CAPITAL MARKETS

Capital markets take time to establish. In none of the emerging economies is there a capital market that approaches the development of capital markets in the West. But countries differ on the amount of encouragement they give to outside and inside investors. For example, Czechoslovakia welcomed the establishment of branches by foreign banks early in its transition. Russia initially prohibited private commercial banking, calling for a delay of at least three years for the establishment of truly private banks. Russia's initial attempt to prohibit private banking failed, but capital hardly moves freely into and out of Russia or most other Eastern European countries at this point. [14]

AGRICULTURE

The privatization of agriculture has varied across countries. As mentioned earlier, China and Poland have been the leaders, with Ukraine initially opting against private agriculture altogether. Agriculture is one area in which establishing private claims to output has had dramatic effects. When individuals were allowed to keep much of the proceeds from the crops they grew, China's growth in output in agriculture was impressive. Russia has made some limited progress here, but much of agriculture still remains under control of the large collective farms.

MONOPOLY

Monopoly has been broken for the most part in retail trade throughout Eastern Europe. The combination of privatization of state retail shops, coupled with the growth of pioneer-style entrepreneurship, has made small retailing a competitive industry. At the other extreme, large monopolistic firms still produce heavy equipment and machinery. In the former Soviet Union, where large and concentrated manufacturing was a central feature of the command economy, there is little more competition in 1994 than existed before the breakup. Progress has been made, however, on reducing the restrictions on imports of foreign goods and equipment, which dilutes the power of the domestic monopolies. Further, because each republic has only a subset of the total manufacturing industries, there has been pressure for continued trade between the former republics and for establishing local competitive suppliers.

PROPERTY RIGHTS AND INVESTMENT

New investment, in both physical and human capital, is the key to rapid economic growth. Investment funds can be generated domestically, through private saving, or from foreign sources. Most transition economies have strongly encouraged and sought out foreign investment, certainly throughout the satellite countries. Hungary, which has a relatively stable government structure, has had the most success in generating foreign investment. The recent successes of the former communists in Hungary's last election, however, may cause concern to investors, both foreign and Hungarian, despite efforts by the new government to reassure concerned parties. Hungary is followed by Poland and the Czech Republic in attracting foreign capital, again consistent with views about the countries' relative stability.

China has also been successful in attracting foreign capital, whereas Russia remains schizophrenic on the subject. Although welcoming the growth and higher standard of living that such capital promises, Russia, in a holdover from Marxist doctrine, remains wary of foreigners. There are suspicions that foreigners will come only to pillage the country of its natural resources, leaving little in return. This view is puzzling in that foreigners are at risk by having their capital in another country. Without protection or the power to influence the government, foreigners risk having their capital expropriated outright or implicitly taken through unfavorable tax treatment. A country that does not like what foreigners are doing can always implicitly or explicitly confiscate the capital.

Contract enforcement is particularly problematic in Russia. Despite the obvious problems associated with having a large criminal class, Greif and Kandel (1994) argue that the criminal class substitutes for the government in enforcing business contracts. Both parties agree that the enforcer will take appropriate action if either side reneges on the contract. Although a substitute, albeit imperfect, for legal contract enforcement, even criminal arbiters cannot guarantee the kind of enforcement that is most needed: the guarantee that the government itself will not renege on its commitments.

Indeed, it is expropriation that investors seem to fear most. When Western businesspeople advise emerging economies, they almost always start by emphasizing the importance of protecting private property, lamenting that governments have not done enough to ensure that investments will be protected from both future government action and criminal elements.[15] Although some governments may be able to reduce or eliminate criminal elements from society, particularly those that hamper business, this has become increasingly difficult to do in Russia. Extortion and other crimes that adversely affect business activity have grown as a result of the inability to enforce formal or informal law. Many believe[16] that disbanding the KGB weakened the government's ability to deal with all crimes, not just political ones. But however difficult the government finds reducing crime, its ability to commit to favorable business policies in the future is even more difficult. Despite any laws that are currently passed, a future government can simply revoke such laws and replace them with ones that are less favorable to

Table 1.2   Ratio of Foreign to Gross Domestic Investment
in Selected High-Growth Countries

Country	Years	Ratio of Foreign/ Gross Domestic Investment
Hong Kong	1970–1989	.058
Singapore	1970–1989	.177
South Korea	1970–1988	.006
Taiwan	1976–1989	.019

SOURCE: Foreign Direct Investments: *World Investment Directory* (New York: United Nations, 1993). Gross Domestic Investments: World Tables, 1993 (Washington, D.C.: World Bank, 1993).

business. There is no obvious way to prevent this from happening. In fact, there is every reason to expect that it will occur, for it happens even in well-established Western governments. In the United States, business-favoring tax cuts initiated by the Reagan administration were recently reversed by the Clinton administration. Whereas it may be more difficult to change law capriciously in a well-functioning democracy,[17] it remains virtually impossible for a government to commit itself in a way that future governments cannot undo. Just as contracts entered into by prior communist governments are not necessarily honored by their replacements, so too can the successors to current governments merely abrogate today's commitments.

Much emphasis has been placed on the role that foreign capital can play in fostering growth, with some countries looking to foreign capital as their perhaps only hope for salvation. But no transition country can expect a large enough inflow of foreign capital to make an appreciable dent on total investment (see table 1.2).

The countries listed in table 1.2 have experienced rapid growth over the past twenty years. Of those, only Singapore has a significant fraction of total investment that was supplied by foreigners, which is not surprising because Singapore's economy is tiny compared with that of South Korea or Taiwan. Although all these countries have experienced rapid growth, none has done it on the basis of foreign investment; virtually all investment was financed through domestic saving. The lesson is that it is unrealistic to believe that growth will come from foreign investment. Foreign investment is more likely to be an indicator that favorable investment conditions are present, but this means that domestic investment is high as well.

CURRENCY CONVERTIBILITY

Countries varied in the speed with which they have gone to a fully convertible currency. Currency convertibility is extremely important, not only because of its implications for international trade but also because of its importance for domestic saving and investment. In countries with high inflation, the ability to denominate loans in foreign currency is a necessary ingredient, as is the existence of a well-functioning market for foreign currency, with high liquidity and many transactions.

In terms of currency convertibility, Poland led the way, followed by Czechoslovakia. Other countries have imposed varying degrees of control over their currencies. In some cases, outside intervention has placed serious constraints on policy makers.

For example, there is little foreign exchange in Ukraine because most enterprises and individuals leave their foreign earnings in accounts in other countries, in large part a result of IMF intervention. In consulting with the Ukrainian government about this policy, we were told that the IMF suggested that Ukrainians require 50 percent of foreign exchange be put up for sale on internal currency markets. In addition, there is a 15 percent tax on repatriated profits and a limitation that individuals cannot buy more than $200 of foreign exchange, and firms must show invoices to buy foreign exchange. All these policies mean that it would be unwise for enterprises to bring back to Ukraine foreign currencies they had earned elsewhere. The effect is that Ukrainians as a whole may own a great deal of foreign exchange but that it is held offshore. If incentives were right, they would bring foreign exchange home, lend it through financial intermediaries, and thereby make it available to any firm that wanted to buy it at market rates. This would be an important step for Ukraine and other countries engaged in such restrictive policies, for, as mentioned earlier, access to foreign currency, or the existence of secure bank accounts denominated in foreign currencies, provides a mechanism through which the financial system can function in the presence of high inflation. Loans can then be denominated in a stable foreign currency, and interest can be earned that will not be subject to highly variable rates of inflation.

APPROPRIATE INCENTIVES IN STATE ENTERPRISES

State enterprises are likely to be a significant part of some transition economies at least through the turn of the century, and, as a result, it is important to make the operation of those enterprises more rational. Specifically, two steps that have been implemented in China[18] are important: First, managerial compensation needs to be tied to the profits of the enterprise. Second, the job security of managers and the workers they supervise should depend on the solvency of the enterprise.

Both are easier said than done. Political pressures exerted by managers can influence legislators. But even if politicians resolve to stand up to strong managerial pressure, implementing compensation and termination schemes poses many difficulties. The calculation of profit is problematic, even in economies with well-established and accepted accounting practices; managers can juggle the books of an enterprise to make it look as though profits are higher than they are in reality. The key word here is *profit*. Although output may be more easily measured than profit, output is the wrong metric; profit values the output at market prices and subtracts the costs of production. A firm might well produce high levels of a good that has a market value less than its cost of production. Increasing output may actually reduce social welfare because society bears costs that are higher than the value of the goods produced. It is necessary to value output, and doing so requires some modern accounting techniques, which are not without problems.

If accounting fails to measure profits accurately, there is one surefire method of providing incentives: If state enterprises are not subsidized but must stand on their own bottoms, no juggling of the books can help loss-incurring enterprises. Eventually, those firms must fail and their managers and workers find themselves unemployed. Given the limited credit markets, this eventuality probably occurs sooner rather than later, so eliminating subsidies provides a backup to any strategic compensation scheme that the state adopts. But letting state enterprises fail requires political resolve and causes unemployment. As a result, an appropriately run unemployment compensation system is a necessary ingredient.

THE SOCIAL SAFETY NET

In the face of tight budgets, the former command economies have reduced the real value of pensions. Russia is particularly notorious for having allowed pensioners' incomes to drop significantly during the first years of the transition. This is not an automatic outcome of budgetary pressure. In the United States, older individuals wield sufficient political power to induce Congress to refrain from cutting their living standards when others are pressed.

More important to command economies are the views of the unemployed or potentially unemployed. Thus, state enterprises have kept their subsidies by threatening to add to the pool of unemployed workers. The workers are extremely resistant to such layoffs, in large part because payments to laid-off workers are not sufficient to make them leave voluntarily.

Germany has gone to the other extreme. In eastern Germany, unemployment benefits are so generous that a huge proportion of the workforce is better off drawing unemployment compensation than working. The Germans, then, made a conscious decision to finance the transition through high unemployment payments to speed the rate at which old, inefficient enterprises can close down and be replaced by a private sector. Many who have been critical of Germany's policies point out that such policies lead to large state expenditures and much income redistribution. Although this is true, such critics ignore the fact that high unemployment compensation may permit a society to take efficiency-enhancing steps that would otherwise be politically infeasible.

If the German approach is adopted, however, some modifications might be useful. If unemployment compensation took the form of severance pay rather than a flow of income based on the number of months unemployed, laid-off workers would have incentives to return to work almost immediately. Because severance pay is a lump sum independent of remaining unemployed, an individual can go back to work without any penalty. Short of that, limits could be imposed on the amount of time during which the high levels of unemployment compensation are earned. After benefits expired, individuals could be provided with welfare payments that are far below unemployment compensation.

Why Slow Growth?

Many politicians in Eastern Europe have made their reputations by arguing that rapid economic reform caused the disruption of the economy and led to falling output. The foregoing should make it clear that there is no evidence to support that claim. If anything, the evidence goes the other way. The countries that have had the best experience in Eastern Europe during the past few years, Poland and the Czech Republic, adopted the most rapid economic reform program by almost any criterion.

Further, within the former Soviet Union, the comparison between Ukraine and Russia is illuminating. Although Russia is hardly booming, its inflation rates have declined, its output decline has slowed, goods are available, and some industries are actually doing well. The same is not true in Ukraine, where better days still seem far off. Russia's reform pace has hardly been breathtaking, but Russia has adopted much more radical economic policies, particularly in the areas of price liberalization and privatization, than has Ukraine.

Finally, China is often held up as the best example of how slow change can encourage growth. But China's change has not been slow in comparison with other countries. China has more private or semiprivate agriculture and industry than any former Soviet republic. In many respects, China's rate of economic reform equaled or exceeded that of Poland and the Czech Republic, especially in adopting important managerial incentives, mimicking the private firms in its

Table 1.3   Percentage Growth Rates, Selected Years in the
             Republics of the Former Soviet Union

	1980–1985	1985–1990	1990	1991	1992
Armenia				−17.4	−52.6
Belarus				−1.2	−10.0
Georgia	4.3	−0.1	−7.3	−20.46	−46.0
Kazakhstan	1.7	2.8	−1.1	−8.5	−14.0
Russia	2.2	1.3	−1.5	−9.1	−19.4
Ukraine	3.6	3.2	0.6	−11.0	−14.7
Uzbekistan			−4.3	−12.8	

SOURCE: *Trends in Developing Economies*. World Bank Book, 1993.

state or quasi-private enterprises. Chinese managerial compensation and job security depend on performance, and the willingness to punish poor performers has been greater than in most countries. China has also not succumbed to political pressure from management and worker groups to protect jobs and incomes at the expense of economic performance.

Economic decline has been pervasive, to be sure. But the declines began before new governments were established in Eastern Europe and well before significant economic reforms were enacted (see table 1.3). An examination of growth in the former Soviet Union reveals that Russia saw a decline in output of 1.5 percent in 1990 and 9.1 percent in 1991, before any economic reforms were instituted. The higher decline in 1992 can be interpreted as continuation of the trend that started a few years earlier. Further, the largest declines in output were in republics that initiated no dramatic economic reforms, namely, Georgia and Armenia. Their declines in large part reflect internal political strife that has nothing to do with the rate at which market institutions were introduced into the economy. Similarly, growth rates in Belarus, Uzbekistan, and Kazakhstan during the 1990s are hardly testimony to the benefits of a slow transition.

If rapid economic change is not the cause of the significant output declines, what is? Much can be learned from looking at Finland and Cuba, where trade with the former Soviet Union was an important aspect of economic life (see table 1.4).

In 1990, Cuba's trade with the former Soviet Union (FSU) was far greater than that of any other country in the table. Finland, too, traded significantly with the former Soviet Union, exporting about the same as France. Finland's economy, however, is about one-tenth the size of France's. Even Germany, whose trade with the FSU was significantly greater than that of Finland, falls far short of Finland on a per-capita basis. Germany employs almost fifteen times as

Table 1.4   Trade with the Former Soviet Union in 1990,
             Selected Countries (in millions of U.S. dollars)

Country	Imports	Exports
Cuba	$6,287	$5,829
Finland	282	267
France	124	278
Germany	531	714
Italy	236	365
Sweden	35	47

SOURCE: Monthly Statistics of Foreign Trade. Paris: OECD, 1985–1993.

many workers as Finland but exported less than three times as much to the FSU. Sweden, which employs about twice as many people as Finland, exported about one-sixth as much as Finland to the FSU.[19]

Cuba and Finland are interesting because they have gone through difficult economic times in recent years. Cuba may be on the brink of economic collapse, and Finland experienced unemployment rates of around 20 percent, virtually unheard of by historical standards. Finland's exports to the FSU had fallen to $128 million by 1992, by which time it was experiencing a deep recession.

Finland has always had a market economy, and neither Finland nor Cuba went through any major political or economic reform program. It is likely that Finland's plight, which was far worse than that of any other comparable West European nation, is a direct result of the disruption of trade patterns that occurred as the Council for Mutual Economic Assistance (COMECON) split apart, the same cause that is at the heart of declines in output throughout Eastern Europe.

The disruption in trade that occurred as COMECON disintegrated was not something that could have been controlled by any individual country. Under the former system, prices at which transactions occurred were distorted.[20] After countries were freed by the Soviet Union from trading at the constrained prices, they could sell to and buy from the rest of the world at market prices. Given this, the countries were essentially forced to face market prices at once, like it or not. Because Czechoslovakia could sell its manufactured goods to Germany at world prices, Romania could no longer expect to buy them at the previously distorted prices. The immediate reality of world prices caused a complete realignment of trade patterns almost overnight.[21]

Once international prices became relevant for international trade, they also became relevant for domestic trade. Even if a small part of the output of one industry were shipped abroad, the ability to sell that output at the world price means that all goods must trade at that price. For example, suppose that the

Czech Republic sells its famous Pilsner Urquell beer to the United States at a price of $20, or 600 koruna, per case. For the brewery to be willing to sell the beer domestically, it must receive the 600 koruna per case or it will export it. Unless controls (such as tariffs or limits) are placed on exporting beer, Czechs will have to pay the international price for beer or have it all shipped overseas. Thus, world prices determine domestic prices, even if only a small amount of trade takes place at those prices.

A complete restructuring of the economy is needed after such a major change in trading patterns but not one of the market versus command economy sort. Rather, there must be a change in the kinds of goods being produced by each country. When countries must buy and sell their inputs and products at world prices, the goods they produced under communism are no longer the goods they can efficiently produce in the new economy. This necessarily implies that some industries will rise while others will fall. The transition to a new industrial structure imposes large adjustment costs in the form of reduced output and layoffs. Eventually, the economies will be stronger as a result of output reorganization. Because real rather than constructed prices affect producers, they will behave efficiently and produce the goods that society wants. Pain is endured during the short run in order to obtain these long-run gains.

Some countries have attempted to patch their command system back together in an attempt to cushion the short-run disruption. These countries erroneously believe that they can reduce pain today at the expense of reduced growth in the future. Unfortunately, that tradeoff is not feasible. Slowing the move to a market economy will not reduce the short-run costs but will only lengthen the time that it takes to enjoy the long-run gains. There is one tradeoff that can be made in the short run, however. Some redistribution, through unemployment compensation and severance-pay programs, can help share the costs of readjustment. Lump-sum payments tend to be less distortionary than payments that depend on the amount of time unemployed. But neither unemployment compensation nor severance pay will eliminate the requirement that the economy fundamentally alter its industrial structure.

Conclusion

The transition period has been difficult for all the Eastern European countries. Although we can specify the ingredients of a successful market economy, the way by which these ingredients are introduced is less well understood. Countries have adopted somewhat different approaches to the transition problem. The Czech Republic and Poland have been leaders in rapid reform. Russia has undertaken some major reform steps but still has a largely state-run economy. Ukraine is at the other end of the spectrum. Not only has Ukraine introduced the market economy slowly, but the Ukrainian government is not yet convinced that it wants or will be forced to have a market economy at all.

Transitions have meant falling output and reduced employment in all the Eastern European countries. But the economic decline is not a result of the speed with which economic reform was undertaken. Rather, the decline in output resulted when the breakup of COMECON made world prices relevant. That countries must buy and sell at world prices means that industry must be completely reorganized. Some industries will rise while others will fall. The process of industrial change brings about short-run declines in output and reduced employment, irrespective of the system under which the reorganization occurs. The long run can expect better times, but there is no way to buy higher output in the short run with reduced output in the long run. Instead, the necessary adjustments must occur, cushioned to some extent by a social safety net.

Notes

1. A few authors have tried to offer plans for managing the transition. Among them are Kornai (1990) and McKinnon (1993).

2. To the extent that individuals who wait in the queue can then resell their goods to others, the amount that managers can extract from the general public will be limited to the difference between the true market price and the current price.

3. See Murphy, Shleifer, and Vishny (1992).

4. A. Anderson in this volume discusses the evolution of the mafia in Russia that resulted from previous corrupt practices.

5. See McMillan (this volume) for a discussion of gradualism in China.

6. Witold Sobkow and Boguslaw Winid, *Questionnaire*, Ministry of Foreign Affairs, Poland, September 1991.

7. UNIDO, *Foreign Investor's Guide to Poland*, chap. 6, "Taxation," p. 71.

8. Miroslav Zozulak, *Prices and Wages Response to Questionnaire*, Ministry of Foreign Affairs, CSFR, September 1991. Material also taken from CSFR, "Scenario of the Economic Reform," 1990.

9. Andrés Márton, Hungarian consul general to Los Angeles, made this statement on May 9, 1994.

10. McLure (this volume) discusses the appropriate tax structure in detail.

11. It is conceivable that a wage increase could actually increase state revenue. If labor supply were sufficiently elastic so that output increased enough to offset increases in labor cost, then state net revenue could actually increase. This, however, means that the wrong allocation of resources had been selected initially.

12. See Stiglitz and Weiss (1983) for a formal treatment of this issue.

13. A number of authors have discussed this problem. One recent example is Edwards and Tabellini (1991).

14. By presidential decree, Yeltsin lifted Russia's curbs on foreign private banks in June 1994.

15. See Anderson (this volume) for a detailed treatment of the rise and effects of organized crime in Russia.

16. E.g., Egor Gaidar argued this in his speech at the Hoover Institution, May 2, 1994.

17. See Lazear (1993) and Diamond (this volume).

18. See McMillan (this volume).

19. Employment data from *Yearbook of Labour Statistics* (Geneva: ILO, 1992) and *Bulletin of Labour Statistics, 1993-4* (Geneva: ILO, 1994).

20. See Lazear (1992).

21. See Collins and Rodrick (1991).

References

Bulletin of Labour Statistics, 1993–4. Geneva: ILO, 1994.

Collins, Susan, and Dani Rodrick. *Eastern Europe and the Soviet Union in the World Economy.* Washington, D.C.: Institute for International Economics, May 1991.

Edwards, Sebastian, and Guido Tabellini. "Explaining Fiscal Policies and Inflation in Developing Countries." *Journal of International Money and Finance* 10 (1991): S16–48.

Employment Outlook. Organization for Economic Cooperation and Development: Paris, 1993.

Kornai, János. *The Road to a Free Economy: Shifting from a Socialist System: The Case of Hungary.* New York: Norton, 1990.

Lazear, Edward. "Interaction between Political and Economic Freedom." In Richard F. Staar, ed., *Transition to Democracy in Poland.* New York: St. Martin's Press, 1993, pp. 111–22.

———. "Prices and Wages in Transition Economies." Paper delivered at In Search of a Transition to a Free Society, Mont Pelerin Society Regional Meeting, Prague, November, 1991. Published as an Essay in Public Policy, no. 29. Stanford: Hoover Institution Press, 1992.

McKinnon, Ronald I. *The Order of Economic Liberalization: Financial Control in the Transition to a Market Economy.* 2d edition. Baltimore: Johns Hopkins University Press, 1993.

Murphy, Kevin, Andre Shleifer, and Robert Vishny. "The Transition to a Market Economy: Pitfalls of Partial Reform." *Quarterly Journal of Economics* 107, no. 3 (August 1992): 889–906.

Organisation for Economic Cooperation and Development (OECD). *Employment Outlook.* Paris: OECD, 1993.

————. *Monthly Statistics of Foreign Trade.* Paris: OECD 1985–1993.

Shleifer, Andre, and Robert Vishny. "Pervasive Shortages under Socialism," *Rand Journal of Economics* 9 (Summer 1992).

Sobkow, W., and Boguslaw Winid. *Questionnaire.* Poland: Ministry of Foreign Affairs, September 1991.

Stiglitz, Joseph E., and Andrew Weiss. "Incentive Effects of Terminations: Applications to the Credit and Labor Markets." *American Economic Review* 73 (December 1983): 912–27.

United Nations Industrial Development Organization (UNIDO), Industrial Cooperation and Investment Promotion Service, in cooperation with the Polish Investment Company S.A. "Taxation." In *Foreign Investor's Guide to Poland.* Warsaw: UNIDO, April 1992.

World Bank. *Trends in Developing Economies.* Washington, D.C.: World Bank, 1993.

Yearbook of Labour Statistics. Geneva: ILO, 1992.

Zozulak, Miroslav. *Prices and Wages Response to Questionnaire.* Czech and Slovak Federative Republic (CSFR): Ministry of Foreign Affairs, September 1991. Material also taken from CSFR, "Scenario of the Economic Reform," 1990.

Appendix

Commonly Used Acronyms

CIS	Commonwealth of Independent States
CMEA	Council for Mutual Economic Assistance
EBRD	European Bank for Reconstruction and Development
EC	European Community: Belgium, Denmark, France, Germany, Greece, Ireland, Italy, Luxembourg, Netherlands, Portugal, Spain, the United Kingdom
G-7	Group of Seven industrialized countries: Canada, France, Germany, Italy, Japan, the United Kingdom, and the United States
GATT	General Agreement on Tariffs and Trade
IMF	International Monetary Fund
KGB	(Soviet) State Security Committee
MFN	Most-favored-nation (trade status)
NATO	North Atlantic Treaty Organization
RSFSR	Russian Soviet Federated Socialist Republic

SELECTIVE CHRONOLOGY OF MAJOR EVENTS IN THE FORMER COMMUNIST COUNTRIES OF EASTERN EUROPE/RUSSIA, 1989–1994

Date	Country	Event
1988		
1988	USSR	Mikhail Gorbachev publishes *Perestroika* in England and New York and *At the Summit*, a book of his speeches and interviews, February 1987–July 1988
December 7	USSR	At United Nations, Gorbachev announces unilateral Soviet manpower/weapons reductions in USSR and Eastern Europe
1989		
January	USSR	Shortages of coffee, toilet paper, laundry soap, sugar, tea; popular support for Gorbachev dropping
January 7	USSR	Announces unilateral destruction of chemical weapons stocks
January 16	Czechoslovakia	Vaclav Havel arrested in Prague's Wenceslas Square (later sentenced to jail)
February	USSR/Afghanistan	Last Soviet troops withdrawn from Kabul
February 16	Lithuania	100,000 celebrate Independence Day in city of Kaunas
March	Vienna	Opening of talks by thirty-five foreign ministers on reduction of armed forces in Europe
March	Hungary	75,000 peaceful prodemocracy demonstrators in Budapest
April	Poland	Solidarity Party legalized
April	USSR	First multicandidate elections in seventy-one years; Yeltsin wins seat in Congress of People's Deputies, with 90 percent support in Moscow; strong voter discontent with Communist Party old guard; apparent support of Gorbachev's perestroika

April 9	USSR/Georgia	Tbilisi massacre: Soviet troops attack crowd of 8,000; gathering began with 150 pro-independence hunger strikers; at least 20 dead; crowds mount to 100,000
Spring	Bulgaria	Expels 300,000 Turks (against Soviet wishes)
Spring	Romania	Food shortages
April–May	China	100,000 jubilant prodemocracy marchers in Tiananmen Square in Beijing ("student revolt"); Deng Xiaoping threatens use of force
May	China/USSR	Gorbachev arrives in Beijing for first Sino-Soviet summit in twenty-four years
May 11	US/USSR	U.S. secretary of state James Baker visits Moscow; Gorbachev says USSR will unilaterally reduce five hundred short-range nuclear weapons in Europe
June	USSR	Yeltsin wins a seat in the Supreme Soviet after 70,000 in Moscow protest his exclusion; millions of Russians watch the parliamentary proceedings on TV
June	Poland	Solidarity candidates sweep elections (Lech Wałesa is Solidarity Party leader)
June	Austria/Hungary	Foreign ministers cut down part of barbed wire at border
June	Romania	Erects eight-foot fence on 260-mile border with Hungary
June 3–4	China	Hundreds of protesters killed in Tiananmen Square
June 16	Hungary	Reburial in Budapest of Imre Nagy (prime minister in 1956), hanged as a traitor thirty-one years earlier
June	China	Twenty-seven spring rioters executed; more than 1,650 people arrested
July	Poland	Inflation at 100 percent; Wałesa turns down compromise offer to share government with General Jaruzelski, who wins election as president; U.S. president George Bush visits Gdansk, offers $119 million in economic aid

SELECTIVE CHRONOLOGY OF MAJOR EVENTS (*continued*)

Date	Country	Event
1989 (*continued*)		
July	Estonia/USSR	Agreement allows Estonia to secede economically; 5,000 non-Estonians protest law establishing Estonian as official language
July	USSR	Tens of thousands of miners in Kuznetsk Basin and elsewhere strike for better pay and more consumer goods; Gorbachev gives in to their demands
July 6	USSR	At Council of Europe meeting in Strasbourg, Gorbachev implies Soviet nonintervention in Eastern Europe
August	Poland	Solidarity-led government in power/first peaceful ousting of a communist regime; intellectual Tadeusz Mazowiecki named prime minister, first noncommunist government head in Soviet bloc in forty-plus years; government deregulates food prices (as farmers demand)
August 23	Latvia	Hands-across-the-Baltics demonstration
September	USSR/US	Yeltsin's first visit to United States; Soviet clothing and watches available at Bloomingdale's in New York City
September	USSR/Ukraine	Independence movement in Ukraine
September 10	Hungary	Allows East German refugees to leave for West Germany through Hungary
August–November	East Germany	More than 100,000 East Germans emigrate to Western Europe
October	East Germany	Fall of Erich Honecker 10/18; 100,000 demonstrate for democracy in Leipzig (two weeks later, 250,000)
October	USSR	Gorbachev fires editor of *Pravda*
October 11	Hungary	Hungarian Communist Party changes its name to the Hungarian Socialist Party

November	US/Poland	Wałesa visits Washington; Congress votes more aid for Poland than Bush had requested
November	Czechoslovakia	Velvet Revolution: largest antigovernment protest in twenty years: 25,000 in Prague confront police, demand end to communism; riot police beat some, but three days later 200,000+ come to Wenceslas Square, then 300,000, then 500,000 (almost one-third of city's population)
November 24	Czechoslovakia	Alexander Dubcek addresses 500,000 in Prague; calls for freedom and democracy; an hour later, Communist Party chief Milos Jakes and entire Politburo resign; crowd jubilant; Karel Urbanek succeeds Jakes
November 10	Bulgaria	President Todor Zhivkov resigns after thirty-five years (spends 1990 under house arrest in granddaughter's mountain villa); successor is reformist apparatchik Petar Mladenov, who favors free elections
November 9	Berlin	Fall of Berlin Wall
November 11	Berlin	Massive prodemocracy demonstrations in East Berlin, with live coverage on East German TV
November 18	East Germany	Government announces that 5,000,000 East Germans have applied for travel documents to West Germany
November–December	Czechoslovakia	Numerous communist leaders purged from power; strong public sentiment for punishment for malfeasance for roles in 1968 Prague invasion
Early December	Czechoslovakia	General strike
Early December	Vatican	Gorbachev meets with Pope John Paul II (unprecedented)
December	East Germany	Growing public sentiment for German reunification; Communist Party dissolves Politburo and Central Committee
December	West Germany	Chancellor Helmut Kohl offers ten-point reunification plan

Selective Chronology of Major Events (*continued*)

Date	Country	Event
1989 (continued)		
December	Lithuania	Parliament moves toward a multiparty system, voting 243-1 to end communist monopoly
December	Czechoslovakia	Dissident playwright Vaclav Havel wants constitution, free elections, market economy, and EC membership; "Havel for President" buttons appear widely
December	Romania	Violent riots in Bucharest
December	USSR/EC	Shevardnadze signs ten-year trade agreement with EC, including gradual lifting of EC quotas on Soviet imports
December 17	Romania	Securitate/secret police massacre civilians in Timisoara (protesting arrest of Laszlo Tokes, pastor of Hungarian Reformed Church there)
December 25	Romania	Nicolae and Elena Ceauşescu executed
1990		
1990	Czechoslovakia	Country name changed from Czechoslovak Socialist Republic to Czech and Slovak Federative Republic; Vaclav Klaus named finance minister, proreform; first return in Eastern Europe of property confiscated after February 1948 communist coup
1990	Hungary	Approximately $700 million in foreign investment
1990	Romania	Approximately 320 cooperative farms closed and taken over by individual farmers

1990	USSR	Communist Party membership drops; by end of year, all fifteen union republics declare sovereignty or autonomy; Yeltsin promotes economist Stanislav Shatalin's 500-day plan for transition to market economy; shortages of consumer goods (e.g., bread, vegetables, cigarettes); distribution breakdowns; Gorbachev v. Yeltsin; ethnic conflicts, including anti-Semitism (more than 170,000 Soviet Jews emigrate to Israel); social democratic parties form in Georgia, Belorussia, Estonia, Latvia, Lithuania, Russia, Ukraine; Baltic republics and Ukraine consider printing own money; multinational food aid begins arriving, latter half of year; Yeltsin's autobiography *Against the Grain*; USSR declares Bulgaria, Cuba, and other satellites must pay for Soviet oil at world market prices and in hard currency after 1/1/91
1990	Bulgaria	National anthem stripped of references to communism and USSR; date of national holiday changed; Stalin-era mass graves discovered
1990	Poland	Inflation estimated at 344 percent
January	USSR/Baltics	Limited economic autonomy granted
January	USSR/Moldavia	Moldavian Republic changes name to Moldova; city of Tiraspol (mainly Russian) votes to become autonomous 1/30
January	Lithuania	Gorbachev visits, attempting to curb movement toward independence; 300,000 demonstrate for independence in candlelight vigil in Vilnius
January	Yugoslavia	Stabilization program implemented to combat hyperinflation, with central authority for money creation
January	Czechoslovakia	Havel becomes president/"Government of National Understanding"

Selective Chronology of Major Events (*continued*)

Date	Country	Event
1990 (continued)		
January	Romania	First concrete steps taken toward market economy/private enterprise; Petre Roman is prime minister of transitional government; government bans Communist Party; Romanian Orthodox Church revitalized; Hungarian-Romanians seek to reestablish Hungarian-language instruction in Transylvania, especially in Cluj area; Soviet foreign minister Shevardnadze visits Bucharest to promise increased USSR oil, gas, electricity, and other assistance
January	Berlin	Twenty thousand anticommunist demonstrators form human chain around Parliament building
January	Japan	Offers $1 billion in loans to Poland and Hungary
January	Hungary	Suzuki Motors of Japan plans new auto plant near Budapest
January	Bulgaria	Communist government resigns; reformists in; former dictator Todor Zhivkov to be investigated on corruption charges
January 1	Poland	Polish zloty devalued and made convertible; wage increase ceilings set; major trade liberalization; plans to privatize state enterprises; prices freed/government subsidies ended for most essentials
January 15	USSR/Azerbaijan	Gorbachev declares a state of emergency, sends 11,000 troops/police
End January	USSR	McDonald's opens in Moscow
February	Bulgaria	"Manifesto on Democratic Socialism" calls for movement toward market economy, with political pluralism and new forms of property; trade unions declare independence from party control

January–March	Bulgaria	Televised roundtable discussions on the future of the country; opposition parties guaranteed media access; Union of Democratic Forces (main opposition party) advocates market shock therapy/immediate complete transition to market economy
February	USSR	Communist Party renounces its constitutional guarantee as sole legal party; 100,000 anticommunist demonstrators in Red Square; large-denomination bills declared worthless
February	Czech/United States	President Havel visits United States; U.S. secretary of state Baker offers economic assistance similar to that offered Hungary and Poland
February	Romania	Mass protests in Bucharest and Timisoara against former communist leaders still in power; trials of former Securitate/secret police officials; four former Ceauşescu government leaders sentenced to life imprisonment; 3,000 miners (whose wages had been doubled) brought in to help quell antigovernment protests; Romanian leu devalued, per IMF/World Bank advice; Vatican envoys visit
February 8	Romania	U.S. secretary of state Baker visits Bucharest; 10,000 nationalist Romanians protest Hungarian-language schools while on same day 10,000 ethnic Hungarians demonstrate in favor (extremist Romanian nationalist organization founded during this period)
February 26	Czechoslovakia	Soviet troops begin pullout, per agreement
March	USSR	Presidential Council (advisers to Gorbachev) supplants Politburo; Parliament passes new property bill allowing stock markets and small business ownership; Supreme Soviet OKs Gorbachev's "proposal for a popularly elected president with new powers to veto legislation, impose a state of emergency or even dispense with Parliament to rule by presidential decree"
March	Czechoslovakia	Requests full membership in Council of Europe and wins interim guest status

Date	Country	Event
1990 (continued)		
March	Hungary	Up to five hundred Hungarian-Romanians a day flee to Hungary after ethnic violence in Romania; Moscow-Budapest agreement for total Soviet troop/weapons withdrawal
March 11	Lithuania	Declares sovereignty; Communists routed in first multiparty election in seventy-two years; Parliament elects Vytautas Landsbergis president; Gorbachev demands renunciation by 3/19; Lithuania refuses, calls on democratic nations to recognize it; USSR sends about one hundred armored vehicles to Vilnius 3/23; United States advises Gorbachev not to use force in Lithuania and orders U.S. diplomats out of Vilnius 3/24; Gorbachev threatens economic sanctions against Lithuania; Bush and Margaret Thatcher meet 4/14 in Bermuda and ask Gorbachev to call off sanctions, but Gorbachev cuts off oil, gas, coal; 6/17 Lithuania agrees to 100-day moratorium on independence and USSR reopens oil pipeline
March 14	Romania	Government takes steps to attract foreign investment; new law allows foreign banks and unrestricted foreign ownership of local ventures
March 15	USSR	Gorbachev elected to restyled presidency
March 18	East Germany	First free elections since Hitler's takeover in 1933
March 19–20	Romania	Ethnic violence in Tirgu-Mures (Hungarian/Romanian)
March 30	Estonia	Declares slow move to independence
April	Hungary	First elections in forty-five years/landslide victory for non-Communists
April–May	Czechoslovakia	Ten-minute anticommunist general strikes
April	Czechoslovakia	State monopoly on foreign trade ended; agrees with EC to lift all trade restrictions by 1995
April	Georgia	Declares independence

April	Germany	Tens of thousands of East Germans protest presence in government of former secret police personnel
April	Romania	Student protests in Bucharest/hunger strikes; State Secretariat for Privatization established to focus on privatizing large state enterprises
April 3	Bulgaria	Communist Party changes name to Bulgarian Socialist Party; advocates moderation, not shock transition, to market economy; abandons Leninist democratic centralism/monopolistic tendencies
April 21	Czechoslovakia	Pope John Paul II visits Cardinal Tomasek of Prague
End April	United States/USSR	New trade agreement concluded in Paris; United States to grant MFN status to USSR, but three weeks later Bush withholds MFN status till Lithuanian question resolved (although he renews MFN status for China 5/90)
May	Albania	Announces freedom to travel, worship
May	Lithuania	Parliament votes to take control of radio and TV
May 1	USSR	Demonstrators denounce Gorbachev/Red Square, Moscow (May Day)
May 4	Latvia	Declaration charting gradual restoration of independence
May 15	USSR	Gorbachev declares Estonian and Latvian independence declarations illegal
May 20	USSR	Decree promoting private home ownership (build-buy-sell)
May 20	Romania	Ion Iliescu of National Salvation Front Party elected president
By end May	Romania	Some 1.5 million Romanians apply for passports under new passports-on-request law, producing floods of emigrants to West Germany (more than 86,000 by August 1990); border restrictions relaxed with Soviet Moldavia; Vatican reestablishes diplomatic relations with Romanian government after forty-two years

Date	Country	Event
1990 (continued)		
May	USSR/United States	Gorbachev and Bush meet in US for major summit
May	USSR	Price hikes create hoarding; Popov becomes mayor of Moscow
May 30	USSR	Yeltsin elected president of RSFSR over Gorbachev's candidate
June	Poland	Beginning of gradual withdrawal of Soviet troops
June–July	Bulgaria	Communist president Mladenov and his prime minister resign (forced out); in first free elections since 1931, UDF leader Zheliu Zhelev elected president; shortly after elections, payments on foreign debt suspended, and Lukanov government begins rationing when basic commodities (sugar, cooking oil, detergent) disappear from shelves
June	Romania	President Iliescu names Petre Roman prime minister; antigovernment demonstrations in Bucharest; Marian Munteanu speaks out; march against state-run TV station; police do not act; hundreds injured by riot police and 10,000 miners 6/14; violent attacks provoke international outcry; freedom of the press threatened; government reluctantly commits (6/17) to totally free and democratic press/radio/TV; United States withholds nonhumanitarian economic aid; EC postpones trade agreement with Romania and excludes Romania from Western aid package for Eastern Europe
June	Russia	Russian Republic votes for sovereignty: Russian law to be above Soviet law
June	USSR	Uzbekistan v. Kirghizia: USSR sends additional 3,000 troops to restore order
June	Hungary	First privatization of state enterprises
June	EC/Dublin	EC considers $15 billion aid package to USSR economy, but Great Britain's reluctance leads to careful study before any commitments
July	USSR	Yeltsin meets with Latvian, Estonian, and Lithuanian presidents in Latvia, promises RSFSR will sign treaties recognizing their sovereignty

July	USSR/Germany	Gorbachev agrees to inclusion of a united Germany in NATO
July	Albania	More than 4,000 Albanians escape or seek asylum elsewhere
July 1	East Germany	East Germany adopts West German deutsche mark
July 9–11	Houston	At economic summit of major industrialized democracies, West Germany and France push for aid to USSR, United States reluctant; each country free to aid as desired
July 10	USSR	Gorbachev rejected as general secretary of Communist Party
July 12	USSR	Yeltsin resigns from Communist Party (as does Moscow mayor Popov)
July 16	Ukraine	Parliament asserts primacy of Ukrainian laws over USSR laws; demands reparations for 1986 Chernobyl disaster
July 21	Romania	Several thousand peaceful demonstrators in Bucharest call for release from prison of Marian Munteanu and others arrested in June (Munteanu was released 8/3); 20,000 small private enterprise firms established by July, 75 percent in service sector
August	Russia/USSR	Gorbachev agrees to work with Yeltsin toward market reform
August	Armenia	Declares independence and calls for own army
August 21	Bulgaria	Closes border to Romanians
August 30	Yugoslavia	Riot police attack Albanian demonstrators
August 30	Tatarstan	Declares independence from Russia
September	Bulgaria	Joins IMF (had applied to IMF and World Bank in February); Lilov elected president of Bulgarian Socialist Party with Lukanov's support; mobs burn and loot Communist Party headquarters
September	Czechoslovakia	Joins IMF and World Bank

Selective Chronology of Major Events (*continued*)

Date	Country	Event
1990 (*continued*)		
September	Romania	Six days of antitotalitarian riots in Bucharest
September	Albania	Nationalists threaten civil war
September	United States/Romania	United States refuses MFN trade status to Romania
September	USSR	Gorbachev restores citizenship of Aleksandr Solzhenitsyn and twenty-two other dissidents; 700,000 oil workers threaten strike
September 20	Romania	New law establishes five types of commercial companies, from simple partnerships to joint stock companies, including system giving each Romanian adult citizen a 5,000-leu ownership voucher
September 24	USSR	Supreme Soviet grants Gorbachev emergency powers for 500 days
October	USSR	Gorbachev awarded Nobel Peace Prize
October	United States/Romania	President Bush does not meet with Romanian president Iliescu at United Nations but meets with all other East European leaders
October	Czechoslovakia	Former Prague Communist Party chief Miroslav Stepan sentenced to two and a half years in prison for abuse of power/suppressing demonstrations of November 17, 1989; citizens issued vouchers for ownership in larger state enterprises being converted into joint stock companies
October	USSR/Moldavia	Disruptions/upheaval
October	Russia	Kalmyk people declare independence from Russia
October	Bulgaria	Lukanov government proposes comprehensive economic reform; strikes/large antisocialist demonstrations

October 3	Germany	Formal German reunification (900-page reunification treaty)
October 16	USSR/Italy	Italian government approves $2 billion aid package for USSR; 11/18, Italy announces $900 million credit line to USSR
October 17	USSR/Ukraine	Ukrainian prime minister Masol resigns after demonstrations of tens of thousands of students/nationalists in Kiev and a one-day strike in September
October 19	USSR	Supreme Soviet overwhelmingly endorses Gorbachev's compromise (moderate) economic reform plan and reconfirms his "power to introduce a market system by decree"; Gorbachev attacks Yeltsin as destructive opportunist; Yeltsin calls for reform to be in hands of leaders of individual republics
October 27	USSR/Spain	Spain promises USSR $1.5 billion credit
November	Bulgaria	Government crisis/fall of Lukanov's cabinet
November	Czechoslovakia	United States approves MFN status; President Bush visits (11/17–18); nearly daily independence demonstrations in Slovak capital, Bratislava
November	Czech/USSR	Finance ministers Vaclav Klaus and Valentin Pavlov agree that on 1/1/91 trade payments will be made in convertible currencies
November	Poland	Ninety-five percent of former Communist Party's wealth nationalized, per public demand
November	USSR	Gorbachev presents draft of new union treaty but five of fifteen republics reject it outright; Russian Republic refuses USSR order to free prices on luxury goods; USSR sends troops to Moldavia; ethnic tensions high; some Russian desire in Dniester area to secede from Moldavia; rationing in Leningrad

Date	Country	Event
1990 (continued)		
November 1	Romania	Government deregulates some prices; clothing/public transport/furniture prices double and footwear prices triple; leu devalued 70 percent; public demonstrations in Bucharest/University Square to protest price increases; Roman threatens to resign; as of this month, 140,000 license requests for small private enterprises, with more than 50,000 approved—80 percent of these in the trade sector
November 25	Poland	Election ends in runoff between Wałesa and Tyminski in December 1990; incumbent Mazowiecki loses
December	Albania	Army suppresses mass demonstrations
December	Latvia	Bombings in Riga
December	USSR	Council of Ministers replaces Presidential Council, reporting directly to President Gorbachev; Congress of People's Deputies gives Gorbachev additional powers (Georgia and Armenia boycott the session); USSR solicits emergency aid from abroad/receives $1 billion in new emergency aid from 12 EC countries meeting in Rome, with strongest support from Kohl and Mitterrand; Russian Republic's Parliament legalizes private land ownership
December	US/USSR	Bush approves up to $1 billion in loans for USSR to buy U.S. agricultural goods
December 9	Poland	Lech Wałesa elected president in runoff election, over surprise second-place Stanislaw Tyminski
December 15	Albania	Statue of Hoxha dynamited
December 20	Bulgaria	Dimitur Popov (nonparty jurist) elected president
December 22	USSR	Gorbachev gives Moldavia 10 days to quell separatism, threatens "necessary measures"

December 25	USSR/Israel	First Moscow-Jerusalem consular relations established since 1967
End December	USSR	Foreign Minister Eduard Shevardnadze resigns, warning of approaching dictatorship; Gorbachev condemns his resignation at this time as "unforgivable"
End December	Bulgaria	Zhelev visits Western Europe, United States, Japan; Zhelev meets with U.S. president Bush, arranges MFN status and donation of 1 million tons of seed corn
December–January 1991	Russia	Yeltsin announces Russia will keep over 100 billion rubles in taxes expected by USSR

1991

1990–1991	Poland	More than 500,000 new private companies in one year
January 1	Czechoslovakia	Auctions begin for small shops and service companies; price liberalization law, with safeguards; new internal convertible currency law
1991	CMEA	CMEA trade arrangements begin to be dismantled officially
1991	Poland	New laws allow 100 percent foreign profit repatriation; Polish-American Enterprise Fund established; Coca Cola to open bottling plants
1991	Hungary	Auctions begin for 16,000 state-owned shops and restaurants
Early 1991	Bulgaria	Most consumer and producer prices liberalized; exchange rate unified and floated
Early 1991	USSR	Shevardnadze's new Democratic Reform Movement includes Shatalin and Popov (Shatalin leaves Gorbachev's service after Lithuanian crackdown)
January	Bulgaria	EC plans to include Bulgaria in Eastern European assistance program; USSR will accept Bulgarian manufactured goods in exchange for 6.5 million tons of USSR gasoline in 1991

Date	Country	Event
1991 (*continued*)		
January	Lithuania	Russian tanks enter Vilnius, 1/13; 13 killed, 100 injured; Radio Vilnius interrupted by military force; Gorbachev refuses Landsbergis's telephone call; thousands defy troops; 1/20, Bush warns Gorbachev against military crackdown in Baltics; some Lithuanian soldiers desert Soviet army
January	Latvia	In Riga, Soviet black-beret militia shoot their way into Interior Ministry; four killed
February	USSR/Russia	Gorbachev calls for Yeltsin's resignation
March	USSR	Yeltsin supported by 280,000 coal miners on strike in Russia and Ukraine
March	Poland	Paris Club forgives 50 percent of Polish debt; United States to reduce Poland's debt by 70 percent
March	Yugoslavia	Student demonstrations in Belgrade; two killed, dozens wounded
March 17	USSR	Seventy-five percent back Gorbachev's union proposal in referendum (boycotted by Armenia, Georgia, Moldova)— twelve republics agree to central bank, free trade, common defense, and coordinated transition to a market system
March 27	USSR	Troops brought into Moscow
March 28	Germany/Czech.	Volkswagen signs deal to rebuild Czech carmaker Skoda, at $6 billion over ten years
By April	Czechoslovakia	Some 300,000 private owners, as compared with *none* a year earlier
April 15	EBRD	Opening of EBRD, led by Jacques Attali: more than $12 billion for Poland, Hungary, Czechoslovakia, Bulgaria, Romania, Yugoslavia, and the Soviet Union
May 1	Russia	Yeltsin successfully negotiates with Kuzbass coal miners to end strike/agrees to privatization

June	Germany	Vote to relocate capital from Bonn to Berlin
June	USSR	Prime Minister Valentin Pavlov defies Gorbachev in Parliament, asks for emergency economic authority
June 11	United States/USSR	Bush announces $1.5 billion in grain credits
July	Croatia/Slovenia	Declare independence from Serbian Yugoslavia
July	London	Gorbachev seeks aid at G-7 meeting (West promises technical assistance but no cash); Bush and Gorbachev agree on arms deal
July	Poland	Communists defeat Wałesa's plan in struggle over election law
July 25	USSR	Gorbachev gives speech in favor of private ownership and free market reform
July 31	Lithuania	Seven die in attack on border post
End July	USSR	Gorbachev announces new power-sharing agreement with ten out of fifteen republics/new union treaty (the missing five are Latvia, Lithuania, Estonia, Georgia, and Moldova)
August	Lithuania/Latvia	Outlaw the Communist Party
August	United States/USSR	Gorbachev and Bush sign 700-page Strategic Arms Reduction Treaty at Moscow summit; Gorbachev declares arms race over
August	USSR	Yeltsin abolishes Communist Party; Gorbachev objects but a day later goes along

Selective Chronology of Major Events (*continued*)

Date	Country	Event
1991 (*continued*)		
August 18–21	USSR	Failed Moscow coup: Gorbachev and family under KGB surveillance at country dacha in Crimea; Vice President Gennady Yanayev declares himself acting president, announces state of emergency; tanks invade Moscow; coup leaders in Kremlin; protesters rally at Parliament building/barricades/some troops and tanks defect to Yeltsin; tens of thousands demonstrate in support of Yeltsin, who climbs on tank, says, "The reactionaries will not triumph," declares coup illegal, calls for general strike and civil disobedience; Gorbachev, in Crimea, listens to British Broadcasting Corporation, Radio Liberty, and Voice of America, which broadcast Yeltsin's call for resistance; thousands protest in Leningrad with support of Mayor Anatoly Sobchak; Yeltsin calls Bush, asks for his help; Bush sends Robert Strauss as envoy to Moscow, convenes National Security Council; United States halts aid; coal miners prepare to strike; by Tuesday, crowds of 150,000 support Yeltsin; putsch tanks leave Moscow; Parliament demands Gorbachev's return to power
August 20	Estonia	Formally declares independence
August 21	Latvia	Formally declares independence
August 22	USSR	Gorbachev returns to Moscow; statue of secret police founder Dzerzhinsky toppled; Boris Pugo, former interior minister and coup plotter (and former head of KGB in Latvia), commits suicide
August 25	Ukraine	Declares independence
August 25	Belorussia	Declares independence
August 27	Moldova	Declares independence
August 29	Estonia	Government officials remove statue of Lenin

End August	Baltics	Russian paratroopers invade but withdraw
August	Germany, Belgium	Favor Western recognition of Baltics
August	Russia/Estonia	Yeltsin recognizes Estonia's independence
By September	Kazakhstan	Declared itself nuclear-free, shuts down Soviet atomic testing facility at Semipalatinsk
September	USSR	Gorbachev names Boris Pankin as the new Soviet foreign minister
September	Azerbaijan	Becomes eighth republic to declare independence
September	United States/Great Britain	Bush and John Major announce six-point Soviet aid plan
September	Three Baltics	Officially gain independence
September	Soviet republics	Agreements between fifteen republics, Gorbachev and Yeltsin
September	Russia	Leningrad renamed Saint Petersburg; Crimean region declares independence
October	Romania	Theodor Stolojan new prime minister
October	Bulgaria	Reestablishes relations with Turkey
October	Former USSR	Eight republics sign union treaty
November	Russia	Yeltsin plans to decontrol prices by end of 1991
November	Germany	Statue of Lenin dismantled in Berlin
End November	Yugoslavia	Vukovar falls to Serbs
December	Ukraine	Leonid Kravchuk elected president

Selective Chronology of Major Events (*continued*)

Date	Country	Event
1991 (*continued*)		
December	USSR	Soviet Union formally disbanded; eleven republics form CIS
1992		
January	CIS	Gorbachev transfers power to Yeltsin; Yeltsin institutes sweeping market reforms, including price decontrols except for bread, salt, gas, coal, and a few other staples; ceilings given for key commodities including milk, bread, fuel oil, and vodka; price of bread quadruples in Moscow state stores; most wage ceilings removed; state stores to be privatized; Yeltsin v. Kravchuk, over Black Sea fleet as possession of Russia or Ukraine
January	Georgia	President Zviad Gamsakhurdia flees violence-ridden Tbilisi for Armenia (had been under siege in Parliament building; rebels set KGB headquarters on fire); more than 100 dead; Yeltsin opposes use of army as peacekeepers in regional disputes
January	Azerbaijan	President Ayaz Mutalibov says Azerbaijan is at war with Armenia (hundreds killed in ethnic violence, 1987–91)
January	Moldova	Ethnic Russians declare own state in Dniester region
January	Russia	Egor Gaidar, minister of the economy, says 21,000 out of about 70,000 small businesses in Russia have now been commercialized
January 3	Yugoslavia	Fourteen abortive cease-fires in six months of civil war so far; warring factions sign U.N.-brokered cease-fire to include U.N. peacekeeping force of 14,000 in Croatia; five peace monitors killed in unarmed EC helicopter blown up by Yugoslav air force
January 16	Bosnia-Herzegovina	Some 1.3 million Serbs declare independence

End January	Washington, D.C.	United States convenes forty-seven-nation conference on aid to former Soviet republics (Yeltsin not invited); Bush pledges additional $645 million in U.S. aid over two years; U.S. Air Force will fly in medicine and food left over from gulf war; conference estimates $30 billion in economic/humanitarian aid is needed
February	Poland	Polish miners in Warsaw protest Wałesa's economic policies
February	CIS	Yeltsin at multination summit at United Nations in New York
February	United States/CIS	Bush and Yeltsin declare their countries no longer enemies but friends; Russians want U.S. technical/financial help in dismantling weapons; U.S. Congress appropriates $400 million to help CIS secure and dismantle nuclear missiles and chemical weapons
February 25–26	Azerbaijan	Armenian forces invade Khojaly area; Soviet troops withdraw
February 29	Bosnia-Herzegovina	Bosnian Muslims and Croats vote for idependence; Bosnian Serbs boycott the vote
March	Albania	First open elections; Socialist Party ousted; hard-liner President Ramiz Alia resigns; widespread unemployment, commodity shortages, looting, food riots
March	Bosnia	Serbian nationalists declare war on Bosnia after Muslims and Croats vote to secede from Yugoslavia
April	G-7 nations	Agree on $24 billion in aid to Russia ($5 billion by United States), with IMF scrutiny
May	Tajikstan	Anticommunist coup
May	Yugoslavia	Breadline massacre in Sarajevo
End June	Czechoslovakia	Czech leader Vaclav Klaus and Slovak leader Vladimir Meciar agree to split state, probably by end of summer
July	Bosnia-Herzegovina	Sarajevo besieged by Serbian nationalists

Selective Chronology of Major Events (*continued*)

Date	Country	Event
1992 (continued)		
July	Yugoslavia	California businessman Milan Panic sworn in as prime minister of new Serbian federation
July	Czechoslovakia	Havel resigns
August	Germany	Erich Honecker, nearly eighty, returns to Berlin to face charges
October	Russia	President Yeltsin takes away Gorbachev's right to travel abroad; Yeltsin issues 148 million privatization vouchers, one per citizen, with face value of 10,000 rubles each
October	Estonia	Lennart Meri, pro–free market, wins presidential runoff
November	Lithuania	Communists voted back into power
December	Russia	Parliament attempts to oust Prime Minister Gaidar against Yeltsin's objections; agreement on referendum 4/11/93; by 12/28/92, new prime minister is Viktor Chernomyrdin
1993		
January 1	Czech-Slovak	Official split
January	Bosnia	President Alija Izetbegovic elected
January	Czech Republic	Vaclav Havel president of new republic
March–April	Russia	Yeltsin, on television, appeals to the people; claims special rule, taking power back from Parliament till popular referendum 4/25, including vote on a new constitution; Yeltsin battles with Parliament/Ruslan Khasbulatov is his chief adversary; Yeltsin agrees to drop April referendum if presidential and parliamentary elections will be held in fall; Khasbulatov decides not to try to impeach Yeltsin; Yeltsin and Vice President Aleksandr Rutskoi exchange verbal attacks

By April	Russia	Approximately 200,000 demobilized troops withdrawn from Eastern Europe; more than 200 American companies have opened Moscow offices, but U.S. business investment in Russia is under half a billion dollars
April	Vancouver, Canada	Bill Clinton/Yeltsin meeting; Clinton offers $1.6 billion in aid (not yet authorized by Congress); Yeltsin accepts
April 25	Russia	Referendum: 66 percent of electorate vote; 57 percent of voters trust Boris Yeltsin, 54 percent support his economic policies; he proposes new constitution, with two newly elected houses to replace Parliament
May	Poland	Wałesa dissolves Parliament after Prime Minister Hanna Suchocka's government loses vote of confidence
May 1	Russia	Procommunist demonstrators violent in Moscow streets
June	Germany	Changes its easy-asylum law
June	Ukraine	Prime Minister Kuchma urges Parliament to *keep* nuclear weapons
End July	Russia	New ruble issued; old rubles must be exchanged at savings banks
August	Georgia	CIA station chief Fred Woodruff shot and killed
August	Poland/CIS	President Yeltsin visits President Wałesa
September	Poland	In elections, former Communists win new role
September	Russia	Anti-Yeltsin demonstrations in Moscow; after one shooting incident, Yeltsin orders militia defending Parliament disarmed; Yeltsin announces new presidential election for June 1994

SELECTIVE CHRONOLOGY OF MAJOR EVENTS (*continued*)

Date	Country	Event
1993 (*continued*)		
By October	Georgia	Shevardnadze now head of state; U.S. intelligence claims that Russian military helped Abkhazian rebel uprising/fighting in early October in city of Sukhumi, which fell to rebels after twelve days; Yeltsin's government denies role
October	Russia	Twelve days after Yeltsin dissolves hard-line Parliament, violent anti-Yeltsin demonstrations; Yeltsin declares state of emergency; Yeltsin sends in tanks against Parliament building (10/11), enemies surrender; 178 die in Moscow battles during the week; 800 wounded; Rutskoi and Khasbulatov jailed
By mid October	Russia	About thirty of its eighty-nine regions no longer paying taxes to central budget
October	Georgia	Abkhazia breaks away, deports 200,000 Georgians; Shevardnadze asks for Russian help
October	Estonia	In first free post-Soviet local elections, former communist Arnold Ruutel is elected mayor of Tallinn; Ruutel's coalition party gains eighteen of sixty-four seats in Tallinn city council versus only five seats for the ruling National Fatherland Party; communist hard-liners lose in city of Narva
December	Hungary	EC Council of Ministers accords associate EC membership to Hungary
December 12	Russia	Parliamentary elections; Zhirinovsky and his Liberal Democratic Party win big, with about 25 percent of vote, but 58 percent approve Yeltsin's new constitution
1994		
January	United States/CIS	Clinton, Yeltsin, and Kravchuk (Ukraine) sign disarmament pact in Moscow
March	Russia	Nixon meets with Rutskoi supporters; Yeltsin cancels meeting with Nixon
Early March	Russia	October putsch leaders released

April	Russia/Azerbaijan	Azerbaijani president Aliyev agrees to Russian troops on Azerbaijan's border with Iran
May	Russia	Aleksandr Solzhenitsyn returns; by May 1994, approximately 40 percent of Moscow apartments privatized
May	Hungary	Communists win absolute majority in elections; Gulya Horn named prime minister
May 29	Germany	Death of former East German leader Erich Honecker in Santiago, Chile
June 13	Bulgaria	Only 34 percent of registered voters vote, so election declared invalid
June 14	Romania	Thousands of Romanian workers, including 10,000 trade unionists, demand 50 percent salary increases, demonstrate in Bucharest against Prime Minister Nicolae Vacarolu
June 22	Russia	Joins NATO's Partners for Peace program for nonmember nations
July 10	Ukraine	Leonid Kuchma wins presidential election

SOURCES:

Newsweek, January 1989–June 1994; *Time*, January–March 1989 and March 1990; *Business Week*, April–June 1991.

Collins, Susan M., and Dani Rodrik. *Eastern Europe and the Soviet Union in the World Economy*. Washington, D.C.: Institute for International Economics, May 1991.

Staar, Richard F., ed. *1991 Yearbook on International Communist Affairs* (25th anniversary edition). Stanford: Hoover Institution Press, 1991: Robert R. King, "Romania," pp. 332–59; John D. Bell, "Bulgaria," pp. 260–69; Carol Skalnik Leff, "Czechoslovakia," pp. 269–82; R. Judson Mitchell, "Union of Soviet Socialist Republics," pp. 359–404.

PART TWO

FUNDAMENTAL COMPONENTS OF ECONOMIC REFORM

2

Macroeconomics in Russia

JOHN H. COCHRANE and
BARRY W. ICKES

Russia faces macroeconomic problems, an apparently calamitous fall in output, and high and variable inflation, along with the microeconomic problems of reform and transition to a market economy. We survey the numbers and conclude that the fall in output, though real, is much less than often supposed. We find reasons for the fall in output in disruptions to the credit and payment systems as they were partially liberalized, excacerbated by a shock to interrepublic trade. The fall in output from these sources is not a necessary part of the transition to market economy; it was avoidable, and steps can be taken to make sure it is not repeated. We stress the link between inflation and the present-value government budget. Declining tax revenues and increasing arrears make us suspect that the current declines in inflation may not last. Finally, we discuss the conundrum of making policies such as a hardening of budget constraints believable, so that firms will act on them.

the current Russian situation, and standard macroeconomic advice—tighten money, run a balanced budget, and so on—is just as obvious and unlikely to be heeded as the standard microeconomic advice to free all markets as quickly as possible. We emphasize three different and often ignored aspects of macroeconomic policy: the dynamics of inflation and present-value government budget balance, the insidious reach of disturbances to the financial and payments system, and the difficulties of making *time-consistent* policy plans.

A macroeconomic observer looking at Russia notices high inflation and an apparent calamitous fall in output. High inflation is easily understood: it is a sign of a government budget that is out of control. Most observers seem to think that lowering inflation is a matter of will, of finding a sufficiently surly director of the central bank. Instead, we emphasize the link of inflation to present and future budget deficits. The surliest minister in the world will have to inflate when the government runs out of money.

The fall in output is more puzzling. Commentators often take for granted that liberalization will imply a period of falling output and living standards before the advantages of markets kick in, but there is little in *economics* to buttress this opinion. Aside from technical counterexamples, economics teaches us that the more freedom the better, so that an economy that liberalizes should do *better* right away. Thus, we have to think about how much of the fall in output is real and then figure out what caused the part that is real. Was it avoidable? What policies can the government take to keep output from falling further?

We start by looking critically at the numbers. We conclude that the actual fall is much less than is apparent. Yet output *has* fallen and certainly has not *risen* as we would expect it to. We review some basic but often forgotten macroeconomics on the source of inflation and the fact that inflation per se is not a reason for falling output. Thus, we search for economically intelligible *reasons* output fell. We find those reasons in the havoc remaining in the still heavily controlled and underdeveloped financial system. These reasons are *avoidable*, they are not a necessary part of the transition from planning to free markets.

A financial system is critical in market economies, so that payments can be made effectively, the state of enterprises can be easily evaluated, and the right incentives for investment (or disinvestment) and output choices are given. Despite this central importance of the financial system for economic reform, development of the financial system has not received a high priority in reform plans. We briefly review the development of the financial system in Russia as it has evolved since the breakup of the Soviet Union.

We tell a story of haphazard partial changes with massive unintended consequences. Starting from a roughly coherent and tightly controlled system, a few parts are liberalized in a first round of "reform." But a half-liberalized system is often worse than either a fully controlled or a fully liberalized system: The liberalization allows people to scheme the remaining controls, and the reform

Figure 2.1   Inflation: Monthly Change in Consumer Prices

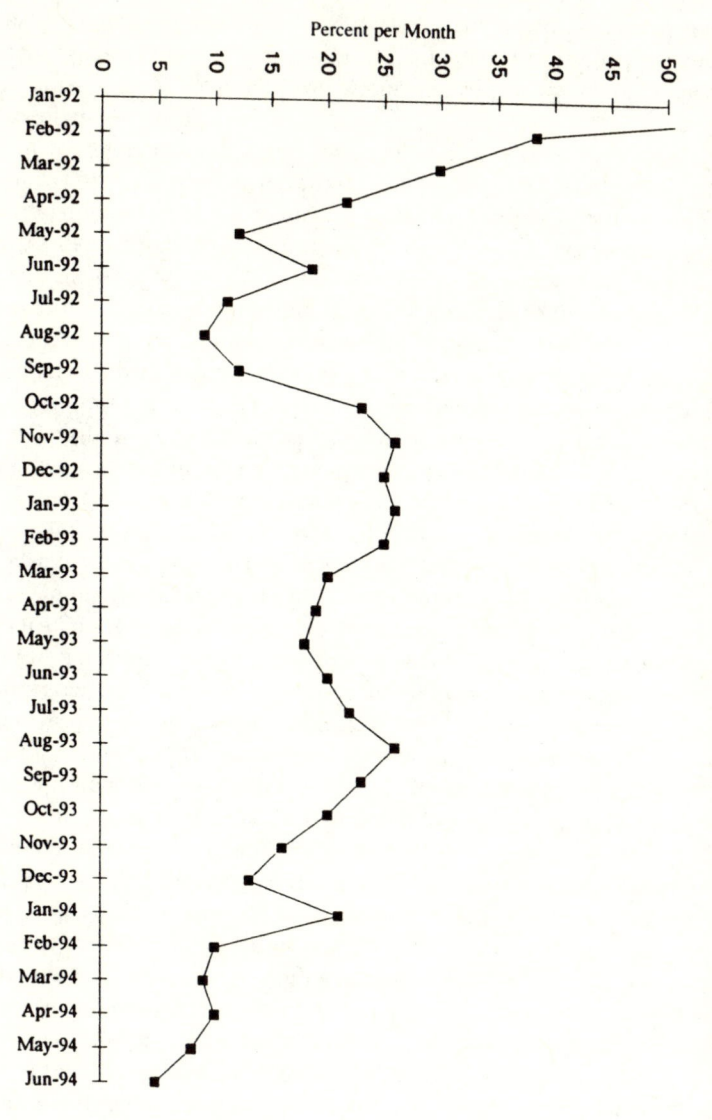

Percent per Month

NOTE: Note that inflation for January 1992 was 245 percent.
SOURCE: PlanEcon X, 8–9, April 1994, Interfax, July 6, 1994.

plan breaks down. A new set of policies is enacted, which break down in the same way. New plans are less and less credible, yet credibility is exactly what a financial system requires to function.

To conclude, we offer some tentative prognostications. Here we are much less optimistic than most commentators who extrapolate current trends. We also comment on possible policy actions.

Recent Macroeconomic History: A Look at the Numbers

One must take great care when interpreting Russian macroeconomic data. Numbers with the same names may have different meanings than their Western counterparts, and data collection methods are different. These are not trivial technical matters: They can lead to a fundamental misunderstanding of the situation.

INFLATION

Measured inflation in Russia has been dramatic since price controls were lifted in January 1992. The price-level shock—a 245 percent increase in the first month—was initially followed by declining inflation rates, confirming the predictions by many observers (including ourselves, Cochrane and Ickes 1992) that price liberalization need not kick off a bout of inflation. But inflation then increased. From the summer of 1992 until the winter of 1993–1994, inflation hovered above 20 percent a month (see figure 2.1). Most recently, monthly inflation has fallen below 10 percent a month, but it remains to be seen whether this reduction can be sustained.

The initial price shock was so large because price controls were lifted following long-suppressed excess demand. During the late Gorbachev period, the government increasingly resorted to money-financed deficit spending. In 1991 the fiscal deficit for the Soviet Union exceeded 19 percent of gross national product (GNP),[1] almost entirely financed by monetization. At the same time, prices in official markets were controlled. Inflation was not zero—even official controlled prices more than doubled during 1991—but money creation far outstripped the rise in prices. Hence, when price controls were lifted on January 2, 1992, the jump in the price level was the inevitable response, the last gasp of Soviet inflation.

Prices were liberalized for most goods, although some staples, milk, and bread and some basic inputs, such as energy prices, remained controlled. After

March 1992 most remaining price controls were lifted, save for energy, although some prices remained controlled by the decision of antimonopoly committees.[2]

After the initial price shock, prices continued to rise, but the inflation rate began to decelerate. The proximate causes of inflation are, of course, increases in the stock of money and central bank credits,[3] and monetary policy was rather tight in early 1992. Figure 2.2 plots money and credit growth along with inflation.

Figures 2.1 and 2.2 suggest three phases. The first period, from the initial price shock to the end of June 1992, was the period of (relatively) tight money. As can be seen in figure 2.2, both inflation and money growth were declining in this period.[4]

One important consequence of tight credit in this period, however, was an explosion of interenterprise debt,[5] from 39 billion rubles in January 1992 to 3.2 trillion rubles six months later. The mechanisms of this explosion are complex, and we deal with them below. Suffice it to say here that enterprises found themselves unable to cover their expenditures; unable to get official government credits, they simply let unpaid bills pile up. As a result of the explosion in arrears, the attempt to maintain a tight credit policy was overturned, and Viktor Gerashchenko, the last head of Gosbank, was brought back to lead the Central Bank of Russia.

The second phase, from July 1992 through December 1993, is a period of relatively high money growth and high inflation. Although fluctuations are apparent, it is evident from figure 2.1 that inflation during this period was typically above 20 percent a month. During this period, credit was rather loose, although it is apparent from figure 2.3 that credit growth slowed during 1993. The interenterprise debts that had accumulated in the first period were basically monetized (paid with newly printed money/new credit) in this period. Moreover, relatively easy money financed continuing losses of many enterprises and postponed a recurrence of interenterprise arrears.

In the current, third phase, inflation has fallen below single digits. Figures for June 1994 show inflation below 6 percent a month. A dramatic reduction in credit growth, as is evident in figure 2.3, is the primary reason that inflation has fallen.

Interenterprise arrears, however, have returned. The total volume of arrears[6] on March 1, 1994, was estimated at 30.9 trillion rubles. Russia's March GNP was 36.9 trillion rubles, so the arrears are about 10 percent of annual GNP. Arrears were 3.8 trillion rubles at the height of the arrears crisis in 1992, estimated variously at 20–40 percent of GNP (see Ickes and Ryterman 1992, 1993), or 62 trillion rubles in today's rubles. Thus, the March 1994 arrears were at least one-fourth to one-half of their level at the height of the crisis. Ominously, arrears now include wage and tax arrears and are more concentrated in loss-making industries.

Until the spring of 1994, interest rates were hundreds of percentage points

Figure 2.2   Growth in M2, Central Bank Credit, and Inflation

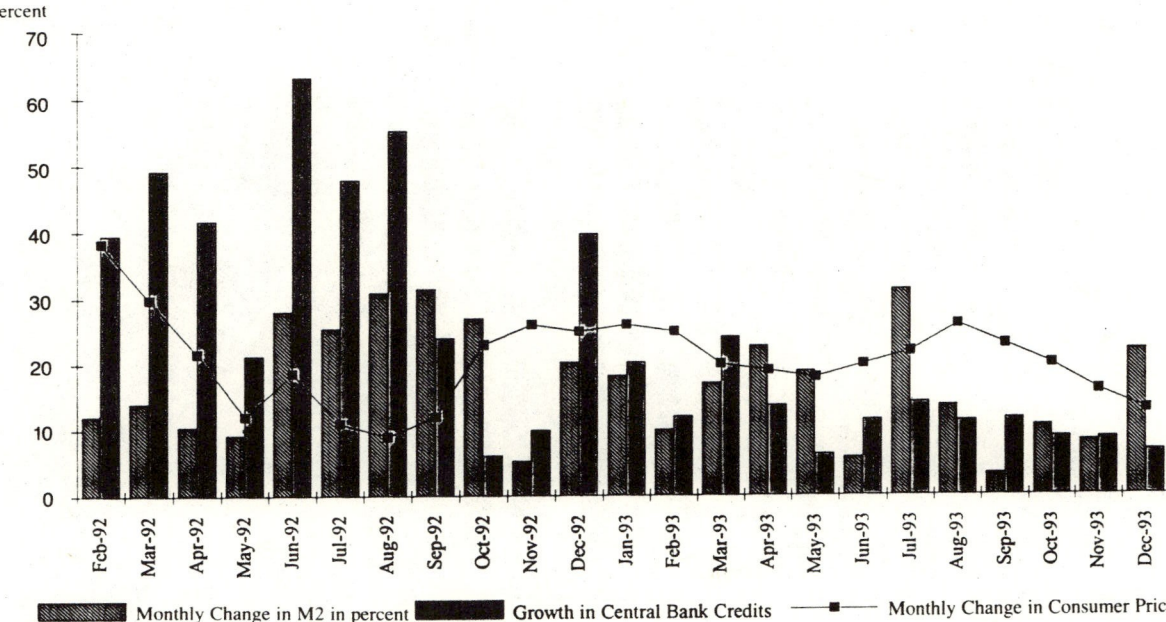

SOURCE: Plan Econ, X, 8–9, April 28, 1994

Figure 2.3   Growth in Real Central Bank Credit

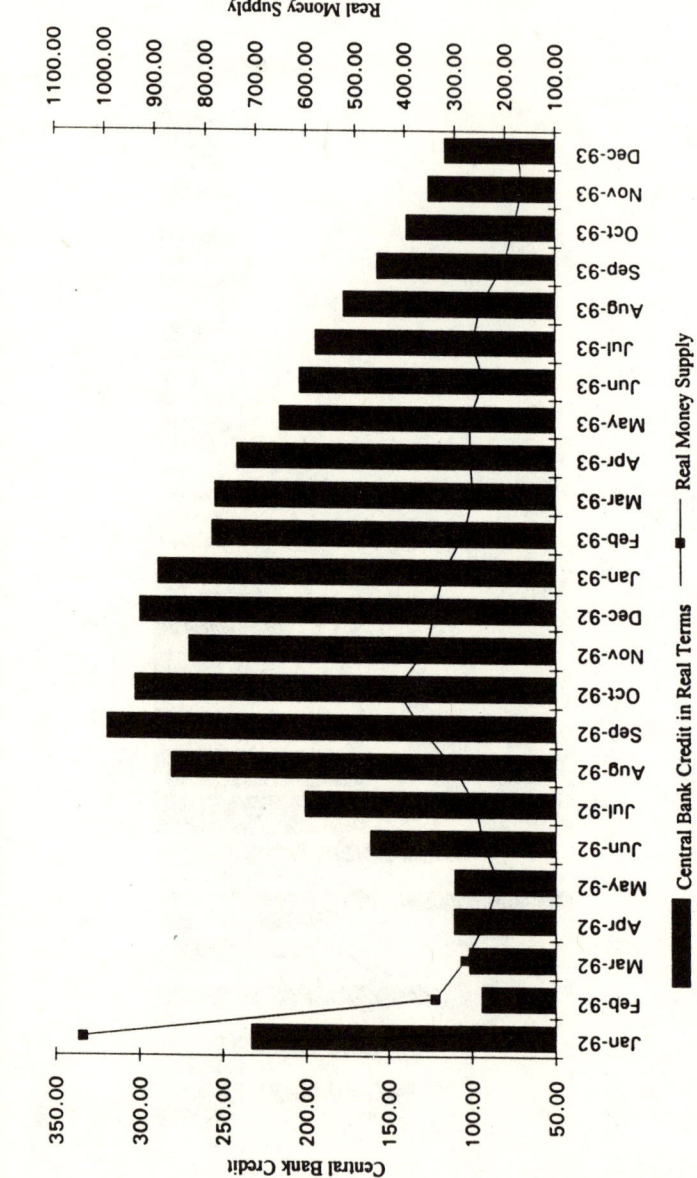

NOTE: Central Bank Credit and M2 Deflated by Consumer Price Index.

less than inflation rates. The discount rate of the Central Bank, for example, averaged around 175 percent a year during 1993, while monthly inflation was over 20 percent (800 percent a year). This means that obtaining credit was tantamount to obtaining a gift; naturally, connections rather than the price allocated such "credit." As a result, the level of interest rates was a poor indicator of the stringency of monetary policy. Interest rates in 1994 have fallen slightly in nominal terms, but owing to the fall in inflation, they are positive in real terms for the first time. The implied monthly rates as of July 1994 are in the 15 percent range, substantially above monthly inflation, which is less than 10 percent. This may not reflect conscious policy as much as slow adjustment of nominal rates to the decline in inflation. Inflation is so volatile, however, that the actual real return on a three-month loan is uncertain.

OUTPUT

Statistics on the fall in output are so large as to be unbelievable. Figure 2.4 presents gross domestic product (GDP), industrial output, and gross fixed investment since 1991. Russian GDP fell 19 percent in 1992 and another 12 percent during 1993. The first quarter of 1994 was down again, 15 percent over the first quarter of 1993, or down at a 20 percent annual rate against the last quarter of 1993. Even the government forecasts that 1994 GDP will be 16–18 percent below the 1993 level. The cumulative fall in GDP since 1990 is more than 40 percent. Compared with the 2–3 percent cumulative falls in GDP in U.S. recessions, these figures seem to indicate a total collapse.[7]

Industrial production has fallen as much or more than GDP. Industrial output fell 16.2 percent in 1993 and it dropped nearly 26 percent in the first half of 1994. As of July 1994, the government forecast that 1994 industrial production will be 25 percent below the 1993 level. Investment has fallen even more steeply, to 30–40 percent of its 1990 level.

The differences between industrial output, GDP, and investment reflect a deeper sense in which output declines are not spread evenly. For example, the first quarter 1994 over first quarter 1993 output decline was 30–40 percent or more in chemicals, engineering, construction, and machine building but less than 10 percent in fuels, electricity, and metallurgy. Production of some consumer durables have even increased—TVs are up 8 percent, and refrigerators, 9 percent.

These facts suggest that the actual situation is not as catastrophic as the GDP or industrial production numbers suggest. The Soviet economy had a vastly overblown industrial sector, dominated by the military-industrial complex, and far too *much*, largely unproductive, investment, reported as high as 40 percent of GDP. At a more micro level, as Cliff Gaddy points out, "the real problem of the Soviet economy was not that it produced too little, too inefficiently, or with too much waste. The problem was that it produced *the wrong things*" (Gaddy

Figure 2.4   Gross Domestic Product, Industrial Output, and Fixed Investment

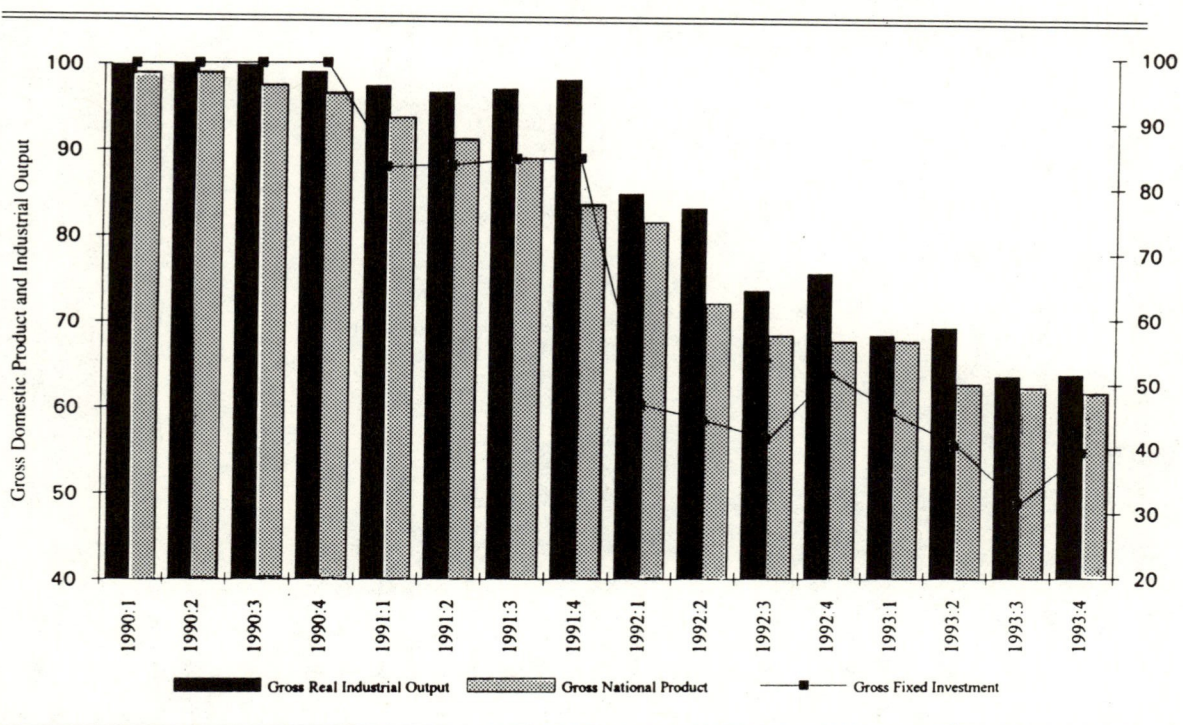

NOTE: 1990:1 = 100.
SOURCE: PlanEcon, X, 8–9, April 28, 1994

1993, 1). To a large extent, the rapid decline in industrial output and investment, especially construction, in old state industries represents a *positive* development.

Furthermore, the statistical system in Russia, which was designed to collect data from state-owned enterprises, is far less able to monitor developments in the new private sector. New firms tend to be concentrated in retail trade and services, which are inherently more difficult to monitor than, say, machine tools. Furthermore, where there was once a strong incentive to report, even overreport, output, both state-owned and privatized firms now have a strong incentive to underreport output in order to evade taxes. Underreporting is an inevitable consequence of very high tax rates and a statistical system that is not sharply cordoned off from the tax authorities. Thus, reports on the fall in industrial output largely reflect the healthy decline in parts of the former state-owned sector. They underreport output in any profit-making enterprise and ignore the rapid development of private businesses.

Finally, the statistical system is geared to the measurement of *raw output*, not *value added*. The plan specified output, and it is very hard to measure value added in a command economy without prices. Although the statistical system is now being changed to measure value added, many Russians still think in terms of industrial production. It is still difficult for many Russians, and many policy makers, to think of services as productive of value.

Value-added calculations are even harder in a high-inflation environment. If costs are incurred two months before output is sold, and inflation is 20 percent a month, then even a break-even proposition will show a 40 percent profit. Indeed, a World Bank survey of Russian enterprises found that all enterprises surveyed were profitable for this reason, even though many were actually on the verge of bankruptcy! In contrast, given the delays in payments, delays in paying wages, long floats in clearing checks, and so forth, it is not always clear in which direction the bias goes. Certainly, the interaction of accounting and inflation is responsible for the fact that measured real GDP always seems to change the most, especially relative to industrial production, when there are big changes in inflation (see figure 2.4).

Industrial production measures are based on raw output, as always. In the United States we are used to the idea that industrial production moves closely with GNP, but this is much less true in Russia. *Raw output* figures are a misleading guide to *value added*, or GNP. If a steel plant loses 100,000 rubles on every ton of steel it sells, every ton decline in its industrial production is a 100,000-ruble *increase* in value added, or national income. Declines in industrial output can be a good thing.

Employment data also indicate a shift away from the state sector and toward the private sector. Much of this is due to privatization of state enterprises rather than actual job changing. Of total employment of seventy-one million, employment in the state sector fell 6.5 million, to 41.5 million in 1993. The share of employment in the state sector fell from 67 percent in 1992 to 59 percent in 1993.

It is surprising how big the state sector still *is*. The privatization program is often regarded as a great success, and observers cite the huge number of enterprises that have been privatized. But the state sector still accounts for half of all employment.

Furthermore, *privatized* is another of those words that conjure up misleading images to Western observers. A "privatized" state firm most often has the same management and workers (typically, they are now the nominal owners); it still receives subsidies and may receive state orders for output; it still uses the dual-monetary system as outlined below; and it expects to be insulated from bankruptcy. Many of these firms have not changed what they produce, their sources of supply, or their customers. Many "privatized" firms *behave* as if nothing has changed.

In summary, much of the apparently disastrous decline in output and industrial production reflects mismeasurement, a healthy decline of the state sector and leaves out important increases in output in the new private and privatized sector.

CONSUMPTION AND LIVING STANDARDS

A 50 percent decline in industrial production in the United States would imply a roughly 50 percent decline in personal income and hence a catastrophic decline in living standards. A direct look at living standards might confirm our hunch that the declines in reported Russian output are overstated.

Figure 2.5 presents estimates of real wages and living standards in Russia. The huge measured decline in living standards during the price liberalization of January 1, 1992, stands out. This measurement, or the equivalent observation that nominal wages rose much less than prices, forms the conventional view that living standards have fallen by 50 percent or more.

Of course, nothing of the sort happened. The overall standard of living in Russia—the level of goods produced and consumed—did not drop from an index of 160 to an index of 40 overnight! Rather, low prices and unavailable goods were replaced by higher prices and many more available goods. The true cost of obtaining goods—waiting in line, and so forth—is not included in the pre-1992 statistics.

Similarly, officially measured, industrial Soviet real wages increased by 79 percent from 1985 to December 1991 (Lipton and Sachs 1992, 220). Increasingly autonomous enterprises raised wages, official prices remained fixed or rose slowly, shortages intensified, and queues lengthened. Prices were much higher in unmeasured parallel markets. The total supply of consumer goods did not increase, so this was no more a period of rising living standards than January 1992 was a dramatic fall.

Figure 2.5   Living Standards

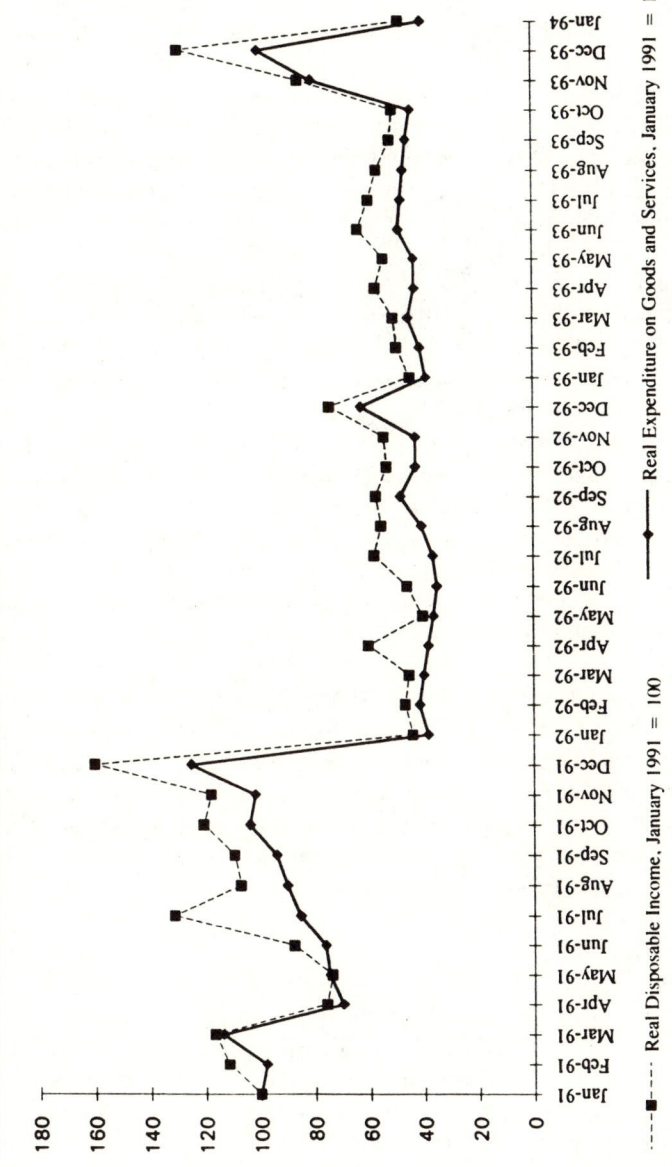

SOURCE: PlanEcon, X, 8–9, April 28, 1994

Moreover, excessive focus on what has happened to these measures of living standards ignores the dramatic increase in choice that price liberalization has brought. With a broader range of choice, consumers can achieve much higher levels of welfare at the same level of expenditure and without the constant waste of time spent waiting in line.

Ignoring the price-induced blips, the trend, or absence thereof, in figure 2.5 is informative. Despite the apparently calamitous decline in industrial production, these measures of living standards appear not to have changed much since January 1992. In fact, the most recent figures show that consumption increased in 1993, real wages rose 11 percent in the first five months of 1994, and the population's savings doubled.

The same picture emerges in retail sales numbers. For example, despite roughly 20 percent declines in output measures, retail sales in constant prices for January–May 1994 are down only 2.4 percent from the same period a year ago. Similarly, household income at constant prices and private consumption were both up in 1994 over 1993.

Unemployment at the end of 1993 was 1.1 percent officially, up from 0.8 percent at the end of 1992. This rate rose to 1.3 percent by March 1994. Alternative measures that use survey evidence give a higher unemployment rate, 5.1 percent up from 4.9 percent a year earlier. Still, these are tiny rates for an economy that has supposedly suffered a 50 percent or more output drop. Other chapters in this volume discuss the employment situation in more detail— whether the "employed" are really working and how much private sector employment there is.

We don't want to imply that everything is rosy. It seems that the overall standard of living is at best staying even, where it should be increasing quickly. The *distribution* of wealth is a big problem. Pensioners' savings were wiped out, and pensions have not been fully indexed. The army and workers in out-of-the-way, one- (dying) industry cities are in trouble. Others are prospering. These are serious problems but not to be confused with the *macroeconomic* problem of a precipitously falling *overall* living standard.

TRADE

Russia has lately been running trade *surpluses*: $17.5 billion in 1993 and a forecast of $16 billion for 1994. Most analysts like trade surpluses, but it reflects bad news in Russia's case. Russia ought to be the focus of massive investment— investment in the *right places*, of course, not dying state industries. But investment from abroad is a capital-account surplus, which corresponds to a trade *deficit*. Russia should be borrowing or selling equity and other assets abroad and *importing* vast amounts of capital goods. That it is running trade *surpluses* is an indication of capital flight and the woeful lack of investment by Russians as well as by foreigners. Russia could even run trade deficits of consumer goods—borrowing from abroad against the higher future income that successful reform will bring.[8] By contrast, the trade surplus may be much lower than reported. To avoid taxes, importers have a large incentive to underreport.

Breakdowns in interrepublic trade have played a critical role in the actual fall in output since 1992. The demise of the Soviet Union did not change the high degree of economic interdependence within the region. The Soviet Union placed greater emphasis on industry rather than region in planning, concentrated industries in search of ephemeral economies of scale, and may even have encouraged economic interdependence for political reasons. The typical state firm received inputs from many different republics and had traditional customers throughout the former USSR. Since the summer of 1992 many of these links have been broken, and enterprise directors have scrambled for new customers and suppliers.

The disruption of interrepublic trade accounts for a large and, we think avoidable, part of the real decline in output. The reasons for the breakdown require a careful analysis of the monetary and payments system, which we undertake below.

GOVERNMENT FINANCES

The success of the stabilization program in Russia ultimately depends on what happens to the fiscal deficit. The deterioration of the fiscal regime in the Gorbachev period was one important cause of that system's demise. Revenues collapsed as the authority of the center declined. The fiscal deficit of the Soviet Union was some 20 percent of GNP in 1991. It is not surprising then that cutting the budget deficit was a top priority of the first Gaidar government.

The extent to which the Russian government succeeded in reducing the budget deficit in 1992 is a matter of dispute because budget accounting in Russia is even more obscure than in Western countries. Import subsidies are a particularly controversial item. The International Monetary Fund (IMF) estimates them to have been 13.8 percent of GDP in 1992. Including this item takes the budget deficit from 7.8 percent to 21.8 percent of GDP on a cash basis and even more on a commitment basis because the government restrained spending below appropriated levels. A survey by the Russian Ministry of Finance (1994) gives much higher numbers for the consolidated budget deficit when measured on an internationally comparable basis. According to this source, the budget deficit was 35.9 percent of GDP in 1992, about half of which was financed by foreign credits.[9] But Sachs (1994) argues that inclusion of foreign-financed import subsidies presents an inaccurate picture of the budget situation because that component of the deficit required no monetization. In contrast, the IMF includes them in their estimates of the Russian budget deficit because these credits are claims on future revenue: Forward-looking people know that these credits will have to be paid off in the future, [10] and consequently their current inflation expectations are affected.

In addition, many funds are off budget—pension, social insurance, employment, and research and development, among others—and are in the hands of government agencies (Delyagin and Freinkman 1993). Although large, these funds seem to be roughly in balance with off-budget expenditures; thus, their inclusion does not change the overall balance by much (Hanson 1994, 18).

It *is* clear that the Russian government succeeded in cutting expenditures, much of them in the defense complex. All measures show that expenditures declined as a share of GDP in 1993, an impressive achievement when we recall that GDP fell by some 12 percent over 1992. Another indicator is the slowdown in Central Bank credits in 1993 (see figure 2.3), about a third of which are provided to the Finance Ministry (industry via commercial banks and other republics each get about a third as well). In March 1994, the Russian government and the IMF arrived at a stand-by agreement on the basis of a government pledge to keep the deficit to 8.6 percent of GDP in 1994. The pledge is certain to be broken, but this deficit is at a much lower level than previously.

But revenues have also fallen since 1992, a trend that increased in 1994. A recent report by the Ministry of Finance, for example, noted that revenues in the first quarter of 1994 were 65 percent of anticipated levels, on the basis of which the budget was formed. This might not be a problem if it were due to a decline in tax rates, leaving room to raise revenue by raising tax rates, but precisely the opposite is true.

Russian enterprises are subject to a 28 percent value-added tax (VAT), a profits tax with an average effective rate of 34 percent, and a wage tax, among many others. These taxes leave little revenue for restructuring and are a healthy encouragement to tax evasion. The decline in government revenues is primarily the result of the fall in output and a decline in the quality of tax collection, despite some of the highest tax rates in the world.

Tax rates, and the rules under which they are applied, have changed frequently. In July 1992, for example, the rules for the VAT were changed, dropping the invoice system. Enterprises could no longer buy inputs for inventories now and claim credits against future tax payments. This change made the VAT more like a sales tax than a value-added tax, applying to loss-making enterprises as much as to profit-making ones. Moreover, this change was retroactive to the beginning of the year. The arbitrary variation in tax structure is important in some of the economic stories we tell below. In particular, it is certainly understandable if enterprise managers are reluctant to invest based on even today's heavy tax rules, figuring that the government will change the rules ex post again and wipe out any profit.

With interenterprise debt and tax arrears mounting, with little room to increase tax revenue, and with a continuing implicit commitment to provide credits for enterprises in distress, one questions whether the government will be able to continue to reduce the deficit.

SUMMARY

Inflation is of course real and substantial. Its uneven pace and uneven nature across goods induces a large and spurious variation in relative prices, distorts the tax system and any accounting, and increases payment system and credit disruptions.

Despite the enormous decline in industrial output, measures of personal income seem flat. Thus, it seems that we are primarily seeing the healthy disappearance of the state industrial sector. However, payments and credit problems, the difficulty of trade across republics of the former Soviet Union and incredibly high tax rates are keeping even well-measured output much lower than it could be.

The government's finances are the most ominous warning for the future. There is a growing stock of interenterprise debt that enterprises expect to be bailed out of tax revenues are falling, and the government is already behind on many payments.

Macroeconomic Frameworks

It is widely assumed that the tighter money and credit policies required to reduce inflation will cause output drops. For a recent example, the Economist Intelligence Unit (1994) says that "the decline in industrial production *resulting from the clampdown on money growth* have proven more alarming" (our emphasis) and that "the alarming figures on falling output—the price paid for declining inflation." Clearly, whether there *is* a tradeoff between output and inflation, what that tradeoff is, and by what mechanism it operates are some of the most pressing macroeconomic questions for the Russian economy.

MONETARY AND FISCAL POLICY

Much macroeconomic policy discussion in Western economies focuses on monetary and fiscal policies that governments undertake to affect business-cycle changes in output, employment, inflation, and exchange rates. It is less commonly realized that most of this framework is irrelevant to the situation in Russia. The *mechanisms* by which monetary and fiscal contractions are thought to cause output declines in Western economies do not operate in Russia's situation.

Fiscal Policy.   Fiscal policy—deficit spending—was once thought to have a direct stimulative power, but few economists think much of this channel anymore. It is clear that if the government raises taxes and spends the money, there will be no expansionary effect: Taking money from us and then giving it back can't help. The idea behind fiscal policy was that if the government *borrows* money from us and then spends it, we will be fooled into thinking we are richer, ignoring the fact that the government will have to raise taxes later on to pay the money back.

Now, economists concentrate on the *distortions* induced by taxes—the fact that people avoid activities like working and saving when the government taxes those activities too much. Borrowing and deficit spending serve a useful purpose in this framework. Borrowing can finance temporarily high government expenditures (such as a war), or it can finance expenditures through a temporary change in the tax system. By borrowing temporarily, tax rates can be kept low and steady. If the government could not borrow, it would have to temporarily raise tax rates to exorbitant levels, which would hurt the economy as people avoided the taxed activities. In the Russian context, we have a great deal to say about the distortions of the tax system.

Monetary Policy.   Contemporary analysis of monetary policy focuses on the possibility that money creation can fool people into producing more than they would otherwise. Some economists think prices are "sticky" so that more money leads to more output, rather than just higher prices for the same output. Other economists think that *surprise* increases in money and all prices can fool companies into thinking that the *relative* prices of their goods have risen and hence into producing more.

There are big arguments over which of the two stories is correct. But one thing is clear: Monetary policy cannot possibly affect output through either channel in Russia today. No economy with inflation at 10-20 percent a month and equally variable has any sticky prices left, nor is anyone likely to be fooled by a spurt of inflation into thinking that the *relative* prices for what he has to sell have risen. Empirical research has long documented that the real effects of monetary policies disappear in high inflation economies (for example, Lucas 1972.)

In summary, whether these business-cycle effects of monetary and fiscal policy exist, and, if so, whether governments can successfully employ them to stabilize fluctuations is a fascinating and ongoing controversy. But it is largely irrelevant to the situation in Russia. The declines in Russian output are hardly attributable to a lack of monetary or fiscal stimulus! Conversely, a sudden monetary or fiscal *tightening* cannot produce a further decline in output *through these usual channels*.

Perverse macroeconomic policies *can* lead to further economic calamities through different channels. Understanding these channels is important to designing or recommending policies to reduce inflation and deficits without further damaging the economy.

First, many industries hang on only by receiving government credits; a reduction in credits must certainly lead to lower output from those companies. However, these credits represent real resources, transferred to money-losing enterprises from elsewhere. Although output in the affected industries will certainly decline, overall, properly measured output and income will rise. It's a fair bet that any other use of the resources transferred to dying state industries will be more productive.

However, firms that would make profits in a free market face severe capital market constraints and heavy taxation in Russia. They face great difficulty in borrowing to finance working capital and more to finance investment. As a result, they operate more in a *cash-flow* constraint, in which each period's expenditures have to be financed by that period's revenues than a conventional *present-value constraint*. (We discuss this financial system and the constraints in detail below.) A credit crunch can drag these firms down along with the losers. *This* is the mechanism to be concerned about in Russia.

This is *not* a problem to be understood as traditional monetary and fiscal policy innovations. Just studying the path of money and credit aggregates or deficit figures will not tell us whether or when Russia's macroeconomic troubles are likely to happen. In addition, it means that credit can be tightened in Russia without macroeconomic consequences, *if* the rudimentary financial system is fixed first.

HIGH INFLATION IS ALWAYS AND EVERYWHERE A *FISCAL* PROBLEM

The most obvious symptom of macroeconomic problems in Russia is high or hyperinflation. Hence, a few basic facts about high inflation are in order.

Governments print excessive amounts of money when they are spending more than they can borrow or receive in direct taxes. In a sense, the budget is always balanced: the *inflation tax* replaces other sources of taxation. Suppose that the government doubles the money stock and that people are only willing to hold the same real amount of money (say, two months' income). Prices double, so the private sector's money balances are worth half of what they were. The government can purchase one month's income with the newly printed money. In this way, the government has transferred real resources — one month's income — from the private sector to itself. It is exactly as if it had assessed a tax on holding money. As we saw above, the government of Russia is raising substantial portions of its revenues from this inflation tax.

Again, inflation in Russia is completely different from that in typical industrialized Western economies. Seignorage revenue—government revenue from printing money or expanding cash-equivalent credit—is trivial in most Western economies. In addition, most credit expansion is *inside* credit, between private parties, not expansion of the monetary base or other government credit. Only a small fraction of the expansion of the money stock represents government revenue. Finally, most Western governments *can* raise more revenue from taxation. Hence, governments typically *can* lower inflation by willfully lowering the rate of money growth and slightly increasing taxes or borrowing to make up the small loss of seignorage revenue. The source of persistent inflation in Western economies is typically the fear on the part of governments that lowering inflation might lead to a recession through one of the monetary channels described above.

In this context, we are used to treating inflation by moral suasion: persuading governments or central banks that they should risk recessions in order to lower inflation. Much policy advice directed at Russia and the former Soviet Union is of this nature. But the situation is different. Money growth cannot be simply lowered by decision of the Central Bank or other authorities, The constraint is not fear of a recession but the lost seignorage revenue.

High inflation ends only when the government either finds other sources of (current or future) revenue or lowers expenditures. Without resolving the *fiscal* problem, advocating monetary restraint is pointless. At best, the government can reduce money growth temporarily, financing a part of expenditures by borrowing at home or abroad, by delaying payments (many state workers have not been paid in months) or some expenditures, by getting advance and usually discounted payment of taxes or other revenue, or by selling assets sooner. But unless the underlying level of tax collections and expenditures changes, these expedients merely postpone inflation. Eventually, the borrowed money has to be paid back, the delayed payments must be made, and so forth. Then, the government has to print even more money, leading to even higher inflation. In fact people may understand that the temporary slowdown in money growth must be reversed. Anticipating higher future inflation, they try harder to lower money holdings now, and so inflation can perversely increase right away!

The bottom line: moral suasion to reduce money or credit creation is pointless. Save the moral suasion for stabilizing the *fiscal* situation and lower money creation must follow.

INFLATION PER SE ISN'T SO BAD

Many discussions of events in Russia and the former Soviet Union presume that inflation is one of the most serious economic problems and hence needs urgently to be corrected. But inflation per se is not that bad. Most important, the vast majority of *cures* for inflation are worse than the disease.

What's bad about inflation? First, people spend too much time taking trips to the bank or money changer. Because cash depreciates fast, people want to hold as little of it as possible. Instead of (say) receiving pay in cash at the beginning of the month and spending it slowly over the month, they will try to convert their cash wages to foreign currency, bank accounts, durables, or anything else that does not depreciate and then convert it back to cash as the need arises. Firms waste time and energy on cash-management activities, avoiding check float, trying to delay payments, and so forth, rather than on productive activities. Both people and firms waste time looking for ways to arrange transactions without money, by using foreign currency, barter, and so forth.

There is a second effect on which economists have speculated but have less quantitative evidence. Inflation is seldom steady but varies from month to month. In this environment, it may be harder for consumers and producers to distinguish *relative* price changes (good or bad deals) from changes in the price *level* (inflation). The economy is obviously less efficient in this circumstance.

These effects—the "welfare costs of inflation" in the economics literature—are real, but they are not that big, a few percentage points of GNP at most. This is an interesting cost to examine in Western economies but does not account for output declines of Russian magnitude.

Furthermore, people in inflationary economies devise all sorts of methods to avoid holding money and to send good price signals. Prices can be quoted in dollars, or one can even pay in dollars. (Some Latin American economies "dollarized" in this way during periods of high inflation.) If that is impractical or illegal, prices can be quoted in dollars and then paid in rubles at that day's exchange rate. People can hold dollars, only converting to rubles at the last moment. Many stores in Russia now have internal currency exchanges for just this purpose! Brazilians adapted to inflation by the widespread use of checks that clear in one day (something you can't do in the United States!). As people make these adaptations to inflation, its costs decline still further.

In the end, inflation per se in an economy with no constraints on foreign currency holdings and transactions can only take away the certainly minor advantages of using a national currency rather than a foreign currency. Inflation is not why economies stop dead in their tracks. In a period of hyperinflation, workers take home their wages in a wheelbarrow full of money at end of day; they rush out to shop, bank, or exchange the money so they don't have to hold it overnight. They might be late for dinner, but they *did* spend the day at work, and they *do* eat dinner when they get home. The German hyperinflation at the end of the First World War, inflation in Israel in the 1970s and 1980s, and some of the Latin American inflations conform to this picture.

THE PROBLEM:
ANTI-INFLATION MEASURES AND FINANCIAL REGULATION

It is the wide range of government policies taken to *combat* inflation, without addressing the underlying deficit, that causes trouble. Further, inflation can wreak havoc with taxes, the payment system, and financial regulations, especially in economies where the financial system is underdeveloped. We conclude that one can substantially improve the Russian economy *without* necessarily stopping inflation. It suffices to allow the financial system to adapt to inflation.

Although inflation per se isn't that bad for the *economy*, it is very bad for the government's finances. If prices did not rise when the government spent newly printed money, it could raise any amount of real resources by money creation. Even if prices rose, but people held the same real quantity of money—be it a month's worth of income, a half year's worth, or whatever—the government could still raise any amount of real resources by raising the rate of money growth and inflation. But as inflation rises, people hold less real money. As anything is taxed more, people use less of it, and money is no exception. Then, a given percentage increase in the money stock results in an even larger percentage increase in inflation. Eventually, a point is reached at which the government raises *less* real resources if it increases the money growth rate. This is the point of explosive hyperinflation.

Governments naturally respond by trying to force people to hold more money. Examples of such policies are limitations on foreign exchange transactions, capital controls, bans on the use of foreign currency for transactions, legal requirements that prices must be quoted in domestic currency, limited or suspended convertibility (if the money was ever convertible in the first place), limitations on the ability to transfer bank accounts to cash, interest rate limitations on bank accounts (so people will be more willing to hold money instead of accounts), and limitations on cash-efficient check, wire, or credit card transactions. Strapped governments also frequently resort to price controls. Price controls hold down the appearance of inflation, which may be useful for political purposes. More directly, when price controls are in place, *money* does not depreciate, so people are more willing to hold it. (If a tomato costs 10 rubles and an hour in line today and 10 rubles and *two* hours in line tomorrow, then there is no pressing need to change rubles into dollars overnight.)

The Soviet Union already maintained most of these policies and to great effect: Soviet consumers held as much as half a year's income as cash, where cash + checking accounts are less than one-sixth of U.S. annual income, and even tinier fractions in economies with Russian inflation rates, like Brazil. A good part of the cumbersome Soviet financial system can be attributed to the government's desire to maintain demand for its currency and hence raise revenue from money creation. Many of these policies are still in effect.

These policies, rather than inflation per se, can stop economies in their tracks. They not only force people to hold rapidly depreciating money, but they destroy the payments and credit systems. The ultimate sign is when people and companies resort to barter, countertrade and other deals to avoid using money. We see all of these in Russia, especially in interrepublic trade.

Further, inflation can cause havoc with the tax, credit, and payments systems. When payments are not indexed, or when interest is not routinely charged on delayed payments, a delayed payment is a payment not made. Hence, there is a large incentive to delay the payment of bills and especially of taxes. In Russia, payments can take three months to clear—three months between when the payer's account is debited and the payee's account is credited. Interrepublic payments can be much worse. With 20 percent inflation, this amounts to a 60 percent tax on all transactions. Such a tax destroys the payments system. But the root cause of the trouble is not *inflation*, it is the rudimentary tax, credit, and payments systems.

Of course, there is a flip side to this. Inflation not only represents a direct tax on money holding but can be used as above to introduce many hidden taxes and reduce many expenditures. Pensions are only slowly indexed, so the inflation amounted to a default on much of Russia's pension obligations. The Russian government actually seems to be pretty good at demanding immediate tax payment but endlessly delaying (nominal) payments, again improving its fiscal situation. In this way, Russian inflation is a device for surreptitiously raising taxes and lowering revenue, as it is in the United States.

We are not arguing for the virtues of inflation. Other things equal, it is not desirable. However, it is important to think clearly about *why* one dislikes inflation. It is not *necessary* that inflation cause great economic dislocation; a well-indexed and dollarized economy can handle very high inflation without great damage. Given that Russia is likely to have high inflation for some time, attention might be better spent on removing the intrusions that interact with inflation to cause harm.

The Russian Financial System

We have argued that inflation per se does not account for the drop in output. Rather, problems with the financial system, some induced or exacerbated by inflation, are the proximate cause of the output drop. This view suggests a closer look at the Russian financial system.

Any financial system serves three functions: It arranges payments between enterprises, monitors enterprise performance, and allocates credit for investment. Any one of these functions can go wrong, and problems in one area can spill over into another. We find that lagging, sporadic, and haphazard reform of the financial system, while rapid changes were taking place in the rest of the economy, has been the primary source of macroeconomic difficulty.

In describing the financial system through various reforms, we focus on the payments system and the nature of enterprise constraints. The latter needs a little explanation. The transformation of state-owned enterprises into independent capitalist firms is one of the essential aspects of Russian economic reforms. The financial constraints faced by enterprises is the critical difference. State-owned enterprises get directives from the government and face what Janos Kornai called "soft budget constraints"—the government bails out any losses. We call this regime a *solvency guarantee* regime. Capitalist firms make autonomous decisions but are forced to make correct investment, output, and other decisions by hard budget constraints. Hence economic reform is the *twin* process of moving control from central planners to enterprise managers *and* hardening budget constraints. Clearly, one without the other is disastrous.

In an ideal world, enterprises can borrow or sell equity to finance worthy projects, working capital, or other temporary variations in cash flow. In an ideal world, then, the "hard budget constraint" is a *present-value constraint*: A firm's present value or net worth must be positive, but it can undergo periods of negative cash flow so long as future prospects are brighter. As we will see, Russian firms are (supposed) to operate in much more stringent *cash-flow constraint*, or *self-finance*, regimes.

Our discussion relates primarily to the state sector and privatized former state enterprises. Although new enterprises do not suffer from many of the problems we outline, they still account for only a small fraction of GDP. In the near term, the performance of the Russian economy still depends on what happens to the former state sector. Hence our task is to understand why output is falling here and how further falls can be avoided.

THE SOVIET FINANCIAL SYSTEM

The financial system of the Soviet Union was organized to meet the needs of centralized planning. One might suppose that a central planning system would not need a financial system. In fact a detailed plan containing various targets that was received from central authorities—the *techpromfinplan*, referring to technology, production, and finance—rather than financial information, played the central role in deciding what enterprises would produce, at what level, where inputs would come from and to whom output would be delivered, what technology to use, how many workers to employ and how much to pay them, and how much the enterprise should invest.

Even under planning, however, a role for finance emerged. The plan could never be implemented as written. Consequently, enterprise directors had to act with discretion. This discretion, in turn, necessitated a means of monitoring their behavior, which provided the basic role for the financial system under the previous regime.[11] By keeping financial records of the transactions made by enterprises, planners could use the bottom line as a monitoring device (*kontrol' rublyom*).

The *techpromfinplan* specified the major financial flows for the enterprise, including profits, loans incurred and repaid, working capital funds, and reserves. When each plan was constructed, the planners decided on the amount of working capital that would be required to produce the plan's target output and provided it in the enterprise's account with its Gosbank branch. But the financial plan served to *support* the production plan. Gosbank's job was to make sure that no enterprise failed to fulfill its plan owing to a lack of available funds.

When an enterprise delivered goods to another enterprise, the seller immediately delivered a payment order to its branch of Gosbank. The seller's Gosbank branch then credited the seller's account. It did not wait for payment to arrive or check to see whether sufficient funds were available in the buyer's account. Importantly for subsequent events, *sellers* rather than purchasers initiated payment. The payment order was then delivered to the Gosbank branch of the enterprise that received the goods. If sufficient funds to purchase the goods were available, the Gosbank account of the purchaser was automatically debited.

There were times, however, when the purchaser's account contained insufficient funds to pay for the delivered goods. In such an event, the payment order was then placed in file number 2 (*Kartoteka Dva*). At the end of the production cycle, Gosbank provided each enterprise account with the net funds necessary to bring it into balance. This action implemented the *solvency guarantee*, or soft budget, constraint.

This system only worked because all transactions flowed within the single bank (monobank). Gosbank could carry enterprise account deficits on its books with no immediate need to settle. Transactions between enterprises could be recorded at the time of transaction, in accounts at different branches of Gosbank, without worrying about payment. No one branch of Gosbank needed to hold reserves to settle imbalances in enterprise accounts. Thus, temporary imbalances in enterprise accounts had no real effects on the flow of production or investment.

The weakness in this system is, of course, the incentive for enterprises to run up losses, knowing they will be bailed out in the end. Worse, directors could easily divert funds to their own uses. Of course, enterprise directors faced many personal and political incentives not to run up too many losses. But, in addition, many puzzling aspects of the Soviet financial system can be understood as useful safeguards against these and other temptations it offered.

The foremost example is the dual-money system. The Soviet financial system strictly distinguished between cash rubles, or *nalichnyye*, and noncash rubles, or *beznalichnyye*. Cash rubles were used to pay wages; noncash rubles were used to pay for inputs. Consumer goods purchases required cash rubles. The incentive rationale for the system is obvious: There's not much point in racking up debts in money that can't be spent on consumption; at the same time, production should never be jeopardized for something as unessential as a lack of funds.[12] In addition, there was less need to monitor managers' employment decisions than to monitor their purchases.

There was a macroeconomic justification as well. The government created sufficient cash rubles to pay wages, at the same time setting the aggregate wage bill to be in (rough) balance with the nominal value of retail goods. It was therefore believed that credit extension to finance production, and the possibility of large ex post bailouts, would have no inflationary consequences. Of course, Russians were and are creative at transforming noncash to cash rubles, so *beznalichnyye* credits led to (at least repressed) inflation. In addition, only recently have discounts for cash payment appeared; the two currencies would not carry the same price unless it was possible to transform one into the other.

In summary, the Soviet financial system was roughly coherent, with many controls (such as the dual-monetary system and only limited autonomy on the part of managers) in place to stop undesirable gaming of other aspects (such as the freedom to rack up debts). Clearly, liberalizing *one* aspect of the system without reforming the others could be disastrous.

FIRST REFORMS: JANUARY–JULY 1992

This system got in trouble as it and the economy were partially liberalized. The collapse of central planning and early reforms following the collapse of the Soviet Union in the fall of 1991, along with the price liberalization of January 1992, gave more autonomy to enterprise directors. The former branches of Gosbank became independent, leading to a proliferation of commercial banks.[13] At the same time, the government said that bailouts were not to be expected and that it would not provide working capital as before. Budget constraints were to be hardened, and enterprises were to keep positive account balances.

Yet the actual system of payments was not much changed. When a seller shipped goods, he submitted a payment order as before. The order followed the same path, from local branch (now typically an independent bank) to a collection center to the Central Bank of Russia to another collection center and finally to the account in the bank of the purchaser. If sufficient funds were available, the payment followed the entire path in reverse. The one crucial change is that the seller's account was not credited until the end of this long process. Payments typically worked through the public mail, so the lag between when a payment order was issued and when the funds arrived in the seller's account could exceed several months. Payment problems were especially acute when suppliers or customers were located in other republics. And as a result of the dual-money system, and the absence of checking accounts or any other financial system, one could not simply short-circuit the cumbersome system, even by so crude and dangerous a means as sending an employee with a suitcase full of cash.[14]

This partial liberalization had several unintended and disastrous effects. First, the long lag between payment and receipt was not a problem when all enterprises and banks were owned by the central government because accounts could be credited before the funds actually arrived. But independent banks could only make payments when there were sufficient funds in the accounts. The lag between payment and receipt suddenly became important because the seller could not use the funds until they were received. Enterprises too far in debt—possibly through no fault of their own—could not pay wages or obtain supplies. Worse, from the government's point of view, they were unable to pay taxes.

Second, payment was still initiated by the *seller* on shipment of goods, whether the purchaser wanted them or not. Managers could just ship supplies, submit payment orders, and force debts on customers that took years to clear up, if ever.

Third, high inflation had a dramatic effect in this environment. Enterprises had no option but to hold working capital in noninterest paying enterprise accounts. Money market accounts paying positive real interest rates were unavailable, and the dual-monetary system prevents enterprises from simply holding foreign currency or other nondepreciating assets. Of course, many enterprises held foreign currency, *offshore,* but as these deposits were illegal, they were of little help in solving internal payments problems. Thus, enterprises were major victims of the inflation tax.[15] Also, during a period of high inflation, delayed payments were devalued. Twenty percent inflation a month and two to three months to receive payment adds up to 50 percent or more lost revenue in the payments system! This alone could bankrupt enterprises that should be solvent.

Given the combination of slow payments and the fact that one could no longer use funds until they actually arrived, the need for liquid working capital exploded. But the Central Bank, in a "tight credit" period, didn't provide working capital. Enterprises could try to borrow from commercial banks, but an independent commercial bank would only lend to an enterprise whose present and expected future solvency is clear or one that can provide easily appropriated and sold collateral. When payments can take two months to clear, it is almost impossible to distinguish an illiquid from an insolvent enterprise. Banks could not tell an enterprise with genuine receivables that would eventually be paid from enterprises whose bills never would be paid. State firms obviously cannot put up state property as collateral; it was equally impractical for privatized enterprises. Consequently, commercial banks did not lend much working capital to enterprises.

Because borrowing or equity sale was not possible, and because any cash saved inflated away quickly, the hard budget constraint amounted to a *cash-flow* constraint, in which a firm must cover all current expenses, including wages, investment, and working capital, out of current revenue A cash-flow constraint seems transparent and easy to enforce, but it is basically impossible for any firm to operate on this basis, even in a stable economy.

The inevitable consequence was an explosion in interenterprise debt.[16] Interenterprise arrears grew by almost a factor of 1,000, from less than 40 billion rubles in January 1992 to 3.2 trillion rubles six months later. Unpaid bills simply piled up in the venerable file number 2; as each enterprise could not get payment from its customers it would in turn be forced to stop paying its suppliers.

In this environment, it was difficult to obtain supplies to keep enterprises going. It was especially difficult to arrange supplies or deliver output across republics of the former USSR. A symptom of the problem was the blossoming of barter deals and other nonmonetary arrangements for obtaining supplies. This chaos contributed to output declines. Our point is that a monetary, macroeconomic disturbance is responsible for at least a large part of the fall in output. It was not the inevitable result of a move to a market economy; it was a happenstance of the way in which controls were only partially lifted. *It could have been avoided.*

This growth in mutual indebtedness became a major concern, not least for the reason that it led to a fall in tax payments, choking economic activity. Most important, because the stock of debt made the announced hard budget regime untenable, the situation was explosive. The government could not distinguish illiquid from insolvent enterprises anymore than the banks could, and as the contagion of debt spread through the economy, a literal enforcement would have meant shutting down 40 percent or more of industrial employment. It also meant that soon-to-be-privatized enterprises might be technically bankrupt. The government was also concerned that workers might obtain shares in a worthless enterprise. But, of course, as enterprises realized that the government could not possibly shut down those in debt, it became all that much easier to pile it up; there is strength in numbers.

JULY 1992

A bailout loomed, but its consequences would be severe. Once a bailout occurs, pronouncements that there will be no future bailouts lose credibility unless there is some drastic change in regime. Moreover, the bailout would naturally lead to a large increase in Central Bank credit to offset the debts of net-debtor enterprises. There being no source of tax revenue for such a bailout, it would necessarily lead to a spurt in inflation. However, if nothing was done the economy would crash, taking enterprises that should stay in business along with those that should in fact be closed.

In the event, the Russian government set up a scheme to net out the arrears built up before July 1, 1992, and bail out net debtors. As a consequence, money growth and inflation accelerated dramatically.

To help prevent a new growth of arrears, the payments system was modified. *Buyers* rather than sellers were to initiate payment. In addition, all purchases were to be *prepaid*. Goods were to be shipped only after payment had arrived. This step, it was hoped, would prevent the outbreak of a new wave of arrears. It was also aimed at stopping enterprises from simply delivering unwanted products to their habitual destinations and then demanding payment. The dual-monetary system was largely maintained, perhaps for the same good reasons.

A sudden change to a prepayment system poses an incredibly difficult problem for enterprises. If the need for working capital was large before, it was even larger now. An enterprise needs a huge source of credit or retained earnings if it is to pay for inputs, wait for the payment to arrive, receive inputs, produce its goods, paying workers all the time, sell the goods, and only receive any revenue after another wait. To make matters still worse, the government also began to require prepayment of taxes in the third quarter of 1992. Although this measure certainly worked to stop the erosion of real tax receipts, it did so at the expense of enterprises' liquidity, something that was already in short supply.

The tautness of this constraint was alleviated, to some extent, by two factors. First, most enterprises continued to ship goods before receiving payment, as before, when dealing with their traditional customers ("historical relations"). Second, the expansionary monetary policy undertaken by the Central Bank of Russia relieved the pressure of living with the constraint. Real Central Bank credit grew rapidly in the second half of 1992 (see figure 2.3). Much of this growth was in targeted credits to specific industries, channeled through commercial banks. Interest rates were well below inflation, so obtaining such credit was profitable and connections were important. The proliferation of commercial banks in this period was (is) primarily an attempt to obtain these Central Bank credits for the benefit of specific enterprises or industries.

With easier credit and the prepayments system, arrears were kept down, but inflation soared. As yet practically no enterprises were forced into bankruptcy, so the government was undertaking a huge subsidy of loss-making enterprises to keep the others liquid. Unless the fundamental causes of arrears are eliminated, policy is caught between a rock and a hard spot. Either the government enforces a tight credit policy to restrain inflation, at the cost of jeopardizing interenterprise payments and, hence, eventually, production, or it softens credit to ease the payments problem, delaying the adjustment of loss-making firms and creating ever-increasing inflation.[17]

1994

As we write, the *system* has not substantially changed. The distinction between cash and noncash rubles persists. Part of the explanation may be that most state and former state enterprises still face soft budget constraints: bankruptcy is not yet a credible threat, though once again there is serious, and maybe even credible, talk under way. Without hard budget constraints, enterprises might increase wages regardless of enterprise profitability,[18] with disastrous effects on inflation.

By contrast, the financial system is quickly adapting to make payments easier.

Banks are developing correspondent relationships so that payments do not have to go through the Central Bank. The economy is dollarizing: Individuals hold much wealth in cash dollars, and dollar-denominated accounts are available to both individuals and enterprises. This is evident in the growth of dollar deposits in the Russian banking system, which have grown from 28 percent of ruble deposits in February 1992 to 75 percent in November 1993 (Sachs 1994, 31). Dollar-denominated transactions can be made quickly and smoothly.

However, a web of complex regulations remains whose unintended consequence is to make life miserable for those who need to make transactions in Russia. The following anecdote (told to Ickes by the director of the enterprise in question) makes the point. An enterprise in Voronezh expected a shipment of parts from Ukraine that had already been paid for. If shipments are not picked up from the railway station within four hours, there is a large hourly fine. The enterprise was not notified that the parts had arrived until eleven hours had passed. However, a customs duty was still due. Alas, the invoice was in Ukrainian karbovanets, not rubles. The customs office was unwilling to accept any calculation of the ruble equivalent, even one that doubled the duty—anything to avoid the mounting hourly fines. The director had to fax Kiev (at least the seller was in Kiev, to which it is sometimes possible to get a phone line!) and finally received an invoice in rubles. But, alas, the duty was more than 500,000 rubles and so could not be paid in cash. The director had to go to the bank to direct that the money be paid. This took three days, even though the enterprise, bank, and customs office were all in the same city.

Early 1994 saw a period of much more stringent credit and hence a decline in inflation to the 10 percent a month range. However, enterprise arrears are rising quickly again. This time may be more dangerous: Not only is interenterprise debt piling up but so are tax and wage arrears. Some privatized enterprises are apparently more willing to incur the wrath of their workers than before; other enterprises simply cannot make wage payments. The tax arrears are part of the plummeting tax revenue mentioned above. In turn, the government is behind in payments to enterprises.

INTERREPUBLIC TRADE AND THE RUBLE ZONE

When the former Soviet Union was replaced by fifteen governments responsible for economic policy, a breakdown in interrepublic trade occurred. Already difficult payments become even more difficult international payments, and political events interfered with trade even further. In an effort to preserve a "common economic space," the new countries (save the Baltics and Georgia) formed the ruble zone to try to reduce the complications.

But efforts to maintain the ruble zone were fraught with difficulties.[19] In 1992, the central bank in each of the new countries could issue *beznalichnyye*, or enterprise rubles. Naturally, each central bank issued credit, as the benefits of credit expansion are felt domestically, while the costs, in terms of inflation, are spread throughout the Commonwealth of Independent States (CIS). Given this fact, it is surprising that inflation was not much worse! The brake was that only the Russian Central Bank could issue cash rubles, which were needed everywhere to pay wages, and the Central Bank of Russia was tightfisted with cash disbursal throughout the CIS.

In the first half of 1992 the large credit issue in the other CIS countries, especially Ukraine, led to large Russian trade surpluses in CIS trade, financed by inflation in Russia. This also exacerbated shortages in Russia. To limit the excessive credit issue, the Russian Central Bank could issue less currency to other central banks to get them to restrain their own issue of *beznalichnyye*. This not only causes loud complaints about a "cash shortage"; it had the unintended effect of delaying payments to Russian enterprises. In July 1992 the Russian government moved to end the automatic financing of these surpluses in the correspondent accounts by fixing strict limits to their size. But this move, when combined with the new prepayment regime, drastically reduced trade between the republics.

The fundamental problem with the ruble zone, at least from the Russian side, was that, as a structural net creditor, Russia diverted significant resources to the other countries, perhaps as high as 10 percent of Russian GDP during the last quarter of 1992. These transfers took two basic forms: exports of petroleum at subsidized prices and deliveries of the common currency. The idea of using a common currency to maintain interrepublic trade had a basic appeal. The problem, however, was how to separate the payments aspects from the fiscal transfers needed to maintain a currency union. This dilemma remained unresolved until the currency reform of July 1993 (the withdrawal of pre-1993 rubles from circulation) rendered it irrelevant.

The appeal of the idea of currency union continues; witness the plans for a currency union between Belarus and Russia. But these plans (as most recently reported) still allow the Belarus central bank to issue rubles. Thus, they don't address the central requirement for a currency union: a clear understanding of who controls monetary emission.

In summary, the sudden disruption of trade brought on by the collapse of the union and the ensuing payments problems is a second culprit for the fall in output. It too did not have to happen, and it too can be avoided in the future.

BANKRUPTCY AND INVESTMENT

We have focused on the payments part of the financial system, and the corresponding need for working capital to bridge the timing of revenues and expenditures, because we think these are the essential parts of the story behind the unusual fall in output. But the role of the financial system in investment and in providing the right incentives for restructuring are the larger long-term story.

In the end, large parts of the former state sector will have to be closed down. Their workers will move to new private sector jobs. Other former state firms will continue but require lots of new investment. The financial system gives the signals for these transformations. Actual bankruptcy or its threat is what closes operations down. More important, and more subtly, new investment can only be marshaled in the presence of an operating bankruptcy mechanism, as we now explain.

In practice, enterprises have little access to capital markets. We mentioned above the problems firms face in obtaining working capital loans: The chain of arrears makes it hard for an independent bank to distinguish the illiquid from the insolvent. Hence, most credit is still simply created by the Central Bank and passed to selected enterprises or industries through "their" commercial banks during loose credit periods and is just less available during tight credit periods.

Even the chain of arrears might not cause problems, however; perhaps loans can be based on collateral, or firms could raise cash via equity sales. Here is where the absence of a bankruptcy mechanism eliminates the potential for a capital market. A state firm can't put up collateral; its managers can't sell state property! Without a bankruptcy mechanism, even a privatized state firm can't put up collateral; in the event of a default, there is no way for the bank to make sure it will get the collateral.

Furthermore, the value-added tax and last-in-first-out accounting mean that even bankrupt firms have substantial tax obligations that are senior to other claims. Thus, a creditor cannot force a bankruptcy to be repaid—the result will simply be to have the assets go to pay taxes. In addition, it is unclear whether wage arrears will be senior to debt in bankruptcy proceedings because there have been so few.

Clearly these problems can be addressed. For example, a bankruptcy could force a loss of control or equity without forcing liquidation. In this way, creditors could recover something or at least discipline management.

Without collateral, equity is an essential ingredient for debt finance. The potential loss of equity in bankruptcy constrains the borrowing behavior of a firm. Before privatization, equity did not exist. And if enterprise directors are uncertain over who will own the firm after privatization, they will try to borrow extensively to keep the enterprise operating; lenders will wisely refuse to extend credit.

In this environment, we would expect firms to try to sell *new* equity to raise cash and finance investment. (We emphasize *new*; the existence of mutual funds that can trade some shares of privatized firms' *existing* equity is only a precursor to a market in which firms can raise capital by selling *new* equity.) This did not happen. Of course state firms can't sell ownership shares. And there were and are a variety of legal impediments for privatized firms. Perhaps more important, selling equity requires some idea of the net worth of the enterprise and the value of potential investment projects. It was and is hard to get any idea of the net worth of enterprises. First, there was and still is great uncertainty over the course of privatization—what the legal status of owners will be. Even more fundamentally, there is great uncertainty over the viability of most enterprises in a market environment. Most firms are still *behaving* much as they did in a state-controlled environment. It is hard to distinguish between those that *cannot* adjust to a market environment and those that simply *choose* not to change because adjustment is costly and the incentives to do so are not yet strong. In addition, the presence of many still-controlled prices, high inflation, and massive arrears make a good accounting of present net worth difficult, to say nothing of the prospects of a new investment or restructuring plan.

In summary, firms have little access to credit or equity financing. As a result, the conventional *present-value* hard budget constraint is in effect a *cash-flow* constraint. The latter is essentially impossible for firms to achieve, so they pile up arrears, in effect relying on interenterprise lending to satisfy working capital needs. Also, because it is impossible to achieve, it is impossible to enforce. And finance for investment or restructuring just does not happen.

Uncertainty, Time Consistency, and Reform

The Soviet Union and now Russia have been on, to use Gertrude Schroeder's phrase, a "treadmill" of reforms that are introduced, quickly fall apart, and are abandoned. The post-Soviet era seems only to have speeded up the treadmill. It is certainly understandable that people are hesitant to believe each regime will last, for example, that an announced hard budget regime will not end in a massive bailout.

THE ECONOMICS OF TIME CONSISTENCY

Economists have studied several aspects of this phenomenon under the broad heading of "time consistency." Here are two basic parables.

1. *Optimal taxes.* At any point in time, a benevolent government's optimal tax policy is to confiscate all wealth and default on its bonds. Thereafter, it promises to never to tax wealth at all and to repay all its debts. This policy is optimal because it induces no distortions; current owners of wealth will be unhappy, but they cannot alter any economic decisions in order to avoid the tax. Savers and workers see no distortions to the accumulation of *new* capital or their efforts.

The hole in this scheme is obvious: *next* year, the government would very much like to go back on its promise, confiscate all wealth, default on its bonds, and promise *again* never to touch wealth or bonds. The plan was not *time consistent*, which will cause the scheme to unravel. Smart people will smell the rat and won't work or save initially because they know the government will break its promise. If the government has a habit of announcing a new stabilization plan every six months or so, people don't even have to be that smart.

2. *An unstable reform.* A government wants to reform its economy by reducing a tax, say, a tariff or an excessive tax on capital. Lowering this tax will raise incentives to invest; thus output will expand, and eventually the government will replace the lost tax revenue with larger and less distortionary income taxes. But if the investment does not occur, then the government will have to rescind the reform to rebalance its budget. Thus investors only want to take advantage of the new investment opportunities if the reform is credible; in turn the reform will only stick if investors believe in it. Each individual investor will only invest if he thinks all the other investors are going to. This game has a *multiple equilibrium*: it is possible that everyone invest and the reform succeeds or that nobody invests and the reform fails. The reform is less likely to succeed if the government has limited access to borrowing or other taxes to bridge the period of lower revenues.

Much of what seems mysterious in government policy amounts to attempts to circumvent these problems. In both cases, the government needs a *precommitment* device—the government finance equivalent of Odysseus's strategy of being tied to the mast to hear the siren's song. Constitutions and traditions are attempts to form such precommitment devices, but of course constitutions can be amended or ignored and traditions violated. (Constitutionalists forget that Liberia and the United States have the same paper organization of government and that the Soviet constitution protected more rights and civil liberties than any other.) Governments can also try to precommit through reputations. Revolutionary governments often honor the bonds of their predecessors, hoping that this will convince bond purchasers of the sincerity of their own promises to repay. Although the potential wisdom of such a move has been known for ages (Alexander Hamilton states it), only recently have economists begun to analyze whether such "reputational equilibria" can be sustained. It turns out they are fragile.

Thus, although it is easy to call for time-consistent policies, it is in fact hard for governments to precommit to actions they may later regret. We offer no magic bullets. But one can at least avoid gross mistakes. No one is likely to trust a reform plan that the government may regret in the future. Complex multistage reform plans are unlikely to work.

TIME CONSISTENCY AND RUSSIAN REFORM

The second parable above is close to the heart of the conundrum facing Russia. As economic activity moves from the state to the private or privatized sector, the method of taxation has changed.

The Soviet Union relied extensively on the turnover tax. This was not a value-added tax; it was simply the difference between the wholesale and retail price of goods. Different tax rates for different goods made it essentially an arbitrary tax that could be used to grab wealth ex post to cover budget surprises.[20] Planning had one virtue, however: arbitrary taxation imposed few (additional) distortions to economic activity.[21] Planners could simply direct investment into a desired area, even if a looming tax would have eliminated private investors.

As the Russian economy becomes increasingly private, the scope for such arbitrary policy is increasingly reduced. In a private economy, agents can much more easily avoid taxed activities, if not evade taxes altogether. Hence, the adverse effects are correspondingly greater.

Most important, decisions to invest, to restructure an enterprise or industry, to move out of dying areas, and so forth all require confidence in the future and confidence that the fruits of these difficult decisions will not be wiped out by some future policy change. But, as we saw above, the economic environment, and especially the structure of taxation, is chaotic. Enterprises can be sure of only one thing: if they find a way to make a lot of money, the government will find a way to tax it.

Increasingly, autonomous enterprises have reacted predictably. Capital is flying out of the country; state enterprises are being carefully stripped of assets. Enterprises are becoming cleverer at avoiding taxes. The managements at many enterprises have, for example, formed new enterprises that sell to the original one to hide income from the taxman (and the statistics). The government is left with fewer and fewer things to tax, so it raises rates more and more. This either halts activity or drives more and more of it underground. The inevitable result is that the government resorts to the inflation tax.

It is not necessarily *current* taxes and policies that drive this behavior but the expectation that *future* policies will confiscate any wealth that comes from legitimate investment or restructuring. Those expectations are unlikely to be changed by statements, promises, new reform plans, or changes in prominent officials. It does not matter how well intentioned the government is; everyone realizes that if the government is bankrupt in a few years it will have to expropriate what it can.

The government is often encouraged to balance its budget to stabilize the economy. If balancing the budget consists only of permanently reducing wasteful expenditures, this may be good advice. But this advice backfires when balancing *current* budgets reduces the present value of *future* income. If the budget is "balanced" by increasing already heavy taxes, by delaying payments that will have to be made in the future, or by refusing credits to industries that the government still promises to bail out if they threaten to go bankrupt, then balancing the budget today increases the burden of *future* taxation. Rational people try to avoid the implied increase in future taxes. In summary, these measures for improving current budget deficits will lead to a *deterioration* in economic performance and a further *delay* in restructuring, precisely the opposite of the hoped-for effects.

Investment as an Option.   The essence of economic restructuring is investment in the broadest sense: inducing economic agents to take actions that are costly or painful today but that will pay off in a future market economy: not just physical investment—building new plants or installing new machinery—but restructuring enterprises, moving to new areas, setting up new institutions, and so forth.

So far, we have only considered how investment responds to its *expected* rewards. But in an uncertain environment, investment decisions are more complex and interesting. Investment opportunities are like an *option*. Investors can decide to invest, not to invest, or *to wait* and see if conditions will improve, in the meantime keeping any wealth they can hidden or abroad.

The option value of waiting depends on two forces: the uncertainty associated with the investment and the profits foregone while waiting. The more uncertain the future, the better it is to wait and see how things turn out. However, the more current profits are foregone by waiting, the better it is to get on with the investment project. Thus, in an uncertain and unprofitable environment, investors may choose to wait to invest, even if the *expected* rewards are high.

Uncertainty with respect to returns is a central feature of economic change in Russia. The policy and regulatory environment, the availability and prices of inputs, what markets will be good opportunities, all these are much more uncertain in Russia than in Western economies. The fact that all other enterprises are simultaneously *restructuring* adds to the uncertainty. Because the economy is in transition, immediate profits are relatively small compared with future profits if reform succeeds Under such circumstances it may be of considerable value to delay investing until more is known.

Clearly, this component of investment makes our multiple-equilibrium reform conundrum even tougher. Even if the expected value of investment is profitable, economic agents may prefer to wait and see if the reform plan sticks before committing themselves. But if agents don't invest, output will not rise, tax revenues will not increase, and the reform plan is guaranteed to fail.

Some Tentative Prognostication and Comments on Policy

It is dangerous to predict events or comment on policies, especially from halfway around the world and facing the inevitable publication lags of a volume such as this one. The past is full of mistaken efforts in which events in

Russia were judged too quickly and mistakenly from habits formed by experience with Western economies. Distant observers failed to realize that the infamous currency confiscation episode of the summer of 1993 was really a mechanism for cutting off subsidies to other republics or that tight credit would simply result in an arrears crisis and a bailout because bankruptcy promises could not be enforced after arrears piled up.

Still, we can't resist a few comments.

Many observers are happy because credit creation and inflation are declining. They may be falling into the same trap as above, thinking that credit is a matter of will rather than present-value budget arithmetic. That arithmetic is gloomy. Tax revenues are two-thirds of forecasts, evasion is widespread, and the government is still expected to bail out loss-making industries. Tax rates are so high that Russia may actually be on the wrong side of the Laffer curve, where higher rates lead to *lower* revenues. The government has fallen behind in paying for goods it has purchased, many enterprises are in tax arrears, and interenterprise arrears are again rising. It is difficult to see how the government can maintain its current policy stance in the wake of these events; a resurgence of inflation seems more than likely.

Many observers are also happy about privatization, looking at the huge number of privatized firms. Privatization is only a step, though perhaps a big one, on the road to reform. Many privatized enterprises continue to behave as if it were "business as usual." To bring about a change in *behavior*, enterprises must have the ability to raise funds. More important, they must face the proper incentives so that they will prefer to restructure. This is where a credible bankruptcy system is crucial. *Financial* reform is thus the key to economic development in Russia, but not enough is happening.

In this environment, it is perfectly rational that not much restructuring is happening and that capital is in flight. Russians understand that desperate government finances can render any restructuring or investment useless, and they know that the future has less to do with character than with constraints. In turn, the fact that there is little investment or increase in taxable income makes the government desperate.

Some observers argue that the Russian government must balance its budget as quickly as possible, that it should raise taxes to do so, and that international aid should be used as a carrot to force these policies. We disagree. Stated tax rates are already some of the highest in the world, and it is unlikely that more revenue can be raised.

Progress on the *present-value* deficit is much more important than reaching quarter-by-quarter targets for lowering reported deficits. Measures that raise deficits for a few quarters or even years *but that solve the long-run budget problems* could result in a flowering of activity. An excessive focus on short-term budget problems that does nothing about the underlying problems will not allay fears of higher future taxes. As we have noted, the government, which faces a multiple-equilibrium reform conundrum, needs to tip the balance against the "wait and see" attitude. The best way to do so is to tackle the root causes of the budget problem.

The most important item on the agenda, then, is for the government to find a way to end its implicit commitment to bail out loss-making industries and to do so credibly. If it can do this, meeting intermediate budget deficit and credit creation targets will be irrelevant; everyone will know that the regime has changed. This is an intricate and political process, so we have no magic bullet, but we can offer a few comments.

First, the government may fear allowing bankruptcies, thinking that bankruptcy must imply liquidation and shutting down huge fractions of industry overnight. But bankruptcy need not imply liquidation. Bankruptcy in the United States is typically an arrangement in which the enterprise *continues to operate* but in which equity holders may lose the value of their equity and control rights, current management may be replaced, and so forth. Russia only needs something similar. Managers must feel that they will lose their positions if performance is not turned around. This kind of bankruptcy is perfectly possible in Russia and need not imply shutting down large fractions of industry. Hence, the government can allow it to happen. In turn, the credible threat that current management may be replaced may induce many firms to restructure.

Any progress in this direction depends, however, on financial reforms that will make it easier to distinguish the illiquid from the insolvent. As we have emphasized throughout, the current state of the financial system makes this difficult. But it is precisely the inability to make this distinction that hamstrings policy. Until the financial system is developed to the point where illiquidity and insolvency can be distinguished, not only will bankruptcy be rare but so will any equity investment and, hence, restructuring.

More generally, the government can make the threat of bankruptcy (and liquidation, too, which will have to happen in many cases) much more credible by taking visible actions to deal with bankrupt firms. In particular, the government could set up a special fund for displaced workers. Setting aside resources to deal with structural unemployment provides a signal that the government means business. Progress also needs to be made on increasing labor mobility. At a minimum, laws can be changed to allow workers more freedom of movement. All these actions help signal that "we're ready to do it." It's not quite a precommitment, but it's better than threatening something one doesn't have the means to do.

Similarly, some observers argue that the Central Bank should continue to tighten credit to lower inflation. This advice may result from confusing the Russian situation with that of typical Western governments. It may backfire. Without changing the financial system, especially the commitment to bail out losing enterprises, tight credit will lead to a mass of arrears. In this situation, a bailout is unavoidable because the babies can't be distinguished from the bathwater. For this reason, *looser* credit may be desirable when the government tries to lower bailout commitments. Without changing the *system*, tight credit merely trades slightly lower inflation today for the certainty of higher inflation tomorrow.

That said, we stress the importance of improvements in the financial system, especially improvements that allow the financial system to weather inflation and bouts of tight credit without arrears piling up. The lesson of the payments crises is that lowering credit and inflation need not imply output declines but will if they cause needless financial system disruption. Some progress is being made, notably increasing dollarization and faster clearing between commercial banks. Progress on credit access is slower, undoubtedly because the fundamentals of collateral and bankruptcy procedures are not in place.

Notes

1. International Monetary Fund (IMF) (1992), p. 67.

2. See Koen and Phillips (1992) for a discussion of what happened to prices after liberalization.

3. The Central Bank of Russia provides direct credit to industries, often via commercial banks. Increases in these credits are one of the most important sources of increasing money stock in Russia. We discuss this mechanism in detail below.

4. The relationship between inflation and lagged money growth in Russia has been noted by Easterly and Vieira da Cunha (1994) and Sachs (1994).

5. The causes and consequences of the arrears crisis are discussed at length in Ickes and Ryterman (1992, 1993) and below.

6. One policy change that took place in July 1992 was the elimination of file number 2, *Kartoteka Dva*, the central record of arrears. Hence, the magnitude of arrears is now just an estimate. Of course, even before 1992 the 3.2 trillion rubles was a lower bound because some enterprises made deals (technically illegal) with suppliers to bypass the official payments system altogether.

7. Sources for the data in this section are primarily the *Radio Free Europe/Radio Liberty (RFE/RL) Daily Report*, July 13, 1994; Economist Intelligence Unit, first and second quarter 1994; *PlanEcon Report*, April 28, 1994; and *Interfax*, July 5, 1994.

8. The trade surplus also reflects concern over external debt. Russia inherited the Soviet Union's external debt ($65 billion at the end of 1991) and has pledged to meet its obligations. Debt service obligations concentrate attention on the balance of trade.

9. See Hanson (1994) for a discussion of this article.

10. Sachs (1994, 26) notes that repayments will be close to $4 billion in 1994.

11. See Grossman (1963). The remainder of this section follows Ickes and Ryterman (1992).

12. Keep in mind that these flows were measured in fixed prices that bore no relationship to opportunity costs. Many important inputs were assigned very low prices. Hence, there was no necessary correspondence between the bottom line and performance in this system. Still it was a good way to force enterprise directors to economize as best they could.

13. One should again beware of familiar-sounding terms. These banks took very few if any deposits, mostly obtaining funds from the State Savings Bank, *Sberbank*, and receiving credits from the Central Bank of Russia. And many had close relations with some enterprises in a particular region or industry.

14. An anecdotal exception may prove the rule: An electronics enterprise in western Siberia had an important supplier in Armenia, which, in turn, depended on an important supplier in Azerbaijan. The Siberian enterprise would load one of its planes (it was a large enterprise) with *nalichnyye* and fly to Baku. After delivering the rubles, it would fill the plane with components for the Armenian enterprise. Because of the war between Armenia and Azerbaijian, however, the plane could not fly directly to Yerevan, having instead to detour into Russian airspace. Then the components would be exchanged for the Siberian firm's inputs.

15. Although enterprises bore the brunt of the tax in absolute terms, most households have even fewer means of evading this tax. See Easterly and Vieira da Cunha for an analysis of the incidence of the inflation tax in Russia.

16. See Ickes and Ryterman (1992, 1993).

17. The timing is crucial in seeing this story. In the first half of 1992, when credit was relatively tight, enterprises were victims of the inflation tax. During this period liquidity was in short supply, and interenterprise arrears exploded. During the second half of 1992, credit was easy, and the enterprise sector was a major recipient of subsidized credit. If one averages over the year as a whole (e.g., Easterly and Vieira da Cunha or Sachs, then it seems as if the enterprise sector was relatively flush. But this misses the true nature of the conditions facing enterprises in 1992.

18. During 1992 and 1993 enterprise directors had an extra incentive to increase wages because the preferred variant of the privatization program implemented in the Russian Federation allowed workers to gain majority control of the enterprise. Hence, to keep their positions, directors needed to maintain the assent of the workers. See Ickes and Ryterman (1994).

19. Goldberg, Ickes, and Ryterman (1994) discuss the implications of the breakup of the ruble zone.

20. For example, a button manufacturer reported in June 1992 that she had faced a 98 percent turnover tax in the Soviet era. Buttons were considered a lot less important than, say, cement. The change to the 28 percent value-added tax made this the most profitable enterprise in the former Soviet Union!

21. Planners could not act in a completely arbitrary manner; they could direct investment and output, but workers and managers had to be provided incentives to supply effort. Consequently, the use of discretionary taxation did have some adverse incentive effects (Litwack 1991).

References

Cochrane, John H., and Barry W. Ickes. "Stopping Inflation in Reforming Socialist Economies: Some Pleasant Socialist Arithmetic." Unpublished, September 1992.

Delyagin, Mikhail, and Lev Freinkman. "Extrabudgetary Funds in Russian Public Finance." *Radio Free Europe/Radio Liberty (RFE/RL) Research Report* 2, no. 48 (3 December 1993).

Easterly, William, and Paulo Vieira da Cunha. "Financing the Storm: Macroeconomic Crisis in Russia, 1992–3." The World Bank, Policy Research Working Paper 1240, January 1994.

Gaddy, Clifford. "Economic Reform and Individual Choice in Russia." Mimeo, Brookings Institution, August 1993.

Goldberg, Linda, Barry W. Ickes, and Randi Ryterman. "Departures from the Ruble Zone: The Implications of Adopting Independent Currencies." *The World Economy* 17 (3 May 1994).

Grossman, Gregory. "Notes for a Theory of the Command Economy." *Soviet Studies* 15, no. 2 (October 1963).

Hanson, Phillip. "The Russian Budget Revisited." *RFE/RL Research Report* 3, no. 16 (6 May 1994).

Ickes, Barry W., and Randi Ryterman. "Financial Underdevelopment and Macroeconomic Stabilization in Russia." In Gerard Caprio, David Folkerts-Landau, and Timothy Lane, eds., *Building Sound Finance in Emerging Market Economies*. International Monetary Fund (IMF)–World Bank, 1994.

———. "From Enterprise to Firm: Notes for a Theory of the Survival-Oriented Enterprise." In Robert Campbell and Andrzej Brzeski, eds., *Issues in the Transformation of Centrally Planned Economies: Essays in Honor of Gregory Grossman*. Boulder, Colo.: Westview Press, 1994a.

———. "The Interenterprise Arrears Crisis in Russia." *Post-Soviet Affairs* (formerly *Soviet Economy*) 8, no. 4 (October–December 1992).

———. "Roadblock to Economic Reform: Interenterprise Debt and the Transition to Markets." *Post-Soviet Affairs* (formerly *Soviet Economy*) 9, no. 3 (July–September 1993).

International Monetary Fund, Economic Review. *The Economy of the Former U.S.S.R. in 1991*. Washington, D.C., April 1992.

International Monetary Fund, Economic Reviews 1993. *Russian Federation*. Washington D.C., June 1993.

Koen, Vincent, and Steven Phillips. "Price Liberalization in Russia: The Early Record." IMF Working Paper, October 1992.

Lipton, David, and Jeffrey Sachs. "Prospects for Russia's Economic Reform." Brookings Papers on Economic Activity 2, 1992.

Litwack, John. "Discretionary Behavior and Soviet Economic Reform." *Soviet Studies* 43, no. 2 (1991): 225–79.

Lucas, Robert E. "Some International Evidence on Output-Inflation Tradeoffs." *American Economic Review* 63 (June 1973).

Ransom, Roger L., and Richard Sutch. *One Kind of Freedom: The Economic Consequences of Emancipation*. Cambridge, Eng.: Cambridge University Press, 1977.

Russian Ministry of Finance (1994). "Russian Finances in 1993: A Finance Ministry Survey." *Voprosy Ekonomiki*, no. 1 (1994): 3–86.

Sachs, Jeffrey. *Russia's Struggle with Stabilization: Conceptual Issues and Evidence*. The World Bank, Annual Bank Conference on Development Economics, April 1994.

3

Democracy and Economic Reform: Tensions, Compatibilities, and Strategies for Reconciliation

LARRY DIAMOND

This essay analyzes the relationship between political democracy and the economic reform process. It first discusses the ways in which capitalism as an economic system and democracy as a political system are related to and reinforce one another. The main part of the chapter considers the tensions and difficulties of achieving economic liberalization either simultaneously with democratization or under democratic structures. Arguments about the desirability of economic reform before democratization are shown to be overgeneralized and to rest on a number of dubious or untenable propositions. In many countries, authoritarianism is not a realistic option for achieving economic reform, and democracies have proven able to pursue difficult economic reforms. But if the reform process is to succeed under democracy, specific strategies must be pursued to reduce the political tensions and obstacles that initially result from reform policies. These strategies include insulating and strengthening the state bureaucracy, instituting a social safety net to relieve the effects of economic adjustment on poor and vulnerable social groups, educating and mobilizing domestic political support for economic reform, and mobilizing international financial and technical assistance for reforming governments.

The Relationship between Capitalism and Democracy

For the past two centuries, few issues in the social sciences have occasioned so much analysis and impassioned debate as the relationship between economic and political systems and, more specifically, the relationship between capitalism and democracy. There are powerful logical, theoretical, historical, and empirical reasons to expect a close association between capitalism and democracy, with a logical relationship flowing almost inescapably from the very definitions of these terms. Capitalism is an economic system based on private ownership of the means of production and the determination of prices and rewards through competition between private producers (rather than through political command and allocation, as under socialism). Democracy is a political system based on the autonomy and freedom of individual citizens, and the determination of public power and policies through competition between groups of citizens, based in parties and interest groups. Economic freedom and political freedom thus would appear, at a minimum, to be natural companions, even if one does not strictly require the other.

Logically, there would seem to be a strong affinity among the marketplace of goods and services in a capitalist economy, the marketplace of ideas in a liberal society, and the marketplace of parties and programs in a political democracy. Underlying each are the fundamental principles of competition and choice; threatening each is the excessive concentration of power in the state. Thus, Lindblom writes that "the liberal notion of freedom was freedom from government's many interventions, and for that kind of freedom markets are indeed indispensable."[1] Going further, Milton and Rose Friedman assert that "economic freedom is an essential requisite for political freedom. By enabling people to cooperate with one another without coercion or central direction, it reduces the area over which political power is exercised. In addition, by dispersing power, the free market provides an offset to whatever concentration of political power may arise."[2]

Historically, it is beyond dispute that capitalism and democracy developed alongside one another in Europe and the United States. Even Karl Marx recognized this. As Peter Berger has observed, "Modern democracy was clearly one of the historical achievements of the bourgeoisie, the rising capitalist class," and in this sense the common Marxist designation of these polities as "bourgeois de-

---

I am grateful for the comments of Barbara Geddes, Edward Lazear, and Barry Weingast on an earlier draft of this paper.

mocracies" remains "*historically* valid."³ This historical relationship has been much more than coincidental; at its core has been the close interdependence between economic and political freedom. As Charles Lindblom has argued, democracy has historically been pursued as a means of affirming, extending, and securing personal liberty, and an important aspect of this liberty has been economic: the right to private property, "freedom to engage in trade and to establish enterprises to pursue the gains of trade, freedom also to move about, to keep one's earnings and assets, and to be secure against arbitrary exactions."⁴ Such minimum freedoms of enterprise, contract, and movement as well as occupational choice are, in turn, essential to the functioning of a market system.

The empirical evidence over the past two centuries, as Peter Berger has observed, also strongly indicates a relationship. Specifically, three generalizations can be made. First, democracy does not seem to be possible without a market economy: "There has been no case of political democracy that has *not* been a market economy."⁵ Moreover, although democracy has coexisted with heavy state intervention in the economy (e.g., India, Israel, and some European countries), extreme protectionism and perversion of markets has been a source of democratic instability in Latin America (and other parts of the Third World).⁶ Second, this conditionality does not appear to be strictly symmetrical: "There have been numerous cases of *non*democratic market economies."⁷ Successful capitalist development is clearly possible under authoritarian rule, and there are (for democrats) a discomfiting number of cases (from Bismarck's Germany to South Korea under the military and Taiwan under KMT one-party rule) suggesting that "when capitalist industrialization is initiated and guided by the state instead of a politically autonomous bourgeoisie, an authoritarian regime can preempt the rise of liberal democracy by co-opting or diverting those groups that would otherwise press for democracy."⁸ Third, however, successful socioeconomic development under capitalism tends to generate escalating—and ultimately almost irresistible—pressures for democratization. Among the capitalist nondemocracies, "those most advanced in their capitalist development (size of market sector of their economy, autonomy of their entrepreneurial class) are also those that have been most exposed to pressures for democracy, leading, in many cases, to the emergence or return of democratic government."⁹ South Korea, Spain, and Taiwan are the classic examples in our time, but Thailand and numerous other developing countries show evidence of the relationship, which is also confirmed by a wide range of quantitative studies.¹⁰

What aspects of a market economy seem essential for democracy? Two fundamental elements stand out. First, democracy requires sufficient private ownership of productive assets to provide a socioeconomic basis for political pluralism and checks on the power of the state. Ceteris paribus, the more these assets are privately owned, the more vigorous will be social pluralism and economic growth. (Some economic growth is essential over time to deepen the legitimacy of democracy, even though new democracies may begin with sufficient legitimacy to weather prolonged periods of economic hardship.) It is theoretically difficult to specify a minimum percentage, but to sustain democracy, an economy must probably be capitalist enough that private ownership accounts for a substantial majority of all production (even in countries such as the European social democracies, where state expenditures are close to half or more of gross national product [GNP]).[11] Second, democracy requires that the prices of goods and services be determined primarily by the forces of supply and demand rather than by political allocation. Bureaucratic determination of prices in a command economy gives the state a monolithic power that hardly seems compatible with democracy and also results in gross economic inefficiencies and shortages that would in any case eventually undermine the legitimacy of democracy.

Beyond these two minimal conditions, further assertions can only be probabilistic. We know that democracy has persisted in many countries with high levels of state economic regulation, protection, employment, and ownership. We also know, however, that these various constraints on private economic investment, production, and competition have been important sources of economic crisis, social conflict, and ultimately political instability. Thus, the more open and market oriented the economy (and the less that political efforts to provide social security and redistribution violate the fundamental principles of the market), the more likely that democracy will be stable and enduring. And thus a fundamental premise of this chapter (and book) is that economic liberalization enhances the long-term viability of democracy, even though it generates certain problems and tensions for it in the short run.

WHY DEMOCRACY AND THE MARKET ARE RELATED

Theoretically, there are many reasons to expect a close mutual association between economic and political freedom, one that is at least partly causal in nature. One reason derives from what Weingast has called the *"fundamental political dilemma of an economic system*: A state strong enough to establish property rights and enforce contracts is also strong enough to confiscate the wealth of all its citizens."[12] As suggested above, the private investment and risk-taking crucial to economic growth in a capitalist system require a predictable social and institutional order in which entrepreneurs have enduring legal protection from the arbitrary exactions of the state and confidence in the political environment. Thus, for there to emerge such a stable and hospitable enabling environment for capitalist investment and production, democracy in all its aspects is not a necessary condition (or a sufficient one), but a strong rule of law does appear necessary, as the World Bank is recognizing in its increasing emphasis on governance.[13] This requires legal and constitutional protections for property rights, contracts, and capital flows that are probably best guaranteed in the long run under a democratic system. "Without the appropriate—and self-enforcing—[constitutional] limits on government, a successful market economy cannot be sustained over the long run."[14] Moreover, liberal democracy, it may be argued, is probably the form of government most conducive to the spirited flow of ideas, people, and resources, which enhances the dynamism of market economies.

Liberal democracy, in turn, seems to require a market-oriented economy because "the dispersion of economic power" inherent in a market economy "creates alternatives and counters to state power."[15] As Robert Dahl argued in an insightful axiom, "The likelihood that a government will tolerate an opposition increases as the resources available to the government decline relative to the resources of the opposition."[16] Unless state power is limited, the individual freedoms so important to democracy by definition cannot be secure. Some would regard the institution of private property as part of the irreducible core of individual freedoms. Even if one does not take that philosophical stance, however, it is clear that state power cannot be effectively limited if the state controls the overwhelming share of the society's economic resources. Moreover, the concentration of economic resources in the state (or any other narrow sector of society) undermines the vigor and authenticity of political competition.

Related to the important roles of private property and the market in limiting state power is the class structure that results from capitalism. A strong, independent capital-owning class (i.e., a bourgeoisie) has long been considered an important bulwark against a hegemonic state and for the protection of individual rights. Historically, Schumpeter observed, the "bourgeois scheme of things limit[ed] the sphere of politics by limiting the sphere of public authority" to the ideal "parsimonious" functions of guaranteeing "bourgeois legality" and providing "a firm frame for autonomous individual endeavor in all fields."[17] "No bourgeois, no democracy," Barrington Moore concluded in his sweeping historical examination, *The Social Origins of Dictatorship and Democracy*, and many scholars since have echoed and cited his formulation.[18] A more recent comparative historical study of similarly impressive scope has questioned the thesis that the bourgeoisie is always prodemocracy, demonstrating that capitalist classes have often backed authoritarian regimes when it served their material interests. More often, the authors suggest, it has been the working class that has pressed forward the expansion of suffrage, political liberties, and democracy.[19] This, too, however, has been a phenomenon of capitalist development, for only in capitalist systems do working-class organizations enjoy sufficient autonomy from the state to mobilize for such rights. Generally, it would seem that both classes are important for democracy and can only achieve political autonomy in a truly capitalist system. Where capitalism is distorted by a heavily protectionist, autarkic pattern of industrialization—as in the Latin American countries that pursued import-substituting industrialization strategies after World War II—democracy is unlikely to be successful precisely because the capitalist and working classes it generates are "dependent and predatory," more committed to preserving rent-seeking distributional coalitions than to achieving economic development or political rights.[20]

This points to a fourth, closely related reason capitalism and democracy are causally related. Tocqueville wrote about the importance of associational life and press freedom to democracy in America almost two centuries ago, and since then theorists and students of democracy have argued that a strong, pluralistic, autonomous civil society is highly conducive to, if not strictly necessary for, effective democracy.[21] Economic systems have their parallel in forms of state-society relations. The command economy seeks control over all corporate economic actors, even if they do not own property. Thus, in a socialist economy, associations of labor, peasants, professionals, students, and other important economic and social interest groups are licensed and directed by the state (or the party that controls the state). In a market economy, such interest groups tend to be much more autonomous and pluralistic, and one might hypothesize that the more market oriented the economy, the more autonomy such groups have. Thus, Peter Berger suggests that "capitalism favors mediating structures. It 'leaves room' for them, precisely because it creates a highly dynamic zone that is relatively autonomous vis-à-vis the state."[22] These autonomous intermediate groups, in turn, further serve to check the power of the state, as well as to develop participatory skills, values, and inclinations among their members. Through both its economic and social consequences, then, capitalism may be necessary for democracy because it defends the boundary between state and civil society.

A fifth reason democracy may require capitalism also relates to the problem of state control over the economy. As a system of institutionalized competition for power, democracy requires that parties and candidates keep their electoral contests within clearly defined legal and normative boundaries and that losers accept defeat, lest the struggle for power degenerate into a Hobbesian war. However, to the extent that the state controls all material resources, opportunities, and advantages—either directly or indirectly, through pervasive regulation and protection—the premium on political power becomes too great to allow for peaceful competition restrained by some framework of mutual trust and shared norms. When the "loss of office means serious [material] losses for major power groups, they will seek to retain or secure office by any means available."[23] This danger was perceptively recognized by Gaetano Mosca when he wrote:

> One of the most important reasons for the decline of the parliamentary system is the relatively huge number of offices, contracts for public works and other [economic] favors . . . which the governing class is in a position to distribute . . . ; and the drawbacks of that system are greater in proportion as the amount of wealth that the government . . . absorbs and distributes is greater, and the

harder it becomes, therefore, to secure an honest living without relying in some respect or other upon public administration.[24]

Evading this conundrum requires more than the superficial structures of capitalism. It requires that the principal means of wealth generation be outside the state, in private ownership of the means of production, and that there exist a genuinely competitive market system. Where the state becomes the primary arena of wealth accumulation—because of its excessive ownership, employment, and regulation—political, bureaucratic, industrial, and commercial elites (along with corrupted and co-opted trade unions and other interest groups) all vie ferociously for the rents controlled by the state.[25] Elections become warfare and corruption flourishes. These distortions have fatally undermined the effectiveness and legitimacy of democracy in the Third World, particularly in postindependence Africa.[26] "A competitive market economy can therefore be justified in sociological and political terms as the best way to reduce the impact of nepotistic networks" and rent seeking.[27]

A sixth causal connection between capitalism and democracy lies at the level of values, beliefs, and ideas. To return to the natural affinities among the economic, cultural/ideological, and political markets, one may hypothesize that the values of competition and freedom of choice, once engendered through the successful operation of a capitalist system (and of the mediating structures characteristic of capitalism), may become generalized to encompass the realms of governance and cultural expression as well. In particular, it appears that successful capitalism generates various types of interest groups—students, professionals, organized labor, and the educated middle class more generally—who demand a say in the decisions that affect their lives and who seek the same participation, responsibility, information, opportunity, and choice in politics that they have in the economy. This raises the interesting question of the extent to which there exists what Peter Berger terms an *economic culture* of capitalism that corresponds in important ways with the political culture of democracy.

This points to a seventh causal linkage between capitalism and democracy, the common need for free and open flows of information. Increasingly in this age of high technology, rapid transactions, complex markets, and global integration, a successful market economy requires—and induces and sustains—a free flow of information. Granted, this information basically concerns economic and business matters, but inevitably this touches on government policy and intentions and thus politics. Moreover, "the granting of one freedom, even if limited and circumscribed, creates powerful precedents for other freedoms. Once economic information begins to flow freely, it becomes impossible to restrict discussion and debate to economic or business topics alone. Inevitably, freedom of economic information will enlarge the democratic space in society."[28]

Finally, as I indicated above, capitalism promotes democracy by promoting economic development. "Economically, a market economy appears more likely to sustain economic growth than a command economy . . . , and hence a market economy is more likely to give rise to the economic wealth and the resulting more equitable distribution of income that provide the infrastructure of democracy."[29] Some of the cultural or value factors that press for democracy may, in fact, result more from such economic and social development than from the operation of a market economy. In addition, economic development presses for democracy because it tends to generate autonomy, pluralism, and activity in civil society (including the flow of information); because it gives rise to a large middle class with a particular interest in freedom and the limitation of state power; and because, under capitalism and separate and apart from more deliberate reforms, it tends to dilute the role of the state in the economy by promoting capital accumulation outside the state. Thus, under capitalism, "even an authoritarian industrializing state . . . will eventually find itself contending with democratic forces unleashed by an assertive middle class that the state itself has indirectly fostered."[30] Capitalist authoritarian states are caught in a kind of catch-22: If they do not deliver economic development, they forfeit their only real claim to political legitimacy; but if they do succeed in modernizing their countries, they eventually become victims of their own success, generating social forces that no longer need the protection or are willing to suffer the constraints of authoritarian rule.[31]

Getting There:
Democratization and Economic Liberalization

There is a strong association in logic and experience between democracy and a market economy and strong theoretical reasons for asserting that this relationship is not coincidental but derives from the basic functional needs and consequences of the two types of systems. Nevertheless, to say that the two systems strongly complement (and may to some extent require) one another does not necessarily imply that the processes of *transition to* democracy and the market economy are necessarily compatible. We learned a generation ago from Samuel Huntington that, although there is a strong association between democracy and modernity, and between political order more generally and modernity, the *process* of modernization can disrupt both democracy and political order.[32] By the same logic, one could imagine that the process of moving from a socialist or statist toward a market-oriented economy could generate powerful disruptive or contradictory effects on democracy. Because democracy and capitalism are highly compatible does not mean that the transitions to them are.

With respect to end goals (as opposed to processes and means), there is more consensus in the world today than perhaps ever before in history. Indeed, the world of the 1990s is remarkable for the degree to which previously widespread regime forms and economic models now lie in ruins, discredited and abandoned. Although the future of democracy is by no means assured, with military, nationalist, and religious fundamentalist forms of dictatorship remaining viable options for organizing state power, communism as a system of rule and a worldwide ideological movement is basically "extinct."[33] A few dinosaurs remain, but without the capacity to reproduce themselves or advance the species.

Even more stunning has been the rejection of state socialist forms of economic organization. It is increasingly appreciated around the world—even in countries such as China and Vietnam, which remain communist in name and formal political structure—that genuine economic modernization, a fundamental transformation of a country's level of economic productivity and wealth, requires the institutions of a market economy. The accumulation of developmental experience and diffusion of economic knowledge have produced a substantial and growing global consensus on a number of core elements of sound macroeconomic policy—including fiscal discipline, broad tax bases with efficient tax administration, competitive exchange rates, liberal trade, and secure property rights—that have been dubbed the "Washington consensus."[34] Countries in the grip of a socialist command economy have required a sweeping and profound structural transformation: freeing prices from state regulation, privatizing productive assets, creating capital markets, instituting effective, liberal forms of taxation and social insurance, and opening the economy to international trade and capital flows (all while maintaining, or creating anew, a stable currency).

The experience of China since the onset of Deng Xiaoping's reforms shows that such a transformation is possible—some would argue more possible or even only possible—under authoritarian rule but not under communist, totalitarian rule. As Kyung-won Kim has observed, for many years China has been in transition to what Robert Scalapino calls an "authoritarian-pluralist" system, which combines undemocratic (even very repressive) management of political power with some considerable space for autonomous activity in the economy and society.[35] Vietnam is at an earlier but increasingly vigorous stage of this softening or pluralization of communism.

To the extent that rapid economic development continues in China, it will increasingly transform the society as well as the economy, giving rise to multiple centers of information, ideas, and resources that will erode the foundations of authoritarian rule. Min-xin Pei has gone so far as to assert that "despite the Chinese hard-liners' pledge to maintain a one-party dictatorship, their regime's internal decay is now irreversible. The Chinese path toward democratization will most likely follow the model of Taiwan and South Korea once China becomes a fully market-based economic system."[36] This then is one path of transition from a (socialist) dictatorship to a market-oriented democracy: sustained economic liberalization and development, under a softer and less monolithic authoritarian regime, eventually undermining that authoritarianism and giving rise (gradually or more suddenly) to a liberal, competitive political regime. It is a path that, as in South Korea and Taiwan, involves a larger and more important economic role for the state than liberal theorists have appreciated.[37]

THE CASE FOR ECONOMIC REFORM
BEFORE DEMOCRATIZATION

In the alternative model of dual transition, economic change follows political change. In Eastern Europe and the former Soviet Union, the rapid and unanticipated disintegration of communist political institutions means that the transition to a market economy must be negotiated within the framework and constraints of (new and shaky) democratic regimes or regimes that at least allow more scope for popular participation and protest.

Conventional wisdom suggests that this is a more difficult path, that "authoritarian governments are better positioned than democratic governments to promote economic liberalization," and thus that economic reform should ideally come first.[38] There are several reasons to presume that "democracy before economic reform" is a more difficult sequence.

First, economic decisions must be made and implemented within the context of new political institutions that have yet to become fully effective or even fully articulated. The dilemma is particularly acute when the transition represents a "revolutionary" displacement of not only a political system but an entire economic and class structure, as in the former Soviet Union.[39] In the aftermath of the downfall of Soviet communism in 1991, the country seemed, in the words of Saint Petersburg's reformist mayor Anatoly Sobchak, "out of control, because the old structures have been destroyed and the new ones have not emerged."[40] For more than two years after the collapse of communism, Russia stumbled on without a new constitution, in a situation of protracted conflict between multiple horizontal and vertical sources of power (horizontally, between President Yeltsin and the Congress, vertically, between the central Russian state and increasingly assertive and rebellious authorities in the local governments and autonomous republics). The failure to adopt a new constitution, form a presidential proreform party, or hold elections quickly in this period was a major blunder on the part of Yeltsin and his democratic allies.[41] Adopting a new constitution and electing a new congress in December 1993 only partially relieved the institutional vacuum, as the long delay played into the hands of fascist and reactionary forces opposed to reform.

Achieving economic reform in the context of a new democracy requires not only a new constitution but the formation of alternative political parties with clear programs, disciplined legislative support, and (ultimately) "large and virtually permanent bases of support among voters." Such a party system is "a crucial condition for a stable democracy" because it provides the conditions not only for effective governance but for meaningful (and peacefully articulated) opposition.[42] The continuing absence of such a stable and consolidated party system has handicapped effective policy making in the postcommunist systems of Eastern Europe and the former Soviet Union and remains one of the greatest threats to the democratic prospect in postcommunist Russia, intensifying problems of ungovernability.[43]

Second, even though communism has disintegrated as a system of government and authority, the communist elite networks and informal power structures (as well as surviving communist party and trade union organizations) retain considerable influence and, in many areas (especially the Central Asian and Caucasian republics), outright dominance. This produces, at a minimum, considerable potential for antiliberalization forces to obstruct or sabotage economic reform. The fact that these forces are often strongest at the levels of the local government and industrial plant creates an ironic twist in comparison with the reform situation in China. Although China remains under formal communist rule, the greater coherence of (surviving authoritarian) political authority there gives the ruling elites greater ability than in Russia, for example, to choose and implement reform policies, while the breathtaking dynamism of the Chinese economy—growing more rapidly than any other in the world—entices elites at all levels to join the bandwagon of capitalist economic activity.

Third, where economic reform comes first, the cases of South Korea and Taiwan suggest that democratization may ultimately proceed more smoothly because the intervening years of economic growth will have created a more favorable set of social and economic conditions, such as a large middle class, a reduction in poverty and inequality, a well-educated population, a vibrant civil society, a more democratic culture, and a strong base of economic resources outside the state.[44]

A fourth reason economic reform appears more difficult when it is preceded by a democratic transition is that democracy is a system of government based on public consent and accountability, whereas economic stabilization and liberalization impose substantial pain on much of the public, at least in the short term. Because economic actors tends to discount future benefits relative to current ones, and because mass publics are poorly informed about the likely future benefits of reform, voters will not voluntarily opt for such painful reforms, it is argued, and will turn out governments that impose them before the policies can generate broad gains.[45] In fact, democracy may suffer from what Weingast calls a "double political uncertainty" concerning not only the identity and policy orientation of the next administration but the viability of the regime itself.[46] This potential political and policy volatility, which increases the risks to investors, constitutes the core dilemma in the debate over the compatibility of democracy and economic liberalization.

Economic growth in the medium to long run requires the implementation of stabilization and liberalization measures that will in the short run impose costs (higher prices for imports, an end to subsidies, reductions in state social services and employment, lower real wages) on large portions of the society and on certain well-defined, politically powerful, and resourceful constituencies (e.g., managers and workers in uncompetitive industries) in particular. Because the costs of economic reform are "immediate, certain, and often concentrated on specific groups," while the benefits "are usually deferred, uncertain, and diffused,"[47] economic reformers face massive problems of obtaining consent in the short to medium run. Not being bound constitutionally to obtain periodic popular consent, authoritarian regimes are claimed to have more scope to look to the long term than democratically elected officials, who must always have their eye on the much shorter electoral cycle. In addition, democratic governments that do initiate economic reform risk being paralyzed (or even brought down) by protests from trade unions and other elements of the urban popular classes, whereas authoritarian rulers typically "demobilize" the groups most likely to protest and can quell protest with new repression if necessary. Thus it was conventional wisdom for much of the 1980s that "a courageous, ruthless, and perhaps undemocratic government is required to ride roughshod over these newly-created special interest groups" for adjustment to succeed.[48]

The paradigmatic case of economic reform in Latin America, in Chile under General Augusto Pinochet, was achieved under an authoritarian regime that was able to implement painful and dislocating economic liberalization measures precisely because it had forcibly excluded most of society—including organized labor and uncompetitive industrialists—from influence over policy.[49] As in Chile, but with less raw repression, economic reform has been imposed unilaterally from the top down in Mexico, where President Carlos Salinas de Gortari has used the monolithic powers of the presidency and his tight control over the hegemonic ruling party and the corporatist labor unions to implement far-reaching privatization and trade liberalization measures. Tensions between economic and political liberalization have been resolved by sacrificing the latter for the former,[50] and President Salinas has frankly conceded that he deferred political democratization because "he needed the immense power he had in the Mexican political system in order to put through . . . economic reforms."[51] President Alberto Fujimori justified his seizure of authoritarian power in Peru in large measure by his proclaimed need to overcome congressional obstruction of his economic reform measures.

FALLACIES IN THE CASE FOR
ECONOMIC REFORM BEFORE DEMOCRATIZATION

Although these problems and tensions are real, there are nevertheless strong reasons for rejecting the generalization that authoritarianism is therefore a more effective political framework for initiating and implementing economic reform policies. There are several fallacies in this deduction that need to be exposed. First, it assumes that authoritarianism would, in the specific countries under discussion, be a politically viable regime form, able to muster the political strength and legitimacy to impose reform policies (assuming also it was committed to reform). It is by no means clear that this would be the case in Russia, Ukraine, Belarus, the Baltics, Poland, Hungary, the Czech Republic, and other postcommunist (and for that matter Third World) countries. Where economic reform has been successfully implemented in authoritarian regimes—in Chile, China, Indonesia, Mexico, South Korea, and Taiwan, for example—there have been relatively coherent elite structures available to design and staff the reforms, and there has been some significant base of political legitimacy for authoritarianism in the society. With the utter discrediting of communist dictatorships in Eastern Europe and the Soviet Union, and of military and one-party dictatorships in Latin America and much of Africa, it is doubtful that new authoritarian regimes in these countries would have the legitimacy in society and the internal coherence and strength to impose serious economic liberalization policies and sustain them over a long period of time. In fact, the illegitimacy, abusiveness, and corruption of authoritarian rule are major reasons the military in Nigeria proved unable to implement effectively its orginal, conceptually far-reaching program of structural adjustment and to build a new political coalition that could sustain it.[52]

Related to this is a second fallacy, that such enduring authoritarian regimes are immune from, or heavily insulated from, political pressures that would obstruct economic liberalization. Precisely when their political legitimacy is low domestically and internationally—and the latter in particular is likely to be the case in the current period—authoritarian regimes must become more sensitive to the political claims of strategic power groups and to the political danger of policies that would incite riots in the streets. In the typical postcommunist and developing country in need of economic reform, those strategic power groups are highly likely to encompass elites whose wealth and income derive from the capture of various rents that would be eliminated with currency devaluation, trade liberalization, price liberalization, and other economic reform measures. And where a weak authoritarian regime is buying social peace only by maintaining subsidies for food, fuel, and other basic commodities and services (thereby barely enabling the urban poor and lower middle classes to cope), it is ridiculous to think that it would be more able than a democratic regime to remove those subsidies. The furious riots and military coup attempt that greeted Kenneth Kaunda's doubling of maize meal prices in 1990 in Zambia are a telling case in point.[53] Developments in Cameroon, Kenya, Zaire, and numerous other countries with embattled, long-serving authoritarian regimes also testify to the general inability of such regimes to sustain a serious reform program (or even to maintain a semblance of fiscal discipline) in the face of popular protest.[54] By contrast, the government of newly elected Zambian president Frederick Chiluba—precisely because it was buoyed by strong democratic legitimacy, an initial "honeymoon period" of widespread popular support, and an overwhelming legislative majority, and because Chiluba had prepared the political ground for fundamental economic change in his election campaign—was able to implement much more far-reaching structural adjustment measures (including removing price controls and subsidies for most commodities) in its first year in office, without rioting or widespread protest. In fact, it tripled maize prices on taking office in December 1991, and subsequently it largely eliminated maize subsidies that had eaten up more than an eighth of the government budget in the final years of the Kaunda regime.[55]

A third fallacy in theories about the inherent advantages of authoritarian rule for economic reform is the assumption that such undemocratic rule in these countries would necessarily bring to or find in power political elites committed to economic liberalization. This assumption is a variant of more general arguments, dating back to the 1960s and 1970s, about the supposed advantages of authoritarianism for economic development. Yet the most recent and exhaustive review of some eighteen comparative statistical analyses of this question since the 1960s finds no basis to conclude that either democratic or authoritarian regimes as a group perform better with respect to economic growth and suggests that it is not regime type "per se that makes the difference but something else."[56] Many recent analyses (particularly drawing from the East Asian development experience) have pointed to state autonomy from private interest group pressures as the most crucial "something else."[57] Authoritarian regimes have certain advantages in this regard. Yet, as Haggard argues, "There are no theoretical reasons to think that authoritarian regimes are *uniquely* capable of solving the collective-action problems associated with development."[58] And, as he also observes, authoritarian regimes vary widely and more often than not are highly penetrated and corrupt. Ultimately, the most obvious "something else" is the right mix of policies. Although there remains debate about the role of the state in this regard, it is increasingly clear that investments in human capital (beginning with universal primary education) have played an important role in stimulating growth, and democracy in principle certainly presents no obstacle to this.[59] Given the regional and cultural location of most states that have recorded rapid, sustained economic growth under authoritarian rule, it may be useful to explore whether there are certain cultural features of East Asian (Confucian) societies that have disposed their elites to use "state autonomy" to pursue self-disciplined, developmentalist policies in the broad national interest, rather than to collect rents for themselves. Temporal factors must also be weighed. The four East Asian "tigers" (Hong Kong, Singapore, South Korea, and Taiwan) and the newly industrializing "miracle" countries (Indonesia, Malaysia, and Thailand) implemented growth-inducing economic reforms at a time when the United States and the Western alliance more broadly were oblivious (if not actually hostile) to issues of democracy and human rights and prepared to shower aid on authoritarian states with a strong anticommunist alignment. Now that the cold war is over, the major bilateral and international aid donors (especially the United States) are much more sensitive to the political nature of regimes, and authoritarian regimes are more likely to pay a price in terms of assistance.

In other parts of the Third World in particular, authoritarian ruling elites typically have material interests (in addition to strong ideological predilections) against economic liberalization. In fact, "the biggest, and certainly the most articulate and politically influential, losers from structural adjustment in many countries are government officials, ruling party cadres, cronies of rulers, and close allies of all three. These are groups whose ability to make effective demands does not decline as regimes become less democratic."[60] In South America, the deep involvement of military officers in running state enterprises gave them a strong material interest against economic liberalization, which was supplemented by the ideological orientation of military officers generally toward nationalism and against liberalism.[61]

To put the issue more generally, "successful economic reform requires a significant degree of credibly limited government," and authoritarian regimes are by their nature less inclined to produce that.[62] The typical authoritarian regime is consumed with rent seeking—manipulating import licenses, foreign exchange controls, subsidies, government jobs, and so on—by high officials, cronies, and clients of the regime, and these people do not figure to give more than polite international lip service to structural adjustment policies that will damage their material interests. Thus, in nondemocratic Zambia, semidemocratic Senegal, and democratic Venezuela alike, it was ruling party activists who mobilized political opposition against economic reforms, forcing either temporary abandonment or significant dilution.[63] In Nigeria, as noted above, the failure and partial abandonment of structural adjustment has occurred under successive military regimes thoroughly dominated by rent-seeking military officers and political cronies. Authoritarianism in Africa has been associated with such staggering abuse and corruption that one could not expect new dictatorships to have any real policy agenda other than their own aggrandizement.[64] In this respect, Africans themselves are now beginning to argue that "postponing democracy does not promote development," that in fact "the absence of democracy is the primary cause of the chronic crisis in Africa," and that open public debate and democratic consensus building would aid the political sustainability of structural adjustment policies by mitigating some of the social costs and enhancing burden sharing.[65] Although democracy certainly does not ensure probity and accountability in governance, it makes them more possible and is probably a prerequisite for them in the African context.

There is every reason to expect that these problems of rent seeking and resistance to reform by entrenched bureaucratic and political elites would be at least as debilitating in the typical postcommunist system of Eastern Europe and the former Soviet Union under authoritarian rule. Even though competitive elections and political pluralism hardly guarantee the displacement from power of the old *nomenklatura*, they do provide an opportunity to challenge them, while constitutional change destroys the old foundations of their power and special privileges. This is a major reason rapid and thoroughgoing democratization seems to be a precondition for economic reform in the more advanced socialist countries of Eastern Europe and the former Soviet Union.[66] In the absence of competitive political mechanisms, it falls entirely to top ruling party elites to confront and overcome resistance from within their postcommunist ranks. And the resistance to reform is likely to be much greater in more industrialized (post)communist countries—where state subsidies for uncompetitive industries constitute a much larger share of gross national product and consumer subsidies and market entry constraints are also more elaborate—than in "backward state socialist economies" like China and Vietnam, whose large agrarian sectors "offer opportunities for a quick breakthrough" to reform with less pain.[67] Moreover, if authoritarian rule emerges in Russia or Eastern Europe, it is likely to take the form of intense nationalist reaction against foreign domination and influence that would evince great hostility to trade liberalization, foreign investment, liberalization of capital flows, and other dimensions of economic opening to the world. Instinctively, then, it would recoil from essential elements of the economic reform agenda.

The initiation of a serious economic reform program requires two political conditions: first, a head of government or set of political leaders committed (whether for substantive or more opportunistic reasons) to basic structural reform and not merely palliative measures, and, second, the political scope for that leadership to break with the past. Across a wide range of countries over the past decade, economic reforms have been most likely to be initiated by "executives who for one reason or another are not beholden to the party, faction, or group that has previously benefited from state intervention."[68] Democracy alone does not guarantee the existence of such an executive free to break with the past, but it makes it much more likely. In fact, Geddes argues, the election into power of a party previously in opposition can provide the latter with a positive political incentive to reform, in that privatization, trade liberalization, and other reforms undermine the accrued material advantages of the former incumbents, "disorganize opponents' support networks, and, at the same time, generate new revenues that they can use to help balance the budget, reduce the debt, and create new distributive networks tied to themselves."[69] Political leaders committed to reform may appear in the guise of economic technocrats, such as Turgut Ozal in Turkey and Carlos Salinas de Gotari in Mexico, whose experience and understanding generate a deep substantive attachment to economic liberalization. More often, they will be savvy politicians, such as Carlos Menem in Argentina, Paz Estenssoro in Bolivia, Jerry Rawlings in Ghana, and Carlos Andrés Pérez in Venezuela, who believe either that there is no realistic alternative or that economic reform will ultimately serve (through both its economic and political effects) their own political ends.[70] External pressure may help to construct the political context that brings leaders to commit themselves to economic reform, but unless it catalyzes or locates a deeply receptive domestic policy environment, the reform policies it induces are likely to be halting and short lived.[71]

A fourth fallacy has to do with the assumption that broad popular interest groups will inevitably oppose the principal elements of an economic reform package. In fact, there has been much variation in the degree of popular opposition, depending on a number of factors. The deeper the "trough" of economic crisis, the more massively apparent will be the untenability of existing economic policies and structures and the readier mass publics will be for serious structural reform.[72] The pervasiveness, profundity, and urgency of economic crisis had much to do with the ability not only of authoritarian Rawlings in Ghana but of democratically elected presidents Menem in Argentina and Estenssoro in Bolivia to launch far-reaching economic stabilization and reform programs.

> In Bolivia in 1985 and Argentina in 1990, hyperinflation had capped a long history of partial or abortive reforms. . . . Ghana had suffered fifteen years of disastrous economic decline by 1983. . . . In none of these cases [including authoritarian Turkey in 1980, democratic Sri Lanka in 1977, and Jamaica in 1980] was there a widespread popular consensus on the precise nature of the necessary reforms. But earlier strategies, including partial or gradual reforms, had proved ineffective or disastrous, and much of the public was prepared to acquiesce or even eager for a change of direction under firm leadership.[73]

The ability of democratic politicians in their election campaigns to level with the voting public and prepare it for tough economic medicine ahead can also do much to preempt popular protest, as the Zambian case shows.

Fifth, political experience of numerous regimes over the past decade or two shows that interest groups inclined to oppose economic reforms, particularly urban trade unions, often lack the political muscle to prevail. Of course, this goes without saying under authoritarian regimes like those in Pinochet's Chile or Mexico, where unions are banned or tightly controlled. However, even under full democratic freedom to operate, trade unions have been sufficiently weakened by general industrial and economic decline and/or sufficiently isolated in their opposition (because other consequences of reform, such as lower inflation and cheaper imports of mass consumption goods, have neutralized opposition from broader urban constituencies) that they have been unable to prevent the imposition of serious adjustment costs, including higher unemployment and lower wages in all eleven of the countries (outside the former communist world) Geddes studied.[74] In postcommunist Eastern Europe as well, "union opposition to initial stabilization and structural reforms . . . was muted, even though real wages dropped sharply."[75] In addition, incoming elected governments may have no political ties or debt to labor and other vested interest groups, and massive electoral defeats, ideological conflicts, and internal rivalries may, at crucial historical moments, render opposition parties and interest groups incapable of mounting effective political resistance to reforms that may cost them and their supporters dearly.[76]

Sixth, it is fallacious to assume that the legitimacy of new democracies is inevitably so weak and fragile that it cannot sustain economic pain without unraveling. For more than a decade (and more in some cases), the response to economic crisis of Latin America's recently restored democracies has been to vote out governing parties rather than to abandon support for demococratic institutions or to embrace extremist political parties and movements.[77] It may be equally fallacious to infer that extremely high rates of inflation, unemployment, poverty, and downward mobility can persist indefinitely without disastrous consequences for democracy; already there are growing signs of democratic erosion and instability in Latin America, including attempted coups in Guatemala and Venezuela and growing polarization and uncertainty in Brazil.[78] Nor should one assume that the Latin American tolerance for prolonged economic hardship under democracy would necessarily be replicated in other regions, particularly the former Soviet Union and some parts of Eastern Europe, where democratic traditions are much weaker. But if new democratic regimes have even a couple of electoral terms to tame inflation, regenerate growth, and relieve economic suffering, that should be enough time if they adopt at the start a radical and comprehensive program accompanied by some kind of social safety net.

Finally, the case for economic liberalization before political democratization should be rejected because the aggregate evidence simply does not support it. The cases of successful economic liberalization under authoritarian rule are surprisingly small in number. If one accepts that the cases of South Korea and Taiwan in the 1960s and early 1970s do not qualify as instances of economic liberalization comparable in scope or urgency to the crisis-ridden economies of today, then the only case of successful economic liberalization under authoritarian rule is Chile.[79] And too much has been made of the Chilean example. For much of the seventeen years of Pinochet's rule, the economy did poorly and economic liberalization was not successfully achieved; in fact it became gravely endangered midway (in 1982), when a deep recession induced a temporary return to interventionist policies. Many of the contributing factors to the regime's ultimate success, such as the intellectual revolution wrought by students of the Chicago school of free market economics and the training (in this tradition) of a considerable core of economic technocrats, could certainly emerge in a democratic context. Moreover, the absence of periodic elections had somewhat contradictory implications for the sustainability of reform policies: "On the one hand, it allowed the government comparatively higher doses of long-term planning. On the other hand, it reduced the need to persuade the population at large of the advantages of reform."[80] As a result of the latter factor, public support for economic liberalization remained weak until virtually the end of Pinochet's time in office.[81] Thus, had a sudden economic downturn or political crisis brought Pinochet's regime down even a few years before it finally exited, the economic reform process might not have been sustained. It is true that authoritarianism proved able—as probably only an authoritarian regime could have at the time—to break the political deadlock in Santiago and crush the power of the trade unions and leftist political forces. But this was a historical situation that is by no means common to all countries, particularly in the world today. Moreover, in the contemporary world, there is much greater political and intellectual agreement than there was in 1973 that socialism *as a system of production* has been a failure and that market institutions are more effective instruments for economic growth and development. This is another example of the danger in generalizing from one historical era to another.

Beyond the highly questionable generalizability of the Chilean case, the performance of authoritarian regimes in Latin America hardly supports the conclusion that authoritarianism is more conducive to economic reform. Barbara Geddes observes:

> Most authoritarian governments fail to liberalize. Of the four Latin American bureaucratic-authoritarian regimes (or five if you count the two episodes in Argentina separately), only Chile carried out a successful structural adjustment. It seems to me highly ironic that one success out of four among bureaucratic-authoritarian regimes and one success (Mexico) out of about a dozen among single party dominant regimes should lead to the conclusion that the least risky strategy for structural adjustment is economic liberalization before political liberalization.[82]

Moreover, previous experience in Latin America with International Monetary Fund standby programs over three decades shows democratic regimes "no less likely to introduce stabilization programs than authoritarian ones, no more likely to break down in response to their political costs, and no less rigorous in their implementation of austerity measures."[83] This is confirmed by more recent South American experience showing that a new democratic regime may actually exhibit more policy discipline than its authoritarian predecessor in dealing with economic crisis.[84] Looking to the experience of structural adjustment in African military and one-party dictatorships, only one case among many emerges as even partially successful—Ghana— while several African democratic regimes, including Zambia and Benin, have already made more progress in structural adjustment than the bulk of African authoritarian regimes.

Few countries have achieved successful economic liberalization in the past twenty years. But in recent years, there does appear to be an interesting, if still tentative, *positive* correlation between democracy and economic liberalization.

> The most radical and far-reaching reforms have been accomplished in Spain and Argentina, both under open, competitive new democratic systems. Very substantial reforms have also been carried out in Turkey (begun during a brief period of military rule, but carried much further by a new democratic govern- ment), Thailand (pushed forward by civilians and opposed by important sectors of the military), Bolivia, Poland, Hungary, and the Czech Republic, all new democracies. In Eastern Europe, the most extensive economic reforms have been carried out precisely in the most democratic of the ex-communist countries. Those countries that have not fully democratized have also resisted economic reform. Significant though still quite incomplete reforms have also occurred in Venezuela, Costa Rica, and Ecuador. Even Brazil and Uruguay, which have strenuously resisted parts of the reform package, have carried out significant trade and exchange-rate liberalizations.[85]

Many of the democracies to which Geddes refers are still in the early stages of economic reform, and it is impossible to know at this point whether their reform programs will be sustained and ultimately succeed. But arrayed against the two or three successes of economic liberalization under authoritarianism are also two or three successes under democracy and a number of other countries that could ultimately be judged successful reformers under democracy. "The empirical record may . . . show that democratic governments have waited to initiate reforms until the costs of resistance imposed by the international economy had reached a very high level, but it does not show that democratic governments cannot carry out successful economic reforms."[86]

If democracy is no less successful—and perhaps at this conjuncture in world history, somewhat *more* so—in implementing and sustaining structural adjust- ment, what are the institutional advantages of democracy that privilege it in some ways over authoritarian rule? First, liberal political regimes, and in particular democracies, benefit from freer, more rapid flows of information and more open, participatory means of determining policy. Although broad popular participation can be an obstacle to effective implementation of stabilization policies (see below), open information and debate are more likely over the long run to yield reform policies that enjoy some public understanding and support, that are better targeted to actual social needs, and that are less compromised by corruption and unfair enrichment of political cronies and special interests. Thus, such policies are more likely to be sustainable because they have a broader base of political legitimacy.[87]

Second, although it threatens the continuity of reformist policies and exposes elected leaders to various societal pressures and demands, the ability to change governments regularly at the polls provides a crucial instrument for shaking up a decadent system. Because democracies tend to produce alternation in power, they are less likely to suffer long-ruling dominant parties whose officials and supporters become "entrenched beneficiaries of economic policies." Electoral alternation may bring to power new parties whose politicians were excluded from the privileges of the old system and can now benefit politically by taking rents away from their bureaucratically entrenched political rivals. Thus, as a general rule, "new governments and outsider presidents are more likely to pursue adjustment policies than are entrenched leaders, . . . [and] most new governments are democratic."[88] This is so, recent Latin American experience suggests, because elections confer on a new government "political capital" to pursue painful but necessary stabilization and adjustment policies, and this capital, or freedom from political constraints, diminishes with temporal distance from the last election.[89]

It is often argued that it is precisely the potential for electoral alternation that makes democratic governments reluctant to impose the short-term costs of economic reform. To be sure, a number of governments implementing economic reform have suffered serious electoral losses, including control of the national government, in a wide variety of countries over the past decade (including Bulgaria, Greece, Lithuania, Mexico, Poland, Russia, Senegal, and Turkey). And some elected governments have pulled back from some aspects of economic liberalization (such as privatization and cuts in state spending and employment) in the face of popular opposition. Yet among her sample of eleven countries (outside the former communist world), Geddes finds that parties that initiated cuts in real income of the working class were defeated in less than half the subsequent elections, a rate that "does not seem larger than would be expected in any sample of elections in similar countries."[90] Remmer shows a much higher rate of electoral alternation for all democratic regimes in Latin America during the 1980s and finds that economic crisis conditions do undermine support for incumbent parties and generate high levels of electoral volatility.[91] But one may surmise that as the structural economic crisis deepens over time, parties that eschew reform will tend to pay a higher political price because economic conditions will be even worse than the short- to medium-term consequences of stabilization and reform.

If economic liberalization is, at a minimum, no less possible under democracy than under authoritarianism, and if authoritarianism confers no clear advantage for economic growth, then there is no *economic* argument for authoritarian rule (and, by most normative standards today, no other argument either).[92] The challenge then becomes one of finding ways to reduce and buffer the costs of economic liberalization policies so as to maximize their viability and sustainability within a democratic framework.

Reconciling Democracy and
Structural Adjustment

It should be apparent by now that authoritarian regimes are, in principle, no more likely to manifest a commitment to economic liberalization programs than are democratic ones. Yet many analysts insist that *if* an authoritarian regime is committed to economic liberalization, it is better suited than a democratic one to implement and sustain it effectively because it is not answerable to public opinion in the short term. The problem for democrats is the disjunction between short-term and invigorating long-term consequences. The challenge for a democracy, then, is to find ways, within the framework and constraints of democracy, to reduce or buffer the short-term costs of reform policies and to find nonauthoritarian functional equivalents for some of the structural features of authoritarian regimes that shield them from the political pressures and protests of affected groups (especially the privileged beneficiaries of previous state intervention). The former strategy involves cost reduction; the latter, insulation of public policy making. To these, democracies can add a third strategy for enhancing the viability of economic reform, which they are in a unique position to undertake: building a positive political constituency for reform through public education and intellectual and political mobilization. All such efforts to devise a political strategy, however, must pay attention to the phased character of the reform process and to the distinctive political problems and requirements of each phase.

PHASES OF REFORM

Economic reforms have a broad common aim: to create the foundations for more vigorous and sustainable economic growth over the long term. But different reforms have served this end in different ways, and the reform process typically follows a certain stylized sequence.

Economic reform involves three distinct types of activity. Initially, crisis-ridden economies require most urgently *economic stabilization* to repress inflation and bring the economy into balance by sharply reducing budget and balance-of-payments deficits and restraining monetary expansion. Sustained macroeconomic balance requires, however, *economic liberalization* to reduce state intervention in the economy and free it up to market forces, both domestically and internationally. And both of these processes require, for their long-term success, *institutional restructuring* to alter existing institutions (e.g., the tax system) and to create new ones (a stock exchange, antitrust and antidumping commissions, export promotion agencies).[93] This third element partly involves strengthening state institutions to enable them to create the physical infrastructure, enhance the human capital, and provide the services (consumer and environmental protection, a social welfare system) necessary for a modern market economy to function well and enjoy consensus support.[94] Unless the regressive effects of reform can be muted by broadening the tax base and efficiently delivering welfare services—key elements of reconstructing the state—the political sustainability of reform will be in doubt.[95]

Both logically and in actual timing, macroeconomic stabilization comes first, although it may be closely followed within a first phase of reform by some elements of liberalization. Stabilization policies are politically difficult because they deliver traumatic shocks—prices soar as subsidies end, currency values plunge, interest rates rise, unemployment swells as state payrolls are slashed. But they are administratively easy to accomplish because they fall within the policy scope of the executive branch and can often be accomplished by presidential decision or decree. By contrast, deeper liberalizing reforms that privatize industries, restructure social security and tax systems, improve property rights, remove monopolies, and restructure labor markets are "immensely more complex," not only technically but also politically, as the "bureaucracy, Congress, the courts, state and local governments, political parties, labor unions, private sector organizations, and other interest groups all get involved."[96] "Moreover, . . . many of the initial costs of stabilization [such as the initial surge in prices] are temporary and spread over much of the population," while "sectoral and institutional reforms usually impose permanent losses focussed on specific groups."[97] Thus phase 2 of economic reform is much more protracted and politically contested. Once substantial structural transformation of the economy is achieved, however, a third phase of reform may become less contested, albeit more incremental in its liberalizing and institution-building tasks.

The phases of economic reform have their complement in the stages of the democratization process, and a vast terrain for theory lies in thinking about how the former relate to the latter. Broadly, democratization can be divided into three stages: *political liberalization*, which opens up at least some limited space for political expression and autonomous organization and action in civil society but within the constraints imposed by a dominant group or party that continues to monopolize control of the state; *democratization*, which subjects state control to regular contestation through free and fair elections, while extending and guaranteeing basic civil and political liberties through a rule of law; and *democratic consolidation*, which normalizes and institutionalizes democratic politics and increases democratic legitimacy to the point where democracy is highly stable and unlikely to break down for internal reasons.

Let us consider a few hypotheses about the relationship between economic reform and the phases of democracy:

1. *Consolidated democracies are less likely to be in need of radical economic*

stabilization and adjustment because, where economies are in such a state of imbalance and crisis as to require such radical measures, democracy is likely also to be crisis-ridden, shallow, and unstable, if it exists at all. In fact, although many of the Organization for Economic Cooperation and Development countries, including the United States, are in need of market-oriented reforms to reduce budget deficits and forms of state intervention that impair long-term economic growth, far-reaching economic liberalization is an issue mainly in nondemocracies or new and unstable democracies. Where economic crisis has gathered to the point where fundamental economic reform is urgently needed, as in Venezuela during the 1990s and Jamaica and Sri Lanka during the late 1970s and 1980s, it has coincided with the *de*consolidation or even near or partial breakdown of democracy. Of course, this hypothesis turns on how narrowly one defines democracy and economic crisis demanding fundamental reform. It could be argued that India today meets both definitions and so contradicts the argument. Yet, strikingly, India has witnessed a progressive deterioration in its democratic functioning in recent years—to the point where it is no longer rated free by Freedom House[98]—and the economic sluggishness induced by many years of statism may be adduced to be one important cause.

2. *Serious economic liberalization would seem to produce or be accompanied by, if it does not require it in advance, at least partial political liberalization* because the legalization of private enterprise, the privatization of state enterprise, the accumulation of capital by private actors, and the freeing up to the market of prices, international trade, and currency values all reduce state power and increase the power of independent forces in society, which must have some level of accurate information and security of property rights in order to operate in the emergent market. This is the situation in which China and Vietnam now find themselves, but it is not clear how far political liberalization must proceed in order for a market economy to emerge. Clearly, democracy itself is not a prerequisite for the emergence of the market.

3. *New and recent democracies are not less able to adopt economic reform policies or more at risk if they do so.* Arguments about their greater fragility and timidity in the face of interest-group pressure notwithstanding, young democratic regimes have been able to adopt economic reform policies without collapsing. In Latin America, they have shown surprising resilience in the face of prolonged economic crisis, which has induced pragmatism and consensus building more than polarization and extremism.[99] So far, economic stress has produced electoral alternation rather than breakdown in young democracies—although there are signs of deterioration in the quality and functioning of democracy in Latin America over the past decade. Precisely because they are new or recently established regimes, they are more likely to have broken or disrupted established power networks with an interest in the economic status quo.

4. *In the aftermath of communist systems in particular, phase 1 of economic*

reform must be accompanied (and in some respects preceded) by radical and rapid political reform to write a new constitution, form new political parties, and elect a new government while sweeping away the institutions of the older order. There are several reasons for this, discussed in part earlier. The transition from communism (or, more precisely, state socialism) involves nothing less than a *revolutionary* transformation of class and state structures. This can only be accomplished if democrats move rapidly and comprehensively on both the economic and the political fronts to create new institutions and demolish the ancien régime when it is in disarray, before it regroups.[100] Moreover, the state in these last decades of communist rule had ceased to represent *any* common national interest, and its collapse left nothing but powerful congeries of rent seekers, utterly contemptuous of law, with the skills and ruthlessness to accumulate enormous wealth, rapidly and illegitimately. Permitting them to do so risks discrediting the entire new order.[101]

Creating a new constitution that enjoys broad popular support and commitment "is a critical political step necessary to underpin the emergence of a new market in the former Communist countries." As noted above, without these institutionalized constraints on the state, "entrepreneurs and investors will not take the risks neessary to make the reforms work."[102] If such a constitution is to be successful in limiting the state and commanding the necessary broad esteem among the citizens, it must be drafted and adopted quickly after the fall of the old order, at that unique historical moment "when citizens are willing to break the previous pattern."[103] Parliamentary elections should then follow relatively quickly, ideally within a few months of the launching of economic reforms, when inflation has been checked and shortages of goods overcome but "before people have gotten worn down by the inevitable costs of transition."[104]

5. *Phase 1 of economic reform—stabilization and early liberalization measures—requires concentrated and autonomous executive power to achieve under democratic auspices* for four reasons. First, because the medicine is so bitter, parties, legislatures, and interest groups are not likely to want to associate themselves with it (even if voters, on the edge of economic desperation, embrace a broad economic reform plank). Second, "the success of a bitter-pill strategy depends on its initial brutality, on proceeding as quickly as possible with the most radical measures," both to blaze past the objections of interest groups that might initially be off balance and to minimize the duration of maximum pain.[105] Third, some stabilization measures do need to be implemented with speed and surprise.[106] And fourth, these new measures need to be embraced during the political "honeymoon" in the first few months of a new administration, when a president (or prime minister) will have maximum political scope to take radical and painful measures, or the opportunity to launch may pass altogether.

In Latin America, where these programs have proceeded the furthest under democratic regimes—in Argentina, Bolivia, and Venezuela—they were implemented mainly through presidential directives or decrees and, in the case of Bolivia in the late 1980s, a state of siege that imprisoned hundreds of union leaders.[107] Seeking to alter expectations suddenly and massively, economic "shock" stabilization programs "took the form of presidential directives planned in secret by technocratic cabinets insulated from social and political pressures."[108]

6. *The second, deeper phase of economic reform requires a more democratic, pluralistic political approach to be sustainable over the long term.* The unilateral approach to decision making, while "necessary to avert economic collapse and initiate needed structural adjustment," becomes less politically effective and more problematic over time, bringing "diminishing returns."[109] "If both economic reforms and democracies are to be consolidated, . . . executive authority must eventually be depersonalized and integrated into a broader framework of contestation and accountability."[110]

Phase 2 marks the end of "extraordinary politics"—when both elites and the mass public are more inclined than normal "to think and act in terms of the common good"—and the return to the "normal" politics of parties and interest groups, when rapid, radical reform becomes more difficult.[111] In contrast to the initiation of reform, which is more likely when politicians and their technocratic allies are insulated from political and interest-group pressures, the consolidation of reform ("stabilizing expectations around a new set of incentives") requires extensive political communication to construct "relatively stable coalitions of political support" and to gain at least the acquiescence of potential opposing forces.[112] Cavalier disregard for the need to build congressional and societal support eventually boomerangs into increasingly intense opposition, and more and more presidential decrees are needed to sustain the process. Authoritarian tendencies in the presidency may swell, as they have in Argentina under Menem. Or congressional opposition may obstruct reform or even find grounds (not often lacking in the strictest legal terms) to lash back at the president and impeach him, as happened in Venezuela, where Carlos Andrés Pérez was even abandoned by his own party. Or, sensing the breadth and passion of popular anger, the military may seek to overthrow the president and the constitutional system along with him—as it twice nearly did in Venezuela in 1992. Or a budding caudillo, fed up with having to deal with congressional objections, may simply seize all power, as Fujimori did in Peru. Whatever the outcome, the failure to educate the public about the necessity for reform, and to build a broad political and societal consensus behind it, leaves policy contested and the new rules of the economic game unconsolidated. In a political system where the government could be turned out at the next election and policy direction suddenly reversed, this undermines the credibility necessary to induce capital to invest in long-term, wealth-creating activities.[113]

7. *Institution building is the premier challenge for the consolidation of both democracy and economic reform.* To achieve the deep positive legitimation and

"normalization" of politics that signal consolidation, democracy needs political institutions—parties, legislatures, courts, state and local governments—that can effectively articulate and aggregate preferences, translate them into policies, and maintain order, justice, probity, and a rule of law. In particular, sustained reform requires a stable and aggregative party system that avoids political fragmentation and polarization (and therefore a proclivity to sharp swings in policy) and is able to produce legislative majorities for reform.[114] By the same token, consolidation of a market economy moves beyond the elimination of harmful forms and degrees of state intervention to create new state institutions and capacities to collect taxes, effect complex privatizations, reconstruct social security systems, and regulate monopolies.[115] The result must be a state that is leaner, more efficient, and technically competent.

8. *A rapid, radical, comprehensive economic reform policy (i.e., "shock therapy") is better not only for the economy but for the consolidation of democracy than more gradual and incremental reform.* It is probably easier to justify this assertion with respect to the economy than to democracy. Communism generated such massive, complex, and interconnected distortions that they are beyond the remedy of gradual liberalization.[116] And it is also true more generally that the quicker that disequilibria and distortions are removed from the economy, the quicker that reform will begin to show positive results that will then become cumulative and self-reinforcing, as market incentives quickly replace the old statist and socialist disincentives. In particular, stabilization and price liberalization measures must be implemented rapidly and decisively if they are going to conquer inflation and breed economic confidence.

Aslund offers numerous other reasons for radical and rapid reform: to attain quickly a reasonable consistency in policy; to give investors, savers, and entrepreneurs confidence "that the new system has come to stay"; to squeeze out corruption and rent seeking; to "transform the intellectual paradigm"; and, as noted above, to get the worst pain over with relatively quickly and "while a sense of crisis and preparedness to sacrifice prevails."[117]

So far, the comparative evidence from Eastern Europe does not show a single case of an incremental reformer performing better economically than countries with radical reform programs.[118] The better economic outcome from radical reform is one reason it is better for democracy. The alternative is not less economic pain but a different, more prolonged, and ultimately probably no less politically destabilizing version of it: high and growing inflation, sharper decline in gross domestic product and slower return to growth, poorer consumption, more disguised unemployment, and new economic inequalities that are less justified by economic performance (and thus more unpopular) than those that result from radical reform.[119] This is more likely to result in outright retreat from economic liberalization, in a return to the stop-and-go, pendular policies that have ravaged Latin America. Inadequate and abandoned reforms are costly; with each failure, confidence erodes and with it the chances for future successful reform (especially under democracy).[120]

This raises explicitly political reasons for democrats to favor radical reform. First, pain that is brutal but begins to subside fairly quickly is more manageable even (perhaps especially) within the context of democracy than pain that is less intense but more prolonged (e.g., across electoral cycles). Second, even with its less intense pain, a gradual reform strategy will still provoke political resistance from entrenched interests (as well as rising anxiety about the potential social costs of reforms still to be implemented), which could produce a political movement to reverse reforms; in fact, it provides antireform interest groups (again, particularly in postcommunist systems) more time to organize and strangle the reform process.[121]

After a certain point, the reform process reaches a point of no return and better sooner than later. The very speed and depth of radical reform results in much economic change (e.g., a large private sector, a convertible currency, an independent central bank) that is virtually irreversible[122]—as is evident in Poland, where even the leftist government that emerged from the September 1993 elections is unable to roll back the basic transformation to a market economy. Moreover, in postcommunist systems radical economic reform also produces salutary and permanent political changes by disrupting, displacing, and shrinking the resource bases of the old communist *nomenklatura* while giving rise to new beneficiaries of the market. Rapid privatization in postcommunist systems, at least initially of small firms, not only quickly stimulates production and provides a new basis for economic growth (most visibly in Poland) but produces a sizable new class of beneficiaries with a stake in reform.[123] Voucher privatization of larger firms also leads to rapid gains in efficiency and generates a still wider social stake in economic reform among numerous small shareholders (including the firms' own workers).[124]

FALLACIES ABOUT ECONOMIC REFORM AND DEMOCRATIC CONSOLIDATION

As considered above, conventional wisdom long emphasized the difficulties of achieving economic reform under democracy and, more recently, the dangers for democratic consolidation (or even survival) of pursuing rapid economic reform. To the fallacies observed above in arguments about the intrinsic advantages of authoritarianism for economic reform, we may add here a few more with respect to the dangers of economic reform for democratic consolidation. The most basic one, of course, is to recall our earlier point that a good number of new or recent democracies have imposed dramatic and austere reform policies and survived. Even if the reforming governments are voted out in every election, rather than only in about half of them, it would not demonstrate the vulnerability of democracy itself, so long as the regime (and popular belief in its legitimacy) held on. Furthermore, when politicians who embrace reform lose public support, we should not necessarily assume a cause-and-effect relationship, especially when discontent increases even as economic conditions improve. The Venezuelan case suggests that riots, demonstrations, plummeting poll ratings, and ultimately attempted coups may represent more the explosion of a long-brewing "sense of outrage toward politicians and public officials," in their duplicity and corruption, than toward reform itself.[125] And defeat at the polls may also owe as much or more to issues other than economic reform.[126] Moreover, successor governments of alternative parties often do not reverse reform policies and may even carry them further.

Second, logically, it does not follow that voters will always refuse to opt for (even radical and comprehensive) economic reform. People will vote for a pro-reform party "if they believe that their future after reforms will be sufficiently superior to the status quo to compensate for temporary deterioration."[127] In particular, if the crisis is acute and an elected government can inspire belief that pain, while acute, will be temporary and that most people will be significantly better off in the long run, the public may broadly support reform policies, even if it did not vote for them (or the government did not campaign for them, as, for example, Menem in Argentina and Fujimori in Peru did not). Moreover, even if voters turn against radical reform, it is again probably only possible after a certain point to slow it, not repeal it. Moreoever, one should not discount the potential for political learning from demonstration effects in other countries and policy failures in one's own. By the time Menem launched his economic reforms, the process in neighboring Chile had produced an economic boom and a broad national consensus. As more countries in Latin America, Eastern Europe, and the former Soviet Union score visible successes with radical reform strategies while others lag behind, political support for radical reform will become easier to mobilize in the laggard countries.

Third, there are some notable theoretical respects in which economic lib-eralization and democratic consolidation are compatible. Both economic reform and democratic consolidation encompass the creation of stable expectations and rules about behavior to guarantee the security of capital when it takes risks to invest and to guarantee mutual security among contending political forces. Both forms of security are best entrenched by a strong rule of law and constitutional order, protected by an independent judiciary. Similarly, "both democratic con-solidation and progress against inflation rest on a common foundation: the rein-forcement of stabilizing expectations."[128] Although cumulative fiscal indiscipline and incompetence may create such conditions of hyperinflation as to require, initially, the imposition of a "shock treatment" from above, the generation of a policy consensus on the need for fiscal discipline to enforce relative price stability can simultaneously serve the cause of democratic consolidation and economic stabilization.

Undoubtedly, there are important respects in which the periodic need to obtain consent from the voters and the ongoing need to allow free expression of protest and representation of interests challenge the ability of a democracy to transform its economic structure and threaten the stability of a democracy that tries to impose reform over broad opposition. But there are many ways of structuring democratic institutions and reform policies to mitigate these tensions and reconcile the contradications between democracy and economic reform. Some of these strategies, at least initially, narrow the scope of democratic processes, yet they occur under the basic framework of democracy and are certainly preferable to authoritarian rule. However, at least two of the methods for reconciliation are explicitly democratic in spirit: responding to the needs of those hurt by reform and building public understanding of the reform process and informed constituencies for reform.

INSULATING AND STRENGTHENING THE STATE BUREAUCRACY

In the context of democracy, it is now widely and compellingly argued that considerable policy insulation and delegation to state technocratic elites is necessary to achieve reform (although some doubts remain about the degree to which democracy can accommodate this state autonomy).[129] As indicated above, strong insulation appears especially important early on, when a stabilization program must be launched along with the beginnings of economic liberalization. In this period, adjustment requires forceful measures about which there cannot be much debate from a technical standpoint. Thus, "a reform policy is not one that emerges from broad participation, from a consensus among all the affected interests, from compromises."[130]

As reforms move into phase 2, more consultation and democratic participation are needed if they are to become democratically sustainable and if they are not to risk lasting damage to the political institutions of democracy. This requires a strategy for political education and mobilization (see below). However, even beyond the period of launching, responsible fiscal and monetary policy will be more likely in a democracy if economic policy making is given some insulation from immediate political pressures and protests and therefore also some discipline and continuity over time. This is not necessarily inconsistent with democratic principles and practice. Most industrialized democracies provide considerable statutory autonomy to their central banks (as several Latin American countries have recently done), precisely so that they can better maintain monetary stability. Public bodies that manage the principal export sectors (Chile's copper, Colombia's coffee, Venezuela's oil) typically enjoy higher levels of political insulation. Many of the new social emergency funds, as in Bolivia and Chile, have also been administered with considerable political autonomy and technical competence (see below).[131] In fact, insulating safety net programs from partisan political manipulation can be consistent with (even necessary for) extensive participation in their design and operation by the poor and the autonomous organizations that represent and assist them.[132]

All these examples involve what Collier calls "agencies of restraint"—autonomous centers of power that "(a) protect public assets from depletion, (b) prevent inflationary money printing, (c) prevent corruption, (d) protect socially productive groups from exploitation, and (e) enforce contracts."[133] Seen in this broader context, the autonomy of such regulatory institutions is not only consistent with democracy but in some respects vital to it. Without judicial autonomy there can be no secure rule of law, and without autonomous audit and oversight institutions to control corruption, it is likely to run amok, destroying the legitimacy of democracy.[134]

A crucial question for policy today is, where does such insulation come from? Under what conditions does it emerge? A number of factors may affect a state's ability to insulate its economic policy-making process, including the extent to which the crisis is perceived as systemic rather than temporary, the administrative capability of the state, the strength of interest groups and clientelistic forces in relation to the state, and the degree of dependence on and assistance from international actors.[135] For safety net programs, insulation has required a strong commitment from the highest levels of government.[136] However, the crucial proximate condition seems to be the emergence among political elites of "a relatively strong consensus" on certain fundamental principles that depoliticizes economic management.[137] "When an objective or an organization becomes sufficiently important in the eyes of the main political actors, implicit or explicit political pacts are often reached to safeguard them against undue political interference and provide them with sufficient resources."[138] Where this has happened, as in Bolivia, Chile, Colombia, and Uruguay, key elements of macroeconomic policy, such as exchange rate management, can be handed over to the insulated technical management of the bureaucracy, and macroeconomic balance can be maintained without abrupt and politically controversial adjustments.[139]

As Moisés Naím has forcefully argued, effective management of the economy requires not only bureaucratic autonomy but considerable enhancement of the administrative capacity, resources, and skill of state elites, not only at the center but at increasingly responsible regional and local levels as well. Improving state capacity requires, in turn, comprehensive reform that transforms the civil service from a resource for political patronage to a career meritocracy, with salaries (particularly at the top levels) sufficiently high to attract and retain highly trained talent. This will be feasible fiscally only with radical reductions in the total number of state employees.[140]

The effective performance of insulated economic policy teams also seems to depend heavily on intellectual and social cohesion within a reformed, meritocratic bureaucracy. Economic reform will gather more vigor and coherence to the extent that civil servants develop informal networks of cohesion inside and outside the bureaucracy and a common political culture or ideology that emphasizes the general public interest over particularistic interests and to the extent that bureaucrats are linked to broader social groups in ways that diffuse this ideology.[141] In recent history, bureaucratic-authoritarian regimes, such as those in Chile, Indonesia, and South Korea, have been more successful in developing such a coherent technocratic policy team than the typical democracy, but if democratically elected officials understand the challenge, there is no reason why democracies cannot do the same. Moreover, in a democracy, technocratic elites in the bureaucracy will have more inclination to reach out to a wider circle of elites in society and so help build a broader base of support and understanding for reform policies. Particularly in the second phase of reform, such a strategy of outreach must involve a two-way dialogue where both political and technocratic leaders listen and learn to some extent from leaders of key constituencies, not abandoning the fundamental logic of their reform efforts but fine-tuning and adapting them in ways that may enhance their political sustainability.

COST-REDUCING STRATEGIES:
SAFETY NETS AND OTHER APPROACHES

The long-term political viability of economic reform will increase to the extent that the costs it imposes on a variety of discrete groups can be reduced or buffered. One approach is to buy off opposition from strategic power groups that are disproportionately harmed, for example, by compensating owners and managers of protected industries that cannot survive the competition that liberalization unleashes and paying extended unemployment insurance to their workers. Unfortunately, measures to buffer the costs of adjustment for owners, middle classes, and formal sector workers are the most expensive and the most likely to involve the old illiberal state subsidies and controls. In addition, many such groups are so deeply embedded in the old structure of privilege that any amount of compensation that could conceivably be offered would probably not suffice to neutralize their opposition.

Social Safety Nets. A different strategy, more efficient and at the same time more equitable, is to create a temporary social safety net to relieve the suffering and insecurity of the most vulnerable and hurting groups at the lower end of the income scale. There are several successful models for this approach. Each targets assistance to the needy (some more effectively than others) rather than subsidizing general consumption or middle-class needs. One dimension of economic reform in Pinochet's Chile that is often neglected in accounts of that "miracle" is the mass-scale public works program from 1975 to 1987, which employed up to 30 percent of the workforce (half a million people) in the worst of the economic recession in 1982. When reform was launched in Bolivia in 1985, the Estenssoro government replaced its "notoriously inefficient" welfare system with an independent Emergency Social Fund (ESF). Bypassing the stilted government bureaucracy and responding to grassroots proposals from community organizations and local governments, the ESF provided income, jobs, school lunches, schools, health posts, and other infrastructure to some one million poor (about a seventh of the population) in its four years of operation. Recently, Zambia has followed a similar approach (influenced by Bolivia's ESF), with safety net programs (primarily for renovation of infrastructure) targeted on the needy that respond to community proposals and encourage self-help. Some comparable type of social safety net could be critical to reviving and sustaining the economic reform process in Poland. It might provide social assistance through municipalities and public works employment to the most depressed regions and revamp the communist welfare system to target health care and social security insurance for the needy, "while introducing private providers and choice of services for those who could afford them."[142]

Targeting assistance on the poor and needy has several appeals. The normative one is obvious. Institutionally, decentralized and demand-based programs can strengthen local government and community organization while incorporating traditionally marginalized groups into the political process.[143] These impacts, in turn, enhance the vitality and legitimacy of democracy. Economically, such policies do not contradict the logic of reform but carry it forward into new dimensions.[144] In fact, without some kind of compensation or relief for the unemployed, reform is likely to suffer, as governments shy away from terminating subsidies and thereby sending uncompetitive industries into bankruptcy.[145] Nor do such programs need to bust the imperatives of fiscal discipline. Some forms of nutritional and health assistance for the poor are relatively inexpensive.[146] And new resources can be generated by the termination of wasteful subsidy programs, the redirection of wasteful military spending, the simplification and enforcement of tax laws, and the imposition (with exemptions for the poor) of user fees for state services.[147]

A well-designed safety net program also helps develop a new constituency for reform while neutralizing some important sources of opposition to reform policies. These political effects are also crucial in strengthening the legitimacy of democracy and mitigating the tensions between the policy imperatives of economic reform and the political processes of democracy. Given the promise and rhetoric of socialist and statist policies, it is perhaps ironic that the poor should emerge as one of the prime potential constituencies *for* reform. Yet state subsidies, economic controls and regulations, and protectionist measures have benefited most the rich and middle classes (and favored sectors of urban labor)—not the poor. "Adjustment measures that seek to reduce those controls and reorient services and subsidies therefore do not threaten [the poor] and may indeed help them,"[148] as will a number of the new policies to reduce poverty and inequality that are consistent with economic reform and sound macroeconomic management. These include improvements in the quality and levels of state investments in education, health, and nutrition; redirections in expenditure from university and secondary to primary and early childhood education and from hospitals to preventive health services; expanded state programs for family planning, rural development, and small business assistance; and greater involvement of local governments, community groups, and business and professional associations in the planning and management of education and other social services.[149]

Not only do safety net programs enhance the compatibility between economic reform and democracy, but democracy may enhance a country's ability to reach the poor effectively with a safety net program. Comparative study shows that these programs are more effective (both in poverty relief and in generating political support for reform) when they involve the participation of the poor and needy and the nongovernmental organizations (NGOs) that represent and work with them, when they encourage public discussion and debate, and when they are politically neutral and administratively transparent.[150] Much of this has to do with particular features of design that provide "at least some institutional autonomy and political insulation coupled with a management approach modelled on that of the private sector."[151] However, participation by individuals and NGOs, as well as public debate and transparency, is clearly more likely in a democracy. In principle, ruling parties in a democracy could well use the programs for partisan ends, as did the populist Peruvian Aprista Party, but such partisanship seems most clearly associated with semiauthoritarian and heavily clientelist one-party dominant regimes like those in Mexico and Senegal (and to some extent Peru under Fujimori).[152]

The targeting of safety net programs does raise some difficult political and moral issues, however. Often the poorest segments of society (the old poor) are the most difficult and costly to reach, and programs that respond to local initiative and demand may give some advantage to more vocal and organized but less needy groups.[153] Such groups, more likely consisting of lower-middle- and working-class elements who have lost jobs, income, and benefits during structural adjustment, could constitute a seirous political challenge to economic reform (and potentially to democracy) if their losses are not cushioned in some way.[154] It is unrealistic to think that all these needs and demands can be met, even to some minimal degree, particularly before growth is vigorously resumed and a fair, efficient tax system is constructed. Inevitably, then, safety net programs will involve difficult trade-offs and may have distributional outcomes something like that of the ESF in Bolivia, which did not reach the formal-sector workers most affected by adjustment (the tin miners) and had a disproportionately low impact on the poorest two poverty deciles.[155] Yet this program nevertheless accomplished much, both in humanitarian terms and in mobilizing new political support for reform.

Other Strategies. A different type of cost-reducing strategy involves sequencing the introduction of the reforms in such a way that the pain is buffered or spaced out temporally. "Postponing import liberalization until after exchange rate reform (and possibly subsidies) have created export opportunities gives both capital and labor a way to make the transition at low cost." This strategy has been employed not only by the Asian "miracle" cases, Japan, South Korea, and Taiwan, but also by successful recent adjusters such as Thailand and Turkey.[156] It does leave in place, however, protectionist forces that might mobilize broad opposition to economic liberalization. Similarly, "a policy sequence that leads to lots of opportunities in the private sector before people are forced out of jobs in the public sector will increase beneficiaries and reduce costs." This is a strategy that Poland appears (wittingly or not) to have employed, in that delays in privatization of large state-owned firms have given time for the private sector (especially in small and medium-sized enterprises) to grow rapidly to absorb the labor of roughly 60 percent of economically active Poles.[157] In contrast, if privatization is delayed too long, it could give time and political capital for opponents to delay it indefinitely. The most sensible general logic for sequencing is to tackle those sectors where reform is most likely to produce positive results quickly in order to generate political support for subsequent more difficult and painful steps.

Another type of cost-reducing strategy involves *equitable cost sharing*. A democratic public must see that the burdens of adjustment are being borne broadly across the society or at least that some groups are not taking unfair advantage of the process. This is why it is important to build up the legal structures of the state to combat corruption and favoritism, to professionalize the civil service for the same purpose, and to modernize the tax system so that the wealthy actually pay.

This leads to a more general point about cost reduction. One important way a young democratic regime can buffer the costs of structural adjustment is through "good governance." People do not live by bread alone. In many of the recently established democracies that are now attempting economic reform, there is a long, bitter legacy of dictatorship and abuse of individual and group rights to which the society at large does not want to return. Governing with accountability, integrity, and respect for public opinion; accommodating differences among disparate parties so that policies can be forged in a coherent and stable manner; implementing an effective rule of law that guards individual rights while maintaining political and civil order; reining in the unaccountable power of the military and local political bosses; and manipulating the symbolic dimensions of democracy in ways that restore national pride—all these are ways that a democratic government can build its political legitimacy and support even while the population is enduring some considerable economic pain. At the same time, as indicated above, securing early on clear constitutional and legal foundations of a new democratic order is vital to creating favorable political conditions for economic reform and to providing the guarantees for property rights, contracts, and free movement of capital and labor necessary for a market economy.

EDUCATING AND MOBILIZING POLITICAL SUPPORT

Ultimately, if economic reform is to be sustainable in a democracy, political support must be generated and mobilized behind it. The *need* to do so may in fact be the reason why economic liberalization can sink deeper political roots of sustainability in a democracy than in a dictatorship, which is contemptuous of public opinion.

Some of the things that need to be done are relatively straightforward. The public needs to be educated, often in the most elementary ways, about how a market economy works and why inflation, budget deficits, overvalued currencies, trade barriers, price controls, subsidies for uncompetitive activity, and other contradictions of market principles damage the collective good over the long term. This requires a concerted campaign to train an effective cadre of business and economics reporters in the mass media who can explain these concepts to the public and interpret and evaluate public policies in light of them. It also requires think tanks, research centers, and economics faculties in the universities that can analyze economic policies and propose alternatives at a higher plane of sophistication, speaking to a more elite audience, from the perspective of a commitment to a market-oriented economy. This is no small undertaking in a region like Africa, where economic understanding is low. It is also a challenge in Latin America, where educational levels are much higher, because so much of the economics profession and social sciences more generally were trained in the theories of Marxism, dependency, and import substitution that ran their economies into the ground. One lesson from the Chilean case is fully consistent with democracy and must be learned by democracies if economic reform is to be sustainable: any kind of major reform of institutional structures involves a battle of ideas as well as policy. If reformers are to prevail politically in the long run, they must prevail intellectually as well.

One of the most promising developments regarding the prospects for democracy and economic reform in the developing and postcommunist worlds is the rapid emergence of supportive institutions in civil society. Think tanks and advocacy organizations with a promarket orientation are proliferating and achieving important policy reforms. The most dramatic success has perhaps been scored by Hernando de Soto's Institute for Liberty and Democracy in Peru, which for the past decade has mobilized massive reseach and thousands of entrepreneurs in the informal sector to reduce Peru's suffocating statism. One consequence of their effforts has been the reduction in the time it takes a firm to gain legal registration—from 289 days to 2![158] Throughout Asia, Eastern Europe, Latin America, and increasingly Africa, independent business groups, think tanks, and press foundations are conducting specialized economic training programs for journalists, judges, corporate directors, potential entrepreneurs, and managers in former state-owned industries, as well as broader educational programs on economics and economic reform for influential constituencies, such as military officers, scientists, students, teachers, and clergy. Some organizations have also initiated economic advisory programs to comment on draft legislation and regulations pending before parliaments or executive authorities. Many of these educational, research, and advisory programs have received funding and technical support from a variety of international donors, such as the Center for International Private Enterprise (CIPE), an affiliate of the U.S. Chamber of Commerce and the National Endowment for Democracy. A CIPE evaluation suggests that the key elements in the success of these programs are accuracy, integrity, clear adherence to market principles, and sound economic cost/benefit analysis.[159]

In a number of countries, business organizations have begun to play influential roles, not only in lobbying directly for reform policies but in educating and mobilizing public opinion for economic reform. Of course, businesses are by no means always promarket; those that benefit from state protection are often among the most implacable opponents of reform. But one way that economic reform generates self-sustaining political momentum is through changes in the nature of interest groups. As reforms progress, they increase the proportion of entrepreneurial to protected firms, creating a growing business constituency for reform.

Democracy involves competition, choice, and debate. Democrats trying to implement economic reform should take these structural features of their political system as a natural advantage, rather than an impediment, an opportunity to build through public dialogue and extended public debate and education a deep and enduring base of support for reform policies and a longer time perspective among the public in its expectations of positive results.

The design and sequencing of reform policies can also help elected governments to build a constituency for reform. Structural adjustment policies in developing countries typically benefit the rural sector, from which wealth has explicitly and implicitly been extracted through policies of price controls, exchange rate overvaluation, and so forth. However, where land and income in the rural sector are highly concentrated, economic reforms may not yield large political returns because the economic benefits are captured by a small portion of the rural population. In such circumstances, implementing "land reforms and other government measures that help small peasants to enter the export market" early on, before or concurrent with exchange rate and other reforms, may generate a much broader distribution of economic benefits and hence a much larger potential base of political support for reforming governments.[160]

More generally, democratic politicians implementing economic reform must have some kind of *political* strategy for building a political coalition or support base for reform over time. This must be related to the task of party building and to calculations of what kind of coalition of "winners" and "nonlosers" from economic reform can produce an electoral majority.

INTERNATIONAL PRESSURES AND SUPPORT

A final factor that can help to reconcile democracy and economic liberalization must come from the international community, in the form of continued pressure to do the right thing and support for governments that pursue, often at great political risk initially, the right policies. Many will no doubt consider Jeffrey Sachs to be overstating the case when he asserts that "countries cannot be transformed without generous and farsighted involvement of the international community."[161] Yet there is a strong logical case for arguing that the more external resources are available to support the construction of market institutions and cushion the pain of transition to them, the more likely reform will be to endure politically and succeed eonomically. In fact, a recent eleven-country study shows that many of the most prominent success stories of economic reform in the developing and postcommunist worlds (Indonesia from the late 1960s, Korea in the 1960s, Chile, Mexico, Poland, and Turkey) received very generous financial aid and debt rescheduling, whereas the successful cases of reform without substantial aid were the already-rich countries of Australia and New Zealand, as well as Poland and Spain with the implicit aid of imminent entry into the European Union.[162]

More often than not, the initiation of economic stablization and liberalization programs has been due to the fact that governments have had no alternative. Even if they believed that continued statism, protectionism, and large fiscal deficits were viable and more socially desirable, international actors (both bilateral and multilateral) on whom they depended for development assistance, debt rescheduling and relief, and other forms of aid would not tolerate it. Although IMF stabilization assistance has always been conditioned on the implementation of more or less orthodox, liberal policies, increasingly all forms of aid carry this condition. External resources are simply no longer available to finance enduring public sector and trade deficits.

At the center of the new political economy of international aid has been an implicit bargain between the creditors and donors on the one hand and the (usually deeply indebted) reforming governments on the other: that if these Third World and postcommunist countries "successfully reform their economies in a neoclassical manner with the direction and help of the [IMF and the World

Bank], then new voluntary bank loans and foreign investment will be available to underpin and sustain the reform efforts. This implicit bargain has failed in most places."[163] Although capital flows did increase to Latin America in the late 1980s and early 1990s (mainly attracted by reform), foreign investment has been slow to enter much of the postcommunist world and Africa in particular. The massive levels of Africa's external debt (relative to gross domestic product) present a particularly difficult problem, both because debt servicing eats up resources badly needed for investment in human and physical capital and because the debt is held by the very international financial institutions (IFIs) that are pressing for reform. "To insist that African countries meet their debt repayments weakens reform, but not to enforce arrangements weakens the IFIs as creditor agencies."[164]

Prospects for reform and democratic consolidation would clearly be advanced around the world by making the bargain real. In the poorest countries, particularly in Africa, debt relief must feature prominently because the debt will never be repaid. A concrete bargain that could do much to facilitate renewed development and to strengthen domestic constituencies for reform would freeze debt service payments in these countries and then retire the debt at some fixed rate (e.g., 10 percent per year) for every year that a country remains committed to democracy and economic reform policies. Specific levels of new aid might also be incorporated into this ten-year commitment. Long-term commitments of this nature offer hope of overcoming the two most serious problems with aid conditionality at present: the lack of adequate resource flows to assist adjustment and the temporary, episodic nature of assistance from international donors. "A temporary reward is a recipe for temporary liberalisation."[165] By contrast, if an explicit longer-term agreement could help lock a country into economic reform policies and democratic institutions for a decade or so, these policies and institutions would have the time to begin to yield concrete results, developing new constituencies of support and self-sustaining political momentum.

Among the most urgent needs for international assistance is to help fund safety net programs. As indicated above, this is far from mere charity to aid the poor abroad (a difficult thing to justify at a time when public dialogue in advanced democracies like the United States is increasingly full of complaints that "we aren't doing enough to meet our own needs here at home"). Its most powerful justification is an investment in a country's economic reform process, therefore in its democracy as well, and therefore also in its long-term political stability and responsibility on the international stage. There is a particularly compelling justification for aiding countries (most of all Russia, but also Ukraine and Eastern Europe) that could have a significant impact on the national security of Europe, Japan, and the United States.

Yet curiously, for the country where the West has the biggest self-interest in the success of reform—Russia—international aid was notoriously slow to be delivered, despite lofty promises of first a $24 billion commitment from the

Group of Seven in 1992, raised to $44 billion in the following year.[166] The failure
of the West to support the economic reform process with the tangible assistance
pledged (which was delegated to the IMF and the World Bank) seriously undermined the agents of reform, led by Yegor Gaidar. In particular, the failure of the
IMF to establish a multibillion-dollar stabilization fund for the ruble as the
Russian reformers expected in early 1992 "undercut the Russian government's
stabilization strategy and severely undermined Gaidar's domesic credibility."[167]
Compare this with the one-billion-dollar stabilization fund Poland got in 1990
to help launch the Balcerowicz plan. As Sachs argues, the IMF's insistence on
seeing demonstrated progress before aid is forthcoming may be poorly suited to
the crisis pressures of "life in the economic emergency room." In fact, the IMF
and the World Bank do not seem to be the appropriate institutions for delivering
assistance whose urgent imperatives rely more on political than technical economic calculations.[168]

In January 1993 Sachs proposed a four-point program for Western assistance
for Russian reform, which seems compelling for the case and also suggests the
kinds of aid that can make a difference: "*real* stabilization support" for the ruble
and a deep debt rescheduling; a support fund for small businesses; several billion
dollars in funds to assist long-term industrial restructuring; and support for social
programs, "mainly unemployment compenstion and job retraining—both to serve
as a political signal and to provide budgetry support, which is crucial to stabilization."[169]

There are more modest ways that the international community is helping as
well. The above-noted efforts of the Center for International Private Enterprise
to assist market-oriented business organizations and training programs are an
important example. From nongovernmental organizations and individual country donors, training and technical assistance are receiving great emphasis, and
still more should be done. It is important, however, to proceed with a low profile
and some sense of humility and sensivity to individual country circumstances
and national pride. We have seen already, in the Russian vote for the neofascist
Zhirinovsky, how tough times and personal hardships can generate acute resent-
ment of foreign models and influences, which is readily exploitable by zealots,
demagogues, and xenophobes. More generally, international actors have to tread
a careful path between firm conditionality and insensitive (and often ill-informed)
imposition of detailed policy prescriptions. Williamson and Haggard seem to
strike the right balance:

> International financial institutions need to allow borrowing countries a substan-
> tial degree of latitude in program design: this should be preceded by extensive
> policy dialogue, and the program should not be approved unless it embodies an
> adequate response to the needs of the situation, but subject to that constraint
> conditionality should be as unnigardly as possible. A team that does not feel it

Date Due

OCT 16 1995			

owns its program is unlikely to pursue it with the enthusiasm and determination that are critical to success, no matter how cleverly or tightly the conditionality terms are defined.[170]

Conclusion

The economic reform process under democracy is going to be messy, conflicted, and protracted. There are going to be setbacks and political defeats along the way. Some countries, perhaps many, are not going to make it, in large measure because their political leaders lack the political commitment, restraint, and skill to see it through. But some of the democracies are going to succeed in implementing a fundamental liberalizing transformation of their economies. And these are going to be the new economic dynamos of the 1990s. There will be variation among them in the role of the state in the economy, for markets are never entirely "free" and economic dynamism has clearly been possible with varying types and degrees of state intervention along the way. But the countries that make it out of the socialist or statist quagmire into vigorous, self-sustaining growth will be those that implement the basic logic of economic liberalization: that open themselves to the world economy, free prices, permit capital to move more or less freely, and allow uncompetitive economic activity to die out in favor of productive efforts that the market sustains and rewards. The success of these economic reformers at economic growth is going to generate powerful demonstration effects, and ultimately these will be the greatest teacher of all. In contrast to the dark forecasts of those who believe that the developing and postcommunist nations must choose between democracy and economic reform, this chapter suggests a very different outlook. Democracy and economic liberalization can be compatible and will succeed together if elected politicians have the commitment and skill to do what is necessary to reconcile them and perhaps the luck to win support from external friends.

Notes

1. Charles Lindblom, *Politics and Markets* (New York: Basic Books, 1977), p. 164.

2. Milton Friedman and Rose Friedman, *Free to Choose* (New York: Harcourt Brace Jovanovich, 1980), pp. 2–3.

3. Peter Berger, *The Capitalist Revolution* (New York: Basic Books, 1986), p. 73. Indeed, it was the neo-Marxist historian Barrington Moore who advanced the proposition, "No bourgeois, no democracy," in *The Social Origins of Dictatorship and Democracy* (Boston: Beacon Press, 1966), p. 418.

4. Lindblom, *Politics and Markets*, p. 164.

5. Peter Berger, "The Uncertain Triumph of Democratic Capitalism," *Journal of Democracy* 3, no. 3 (July 1992): 9. Emphasis in the original.

6. Carlos Waisman, "Capitalism, the Market, and Democracy," in Gary Marks and Larry Diamond, eds., *Reexamining Democracy: Essays in Honor of Seymour Martin Lipset* (Newbury Park, Calif.: Sage Publications, 1992), pp. 140–55.

7. Berger, "Uncertain Triumph of Democratic Capitalism," p. 9.

8. Kyung-won Kim, "Marx, Schumpeter, and the East Asian Experience," *Journal of Democracy* 3, no. 3 (July 1992): 25.

9. Larry Diamond, Juan J. Linz, and Seymour Martin Lipset, *Democracy in Developing Countries: Africa* (Boulder, Colo.: Lynne Rienner Publishers, 1988), p. xxi.

10. Larry Diamond, "Economic Development and Democracy Reconsidered," *American Behavioral Scientist* 35, nos. 4 & 5 (March–June 1992): 450–99; reprinted in Marks and Diamond, eds., *Reexamining Democracy*, pp. 93–139. For the original formulation of the thesis, see Seymour Martin Lipset, "Some Social Requisites of Democracy," *American Political Science Review*, March 1959, pp. 69–105.

11. Writing a generation ago, Robert Dahl argued that it was not private ownership per se but a "pluralistic social order" that is necessary for democracy. The true obstacle to competitive politics lies not in the structure of ownership, he maintained, but in highly centralized direction of the economy, which negates pluralism. Looking to the Yugoslav model, he speculated that decentralized socialist economies might provide a model that could accommodate sociopolitical pluralism and hence polyarchy (liberal democracy). Robert A. Dahl, *Polyarchy: Participation and Opposition* (New Haven: Yale University Press, 1971), pp. 60–61. However, the Yugoslav model never did accommodate real political pluralism and failed economically as well. Dahl now argues that "the Yugoslav experience does not settle the question of whether democracy might be compatible with a 'socialist' market economy based on some form of decentralized 'collective' or 'social' ownership and control." Robert A. Dahl, "Why Free Markets Are Not Enough," *Journal of Democracy* 3, no. 3 (July 1992): 82–83. However, it is difficult to imagine that an economy could truly be decentralized and competitive without protecting private property rights, even though many firms might be owned collectively by their workers.

12. Barry R. Weingast, "The Political Foundations of Democracy and the Rule of Law," unpublished paper, Hoover Institution, 1993, p. 42. Emphasis in the original.

13. For example, its recent publication, *Managing Development: The Governance Decision* (Washington, D.C.: World Bank, 1991), states: "The rule of law is a key element of predictability and stability where business risks may be rationally assessed, transaction costs lowered, and governmental arbitrariness reduced" (p. iii). Quoted in Seymour Martin Lipset, "The Social Requisites of Democracy Revisited," 1993 Presidential Address to the American Sociological Association, *American Sociological Review* 59, no. 1 (February 1994): 15.

14. Weingast, "Political Foundations of Democracy," p. 28.

15. Samuel P. Huntington, "Will More Countries Become Democratic?" *Political Science Quarterly* 99, no. 2 (Summer 1984): 204.

16. Dahl, *Polyarchy*, p. 48.

17. Joseph Schumpeter, *Capitalism, Socialism and Democracy*, 3d ed. (New York: Harper and Row, 1950 [1942]), p. 297.

18. Barrington Moore, *The Social Origins of Dictatorship and Democracy: Lord and Peasant in the Making of the Modern World* (Boston: Beacon Press, 1966), p. 418; Lipset, "Social Requisites of Democracy Reconsidered," p. 2.

19. Dietrich Rueschemeyer, Evelyne Huber Stephens, and John D. Stephens, *Capitalist Development and Democracy* (Chicago: University of Chicago Press, 1992).

20. Waisman, "Capitalism, the Market, and Democracy," p. 151; see also pages 144–48.

21. Alexis de Tocqueville, *Democracy in America*, vol. 2 (New York: Vintage Books, 1945 [1840]); especially book 2, chaps. 5–7, pp. 114–28. See also Huntington, "Will More Countries Become Democratic?" p. 204; Seymour Martin Lipset, *Political Man: The Social Bases of Conflict* (Baltimore: Johns Hopkins University Press, 1981 [1960]), p. 52; Larry Diamond, "Civil Society and the Struggle for Democracy," in Diamond, ed., *The Democratic Revolution: Struggles for Freedom and Pluralism in the Developing World* (New York: Freedom House, 1992), pp. 1–27; and Diamond, "Rethinking Civil Society: Towards Democratic Consolidation," *Journal of Democracy* 4, no. 3 (July 1994): 4–17.

22. Berger, *Capitalist Revolution*, p. 85.

23. Lipset, *Political Man*, p. 51.

24. Gaetano Mosca, *The Ruling Class: Elementi di Scienza Politica* (New York: McGraw Hill, 1939 [1896]), p. 143.

25. Richard L. Sklar, "The Nature of Class Domination in Africa," *Journal of Modern African Studies* 17, no. 4 (1979): 531–52.

26. Larry Diamond, "Class Formation in the Swollen African State," *Journal of Modern African Studies* 26, no. 1 (March 1988), and Diamond, *Class, Ethnicity and Democracy in Nigeria: The Failure of the First Republic* (London: Macmillan; Syracuse, N.Y.: Syracuse University Press, 1988); Richard Joseph, *Democracy and Prebendal Politics in Nigeria: The Rise and Fall of the Second Republic* (New York: Cambridge University Press, 1987).

27. Lipset, "Social Requisites of Democracy Revisited," p. 2.

28. John Sullivan, "Business Interests, Institutions, and Democratic Development," paper presented to the *Journal of Democracy* Conference on Economic Reform and Democracy, Washington, D.C., May 5–6, 1994. Revised versions of this and all subsequently referenced papers from this conference appear in the *Journal of Democracy* 5, no. 4 (October 1994).

29. Huntington, "Will More Countries Become Democratic?" p. 205.

30. Kim, "Marx, Schumpeter, and the East Asian Experience," p. 29.

31. Larry Diamond, "Beyond Authoritarianism and Totalitarianism: Strategies for Democratization," in Brad Roberts, ed., *The New Democracies: Global Change and U.S. Policy* (Cambridge, Mass.: MIT Press, 1990), p. 236. See also Larry Diamond, "The Globalization of Democracy," in Robert O. Slater, Barry M. Schutz, and Steven R. Dorr, eds., *Global Transformation and the Third World* (Boulder, Colo.: Lynne Rienner Publishers, 1993), pp. 31–70.

32. Samuel P. Huntington, *Political Order in Changing Societies* (New Haven, Conn.: Yale University Press, 1968); and Huntington and Joan Nelson, *No Easy Choice* (Cambridge, Mass.: Harvard University Press, 1976).

33. Kenneth Jowitt, *New World Disorder: The Leninist Extinction* (Berkeley: University of California Press, 1992).

34. John Williamson, "Democracy and the 'Washington Consensus,'" *World Development* 21, no. 8 (1993): 1329–36.

35. Kim, "Marx, Schumpeter, and the East Asian Experience," p. 26; for Scalapino's model, see Robert A. Scalapino, *The Politics of Development: Perspectives on Twentieth-Century Asia* (Cambridge, Mass.: Harvard University Press, 1989), and Scalapino, "National Political Institutions and Leadership in Asia," *The Washington Quarterly* 15, no. 4 (Autumn 1992): 157–72.

36. Min-xin Pei, "Societal Takeover in China and the USSR," *Journal of Democracy* 3, no. 1 (January 1992): 116. For a different view, see Maurice J. Meisner, "A 'Capitalist' China Does Not Ensure a Democracy," *Los Angeles Times*, June 5, 1994, pp. M1 and 4. Meisner asserts that the heavily state-dominated nature of China's peculiar form of capitalist development has given rise to a new bourgeoisie that "is not only a creature of the communist state and its policies but is actually largely composed of party-state officials (or ex-officials), their relatives and friends." Even truly private entrepreneurs are heavily dependent on state patronage. Such a dependent bourgeoisie, he argues, will hardly be a force for democratic development. For similar arguments about the apathy or resistance to democratization on the part of the bourgeoisie in many developing countries, see Rueschemeyer, Stephens, and Stephens, *Capitalist Development and Democracy*.

37. Stephan Haggard finds, for example, that in Korea, Taiwan, and Singapore, "state institutions played a critical role in easing entry into international markets by providing information, support, and guidance." *Pathways from the Periphery: The Politics of Growth in the Newly Industrializing Countries* (Ithaca, N.Y.: Cornell University Press, 1990), p. 268. Another influential work in this regard is Robert Wade, *Governing the Market: Economic Theory and the Role of Government in East Asian Industrialization* (Princeton, N.J.: Princeton University Press, 1991). A recent influential work that acknowledges the insights of this revisionist perspective while also advancing many tenets of the neoclassical emphasis on "getting prices right" is the World Bank's *The East Asian Miracle: Economic Growth and Public Policy* (New York: Oxford University Press, 1993).

38. Samuel P. Huntington, "What Cost Freedom? Democracy and/or Economic Reform," *Harvard International Review*, Winter 1992–93, p. 12.

39. Michael McFaul, "The Causes and Consequences of the 'End of Market Romanticism' in Russia," paper presented to the Council on Foreign Relations, Washington, D.C., March 31, 1994, pp. 3–7.

40. Quoted in Pei, "Societal Takeover," p. 116.

41. McFaul, "Causes and Consequences of the 'End of Market Romanticism.'"

42. Seymour Martin Lipset, "Reflections on Capitalism, Socialism, and Democracy," *Journal of Democracy* 4, no. 2 (April 1993): 47, and Lipset, Social Requisites of Democracy Revisited," p. 14.

43. Michael McFaul, "The Morass in Moscow: The Democrats in Disarray," *Journal of Democracy* 4, no. 2 (April 1993): 17–29, McFaul, "Is Russian Democracy Doomed? Explaining the Vote," *Journal of Democracy* 5, no. 2 (April 1994): 4–9.

44. Diamond, "Economic Development and Democracy Reconsidered," in Marks and Diamond, eds., *Reexamining Democracy*, pp. 93–139; for specific country effects, see, for example, T. J. Cheng, "Democratizing the Quasi-Leninist Regime in Taiwan," *World Politics* 41 (1989): 471–99.

45. This argument is summarized in Leslie Armijo, Thomas J. Biersteker, and Abraham F. Lowenthal, "Democratization and Market-Oriented Economic Reform: Complementary or Contradictory?" paper presented to the *Journal of Democracy* Conference on Economic Reform and Democracy, Washington, D.C., May 5–6, 1994, pp. 32–34.

46. Personal memorandum from Barry Weingast, August 9, 1993.

47. Joan M. Nelson, "The Politics of Economic Transformation: Is Third World Experience Relevant in Eastern Europe?" *World Politics* 45, no. 3 (April 1993): 434.

48. Deepak Lal, *The Poverty of Development Economics* (London: IEA Hobart Paperback, 1983), p. 33, as quoted in Nicolas Van de Walle, "Political Liberalization and Economic Policy Reform in Africa," Working Paper No. 3, Michigan State University Working Papers on Political Reform in Africa, July 1993, p. 5.

49. Eduardo Silva, "Capitalist Coalitions, the State, and Neoliberal Economic Restructuring," *World Politics* 45, no. 4 (July 1993): 526–59.

50. Stephan Haggard and Robert R. Kaufman, "Economic Adjustment and the Prospects for Democracy," in Haggard and Kaufman, eds., *The Politics of Economic Adjustment* (Princeton, N.J.: Princeton University Press, 1992), pp. 337–38.

51. Huntington, "What Cost Freedom?" p. 12.

52. Larry Diamond, "Nigeria's Search for a New Political Order," *Journal of Democracy* 2, no. 2 (Spring 1991): 54–69, and Diamond, "Corruption: Nigeria's Perennial Struggle," *Journal of Democracy* 2, no. 4 (Fall 1991): 73–85; Diamond and Oyeleye Oyediran, "Military Authoritarianism and Democratic Transition in Nigeria," *National Political Science Review* 1, no. 1 (1993): 221–44; Peter Lewis, "The Politics of Democratic Failure in Nigeria," Working Paper No. 8, Michigan State University Working Papers on Political Reform in Africa, March 1994; and Thomas Biersteker, "Structural Adjustment and the Political Transition in Nigeria," in Biersteker and Peter Lewis, eds., *Economic Crisis, Structural Adjustment and Political Transition in Nigeria* (forthcoming).

53. Michael Bratton, "Zambia Starts Over," *Journal of Democracy* 3, no. 2 (April 1992): 85; and Carol Graham, "Democracy, Adjustment and Poverty Reduction in Africa: Conflicting Objectives? The Experiences of Senegal and Zambia," paper presented to the Johns Hopkins SAIS Conference on Democratization in Africa, April 1994, p. 15

54. Van de Walle, "Political Liberalization and Economic Policy Reform in Africa," pp. 8–9.

55. Graham, "Democracy, Adjustment, and Poverty Reduction in Africa," pp. 18–19.

56. Adam Przeworski and Fernando Limongi, "Political Regimes and Economic Growth," *Journal of Economic Perspectives* 7, no. 3 (Summer 1993): 65. In her study of

152 LARRY DIAMOND

Latin American economies during the debt crisis of the 1980s, Karen Remmer similarly finds "no basis for asserting that authoritarian regimes outperform democracies in the management of economic crisis"; in fact, democracies had slightly better (but not statistically significant) economic growth and wage performance and "achieved a far better record at avoiding acute economic crises in the first place." Karen L. Remmer, "Democracy and Economic Crisis: The Latin American Experience," *World Politics* 42, no. 3 (April 1990): 333, 334.

57. *Pathways from the Periphery*; Dani Rodrik, "Political Economy and Development Policy," *European Economic Review* 36, no. 2/3 (April 1992): 329–36.

58. Haggard, *Pathways from the Periphery*, p. 256. For a similar perspective with respect to economic reform, see Thomas R. Callaghy, "Vision and Politics in the Transformation of the Global Economy: Lessons from the Second and Third Worlds," in Robert O. Slater, Barry M. Schutz, and Steven R. Dorr, eds., *Global Transformation and the Third World* (Boulder, Colo.: Lynne Rienner Publishers, 1993), p. 168 and passim.

59. World Bank, *The East Asian Miracle*.

60. Barbara Geddes, "Economic Liberalization and Democracy," paper presented to the *Journal of Democracy* conference on Economic Reform and Democracy, Washington, D.C. May 5–6, 1994, p. 13.

61. Ibid. This military resistance to economic liberalization, Geddes observes, was evidenced not only in Argentina, Brazil, and Uruguay but in Thailand, Turkey, "and even South Korea and Chile."

62. Personal memorandum from Barry Weingast, August 9, 1993.

63. Geddes, "Economic Liberalization and Democracy," p. 16. It could be argued that Venezuela's inclusion in this list does not contradict the argument about the advantages of democracy for economic reform because Venezuela's has been an increasingly narrow and hierarchical democracy, dominated by small circles of political bosses in the two major parties, what Venezuelans have dubbed a "partidocracia." See Michael Coppedge, "*Partidocracia* and Reform in Comparative Perspective," paper presented at the conference "Democracy under Stress: Politics and Markets in Venezuela," sponsored by the North-South Center in collaboration with the Instituto Venezolano de Estudios Sociales y Politicos, Caracas, November 9–11, 1992, pp. 25–26.

64. Diamond, "Class Formation in the Swollen African State"; and Diamond, "Corruption: Nigeria's Perennial Problem," *Journal of Democracy* 2, no. 4 (October 1991): 73–85.

65. Claude Ake, "Rethinking African Democracy," *Journal of Democracy* 2, no. 1 (Winter 1991): 35.

66. Anders Aslund, "The Importance of Democracy for the Economic Transformation of the Post-Communist Countries," paper presented to the *Journal of Democracy* conference on Economic Reform and Democracy, Washington, D.C., May 5–6, 1994.

67. Min-xin Pei, "Reform and Neo-Autocracy," paper presented to the *Journal of*

Democracy conference on Economic Reform and Democracy, Washington, D.C., May 5–6, 1994, p. 15; see also Huntington, "What Cost Freedom?" p. 12.

68. Geddes, "Economic Liberalization and Democracy," p. 17.

69. Ibid. pp. 17–18. The election of political outsiders can also create problems for reform, however, as we explore below. If newly elected presidents do not enjoy the backing of at least a moderately coherent majority party or coalition in the legislature, they may be unable to sustain the reform process that they initiate.

70. Nelson, "Politics of Economic Transformation," pp. 434–35.

71. Ibid., p. 435; Van de Walle, "Political Liberalization and Economic Policy Reform in Africa," pp. 7–9.

72. Thomas R. Callaghy, "Lost between State and Market," in Joan Nelson, ed., *Economic Crisis and Policy Choice* (Princeton, N.J.: Princeton University Press, 1990), p. 263. Thus did Callaghy argue in 1992 (in what seems an increasingly astute assessment with the passage of time) that "only major social and economic crisis" would be likely to give rise to a broad and informed domestic constituency for macroeconomic restraint and reform in Nigeria ("Democracy and the Political Economy of Restraint and Reform in Nigeria," paper presented to the Hoover Institution/AID Conference on Economy, Society, and Democracy, Washington, D.C., May 6–9, 1992, p. 39).

73. Nelson, "Politics of Economic Transformation," p. 437.

74. Geddes, "Economic Liberalization and Democracy," pp. 8–12.

75. Neslon, "Politics of Economic Transformation," p. 451.

76. Ibid., pp. 436–37, 450–51.

77. Karen L. Remmer, "The Political Impact of Economic Crisis in Latin America in the 1980s," *American Political Science Review* 85, no. 3 (September 1991): 777–800.

78. Larry Diamond, "Democracy in Latin America: Degrees, Illusions, and Directions for Consolidation," in Tom Farer, ed., *Beyond Sovereignty: Collectively Defending Democracy in a World of Sovereign States* (Baltimore, Md.: Johns Hopkins University Press, 1995); Bolivar Lamounier, "Brazil at an Impasse," *Journal of Democracy* 5, no. 3 (July 1994): 72–87; Haggard and Kaufman, "Democracy and Economic Reform in the 1990s," paper presented to the *Journal of Democracy* Conference on Economy, Reform, and Democracy, Washington, D.C., May 5–6, 1994, pp. 3–5

79. Geddes, "Democracy, Labor, and Structural Adjustment," paper presented to the Berkeley-Stanford Workshop on Reconfiguring State and Society: Social and Political Consequences of Liberalization in Comparative Perspective, April 22–24, 1993, p. 2. She argues for disqualifying Korea and Taiwan because of the continued high levels of state intervention in the economy and because "the costs of the transition of the populations of Taiwan and South Korea were quite small compared to the costs now being paid by those going through the transition. [Import-substituting industrialization] had not gone as far in these countries and had not created such extensive vested interests, and in both cases labor had been suppressed previously for political reasons, so large wage cuts did not accompany the transition."

80. Juan Andres Fontaine, "Economic and Political Transition in Chile, 1970–90,"

paper presented to the Hoover Institution/AID conference on Economy, Society and Democracy, Washington, D.C., May 7–9, 1992, p. 32.

81. Ibid.

82. Geddes, "Democracy, Labor, and Structural Adjustment," p. 3.

83. Remmer, "Democracy and Economic Crisis," p. 318. For the evidence, see Karen L. Remmer, "The Politics of Economic Stabilization: IMF Standby Programs in Latin America, 1954–1984," *Comparative Politics* 18 (October 1986): 1–24.

84. Remmer, "Democracy and Economic Crisis," pp. 328–32.

85. Barbara Geddes, Memorandum prepared for the Workshop on Political and Economic Liberalization, University of Southern California, May 21–22, 1993, p. 1. See also Geddes, "Economic Liberalization and Democracy," pp. 4–6.

86. Ibid.

87. For a summary of arguments along these lines in the African context, see Van de Walle, "Political Liberalization and Economic Policy Reform in Africa"; and also Haggard and Kaufman, "Democracy and Economic Reform in the 1990s," p. 9.

88. Geddes, Memorandum prepared for the Workshop on Political and Economic Liberalization, p. 2.

89. Karen L. Remmer, "The Political Economy of Elections in Latin America, 1980–91," *American Political Science Review* 87, no. 2 (June 1993): 393–407. Remmer thus concludes that competitive elections in the region enhance rather than undermine macroeconomic management in a kind of mirror image of the political business cycle characteristic of advanced industrial democracies.

90. Geddes, "Economic Liberalization and Democracy," p. 12.

91. Incumbent parties lost in sixteen of the twenty-one elections between 1982 and 1990; Remmer, "Political Impact of Economic Crisis in Latin American in the 1980s."

92. In fact, even if there were moderate economic costs (in greater difficulty of economic liberalization and slower growth) to democracy, it might still be preferred from many normative frameworks because of the benefits it provides in terms of individual liberties and political freedom.

93. While the distinction between stabilization and liberalization is conventional and widely accepted, former Polish finance minister and prime minister Leszek Balcerowicz emphasizes the distinctive nature of this third type of reform, for which former communist countries have a particularly massive need. Leszek Balcerowicz, "Democratisation and Market-Oriented Reform in Eastern Europe," paper presented to the *Journal of Democracy* Conference on Economic Reform and Democracy, p. 11.

94. Moisés Naím, *Paper Tigers and Minotaurs* (Washington, D.C.: Carnegie Endowment for International Peace, 1993), pp. 144–45, 152–54; Naím, "Latin America: Post-Adjustment Blues," *Foreign Policy*, no. 92 (Fall 1993): 133–50; and Naím, "Latin America's Journey to the Market: From Macroeconomic Shocks to Institutional Therapy," paper presented to the *Journal of Democracy* Conference on Economic Reform and Democracy.

95. Adam Przeworski, *Democracy and the Market* (Cambridge: Cambridge University Press, 1991), p. 161.

96. Naím, "Latin America: Post-Adjustment Blues," p. 138; see also his "Latin America's Journey to the Market," pp. 5-11.

97. Joan Nelson, "Market Reforms and Democratic Consolidation," paper presented to the *Journal of Democracy* conference on Economic Reform and Democracy.

98. Freedom House, *Freedom in the World: Political Rights and Civil Liberties, 1993–94*, pp. 303–7.

99. Remmer, "Democracy and Economic Crisis," and Remmer, "Political Impact of Economic Crisis in Latin America in the 1980s." Moreover, Remmer finds that newly established democracies in Latin America did not perform worse economically than authoritarian regimes and outperformed them "in promoting growth, containing the burden of fiscal deficits, and limiting the growth of the debt burden." "Democracy and Economic Crisis," p. 327.

100. McFaul, "Causes and Consequences of the 'End of Market Romanticism,'" pp. 3–20.

101. Aslund, "Importance of Democracy," pp. 2–4.

102. Weingast, "Political Foundations of Democracy," p. 28.

103. Ibid., p. 41. See also Aslund, "Importance of Democracy," p. 6. He suggests that an additional reason to move rapidly toward a new constitution is that the earlier it is adopted, "the less various political forces will know about their potential strength, and the more equitable the constitution is likely to be and the better it is likely to function."

104. Aslund, "Importance of Democracy," p. 22.

105. Przeworski, *Democracy and the Market*, pp. 183 and 157; Haggard and Kaufman, "Introduction: Institutions and Economic Development," in Haggard and Kaufman, eds., *Politics of Economic Adjustment*, pp. 18–19. As Aslund observes, "The population is usually prepared to accept a fair amount of sacrifice for some time, but they are not prepared to take it for long." "Importance of Democracy," p. 14.

106. "If everyone knows that the price of a particular commodity will be deregulated, there will be a rush on it before the measure is adopted." Measures to freeze wages and/or prices, to freeze savings, to switch the currency, and so on, will also trigger panics that will undermine them if they are announced in advance. Przeworski, *Democracy and the Market*, p. 183, note 56.

107. Juan Carlos Torre, "The Politics of Economic Crisis," *Journal of Democracy* 4, no. 1 (January 1993): 111–12. On the Venezuelan experience, see Naím, *Paper Tigers and Minotaurs*.

108. Torre, "Politics of Economic Crisis," p. 108.

109. Ibid., p. 113

110. Haggard and Kaufman, "Democracy and Economic Reform in the 1990s," p. 15.

111. Balcerowicz, "Democratisation and Market-Oriented Reform in Eastern Europe," p. 20; see also Naím, "Latin America's Journey to the Market."

112. Haggard and Kaufman, "Institutions and Economic Development," pp. 19–20; see also Naím, *Paper Tigers and Minotaurs*, pp. 150–52.

113. Torre, "Politics of Economic Crisis," p. 113. Even for the paradigmatic case of economic reform under authoritarian rule, this failure "to persuade the population at large of the advantages of reform" left public support for reform quite weak and the process politically vulnerable until near the end of Pinochet's time in office, when the economic

benefits of reform finally blossomed. Fontaine, "Economic and Political Transition in Chile, 1970–90."

114. Haggard and Kaufman, "Economic Adjustment and the Prospects for Democracy," pp. 342–48, and "Democracy and Economic Reform in the 1990s," pp. 19–20. A variety of electoral systems (and specific party systems from two-party to moderate multiparty) can produce this effect; the key is to find the appropriate system for each country and avoid institutional forms that have demonstrated logical and empirical flaws (such as the combination of presidentialism and proportional representation).

115. Naím, "Latin America's Journey to the Market," pp. 7–9; see also Haggard and Kaufman, "Institutions and Economic Adjustment," and other essays in their edited work, *Politics of Economic Adjustment*.

116. Aslund, "Importance of Democracy," pp. 10–11.

117. Ibid., pp. 13–15.

118. Balcerowicz, "Democratisation and Market-Oriented Reform in Eastern Europe," p. 17.

119. Ibid., p. 19; Asland, "Importance of Democracy," pp. 15–20.

120. Przeworski, *Democracy and the Market*, p. 169.

121. Carol Graham, "Beyond the New Poor/Old Poor Trade-Off: New Coalitions for Economic Reform," paper presented to the Annual Meeting of the American Political Science Association, September 1–4, 1994, pp. 10, 20–21.

122. Balcerowicz, "Democratisation and Market-Oriented Reform in Eastern Europe," p. 24.

123. Sullivan, "Business Interests, Institutions, and Democratic Development."

124. Joseph Blasi, "Privatizing Russia—A Success Story," *New York Times*, June 30, 1994.

125. Naím, *Paper Tigers and Minotaurs*, p. 11.

126. Nelson, "Poverty, Equity, and the Politics of Adjustment," in Haggard and Kaufman, eds., *Politics of Adjustment*, pp. 253–58.

127. Przeworski, *Democracy and the Market*, p. 164.

128. Laurence Whitehead, "Democratization and Disinflation: A Comparative Approach," in Joan M. Nelson et al., *Fragile Coalitions: The Politics of Economic Adjustment* (Washington, D.C.: Overseas Development Council, 1989), p. 91.

129. See, for example, the essays in Haggard and Kaufman, eds., *Politics of Economic Adjustment*, particularly those of the editors, "The Political Economy of Inflation and Stabilization in Middle-Income Countries" (pp. 270–313), and John Waterbury, "The Heart of the Matter? Public Enterprise and the Adjustment Process" (pp. 182–217), and the introduction by the editors (pp. 18–27); see also Thomas R. Callaghy, "Vision and Politics in the Transformation of the Global Political Economy: Lessons from the Second and Third Worlds," in Robert O. Slater, Barry M. Schutz, and Steven R. Dorr, eds., *Global Transformation and the Third World* (Boulder, Colo.: Lynne Rienner Publishers, 1992), pp. 161–257, especially pp. 166–70 and 239–44, and on Latin America, pp. 197–207. Callaghy particularly emphasizes the difficulties of achieving under democracy the

necessary insulation of "economic teams from [political] pressure, opposition, and requests for particular exceptions" (p. 168, also pp. 239–44).

130. Przeworski, *Democracy and the Market*, p. 183.

131. Naím, "Latin America's Journey to the Market," p. 33.

132. Graham, "Beyond the New Poor/Old Poor Trade-Off."

133. Paul Collier, "Africa's External Economic Relations, 1960–1990," in Douglas Rimmer, ed., *Africa 30 Years On: The Record and Outlook after Thirty Years of Independence* (London: James Curry Ltd., 1991), p. 155.

134. On the latter point, see Larry Diamond and Marc F. Plattner, eds., *The Global Resurgence of Democracy* (Baltimore, Md.: Johns Hopkins University Press, 1993), section 3, "Political Corruption and Democracy," pp. 193–244.

135. Callaghy, "Vision and Politics," in Slater et al., eds., *Global Transformation*, pp. 166–67.

136. Graham, "Beyond the New Poor/Old Poor Trade-Off," p. 19.

137. Remmer, "Political Economy of Elections in Latin America," p. 402.

138. Naím, "Latin America's Journey to the Market," p. 33.

139. Remmer, "Political Economy of Elections in Latin America," p. 402.

140. Naím, "Latin America's Journey to the Market," pp. 23–26. On this point, see also Callaghy, "Visions and Politics," in Slater et al., eds., *Global Transformation*.

141. Callaghy, "Vision and Politics," pp. 169–70.

142. Carol Graham, "Safety Nets and Market Transitions: What Poland Can Learn from Latin America," *Brookings Review*, Winter 1994, pp. 37–39; and Graham, "Democracy, Adjustment and Poverty Reduction in Africa," pp. 19–20. See also Graham, "The Politics of Protecting the Poor during Adjustment: Bolivia's Emergency Social Fund," *World Development* 20, no. 9 (September 1992); and Graham, *Safety Nets, Politics, and the Poor: Transitions to Market Economies* (Washington, D.C.: Brookings Institution, 1994).

143. Graham, "Beyond the New Poor/Old Poor Trade-Off," and Graham, *Safety Nets, Politics, and the Poor.*

144. As Haggard and Kaufman note, the World Bank has long "advocated more effective targeting of anti-poverty programs . . . and has increasingly emphasized the role of education and health policy not only in alleviating suffering but as an input to growth as well." "Democracy and Economic Reform in the 1990s," p. 11.

145. McFaul, "Causes and Consequences of the 'End of Market Romanticism,'" p. 21.

146. Nelson, "Poverty, Equity, and the Politics of Adjustment," p. 232.

147. Ibid., p. 260.

148. Ibid., p. 232.

149. Inter-American Dialogue, *The Americas in 1993*, pp. 47–53; Nelson, "Poverty, Equity, and the Costs of Adjustment," pp. 239–44; Naím, "Latin America's Journey to the Market," pp. 21–23, 26–27, 30–31.

150. Graham, "Beyond the New Poor/Old Poor Trade-Off," pp. 2, 16, 19–22.

151. Ibid., p. 18.

152. Ibid., p. 5–6, 14, 19–20.

153. Ibid., pp. 1–2.

154. Haggard and Kaufman, "Democracy and Economic Reform in the 1990s," pp. 12–13.

155. Graham, "Beyond the New Poor/Old Poor Trade-Off," p. 3.

156. Geddes, "Democracy, Labor, and Structural Adjustment," p. 11.

157. Ibid., p. 12. Aslund argues that privatization is a less urgent priority in phase 1 of reform than liberalization and economic stabilization because "enterprises will do little regardless of ownership until money has become scarce." "Importance of Democracy," p. 12.

158. Sullivan, "Business Interest, Institutions, and Democratic Development."

159. Ibid. Press training programs are also more successful, Sullivan observes, where they involve local media organizations as cosponsors, provide debate between competing viewpoints, and involve a mixture of professional backgrounds in the teaching.

160. Geddes, "Democracy, Labor, and Structural Adjustment," p. 11.

161. Jeffrey Sachs, "Life in the Economic Emergency Room," in John Williamson, ed., *The Political Economy of Policy Reform* (Washington, D.C.: Institute for International Economics, 1994), p. 504.

162. John Williamson and Stephan Haggard, "The Political Conditions for Economic Reform," in Williamson, *Political Economy of Policy Reform*, pp. 566–67.

163. Callaghy, "Vision and Politics," pp. 173–74.

164. Thomas M. Callaghy and John Ravenhill, "How Hemmed In? Lessons and Prospects of Africa's Responses to Decline," in Callaghy and Ravenhill, eds., *Hemmed In: Responses to Africa's Economic Decline* (New York: Columbia University Press, 1993), p. 526.

165. Collier, "Africa's External Economic Relations, 1960–1990," p. 161.

166. As of early 1994, Sachs estimates, the West had transferred only about 1/7 of the resources pledged. Jeffrey Sachs, "Betrayal," *New Republic*, January 31, 1994, p. 14.

167. McFaul, "Causes and Consequences of the 'End of Market Romanticism,'" p. 33.

168. Ibid., p. 31.

169. Sachs, "Life in the Emergency Room," p. 521. This paper was delivered at the conference hosted by the Institute for International Economics in January 1993. For a similar and more recent perspective, emphasizing the funding of social safety net programs based in major regional cities throughout Russia (with parallel transfers of Russian subsidies for state enterprises into the safety net programs), see McFaul, "Causes and Consequences of the 'End of Market Romanticism," pp. 34–35.

170. Williamson and Haggard, "Political Conditions for Economic Reform," p. 566.

4

Privatization in the Former Soviet Empire

The discovery that privately owned firms perform better than state-run enterprises has led to a worldwide privatization movement. Chile, Great Britain, and more recently many European and Latin American countries have sold state companies to private owners. The former Soviet Union and its satellite countries, weighed down with inefficient, costly, government-owned concerns, have either initiated major programs to divest the state of these albatrosses or have plans to do so. In most countries the conversion of small retail shops to private ownership has been relatively easy and quick. In contrast, the obstacles to privatizing large companies are immense. The people lack the capital to purchase the firms, stock markets are in their infancy and lack liquidity, and selling state corporations to foreigners raises xenophobic passions. The only workable solution is a mass privatization program. The Czech Republic, Russia, and Lithuania have provided their citizens with vouchers to purchase state companies. These policies have been highly successful. The Russian scheme has shifted about two-thirds of small businesses and nearly half the large industrial concerns from state ownership to the private sector. Although these efforts might still fail, the outlook is encouraging.

THE COLLAPSE OF THE COMMAND ECONOMIES brought on by crumbling industry, discordant incentives, and an enervated proletariat has accomplished what atomic weapons, summit diplomacy, and the Central Intelligence Agency (CIA) could not: the overthrow of communism. Within the surviving economic decay, however, lies the malignancy of a multitude of state concerns, burdening the industrious, the innovative, and the innocent. For reform to succeed, the system must be stripped of the bureaucracy of its industrial institutions.

The erstwhile East bloc countries of Central and Eastern Europe confront daunting obstacles in converting their economies to a market system. The threat of hyperinflation looms; traditional markets in Council for Mutual Economic Assistance (Comecon) countries have dried up; the Soviet Union has split into quarreling republics; government bureaucracies staffed with former communist officials oversee all changes; and communications and transportation systems are antiquated, rundown, and totally inadequate for a modern market economy. These burdens afflict economies saddled with bloated, unproductive enterprises. These government-owned monoliths are overstaffed and grossly inefficient, use obsolete technology, and manufacture shoddy products unsalable in world markets. Many should be closed; others need restructuring; all require conversion to private ownership. Most states of the former Soviet Empire have been wrestling with the problems of privatizing their giant monopolistic plants, their decrepit infrastructure, and their bad distribution systems.

The process of privatization has at least begun in most of the former communist states. Their goal of a modern market system—or, as they put it, "a normal economy"—drives the most ambitious programs ever tackled to shift resources from state hands to the private sector. Although program planners have drawn on the experience of Chile, Great Britain, and other occidental countries in selling public enterprises, in the main they have found those models inadequate. It is too early to judge the outcome, but the speed of privatization in a few states offers hope for the rapid organization of a private enterprise system. Other countries are still caught in a web of bureaucracy, stifled by political infighting, and riven by a failure of will.

These former Marxist states began their reforms with none of the prerequisites of a free enterprise system. To achieve strong growth, a market economy requires secure property rights, that is, the legal freedom to alter, improve, or alienate one's possessions, including land—to develop, sell, buy, mortgage, bequeath, donate, or lend—and a legal system that will both protect these rights and enforce contracts. Enforcing contracts necessitates an independent judiciary capable of defending an individual's property from state encroachments. Limits on the utilization of land and assets must be narrow and well defined. In addition, the former communist countries need to legislate a commercial code, antitrust statutes, and bankruptcy laws and to legalize private property while providing a stable tax and regulatory environment.

Unless these governments transfer ownership of their enterprises to private hands, even flawless macroeconomic policies will fail for some time to prevent their economies from continuing to deteriorate. Investment will be inefficient; workers will be underemployed; productivity will stagnate or decline. Although a policy of encouraging the formation of private firms owned by citizens and foreigners will diminish the state sector over time, it will take many years to alleviate significantly the infirmities of the economy. An aborted privatization program will create a serious drag on the economy for decades and retard the eventual convergence of those economies with Western Europe. Moreover, if the process is allowed to drag on too long, state enterprises will pressure the government to protect them from foreign and domestic competition. Experience worldwide betokens that governments too often will provide such shelter. The result will be continued paralysis and inflation.

Not only are Russia, the former Soviet republics, and the USSR's former satellites moving toward reducing the scope of government in economic affairs, but many countries, from such bastions of capitalism as Singapore, Taiwan, and Japan to the more leftist states such as Italy, Greece, France, and most of Latin America, are hawking state-owned concerns. Since 1983 Malaysia has sold stock in some seventy-three enterprises and is continuing its privatization effort. The Communist Chinese government has announced plans to auction two hundred failing government-owned companies, most of which are unprofitable as a result of large workforces, inflexible managements, and interference from local bureaucrats.

This privatization process commenced in the early 1970s, when the Chilean military overthrew the former Marxist-socialist government and set out to return land, property, and companies that the state in the previous decade had sequestered. Margaret Thatcher during the 1980s pressed a program that included selling public housing to its tenants, turning public utilities into private ones, and returning to individual ownership much of the British industry nationalized earlier by the Labour government. Today, as already mentioned, privatization is sweeping the globe. The old beliefs that socialism was the road to riches and that the government could manage business as well as greedy capitalists have died a well-deserved death.

The problems facing the former communist states, however, are unprecedented. Most of the former bloc economies have had meager experience with the private sector over the previous forty years; the Soviet Union had banned the free market for more than seventy years. Virtually no one today in Russia remembers a peacetime, private economy. Never in history has any country made this transformation. Previous privatizations have been small by comparison and implemented in the context of market-based economies.

Chile, which had implemented the most ambitious privatization effort in the world before the fall of the Berlin Wall, started with a basically capitalistic system in which more than 60 percent of the economy remained in private hands. Even though the state sector was large by noncommunist standards, the government had only recently nationalized much of it. Great Britain labored a decade to privatize about 5 percent of its economy. It took Chile fifteen years to move about 23 percent of its gross national product (GNP) from government ownership into private hands (Hachette and Lüders 1993, 4). Moreover, Western countries have had the benefit of free markets in labor and housing, stock exchanges, meaningful accounting records, and a substantial number of individuals with extensive assets who could purchase shares in new companies.

None of these conditions exists in countries attempting to throw off Marxism. At the time of the collapse of the Soviet Empire, the state in all these former communist countries owned and controlled between 80 and 100 percent of their economies. Even today, four years after the fall of the Berlin Wall, the Polish government, which has implemented the most successful economic reforms, still accounts for about half of the country's total output and an even larger proportion of industrial production.

Importance of Private Enterprise

A private economy offers several potent benefits over a state-directed one. A competitive free enterprise system is more efficient, that is, it produces more goods with fewer inputs, than a publicly owned and managed economy. It also secures a base for freely elected governments. No democracy has ever flourished in a country in which the state owns the great majority of property. In addition, private economies, contrary to the teachings of socialists, are more likely to maintain cleaner environments than communist countries.

For an elected system of government to work, an opposition must be able to mount a challenge to the party in power. In a democratic system voters must have information about the existence and platforms of the various candidates. If all or almost all property is in state hands, an alternative party or parties will be unable to obtain resources to publicize their programs that are free of government control. When all work for the state, opposition to government officials can be dangerous to one's livelihood, liberty, or even life.

The cleaner environment under a capitalist system rests on two factors. Profit-maximizing firms attempt to minimize wastes, which are costly and polluting. Moreover, given the existence of private centers of earnings and wealth, environmentalists can raise the resources to pressure politicians to enact pollution controls; in addition, they can propagandize their cause. The results are unambiguous: Western Europe is noticeably cleaner than Eastern Europe.

A large private sector also yields a more dynamic economy. Although in principle a state-owned enterprise could achieve the same level of efficiency as a private firm, especially if it faces strong competition from active rivals, in practice public companies are likely to be inefficient, slow to innovate, bureaucratic, overstaffed, and often unprofitable even when granted a monopoly. To generate the pertinent inducements for solid economic performance, the means of production must be privately owned. People and institutions respond to incentives. The motivations influencing a government operation differ significantly from those driving a profit-making, privately owned concern.

Owners of businesses with hired managers face the problem of ensuring that the people in charge operate the activity in the manner best designed to promote the equity holders' well-being. Company executives, like everybody else, act to promote their own interests. They may seek higher salaries, choice perks, or easier relations with potentially troublesome forces, such as organized labor. Private firms and corporations treat this principal-agent problem by offering the managers bonuses, stock options, and long-term contracts that tie the executives' interests to that of the firm's. In other words, companies attempt to provide their executives with a significant financial interest in maximizing the value of the company. In the United States, stockholders also rely on financial oversight by an active market. If the company officials neglect the value of the assets, the price of the shares will slide, depressing the value of their options and making the firm vulnerable to a takeover by outside raiders. Ultimately, competition with other firms will force the business to become efficient.

Even if the state instructs a government company to maximize profits and to simulate a private firm, the outcome is likely to fall short. The public as owners of a business cannot rely on stock options or takeovers as a means of disciplining its managers. Often the state protects its protégés from rivals, frequently bailing them out when they are in the red. Consequently, competition can rarely be counted on to ensure the good behavior of state-owned firms. In addition, since everyone owns the firm, no one will take much interest in its productivity—as long as it does not raise prices. If the state concern enjoys a monopoly, as often happens, there is nothing the government can do to ensure that management maximizes profits.

All too often government officials in the former centrally directed command economies have proposed the "corporatization" of state enterprises. As the planners see it, this is a step on the way to privatization. Government concerns will be transformed into corporations with boards of directors, appointed by state officials, who will oversee managers instructed to earn profits. Ukraine, for example, has adopted this policy without as yet initiating any serious privatization.

As indicated, it is unlikely that corporatization will bring efficiency or even greatly improved economic performance.

Moreover, government officials rarely require a state firm to act like a private profit-making entity. Unless such an arrangement is written into law or the constitution, politicians will employ the company to reward their friends and punish their enemies. Keep in mind that politicians, bureaucrats, and government officials, like people in the private sector, are interested in promoting their own well-being. Often they will rationalize this position, noting that "to do good, they must do well." Benefiting their colleagues or supporters will help them remain in office so that they can "promote the public weal."

The directors of government-owned firms normally attempt to please their political overseers; if the companies are worker managed, they favor the employees. In either case they will be unlikely minimize costs or maximize profits through catering to the consumers of their products. Politicians seek to build support by encouraging government agencies to employ a large number of well-remunerated workers. Government firms the world over are much more reluctant than private ones to lay off excess workers even if suffering losses.

Seldom does a government-owned firm have much incentive to cater to consumers; satisfied customers would undercut requests for more state funds "to improve service." Unless the company's customers are in a position to aid political leaders by subsidizing election campaigns, turning out volunteers to support candidates for office, or influencing many voters or supporters, the public firm will pay little attention to buyers of its products.

In a democratic state, politicians naturally employ state corporations to help those that can benefit the official at the next election. Even dictators find that rewarding those who support the regime can help preserve their power. In nondemocratic regimes, building support is vital to leaders, and they will manipulate state enterprises to garner that backing. Although a ruthless dictator can remain in power by force, it is less costly and in the long run cheaper to forge approval among at least some groups in society.

If the government requires that a publicly owned concern compete in the market with other companies and provides management with incentives to maximize profits, a state firm can be moderately efficient. Even in this unusual case, officials and politicians are less likely to supervise company executives actively and will exert less pressure to maximize profits. As a consequence, even under the best of circumstances, public concerns will be less vigorous in checking costs and providing optimal service. Unfortunately, politicians rarely require companies to go this far in mimicking private competitive firms. Bureaucrats garner few benefits from simply managing a firm competing with others in the market. Government officials can often gain more if they authorize a state monopoly, which can exploit its position to provide benefits to political leaders.

State-owned firms have performed best when forced to vie with private firms for business in the world market. Too often, however, nationalized companies have failed to compete adequately, and governments have resorted to subsidies. When state-run firms are in the red, politicians resist pruning employment or liquidating money-losing operations. Moreover, governments have generally compounded the inefficiencies of state operations by prohibiting competition, thus leading to even less discipline and more waste. Monopoly in general breeds excessive costs, a lack of attention to the public, high prices, and poor service. When the government owns and manages the operation, which it does typically with little regard for consumers, it exacerbates the ill effects of monopoly. A few favored groups may benefit greatly from this arrangement; virtually all could profit were the operation privatized and competition allowed.

Public companies are typically free from profitability constraints; they can always call on the state for aid. Because the taxpayer will pay for generous settlements, these officials face little incentive to resist labor union pressures. It is ironic, therefore, that there appears to have been more labor strife in the state-owned coal mines of Great Britain than in the privately owned pits in the United States.

Because the national treasury will simply confiscate any profits without benefit to the company or its workers, it is senseless for a government enterprise to do more than break even. Aside from pleasing their political superiors, the directors can normally find many worthwhile benefits to award themselves or their workers. Managers of state concerns, knowing that having labor on their side in disputes with politicians can be helpful, often curry favor with union leaders. As mentioned above, the absence of market discipline enables public corporations to employ more workers than needed and to be generous with wages and benefits while accumulating management perquisites.

One of the most debilitating socialist compromises can be worker ownership (see Kornai 1990; "Perestroika Survey" 1990; Schroeder 1988). A number of Marxist-oriented nations have experimented with employee-owned enterprises with unfortunate outcomes. It was a disaster in Yugoslavia. As generally practiced, workers can neither alienate their rights nor retain them if they leave the firm. If they quit, are fired, or retire, they lose their equity interest. In such cases the employee owners have only a short-run viewpoint. As long as they are with the company, they are concerned that the firm stay in business, but they have no abiding interest in its future. As a consequence, if employees possess title to the enterprise, company officials will favor workers over investment or sales. Executives of these labor-owned enterprises will commonly indulge their employees, disbursing generous salaries and guaranteeing no layoffs. Workers prefer high pay to investments, especially if new equipment means a substitution of capital for labor, with the result that the physical plant deteriorates and becomes obsolete. Worse still, if the company has access to government subsidies, it will inflate worker compensation almost without limit. Only if the working men and women are free to sell their stock or pass it on to their heirs will a worker-owned company operate like any other privately owned corporation. In that case, worker ownership will be synonymous with stockholder ownership.

A number of other factors contribute to the poor performance of public companies. When the government owns an enterprise, the regulators and the regulated are the same. Although American academics often allege (Stigler 1971; Peltzman 1976), with good reason, that regulated enterprises capture the regulators, if the state owns the operation, no semblance of an independent check on the company exists.

In addition, the prices charged by state-owned firms are subject to political pressures. Anytime a government enterprise raises its charges, the public reacts quickly, and elected leaders may suffer repercussions at the polls. In much of the world, public firms lose money. Partly they run in the red because managers encounter few incentives to keep costs under strict controls; partly they lose money because they have objectives other than profit maximization; and partly they need subsidies inasmuch as raising prices is a politically upsetting act—consumers of the product will often demonstrate or riot in the street. Many oil-producing states have found that shaving gasoline subsidies is fraught with danger and can lead to violent street demonstrations.

In contrast, large state enterprises can evolve into a source of power. With great resources at their command, a large labor force that can be mobilized, and many customers to incite, major public concerns can be politically influential. In nondemocratic countries such institutions may have almost as much power as the military. Whenever the Argentine government, for example, threatened either to privatize or to curtail subsidies to the large state monopolies, unionized workers would hobble Buenos Aires in protest.

Private businesses are free of most of these vices. The discipline of the market dictates that privately owned firms must proffer products as useful as or better than those of their competitors; they must satisfy consumers; and they must keep expenses below prices. In fact, private managers must maximize profits to avoid being driven out of business or removed from control. As a consequence, private competition is the only guarantee of efficient enterprises that can make a country productive and rich.

Corporations owned by individuals, private partnerships, and individuals in business for themselves must cover their expenses with their sales. To remain profitable, they cannot cater to political groups, they cannot pamper workers, they cannot bribe labor leaders. They must concentrate on satisfying their customers. If market demand falls, they will slash their workforce. If consumers fancy a different mix of products, they will revamp their output. Their attitude toward government officials depends on the influence such people have over the fortunes of their company. If the state runs a laissez-faire economy, then private business can safely ignore the pleadings of politicians. In contrast, if the government regulates much of their activity, the directors of private concerns must take seriously any requests from officials.

THE EVIDENCE

Although most studies fail to find any relationship between democracy or dictatorship and economic growth, one economic analysis determined that, from 1960 to 1980, politically open societies, which have strong property rights and a market allocation of resources, experienced three times the growth rates of economies without free markets or free political conditions (Sirowy and Inkeles 1990; Scully 1988). Comparisons of nonmarket or highly regulated economies and free markets demonstrate overwhelmingly the superiority of free markets. When the Berlin Wall fell, for example, the measured value of East German per capita income was about half that of West Germany's, even though both economies started at the same level in 1945. Moreover, shorter vacations and longer work-weeks in the East, coupled with higher labor force participation rates, meant that the population labored longer for that sorry level of earnings. Consequently, the real living standards of East Germans amounted to considerably less than half those of their Western counterparts. In addition, East Germany was an ecological disaster.

Ownership makes a considerable difference in economic performance. A large body of literature has compared the effectiveness of privately owned firms with that of firms in government hands (Boardman and Vining 1989; Hanke 1985; Clarham 1987; Clarkson 1972; Alhlbrandt 1973; Bennet and Johnson 1979; Stevens 1981; Bennett and Di Lorenzo 1983). Private firms almost always outdo their government peers. Two economists, Anthony Boardman and Aden R. Vining, analyzed the five hundred largest non-U.S. industrial firms, all of which were operating in competitive environments but of which a substantial minority were owned either in part or entirely by a government. The authors found that "large industrial MEs [mixed enterprises] and SOEs [state-owned enterprises] perform substantially worse than similar PCs [privately owned corporations]."

Surely the most telling evidence on the effects of government control and ownership emanates from the actual experience of nationalized firms in comparison with unregulated private-sector companies operating in the same field. After examining a good bit of the data on the subject, John Hopkins economist Steven H. Hanke concluded that in virtually all cases private firms performed better than government enterprises. For example, Australia has two domestic airlines operating under almost identical conditions, but the privately owned carrier has significantly higher productivity than the publicly owned one. A comprehensive study of state privatization done for the Florida Chamber of Commerce (Clarham 1987) revealed that, for some eighteen public service categories, the savings resulting from privatization ranged from 8 percent for waste-water treatment to 77 percent for emergency medical services.

Professor of economics Kenneth Clarkson established that private, for-profit, hospitals have a notable advantage over nonproprietary hospitals. Nonprofit institutions use less market information than do those that are private. Public hospitals prefer managers who have degrees in administration, while private institutions are satisfied with those who can supervise the operation efficiently even if they lack formal credentials. Municipal and county health care facilities rely on polls rather than market response to judge performance. They also tend to give more across-the-board pay increases rather than increases based on individual performance. For the same illness, patients are kept in public institutions for longer periods without any measurable improvement in health care.

Scottsdale, Arizona, has contracted with a private firm for fire protection. One analysis demonstrated that fire protection in Scottsdale was half as costly as a city-owned service (Alhlbrandt 1973). Studies of refuse collection have shown that private contractors charge significantly less than municipally owned collectors. According to research by economists James Bennett and M. H. Johnson, private firms that sell trash collection to homeowners deliver less expensive, more efficient, and superior services. The U.S. Department of Housing and Urban Development found (Stevens 1984) savings of 37 to 73 percent from employing private contractors for tree cutting, trash collection, asphalting, and public transit. The department reported that privately operated bus lines were 40 percent cheaper than publicly owned lines. In another paper, economists James Bennett and Thomas Di Lorenzo determined that government-owned hydroelectric plants were 20 percent dearer than privately owned plants. They were also slower to innovate.

THE FAILURE OF GOVERNMENT OWNERSHIP

Many governments have opted for public ownership of key industries, not only those considered to be natural monopolies. In all too many countries, the state has owned oil companies, airlines, steel mills, and coal companies on the grounds that these activities are essential to the well-being of the nation. In most cases the results have been poor. In virtually all instances, the state-run firms employ excessive workers compared with private companies. Moreover, these employees are often very well paid, with the resulting bloated payroll coming at the taxpayers' or ratepayers' expense. In addition, because elected officials appoint managers on the basis of their politics, not their competence, these nationalized firms frequently provide a dreadful level of service. For example, acquiring a telephone from the state monopoly in many countries (without resorting to bribery) necessitates years of waiting. Once the phone is installed, service is more expensive and less reliable than in the United States, where telephone companies are privately owned and profitable. Not only do these national telephone monopolies deliver miserable service at high prices, but they lose money in the process! In many Third World countries with inadequate state telecommunication systems, private cellular telephone companies have done a landslide business. The wretched performance by publicly owned utilities explains why so many countries are privatizing their public monopolies.

Those countries with the most state-owned businesses have suffered the most in terms of poor service and slow growth. Marxist states had and have made a religion out of public ownership of the means of production, enduring as a consequence inadequate growth and inefficient economies. Not only socialist governments but virtually all states have founded publicly owned enterprises or have nationalized private companies. In many cases, the government has taken over major private corporations that were floundering, such as the U.S. government acquisition of the Penn-Central Railroad, which became Conrail. In other public takeovers politicians have maintained that critical industries should be in official hands for national defense or social reasons—even though government management normally results in less efficient service. The state runs postal services in almost every country—probably the better to monitor communications among its citizens.

Governments have generally schemed to control communications and transportation, thus strengthening the regime. Public ownership of the media almost always leads to a progovernment slant for radio and television. Even in the United States, where communications have long been in private hands, the Federal Bureau of Investigation (FBI) has requested that Congress require telecommunications companies to provide the technology to facilitate wiretapping—at a cost to the telephone user. In other words, the FBI wants telephone consumers to pay so that it can eavesdrop! It would be much simpler if the government owned the phone system!

Thus, if the former communist countries are to become prosperous, democratic, and free of bureaucratic intrusions, they must privatize their bloated state economies. The large government sector, with its inefficient plants, its money-losing enterprises, and its resource-wasteful activities, acts as a drag on the rest of the economy and taxes the budding free enterprise sector. The albatross of public enterprises retards strong economic growth.

As stressed above, this transformation is virtually without precedent. Chile, during the 1970s and 1980s, affords the nearest example of a country that has privatized a major portion of its economy. Starting in the early 1980s, the British, under Prime Minister Margaret Thatcher, undertook a well-publicized denationalization program that has been widely imitated. Governments around the world are striving to rid the state of commercial enterprises by shifting the firms to the private sector. Just four decades ago, however, the dominant ideology was quite different.

The Privatization Movement

Prevailing views on the free market's ability to deliver adequate goods and services at reasonable prices significantly affect the scope of government ownership. As an aftermath of the Great Depression and the Second World War, a sizable portion of the public in the occidental world judged private enterprise to be a seriously flawed system that required either strict state oversight or government ownership of crucial industries. Many intellectuals rejected capitalism totally, opting for collectivism. Fabian socialists contended that public companies would enjoy lower costs than private firms, which must earn profits. In addition, left-wing supporters claimed that state-owned companies would be managed in the interests of both consumers and workers, resulting in less labor strife and better products. African intellectuals, who later went on to dominate their countries, imbibed socialism on the Left Bank in Paris or in the lounges of the London School of Economics.

The former Marxist countries, of course, nationalized their industries under the ruling dogma of their societies. They believed that private property was theft, that the state could run the economy more efficiently than a free market, that only when all the means of production were in the hands of the *people* could economic justice be secured. Thus communist governments prohibited private enterprise, took possession of most firms operating at the time they achieved power, and nationalized land and much of the housing. In principle, the public owned everything; in practice, no one owned anything. As a result, the care and maintenance of buildings, machinery, and land were neglected. For a while, these states achieved a moderately good rate of growth by devoting more and more labor to production and through forcing the public to save much of its earnings by offering it little in the way of consumer goods. Ultimately this strategy reached a limit; economic performance slowed and began to deteriorate.

At the end of the Second World War, much of the intellectual community and the educated public presumed that socialism was the wave of the future. Slowly, over the next three decades, the views of opinion makers and educators began to shift, becoming more sympathetic to capitalism, and, since the mid-1970s, the world has enjoyed a trend toward privatization. Several reasons account for this ideological conversion. Academics and then the public learned that factors other than the public's well-being exert influence on politicians and government officials. Voters came to understand that the ambition to be elected or reelected afforded the main motivation for politicians in democratic societies. The public choice literature and various studies of state ownership contributed strongly to this shift in view (e.g., Downs 1957; Buchanan 1968, 1972).

The consistent failure of the nonmarket economies to produce an adequate standard of living, vigorous economic growth, freedom, or even equality increased the disillusionment with socialism. Many Western countries had experimented with nationalization of major industries, often with calamitous results. State-owned enterprises did not ameliorate the lot of workers but did contribute to sizable budget drains. Labor strife was as common under government ownership as it had been when the companies were private. Under state control the quality of service or products failed to improve and often deteriorated. Government-owned firms were often inefficient and slow to innovate. The public's perception grew that the officials running these enterprises were primarily influenced by powerful interests. Good service, high quality, and low costs came in a weak second!

The Chilean government embarked on the first major privatization effort in the modern world, but its efforts and successes are little known outside Latin America, where a number of states have begun to copy the program. A recent book by Dominique Hachette and Rolf Lüders, *Privatization in Chile: An Economic Appraisal,* should bring that success to the English-reading public. Although Chile was first in its reforms, the British success has given rise to the worldwide movement. The experiences of Santiago and London in privatizing a large number of their state-owned companies yield salient lessons.

CHILEAN PRIVATIZATION

After the overthrow of the Marxist regime of Salvadore Allende by the military, Augusto Pinochet inaugurated a program to return government enterprises to the private sector.[*] The Allende government had multiplied state ownership from 68 concerns in 1965 to 596 in 1973, when General Pinochet led the army coup. Between 1965 and 1973, the proportion of the economy in the public sector ballooned from 14 percent to 39 percent of gross domestic product (GDP). In the late 1960s, under the guise of land reform, the state expropriated and managed much of the farming—about 60 percent of irrigated land; during this period the government "Chileanized" the copper mining industry. In the end government bureaucrats were running 325 industrial firms and 18 banks, including virtually all the important financial institutions. By 1973, state enterprises represented 100 percent of the electricity and gas GDP, 85 percent of the finance and mining GDP, 70 percent of the transportation and communications GDP, and 40 percent of the industry GDP.

---

[*]The discussion of Chilean privatization is based on Hachette and Lüders.

Since the 1930s the Chilean government had owned and operated many concerns in traditionally government-owned or regulated sectors, such as railroads, telephones, waterworks, schools, and hospitals. The state had built a steel company, constructed housing, and founded the electric utility. The acceleration in government intervention after 1965 and especially after 1970, when the socialist government took power, however, was unparalleled.

During the military rule the government undertook two waves of privatization. Originally Pinochet set out simply to restore to their previous owners the firms nationalized between 1965 and 1973, including farmland. As officials strove to return expropriated property, the previous owners balked and demanded credit on the grounds that the socialist regime had depleted their working capital. Santiago agreed and granted loans to finance the acquisition and operation of the transferred companies.

The military also ordered all state enterprises to operate on a profit-making basis. Public functionaries raised utility prices to eliminate a large drain on the treasury. Government subsidies for inefficient concerns were shaved, and by 1978 only housing and programs for reforestation continued to win government aid. After the coup, the authorities gradually opened the economy to competition from abroad, subjecting much of Chilean industry to market pressures for the first time. The economic planners canceled bans on imports and slashed tariffs from levels as high as 750 percent to a uniform 10 percent. The state abolished multiple exchange rates and price controls.

The Pinochet regime had a variety of objectives for its privatization program. In the first period, the main objective was to return property that it deemed stolen by the previous Marxist government. In addition the state, needing the revenues garnered from the sale of public enterprises, wanted urgently to eliminate the budget-draining subsidies that inefficient, bureaucrat-run companies were demanding. The economic experts who drew up the plan expected that the privately managed companies would be much more productive and efficient than the state-operated enterprises had been. Initially the goal of privatization was confined to those properties nationalized under the Allende regime. As it succeeded officials became bolder and added more government-owned firms to the list.

Between 1975 and 1979, the state privatized 207 concerns in finance, industry, wholesale, and distribution. During this period, the military leaders restored 80 percent of all publicly owned companies to the private sector. The proportion of national income accounted for by government firms dropped from 39 percent in 1973 to 24 percent in 1981.

In addition to privatizing industry, the Pinochet administration dramatically transformed the ownership and operation of a variety of other activities. Officials returned virtually all the land expropriated in the 1960s and early 1970s to the private sector, restoring it to the original owners, selling small plots big enough to support a family to farm workers at a subsidized price, or auctioning the property. For the first time the government legislated private property rights in water and irrigation, authorizing the purchase and sale of such privileges.

In a unique privatization initiative, state economists fashioned a private sector social security system, partly privatized medical care, subsidized the sale of public housing, and opened up education to nongovernmental competition through a voucher scheme. Private universities have blossomed as a result. Perhaps the most beneficial and innovative policy, however, has been the creation of a private pension plan for all Chileans. Under this program, the law requires that all workers contribute 10 percent of their earnings to one of the government-approved pension plan companies. These institutions, which are private, for-profit concerns, compete to secure the deposits of workers by offering high returns and quality service. For those workers who had been paying into the government-managed pay-as-you-go scheme, the administrators estimated the present value of their past contributions and then contributed stock in the newly privatized companies equal in value to those contributions.

This system has been a great success and generated strong savings for the Chilean economy. Workers are pleased with the result—as the stock market has risen so have pensions. The state still guarantees a minimum retirement allowance for the poor, paid for through general taxes.

The U.S. recession of 1981–1982, policy errors by the Chileans, and a sharp decline in copper prices led to a severe depression in 1982 and 1983. Many firms that had been privatized in the first period floundered, forcing the government to renationalize them. This led to a new program of privatization, which eschewed offering credits and demanded cash. After 1983 officials relaxed the ban on foreign ownership and encouraged outside investments.

Learning from the earlier period, the administrators of the program expanded their objectives in this second period to include strengthening the capital market, spreading ownership among a broader sector of the public, and generating resources for infrastructure investment and reductions in the national debt. The economists who planned the operation strove to build public support for the activity by ensuring that the workers as well as the well-to-do had a chance to share in the benefits of privatization. In addition, they determined not to fund privatization mainly through loans.

During the second phase of privatization the Chilean government instituted a variety of novel privatization techniques to satisfy its new objectives. In this period the administrators discounted shares to workers in the firm being privatized, peddled the company or shares to pension funds and other financial institutions, auctioned the shares or the whole company, or sold the stock in small blocks to the public with long-term credits and generous investment tax write-offs. "Worker privatization" guaranteed that the firm would repurchase the shares at the original price at the time of their retirement if the workers so chose. Employees could hardly lose under this scheme: if the stock rose, they could sell in the open market; if it fell, they could recover what they had paid. As a result, by 1989, the government retained only 45 of the 596 companies that it had owned or managed in 1973, and the share of state enterprises in GDP had plummeted from 39 percent at the start to 16 percent.

Many of these privatizations aroused vigorous political opposition because they included concerns that had been in state hands for decades. In some cases, such as the steel plants, the government had founded the firm. Thus the administrators of the system moved slowly to privatize these enterprises, often advertising that only 30 percent of the shares would be divested. After transferring that equity to individual owners, civil servants announced the sale or transfer of a further 19 percent, with the state still retaining a majority of the stock. Following the divestiture of those shares, officials would market another 2 percent, giving the private sector control. The government then sold the remainder relatively quickly in the stock market.

Chile's program has been so successful that other Latin American countries have begun emulating it. Moreover, after the military government peacefully turned over power to an elected civilian regime, the new administration pledged to maintain the reforms and continue with privatization. Property ownership is now more widely spread than ever before, creating support for the market system.

The Chilean privatization demonstrates that, if the government finances the sale of companies, the state risks taking back the enterprises and that it is possible to set up a successful private social security system. In addition, broadening property ownership is essential for maintaining a private enterprise economy. Most observers credit the privatization program and the other economic reforms for Chile's outstanding economic performance in recent years.

UNITED KINGDOM PRIVATIZATION

Well before the reforms in Eastern and Central Europe, the Conservative government in Great Britain embarked on a privatization program to roll back the socialist policies of the previous Labour government. Although the British did sell a few firms outright or some portion of the equity to employees, in the main the Thatcher government offered most of the shares through the London exchange. To ensure the program's popularity and the success of the sale, much of the assets were deliberately underpriced and often the state restricted the number of shares that any individual could acquire. The Thatcherites intended and largely succeeded in disseminating ownership, constraining any future Labour government from renationalizing those companies. Labor unions generally opposed the effort, but, by offering workers equity in their firms at below-market levels, the Conservatives succeeded. Despite union opposition, for example, more than 90 percent of eligible British Telecom employees bought shares proffered at a discount. As the experience of the Thatcher government attests, privatization involves more than simple economics; the policy must take into account political ramifications. Building public support for divesting the state's assets is crucial to privatization's success.

By 1990, Margaret Thatcher's government had transferred about 5 percent of the British gross domestic product and roughly a similar proportion of the workforce to the private sector. Those sales constituted more than one-third of the government's assets. As a result of privatization, the proportion of the population that owns stock has tripled, to about 20 percent.

Although impossible to prove, I believe that in the 1980s the United Kingdom's privatization program reinforced its vigorous economic expansion. During that decade, London transformed England from the "sick man of Europe" to the Continental country enjoying the best growth. Scrapping government regulations and shifting public enterprises into the private sector in effect created higher incomes for the British. This gain, which was spread over the decade, spawned much higher growth during the period of the reforms. Those changes may or may not lift the United Kingdom's long-run rate of growth, but they did boost the British people's living standard (Stevenson 1994).

PRIVATIZATION ELSEWHERE

The collapse of communism proved that collectivism was unworkable. Former communist states in Africa as well as in Eastern and Central Europe moved to oust Marxist regimes. Even in noncommunist countries, governments embarked on privatizing existing public enterprises, recognizing that they could no longer afford to support inefficient and wasteful state corporations. With the success of privatization efforts in Chile and Great Britain, public opinion has begun to shift away from viewing state ownership as a simple alternative to private ownership. Although not completely impotent as an ideology, socialism has been severely weakened. Fortunately, communism is virtually dead as a system and remains only a flickering revolutionary cause in a handful of poor Third World nations and an intellectual exercise at some universities.

Thus, the movement to privatize has been gaining steam around the world. In the United States during the second half of the 1980s, the federal government sold Conrail, the state-owned railroad taken over in the 1970s after the failed merger of the New York Central and Pennsylvania Railroads. In the 1990s, the French, Italian, Mexican, and Argentine governments all instituted privatization programs. Public officials have peddled airlines, telephone companies, railroads, and banks to eager investors. The Argentine state, for example, has disposed of $5.3 billion worth of assets and, as I write, is offering to sell a zoo, gas and water utilities, two steelmakers, railroads and subways, a television station, a hotel, and the national mint (Kamm 1993). Most of the former communist countries in

Central and Eastern Europe, as well as Russia and parts of the old Soviet Union, have launched major privatization programs.

How to Privatize

Privatization is so complex, knotty, and tough that nations have been driven to experiment with alternative approaches. From an economist's point of view the method may be unimportant. Once a firm is privately owned, those business men and women who can earn the most from its resources will eventually buy it or be hired by others to run it. Such a step will maximize the value of the asset. Only an economist, however, would say that the process doesn't matter. To succeed, privatization must appear to be equitable; it must afford the taxpayer a fair return; it must satisfy at least in part the claims of groups involved in the enterprise; and it must not excessively endanger the well-being of workers or managers. Too many privatization projects have failed because public support for them was absent.

A successful, large-scale divestiture of state property requires a major public figure to champion the plan. In Chile, General Pinochet strongly backed the "Chicago" economists who spearheaded the reforms. In the Czech Republic, Vaclav Klaus, an enthusiastic supporter of a private market, rammed through the parliament and then implemented the most successful privatization program in Central Europe. Leszek Balcerowicz, another fervent supporter of free enterprise, masterminded the "shock therapy" that freed the Polish economy and set the stage for the subsequent privatization of its industry. In Russia, Boris Yeltsin has furthered the most ambitious privatization scheme in the world.

Those less dedicated to the concept can twist the term *privatization* to include mutations of one form of state ownership into another. Government officials often claim to have privatized an enterprise when all they have done is shift some portion of the state's equity to other entities that are directly or indirectly government controlled. In many former communist countries, privatization has sometimes consisted of transferring part or all of the ownership from a government department to an "independent" state-owned firm. For example, in Russia a group of state firms may organize a "commercial" bank. The purchase of equity in a public concern by such a financial institution fails to shift ownership to the private sector. Even if the recipient of the stock is genuinely a private person or firm, is the enterprise private if the buyer controls less than 100 percent? If individuals own a majority of the shares, if the government keeps only a minority position, and if—a big if—the public officials refrain from involving themselves in the operations of the business, then the firm may be considered private. All too often, however, the state maintains a strong interest and may aid the company if it experiences financial troubles. More troubling, it may also be ready to lean on the enterprise to keep it from any major restructuring. True privatization must leave a firm under the control of private individuals who will reap the benefits of wise decisions and suffer the losses of poor ones.

Western advisers have debated whether state-run enterprises should be restructured *before* privatization. Margaret Thatcher's program attempted to make each firm that was being offered for sale profitable before it was taken to market. A restructured enterprise earning profits is obviously a more attractive investment than a government concern hemorrhaging money. Many economists, however, contend that to do the same in the former East bloc countries would slow the process and throw roadblocks in the way of privatization. Those countries opting for mass programs have determined to eschew restructuring and assume that private owners will have the will and ability to fire workers, lop off inefficient operations, and close money-losing facilities. Those officials may be right: It is probably more difficult for a government to make those decisions than for an owner, but in neither case is it easy.

Inasmuch as the socialist governments built many of those facilities as monopolies, government officials and privatization experts have fretted about the lack of competition that such concerns will face when privatized. Most foreign advisers have recommended opening up the country to imports and authorizing foreign investment to provide competition. Free trade, however, is unlikely to be a realistic option no matter how beneficial it would be in the long run. Probably more than half the industries could not survive world competition, and unemployment would zoom. As discussed below, there is no place for much of the redundant workforce to go.

Often the government can increase competition through improving transportation facilities. In much of the former Soviet Empire, highways and railroads are in dreadful shape. A single bakery, construction firm, and cement plant may service each city. If transportation costs are reduced, local monopolies will face new rivals and have to improve their prices and services. As newly privatized firms cut their labor force, the state may find it beneficial to employ redundant workers in building or improving transportation networks.

Government officials in these countries are concerned about dominant producers. Marxist dogma taught that capitalism was riddled with monopoly; thus the holdover communist officials see monopoly under every bed. In Ukraine, which may be an extreme example, the government treats every industry in which one firm controls more than 35 percent of the market as a monopoly and regulates its prices. According to this rule, one-third of the Ukrainian economy is subject to price control!

A private monopoly, however, may be less pernicious than one that is public. If the state erects no roadblocks to new competition and permits imports, a private firm without domestic competitors cannot excessively exploit consumers. If such a private firm earns unusually high profits, it will attract competitors, including foreign ones. Moreover, in the privatization process, the government can take into account potential monopolies. Many large state enterprises are vertically integrated, with the core company owning many suppliers. In the former Soviet Union, for example, the military produced consumer goods for its officers, steel for its tanks, iron for the steel, and housing for its workers. Rather than selling such enterprises whole, the authorities can divide each firm into small, viable components and offer them for sale. If there are significant economies involved in the joint ownership of some parts, buyers will then have the incentive to merge such facilities.

The privatization mechanism depends on the value of the property, the state of the financial markets, and the wealth of the citizens. Each country has divided its privatization into small and large. Small privatization covers divesting petty enterprises, mainly retail businesses, including services and small manufacturing. Large privatization, then, consists of the denationalization of major enterprises, principally those that will become joint stock companies. In addition, after the iron curtain fell, those people whose properties in the former Soviet satellite states were expropriated after World War II lodged claims for restitution.

REPRIVATIZATION

In all the former communist countries, except the republics that once constituted the Soviet Union, the government is under significant pressure to return property to former owners. *Reprivatization*, as it is dubbed, has a strong constituency of previous owners demanding the restoration of a significant number of small businesses. In Czechoslovakia, past proprietors and their families could demand up to 30 percent of all small businesses. After forty years, however, sorting out titles can take considerable time. Changes have taken place: in some cases properties have been improved at state expense; in others they have been allowed to deteriorate. After roughly four decades, several people may claim a particular business.

Germany's efforts at restitution in its eastern sector demonstrate that attempting to return assets to their original owners can hinder investment. Uncertainty about whether a previous owner will appear after a new proprietor has invested in improving the property can bedevil privatization. More than 1,200,000 Germans have made claims against property in the former communist sector, but less than one-quarter of those have been settled ("Property Wrongs," 1993, 33). Authorities acknowledge that it may take ten *more* years to adjudicate all the claims. To further the program, German officials have had to warrant buyers from claims by precommunist owners. In addition, because much of the land has been seriously polluted, the state must offer investors and previous owners immunity from any cleanup costs.

Perhaps based on the East German experience, both Hungary and Poland have decided to forgo restitution and simply provide compensation. Poland has yet to legislate any reprivatization, although the government has proposed a statute that would allocate privatization bonds to former owners. The Hungarian parliament has enacted a program to return farmland. The Czech government, in contrast, is returning all property nationalized or expropriated by the Communists, including farmland, or providing compensation when restoration is impossible (Frydman, Papaczynski, and Earle 1993, 70–91).

A major complication in any reprivatization is determining which previous owner from what period should receive compensation. Hungary, for example, debated whether to provide restitution (or compensation) to Jews expropriated in 1938, to Hungarian-Germans who lost their property in 1945, or to Hungarians expropriated by the Communists after 1948. Ultimately the Hungarians, like the Czechs, decided to provide compensation only for those who lost property to the Marxists. The German law provides for restitution or compensation for properties expropriated between 1933 and 1945 (under the Nazis) and properties taken between 1949 and 1990 (under the East German government) but not for those assets confiscated while the Soviet Union was occupying the land.

SMALL PRIVATIZATION

Most of the former East bloc countries are auctioning small businesses to the highest bidders, although Hungary and the Czech Republic have restricted such sales to their citizens. Russia has been considering employing vouchers even for retail businesses. In virtually all states, local authorities handle the sale of the properties, and what is actually transferred in such small privatizations is usually a five- or ten-year lease, the name of the store or enterprise, and its inventories and fixtures. The building and land remain in state or local government hands.

Employees of these concerns frequently assert a right to the properties and demand to be given priority in purchasing the assets. Nonemployees contend, however, that these workers should be given no special allowances. The public resents retail clerks for having been discourteous to patrons in the past and for having taken advantage of their positions for personal profit. As a result, the Czech government decided to give no edge to employees bidding for properties at auctions. For other countries, the process has been more complex, and, in many cases, local authorities have awarded special privileges to managers or workers. In Russia observers complained that handing stores over to their employees changed nothing but that when the stores were sold, the buyers made significant improvements.

The employees and the general public both fear that small firms will be auctioned to former communist officials, the *nomenklatura*, or black marketers because they are the only people with funds. Few others have been in a position to save and accumulate capital. Thus the public is unhappy with peddling these small enterprises to the highest bidder, but no one offers a better alternative. Romania, Lithuania, and Mongolia have determined to use vouchers for small enterprises as well as large. Auctioning property for coupons eliminates the advantage of the mafia in acquiring shops but will probably beget multiple ownership. Unfortunately small businesses are usually better run if owned and managed by a single individual or by a small partnership; having many proprietors may complicate retail operations and lead to a less than optimum use of resources.

If the building in which the service or retail establishment operates remains in government hands even after it has been privatized, property rights may still be poorly defined. In Poland, for example, local governments have awarded stores to the highest bidders, only to reclaim the properties later when other, better offers developed. Nevertheless, the Polish government has affirmed that it has converted about 90 percent of its retail establishments to private ownership, mainly through local auctions or the creation of new shops.

HOUSING AND AGRICULTURE

Although much attention has focused on privatization of industry and commerce, housing is another important sector that needs to be returned to private hands. Without a private rental market and individual homes, the labor market suffers from a lack of flexibility. Enthusiastic advocates of the free market face daunting political difficulties in shutting down a major company that dominates an area because laid-off workers are unable to move to cities where jobs exist but housing does not.

But privatizing housing creates opposition from existing tenants. Because rents for government apartments are often so low that they fail to cover maintenance expenses, privatizing flats—even if they are given to the tenants—can be unpopular, and selling housing to nonresidents can produce widespread resistance.

The conversion of housing to private property is taking place, however, although in a disorganized and unsystematic fashion. On the outskirts of Moscow, entrepreneurs are building apartments and exchanging them for shared accommodations in the center of the city. Those real estate speculators then renovate the newly freed space and sell the refurbished flats to foreigners or newly rich Russians. This new market arose early in 1992 after the city authorized transactions in former state-owned apartments. In 1993 city authorities privatized nearly 40 percent of Moscow's apartments (Bohlen 1993).

Lithuania has successfully employed vouchers to privatize housing (Girnius 1992). In 1991, the parliament authorized the distribution of the privatization certificates to its citizens. Starting early in 1992, the government put up for sale apartments and houses in which all occupants had agreed to the privatization.

The state fixed the prices on the basis of construction costs, although large apartments or houses carried a premium. Using the vouchers only citizens could buy the housing, and they had to make a cash down payment of 10 percent. This program has been highly successful in creating a substantial private housing stock.

Little Western attention has been devoted to reforms in agriculture. Given that China began its move toward a market system by lifting restrictions on peasant farming, this lack of attention is surprising. Except Poland, which maintained a large private-sector agriculture throughout the communist era, the former command economies suffer from inefficient and unproductive state and collective farms. Russia, which exported grain before the 1917 revolution, must now beg for credits from the United States to import enough to feed itself. Russian policy makers, however, claim that the immense farms in the former Soviet Union cannot easily be subdivided into smaller family plots and that the tractors are too big to use on a family farm. Moreover, few agricultural workers want to give up the security of a state or collective farm for the uncertainties of self-employment. State farms dispense pensions, vacations, housing, and often medical care. If a worker becomes a private farmer, he or she must purchase the seed and fertilizer from a government company whose managers may be biased against individual farming, rent agricultural equipment from the collective or state farm, and sell the output to a state buyer who will dictate the price. Few farmworkers want to make the effort. Yet without agricultural reform there is little chance that farming can be restored to efficiency.

Restitution also plagues agricultural privatization, especially in the former satellite countries of Eastern and Central Europe. The heirs to farmland in many cases want their property returned. The terrain, however, is currently occupied by cooperative or state farmers who resist leaving because they have lived there for decades. In most countries state officials have so far failed to establish a significant private farming sector.

OPEN SALES

For large industrial enterprises, governments have employed two basic methods of privatization, albeit with innumerable variants. The traditional approach, pioneered by Chile and Great Britain, has been to sell state enterprises or assets, sometimes at a discount, to garner political support. Political leaders have vended public firms through auctions, tender offers, stock market flotations, cash deals, and lease-buy arrangements. Governments have peddled these assets to private firms, rich individuals, foreigners, workers, and the general public. A major advantage of selling is that the state collects often much-needed revenues. Moreover, an open sale of an enterprise will normally result in the person or persons buying it who can most efficiently exploit it by installing efficient managers to maximize his or her return. The drawbacks of traditional methods of divesting state enterprises are mainly political; virtually any sale that is not an open auction brings charges that the government is giving away valuable property. Disappointed buyers often claim that officials are favoring certain groups or individuals. If foreigners are permitted to buy, xenophobia raises its ugly head; if sales are restricted to citizens, revenues will be lower than the maximum possible and resources may be employed less than optimally.

For most of Eastern and Central Europe, the traditional methods of privatizing, such as selling the stock of the enterprise on the bourse, are impossible. In those countries capital markets are either nonexistent or in their infancy. Hungary, Poland, and the Czech Republic do have new stock exchanges, but they are small and lack liquidity. In Russia and Ukraine commodity exchanges have sprung up that claim an ability to trade in stock, although none do. Poland has opened a bourse in the former headquarters of the Communist Party. Stock exchanges, however, cannot touch the underlying problems: the public lacks the assets to purchase large firms, and the trading floors lack the liquidity to finance major public offerings. Moreover, the only people with money are either black marketers or former members of the *nomenklatura* who used their positions for personal enrichment. Selling assets to these groups is unpopular and might halt privatization.

Without a market to price assets, a major issue in selling enterprises to foreigners or to those few with wealth is the valuation of said enterprises. Most government firms are overstaffed and use obsolete technology, and what they are worth depends on future earnings, an uncertain sum under the best of circumstances. Proper valuation is important because almost any sale results in charges that the government disposed of the company too cheaply. Such assertions lead cautious bureaucrats to overprice the property. As a consequence sales are likely to be slow.

Although a common solution has been to hire Western accounting firms, such as Price Waterhouse, Arthur Andersen, or Baker & Mckenzey, to do the evaluations, bureaucrats and the general populace in these countries fail to realize the uncertainty involved in any valuation, even that of a private firm in a market economy. Furthermore, appraising these state enterprises is all but impossible because they have never collected the proper data, that is, figures on costs of inputs, capital expenditures, and sales, or employed the concepts of cost and profit inherent in market-based companies. Prices in the past failed to reflect economic realities; the bureaucracy simply set them arbitrarily.

Although authorities in these countries emphasize the importance of privatizing quickly, traditional methods will take years. Some of the more optimistic time schedules put forward envision ten years to privatize about 50 to 70 percent of an economy; at the rate Hungary has been privatizing, it will take one hundred years. Although their schedules are faster than any previous government divestment, they are too slow to inaugurate an economy that can compete on the world markets and yield significantly higher incomes for the population. Only a mass privatization program employing vouchers can achieve rapid privatization.

MASS PRIVATIZATION

Distributing vouchers to the public to purchase shares in state-owned companies constitutes the other method of large-scale privatization. As state firms come up for transfer to the private sector, individual coupon holders can bid on them. One rationale behind such a mass privatization program is that the public, in theory, owns all government enterprises and should therefore be given title to them. In addition, all citizens will gain from the program, even if they simply sell their vouchers—thus building support for divesting public companies. Besides, voucher privatization seems egalitarian; it allots each individual, no matter how wealthy, an equal claim on state enterprises. Although the rich may be able to buy additional coupons or, subsequently, an increased proportion of shares in privatized enterprises, the initial distribution of stock limits the advantage of those who have acquired wealth illegally or unethically. Another advantage of this approach is that the authorities need not value companies before the auction; the voucher sale will determine a firm's relative worth. The program also makes it possible to exclude foreigners from the auction, a popular step. Finally voucher privatization can proceed much more quickly than selling individual companies; speed is vital if the economy is to shed these millstones.

People have suggested, not seriously, that the state simply issue every citizen one share in each government enterprise, thus officially transferring the operation to the private sector. This proposal guarantees that everyone would own a minute sliver in all enterprises but that no one would exercise control over the managers. The bureaucrats who currently run the firms would continue to do so, and nothing would have changed. To ensure that managers are properly supervised by the owners, some concentration of ownership is necessary. Thus these voucher schemes are predicated on the assumption that individuals and mutual funds will mass their certificates in a few firms that they can govern.

Voucher privatization produces no cash for the government and/or the enterprise, a major drawback. To raise funds, the state sells only a portion of the enterprise for coupons, retaining some ownership to market later for much-needed revenues. One reason the Hungarian government was reluctant to initiate a mass privatization program was that its treasury craved the funds from sales.

By the summer of 1993, notwithstanding the absence of any state revenues from these schemes, virtually all former communist countries in Eastern and Central Europe were planning or implementing mass privatization programs, not all of them voucher schemes. Although each country has employed different rules, voucher privatization has been tried or is planned in Bulgaria, Romania, Czechoslovakia, Mongolia, Russia, and Lithuania. Hungary for a long period refused to contemplate any mass privatization plan, asserting that vouchers were basically a socialistic idea. In August 1993, however, officials announced that in 1994 they were going to provide all their adult citizens with interest-free credit of 100,000 forint (about $1,000) to purchase shares in Hungarian state enterprises (Clegg 1993). Poland plans a unique mass privatization employing selected mutual funds as intermediaries. Ukraine has a coupon scheme on the drawing boards. Estonia, a holdout on mass privatization, contracted with the Treuhandanstalt—the German agency charged with privatizing enterprises in the former East German regions—to sell its state-owned companies. As of August 1993, however, the German bureaucrats had disposed of only twenty Estonian companies (Michaels 1993). Nevertheless, during 1994 they continued to sell additional enterprises.

Only the Czechs, the Lithuanians, and the Russians have actually organized and implemented a voucher scheme. Since its elections in 1991, Poland, which had led the way in economic reforms, has suffered political gridlock. At the end of August 1993, Belarus finally enacted its first law setting out the objective of privatization.

Even though vouchers are redeemable only through an exchange for shares in state enterprises, some governments, such as Russia's, have authorized trading in these coupons. Others countries have countenanced only their pooling in mutual funds. The rationale for prohibiting the open sale of vouchers—"if vouchers can be sold, the rich few will buy all the vouchers and acquire dominance in stock ownership. The poor will be deprived of an opportunity to obtain a stake in their economy"—manifests little economic sense. All systems, of course, authorize trading in stock after it is issued (usually allowing foreign purchases) that, by the same argument, would concentrate ownership and again would disinherit the poor! Nevertheless, the prohibition on selling presents a facade of protecting the ignorant, the gullible, and the elderly and is generally popular. But in practice trading will take place, and, if illegal, sellers will realize an even shabbier return than in an open market.

In Czechoslovakia the original voucher program covered state enterprises throughout the country and was open to all federal citizens, but only Prague has persisted with privatization since the "velvet divorce." Slovakia has been mired in indecision. The Czech government's program, however, through vouchers, has divested itself of more firms in one year than Chile did in sixteen years or Great Britain in ten. The Russians claim even greater success—81,000 of the nearly 200,000 state concerns have been sold for vouchers including most retail establishments (Whitney 1993). In September 1993, the Lithuanian government announced the privatization of 3,800 state companies—68 percent of all such firms (Girnius 1993).

The Hungarian experience is instructive. Initially the government and various ministries peddled a number of state enterprises to large foreign corporations, many of which promptly resold their acquisitions for a great deal more money than the original purchase price. In addition, company managers took a number of state firms private, enriching themselves in the process. Insider takeovers often led simply to a semblance of change without substance. The now "privatized" firms still demanded state subsidies; lacking them many would have been unable to stay afloat. This sorry record led to a public backlash against privatization, resulting in the creation in 1990 of the State Property Agency (SPA), which was charged with overseeing the divestiture of state assets. Since that time, the SPA has struggled to rid the government of various enterprises. The results are unclear. Many so-called privatizations consisted of the transfer of partial ownership of a company to another state-owned enterprise. The outcome has been highly unsatisfactory, and progress in transferring government assets to the actual private sector has been slow—in three years the officials have disposed of only 17 percent of state property ("Budapest Tries to Sell Hungarians on Capitalism" 1993). Buyers have frequently been foreign corporations, which has caused a backlash. This lack of progress has forced the government to rethink its opposition to mass privatization.

Privatization Roadblocks

The centrally controlled command economies of the past erected mammoth plants to take advantage of any scale economies, and whole regions were responsible for producing certain goods needed throughout the eastern bloc, rendering them monopolies. Moreover, the communist bureaucrats required that each economy accept the shoddy products manufactured by others, but with the opening to the West, countries can now buy well-made articles, if they have the currency, rather than accepting the slipshod commodities fabricated by their neighbors. In addition, trade between the former members of Comecon and within the former Soviet Union has collapsed as each demands that the others pay in hard currency. Thus these giant plants, which formerly supplied much of the Soviet bloc, now face shrinking markets. Many state-owned behemoths are inefficient and should be bulldozed, but they employ too many people for the governments to close them cavalierly. If the state sells them, however, a private owner will certainly lay off most workers, curtail output, and hoist prices to monopoly levels.

Even though each former East bloc country is different, all encounter similar hurdles in making the transition, one of the most important of which is that property rights are not well defined. Although the state nominally owns all productive assets, in fact no entity possesses clear title. Typically workers and managers have treated the firm as their own property, and employee opposition can stall or slow the most ambitious denationalization programs. Because a typical firm employs excess labor, workers fear wholesale layoffs, in many cases, as much as two-thirds. If the firm is unprofitable, a private employer may shut it down completely; if it is profitable, the employees will covet the assets.

In both Poland and Hungary, workers can hinder or prevent privatization because, in the 1970s and 1980s, in an effort to provide a more flexible system, the Communists in those countries converted most firms into enterprise councils, with laborers electing large numbers of the directors. As a result, the employees have been dictating the major decisions and assuming that they own the firms. Thus to privatize, the government is forced to "renationalize" the companies to convert them into corporations that can be marketed. If workers oppose the transformation, however, the laws in both countries make it difficult to convert to a joint stock company.

Because workers can neither sell the assets nor retain claim to them once they depart the firm, the enterprise councils have favored wage increases over investments. Consequently, plants and equipment have become outmoded, de-capitalized, and deteriorated. Officially, the state still has title to the property, but public officials have retained little say in the allocation of resources. Many plants are so decrepit that they have no economic future, and thus attempts to privatize them are futile. Even in Czechoslovakia and Russia, which never experimented with worker management, employees still behave as owners of the factories, with similar disastrous results.

In contrast, some workers in failing enterprises look to privatization, especially a joint venture with a foreign firm, as salvation. The Warsaw government imposed a tax on increases in real wages by any state-owned firm; consequently, many Polish state employees see privatization as the only way of raising wages.

Even if the state is the official owner, which governmental body controls the assets may be uncertain. Various ministries, regions, and localities may claim title. To convert an enterprise to private ownership, a national privatization agency may have to dispute property rights with a powerful and reluctant government ministry or with possessive local or regional bureaucracies. As a result, investors may be uncertain with whom to negotiate. In Czechoslovakia before the breakup, for example, both the Czech and the Slovak governments contested mineral rights with the federal government, and property claims by various governmental bodies hinder foreign investments and business in Russia.

Major Privatization Programs

The three best-defined mass privatization programs among the former Soviet bloc—the Polish, the Czech, and the Russian—are described below. They differ significantly and may all ultimately fail. Nevertheless, the two that have begun are progressing rapidly and remarkably. Unless brought down by fraud, the opposition of entrenched interests, or simply a loss of will, their future appears bright. None of them, however, including the Czech program, has tackled the problem of giant, inefficient, ramshackle plants producing shoddy goods that would be better scrapped than sold.

POLISH ECONOMIC REFORMS

Poland exemplifies the political difficulties of privatization and economic reform.* On January 1, 1990, the government inaugurated its "shock therapy," designed to shift quickly from a centrally directed command economy to a market-driven private enterprise system. Under the strong direction of Leszek Balce-rowicz, the authorities lifted controls on prices, legalized private property and enterprise, opened the country to trade with the West, cut the budget deficit, boosted interest rates above the rate of inflation, levied a tax on any significant boost in state companies' wages, and started privatizing business. Over the next year and a half, Poland led the world in economic reforms. In a short period of time approximately 90 percent of all retail trade became private. Small and medium-sized businesses sprang up. By the middle of 1993, the private sector employed 60 percent of all workers and produced close to 50 percent of national output ("World Wire: Poland Tallies Its Sell-Offs" 1993). Three years after its shock therapy, Poland is enjoying economic growth for the first time since the downfall of communism and, for the year 1993, realized the best economic performance of any country in Europe.

Privatizing small business was simple in that regional authorities auctioned the shops and enterprises. Generally, however, the governments sold only leases on the operations, imposing restrictions on the new owners, such as requirements to continue to carry certain types of goods. The economic reformers planned that the small privatization would be quickly followed by a divestment of medium to large enterprises, which officials intended to transform from worker-managed enterprises into corporations owned by the state and then sell them in a British-type privatization. It soon became evident, however, that this policy was doomed to failure as workers and managers could frustrate the transformation and as the public—except those who had acquired capital illegally—possessed no funds with which to purchase the companies. Through September 1993, the government vended nearly 2,400 companies out of 8,441 for about $473 million ("World Wire: Poland Tallies Its Sell-Offs" 1993).

The government established four paths to privatization for medium and big

---

*Background material on Poland can be found in Frydman, Papaczynski, and Earle 1993.

enterprises: (1) The managers could turn the company into a corporation that could sell its stock on the exchange. (2) The concern could sell its assets directly to a buyer—foreign or domestic. Often managers and workers founded a separate firm to lease the enterprise with ownership transferring to the new enterprise at the end of a specified period. (3) Workers and managers could buy the concern directly through some type of management buyout. (4) The government could privatize the enterprise through the mass privatization program. Participation in the privatization program, however, was and is voluntary.

In the fall of 1991, to reform the parliament, which still contained many delegates appointed by the Communists, the country held an election for new legislators. Attempting to ensure that many of the existing members would win seats, the old parliament prescribed a strict proportional system in which even the smallest parties would be represented. As a consequence, the new legislature split into a multitude of factions, unable to address the issues of privatization. After reforming the election law, the government held a second election in the fall of 1993 that produced a less fractured parliament—although one less dedicated to vigorous economic reform.

Since the 1991 election, President Lech Wałesa and four different prime ministers have supported a unique mass privatization program. Finally, in May 1993, the parliament enacted the plan for shifting large and medium-sized businesses from the public sector to the private. Unlike the mass privatization programs initiated elsewhere, the government apparently felt that Polish citizens could not make sensible investment decisions using vouchers. As a substitute for direct participation in privatization, the government set up about twenty investment funds, run by experienced Western financiers, to receive shares in corporations' being privatized. Compensation for the Western directors depends on the success of their funds.

Each investment fund will control 33 percent of the shares of some fifteen to thirty former state companies, with 27 percent of the shares spread among the other investment houses. The investment funds will choose the concerns in which they will take the lead through a National Football League–type draft; in other words, each fund will take turns choosing, among the enterprises in the program, those companies they prefer to oversee. The program grants workers up to 10 percent of the equity in each firm while the government temporarily retains the remainder. The lead funds—those possessing one-third of the stock in their corporations—will act as advisers and supervisors of the various businesses, appointing directors and senior managers. Those trusts will be able to trade the unlisted shares among themselves.

For a modest sum, adult Poles will be able to purchase a certificate giving them ownership in each of the twenty funds. Buyers of the certificates can sell their rights. A year after the program commences, the rights to each fund can be sold separately and the shares of the underlying companies will be available on the Warsaw bourse. The delay is intended to develop a record so that Polish investors will have more information in choosing companies. The fate of this mass program in the new parliament is uncertain.

CZECH PRIVATIZATION

In the summer of 1992, Czechoslovakia pioneered the first mass privatization program in the world.* In 1991, more than a year before the enactment of that program, the federal government of Czechoslovakia had legalized private businesses, requiring only that they register with the government. Entrepreneurs could freely hire unlimited numbers of workers. A commercial code passed in January 1992 regularized private transactions.

The Czech government has instituted an innovative approach to privatizing major enterprises. Although the state is open to tenders from foreign buyers, public officials have slated most public companies for voucher privatization. Under that program the government has sold vouchers usable only for the purchase of shares of stock in state enterprises. Any citizen eighteen years or older could purchase the vouchers, each of which contained a thousand coupons, for about $1.20 at the then exchange rate and could register the coupons for $34.00 to cover administrative costs. (Although these expenditures are trivial to Americans, they equal about one-quarter of the Czech average monthly wage.) Despite its potential profitability, the public showed little interest in the scheme until an entrepreneur, Viktor Kozeny, offered to buy any coupons deposited with his fund, the Harvard Capital and Consulting Fund (no relation to the university), one year after the sale of the companies at *ten times the original price*.

In the first round, about 8.5 million Czechoslovakian citizens—more than half the people in the two republics and 79 percent of the eligible population—purchased coupons to participate in the program. (The law prohibits trading in vouchers.) Individuals exchanged about 72 percent of the vouchers purchased for shares in the 437 investment funds that sprung up (Frydman, Papaczynski, and Earle 1993, 86). Without these funds, it is unlikely that the scheme would have succeeded. It is worth noting that the authorities failed to anticipate the importance of these investment trusts and imposed practically no regulations on them. During the second round, which began in the fall of 1993, about 2.5 million Czechs bought vouchers to purchase shares in about seven hundred companies slated for privatization (Pehe 1993b).

The mutual funds can secure control by investing heavily in certain enterprises, although the program limits them to no more than 20 percent of the stock

---

*Background material on Czechoslovakia can be found in Frydman, Papaczynski, and Earle 1993.

in any one firm. Thus these institutions alleviate the principal-agent problem discussed earlier. Harvard Capital, which is the second-largest trust, has concentrated its investing in only fifty-one companies; for thirty firms it has purchased near the maximum 20 percent ownership (King 1993, 8). The thirty-year-old Kozeny, as head of the fund, vows to wield his leverage to force reluctant managers to pare their workforce by about 30 percent and to fire many directors.

In addition to coupons the privatization program has employed several other methods to shift enterprises to the private sector. Initially, the Finance Ministry ordered all state companies to prepare for privatization. They could sell the firm or part of its assets through a tender or an auction; they could elect to hawk their shares, again through a tender or an auction. Alternatively, they could suggest a direct sale of part of the properties or the entire company or propose transferring the firm to municipal governments or health and pension institutions. The government stressed that it was open to any procedure that would result in the divestiture of the equity. In many cases companies and would-be buyers advanced competing projects, leaving federal and republic officials to decide how to dispose of the state enterprise's equity. The program restricts employee ownership to less than 10 percent. Companies elected predominantly to convert to joint stock firms (corporations) in preparation for coupon privatization.

Through the voucher program the Czech Republic has sold nearly a thousand concerns. In the first round of bidding, the state calculated the value of the companies to be awarded for coupons and issued stock in proportion to that estimate. The initial price was pegged at three coupons a share for each corporation, and individuals and mutual funds chose how many shares of which firm they would request. At the end of the sign-up period, public officials calculated the number of shares desired compared with the number offered. If the public demand equaled the shares proffered, the officials allocated each coupon purchaser the requested shares; if orders exceeded the offering by less than 125 percent, they prorated the equity. For companies oversubscribed by more than 125 percent, the officials withdrew the stock from the market and marked up the price for the next round. If the public solicited fewer than the number of shares offered, those that bid received stock at the initial price of three coupons a share and the remaining equity was discounted for the next period. The authorities carried out several rounds; thus, through a series of offerings, the program achieved a market clearing price.

When the first phase of the Czech program was completed, 988 state-owned corporations were safely in the private sector (Stevenson 1993a, D8). At the end of May 1993, some months after the first round was completed, the government began distributing shares in those businesses to the funds and to individuals (Prague officials had delayed issuing shares because of a dispute with Slovakia). The shares are now selling on the nascent Prague stock exchange, and the Czech privatization ministry has announced the next phase of the program, scheduling some 770 additional companies for coupon auction (Pehe 1993a).

Perhaps unwisely, many of these funds, not only the Harvard one, promised to redeem shares at some multiple of the original price. Few of these investment companies, however, have any appreciable capital with which to honor their pledge. If many subscribers demand remuneration, these investment houses may be forced to liquidate a significant portion of their holdings. Given the lack of liquidity in the Czech financial markets, stock prices may plummet and some or perhaps many of these funds may go under, taking with them the claims of a large number of investors. A significant collapse could discredit and endanger the whole program.

RUSSIAN PRIVATIZATION

Of all the former communist states, Russia has encountered the most daunting political hurdles in reforming its economy. The continuing power struggle between parliament and President Boris Yeltsin has debilitated governance in the erstwhile superpower, reducing the state to near anarchy and ultimately leading to the suspension of the legislature and its violent takeover. Beginning in the fall of 1992, the president employed executive decrees to implement a voucher privatization program designed to transfer a huge portion of Russian industry to private hands almost overnight. Yeltsin is running a mammoth going-out-of-business sale to move as many state firms as possible into the private sector before the Communists and the bureaucracy can stop him. He and his colleagues, in an effort to guarantee the transformation to a market economy, aspire to build quickly a constituency for privatization by creating a large group of individual owners that will restrain parliament from reimposing a state-controlled system.

After narrowly enacting the voucher program, parliament subsequently strove to undermine it by voting to transfer authority for privatization to state ministries unsympathetic to denationalization. The central bank, controlled by parliament, openly discriminated against private firms. In addition, local administrations, often still ruled by Communists, are attempting to block change, and, outside Moscow, central control is weak. Large firms run by powerful industrialists oppose privatization because it might curb their state subsidies and lead to major restructuring. The managers of these enterprises are maneuvering to take over control and ownership themselves. The situation is chaotic at best.

To illustrate the major quandaries facing privatization and the Russian economy, let us look at the Russian steel industry. By Western standards, virtually all ferrous metal companies are bankrupt. Without credits from the Russian central bank, many such firms would simply shut down. Steel plants are the only employers in such heavily polluted cities in Siberia as Novokuznetsk and Magnitogorsk, employing about a million workers. Serafim Afonin, an executive of the Russian State Committee for Metals, has maintained that the industry earns about 50 percent of its costs and that subsidies for the ferrous metal industry in 1992 amounted to $1 billion U.S. dollars (Crombie 1993). Moving the workers elsewhere, given the shortage of housing and the lack of a rental market, is impossible. Even if streamlining the plants to lower their costs were feasible, the market for iron and steel is too small to absorb more than a fraction of potential output, now that the military is no longer building huge quantities of tanks. The Russian ferrous metal plants are capable of producing 94 million tons of steel a year, or roughly the equivalent of one ton per adult, compared with a U.S. capacity of about one-quarter of a ton per adult. Even though the plants slashed production in 1992, six months later about 30 percent of the output remained unsold, and little of the steel is of sufficient quality to be exported. Given such problems, the state has made no plans to privatize these dinosaurs and the central bank continues to hand out subsidies, leading to more inflation.

Under the Russian privatization program every man, woman, and child is endowed with a voucher displaying a nominal value of 10,000 rubles, but those rubles can only be exchanged for stock in companies being privatized (Chubais 1993). As public enterprises are put on the auction block, individuals and investment funds can bid for shares with the vouchers. Unlike the Czechs, the Russians allow people to buy and sell these certificates freely. Initially, the price for vouchers fell to about 40 percent of their face value, or about $40, which partly discredited the plan. After the winter of 1993–1994, however, the nominal value climbed to nearly 10,000 rubles, but rapid inflation has pared the real value of these claims; by the fall of 1993 at the then current exchange rate they were worth roughly $10. By November 1993 vouchers were selling for about $27 (Stevenson 1993b). Nearly 98 percent of the 150 million Russian citizens have acquired these vouchers (Efron 1993).

Not all the shares will be auctioned through vouchers. Workers and managers can purchase 51 percent of the stock at subsidized prices. Alternatively, if workers prefer, the state will give them 25 percent of the stock but without voting power. The state reserves 20 percent of the equity for future cash sales. If employees buy the 51 percent to which they are entitled, the remaining 29 percent will be available for coupon privatization. Thus both employees and the public have a chance to acquire shares in the newly private companies. If the managers take a large portion of the equity, they are likely to focus on profit maximization rather than looting the corporation at the expense of the owners.

Like the Czech program, the Russian privatization program has attracted about 550 investment funds, but the government regulates them more closely than the Czech government does (Bush 1993). By the summer of 1993, these investment houses, more than half of which were established that year, had acquired 25 million vouchers and invested about eight million 10,000-ruble coupons in concerns that the state is divesting.

President Yeltsin decreed that state corporations sell at least 29 percent of their shares to the public for vouchers. Parliament asked the Russian Supreme Court to rescind this order. The president also set up the State Property Committee (SPC), charging it with oversight of the voucher program, but parliament voted to strip the committee of its authority. This struggle for power left the program's status in limbo and provided cover for those bureaucrats who wished to slow the process, until Yeltsin brought in tanks to subdue the cantankerous legislators. Ignoring parliament, the SPC instructed regional authorities to identify all hopeless enterprises, forget them, and concentrate on selling the remainder without any restructuring. To what extent local officials have been following Yeltsin's and the SPC's directives is unclear.

On a hopeful note, the Russian legislature has legalized the right to own, sell, and mortgage land ("World Wire: Russia Allows Land Ownership" 1993). Although foreigners cannot own land, they can lease it for ninety-nine years. Real estate ownership could induce significant growth in private agriculture, which to date has been slow to spread.

The small-scale privatization program began in 1992, and, by the end of the year, nearly 14,000 shops out of an estimated total of 123,000 had been sold (Hays 1992). The program has moved forward rapidly, and by the fall of 1993 local communities had disposed of about 50,000 small enterprises. In total the state sold about 81,000 enterprises in 1992 and 1993 (Whitney 1993). According to Anatoly Chubais, the deputy overseeing privatization, by the end of the program on June 30, 1994, about 140 million Russians would have invested their vouchers, more than two-thirds of all small firms had been privatized, and 70 percent of midsized and large firms would have been sold for vouchers ("World Wire: Russia to Rush Sell-Offs" 1994; Vinton 1994). These include such very large firms such as ZIL auto manufacturing company, with over 100,000 workers; the Uralmash, a heavy engineering corporation employing 30,000 men and women; and the Dzerzhinsky tractor plant, with 27,000 employees.

Each city or region is responsible for establishing a property committee to oversee the transfer of retail stores to private hands either through tender offers or auctions. Employees can receive a 30 percent discount on the price of the shop and have three years to pay the total (Chubais 1993). As a result, worker cooperatives have purchased about 60 percent of the stores. In all too many cases, however, local authorities have stood in the way of such privatizations, and thus many have consisted simply of leasing a retail outlet for five years with the prospect that the "owner" will have to compete again at the end of that period for a renewal. Typically, the city or region retains ownership of the building and land.

An early example—a baking company—demonstrates some of the hazards and uncertainties of the privatization process. In December 1992, the state sold 44 percent of the shares of the Bolshevik Biscuit Company for vouchers; employees and managers purchased the remainder (Hays 1992, A18). As long as the employees' stock is fully alienable, this firm has truly been privatized; but if workers' ownership is contingent on their employment, inefficiencies are bound to develop. Moreover, if the firm finds itself in financial difficulty, the state may still step in to bail it out, which diminishes the incentive to carry out any painful restructuring. (Even in the capitalist U.S. of A., the government aided Chrysler and Lockheed rather than letting them go through bankruptcy!) In addition, the Western privatization aid package is providing this bakery with an export credit from Italy that requires it to purchase its equipment from that country ("Russian Industry: How Not to Help Bolshevik Biscuit" 1993). Whether Italian ovens together with a subsidized loan make sense for this new firm is unclear.

Unfortunately, the voucher program brings with it no new cash to invigorate the newly privatized enterprises. Russia is looking to the West to supply the capital needed to upgrade these firms, but state-supplied resources carry all the problems of government involvement. Whether these Western funds can be invested, loaned, or granted efficiently remains to be seen. The Russian government envisions local and foreign venture capitalists managing the aid and applying commercial principles when investing those assets. As the Bolshevik Biscuit aid package illustrates, however, too many of these funds come tied to foreign exports, which are unlikely to be what is most needed. Where venture capitalists have been most successful, they have risked their *own* resources; they will be unlikely to maintain the same rigor using taxpayer money. The foreign aid, however, could usefully finance technical assistance and training for Russian businesspeople.

The Russian public remains skeptical of the privatization program. It sees state apparatchiks acquiring state property cheaply by bribing bureaucrats and then reselling it for multiples of the original price, with the earnings often deposited abroad. Many also suspect that the Russian mafia is cornering the vouchers and securing all the good enterprises. Corruption and charges of corruption are commonplace.

Despite the ambiguity and contradictory statistics coming out of Russia, the Yeltsin program appears to be gaining momentum and may yet build support for a market system. The program provides something for everyone. The pensioner on the street can sell his or her voucher for food or vodka. Executives of successful companies can purchase a majority of the stock. The investment funds and the ability of those with cash—whatever its source—to buy large blocks of vouchers ensure that ownership is sufficiently concentrated for good management.

Yet formidable political and economic forces are arrayed against privatization—especially mass privatization. Many, if not most, privatized firms will fail. Eager investors may then become disillusioned with the market system and the public repudiate the whole effort. If this happens Russia's future will be grim.

The Russian economy has been in decline for at least a decade, perhaps longer, although in the last few years output has been falling faster than previously.

Many blame the economic reforms, but they may not be responsible. After the breakup of Comecon in 1990, trade with former communist countries contracted sharply. In 1991, when the Soviet Union came apart, many republics declared independence and introduced their own currencies. Increasingly, each former entity of the Soviet Empire has demanded that its exports be paid for with hard currencies, resulting in a sharp cut in trade and a concomitant drop in production. It is worth noting that Ukraine, which was the first republic—excepting the Baltic states—to issue its own currency but which has implemented virtually no reforms and failed to inaugurate a privatization program, has suffered an even larger collapse in output than Russia.

Conclusion

Privatization is imperative if the former socialist states are to join the modern world, achieve vigorous growth, and sustain a democratic way of life. Unless those countries eliminate their publicly owned dinosaurs, their economies will be saddled with costly drags on their growth. The abandonment or failure of privatization will probably condemn those countries to the Latin American diseases of stagnant growth, periods of hyperinflation, weak democratic governments followed by strong-man rule supplanted by weak elected regimes.

Unfortunately, the public may lack the will to see the process through to a successful conclusion. Lithuania, which has moved fastest among the Baltic countries to convert to a market economy, during the winter of 1992–1993 voted in the Communist Party. In Poland, the electorate has also chosen Marxists to rule the state. In the December 1993 Russian parliamentary elections, those opposed to rapid reform secured a majority and the most liberal reformers came in second to the neofascist party. In both Lithuania and Poland, however, the Communists ran as social democrats and promised to support market reforms but at a slower pace; in Poland they had voted in the May before the elections to support the mass privatization program. Even in Russia the anti-Yeltsin parties only propose slower progress toward a market, not abandoning it. In Lithuania privatization is continuing at a rapid clip. Almost everywhere, the voter, given a choice between going slowly or privatizing quickly, has elected gradual change. Only in the Czech Republic has the citizenry supported a strong program of reform.

The difficulties in shifting from a centrally controlled to a market system are formidable. Most of the available evidence, however, demonstrates that speed and determination are essential and effective. Those states such as Hungary that have attempted to implement reforms gradually have made little progress. In contrast, the Russian program—chaotic, messy, quick—just might succeed. The

Czech plan also appears to be a winner, although, as in Russia, scandals, defaults, or fraud could scuttle the initiative. Even if the process ended abruptly, the state sector has shrunk considerably. With the ex-communists' win, the prospects for Poland look dicey. Nevertheless, progress is being made: even in Poland, Lithuania, and Russia the former Marxists support moving, albeit slowly, to a market system. Given strong leadership, the eastern bloc states may yet join the West with growing prosperity and democratic governments, cutting the risks of war, creating viable trading partners, and yielding higher incomes for the whole world.

References

Alhlbrandt, R. "Efficiency in the Provision of Fire Services," *Public Choice* 28, no. 2 (Fall 1973): 1–15.

Bennett, J. T., and T. J. Di Lorenzo. "Public Employee Unions and the Privatization of Public Services." *Journal of Labor Research* 4, no. 1 (Winter 1983): 33–45.

Bennett, J. T., and M. H. Johnson. "Public versus Private Provision of Collective Goods and Services: Gorham Collection Revisited." *Public Choice* 34, no. 1 (Spring 1979): 55–63.

Boardman, Anthony E., and Aden R. Vining. "Ownership and Performance in Competitive Environments: A Comparison of the Performance of Private, Mixed, and State-Owned Enterprises." *Journal of Law and Economics* 32, no. 1 (April 1989): 1–33.

Bohlen, Celestine. "Moscow Privatization Yields Privacy and Problems." *New York Times*, February 28, 1993, p. 1.

Buchanan, James M. *Perspectives in the Study of Politics*. Chicago: Rand McNally, 1968.

———. *Theory of Public Choice*. Ann Arbor: University of Michigan Press, 1972.

Bush, Keith. "Role of Investment Funds in Privatization." *Radio Free Europe/Radio Liberty Daily Report*, August 10, 1993, p. 1.

Chubais, Anatoly B. *The State Committee of the Russian Federation for the Management of State Property: Annual Report 1992*. Moscow: State Committee of the Russian Federation for the Management of State Property, 1993.

Clarham, K. et al. *The Role of Privatization in Florida's Growth*. Tallahassee, Fla.: Florida Chamber of Commerce Foundation, 1987.

Clarkson, Kenneth. "Some Implications of Property Rights in Hospital Management." *Journal of Law and Economics* 15 (October 1972): 363–84.

Clegg, Nick. "Hungary's Privatization Falters after Flying Start." *Financial Times*, October 19, 1993, p. 4.

Crombie, Robert. "Collapsing Steel Industry Still Propped by Subsidies." *Moscow Times*, business section, June 9, 1993.

Downs, Anthony. *An Economic Theory of Democracy*. New York: Harper, 1957.

Efron, Sonni. "Yeltsin to Broaden the Scope of Privatization." *Los Angeles Times*, May 15, 1993.

Frydman, Roman, Andrzej Rapaczynski, and Johan Earle. *The Privatization Process in Central Europe*. New York: Central European University Press, 1993.

Girnius, Saulius. "Lithuania Sets Ambitious Goals." *Radio Free Europe/Radio Liberty Research Report, Privatization: A Special Report* 1, no. 17 (April 24, 1992): 67–72.

———. "Slezevicius Addresses Seimas." *Radio Free Europe/Radio Liberty Daily Report*, September 15, 1993, p. 6.

Hachette, Dominique, and Rolf Lüders. *Privatization in Chile: An Economic Appraisal*. San Francisco: International Center for Economic Growth, 1993.

Hanke, Steve H. "The Literature on Privatization." In *The Privatization Option*, Heritage Lectures 42, ed. Stuart Butler. Washington, D.C.: Heritage Foundation, 1985.

Hays, Laurie, "Once Again, a Bolshevik Could Help Overthrow the Old Regime in Russia." *Wall Street Journal*, December 9, 1992, p. A18.

Inkeles, Alex. "Industrialization, Modernization and the Quality of Life." *International Journal of Comparative Sociology* 34, nos. 1–2 (January–June 1993).

Kamm, Thomas. "Four Big Argentine Firms Stake Future on Role in Nation's Privatization Push." *Wall Street Journal*, March 10, 1993, p. A10.

King, Neil, Jr. *"Power Broker*: Czech Financier Raises Enormous Stock Fund, Storm of Controversy." *Wall Street Journal Europe*, August 13–14, 1993, pp. 1 and 8.

Kornai, János. *The Road to a Free Economy*. New York: Norton, 1990.

Michaels, Daniel. "Privatization: Estonia's Industry Sell-Off Guided by Treuhand Team." *Wall Street Journal Europe*, August 30, 1993, p. 4.

Pehe, Jiri. "Czech Launch Second Wave of Voucher Privatization."*Radio Free Europe/ Radio Liberty Daily Report*, September 30, 1993a, p. 4.

———. "Economic News from the Czech Republic." *Radio Free Europe/Radio Liberty Daily Report*, November 16, 1993b, p. 4.

Peltzman, Sam. "Toward a More General Theory of Regulation." *Journal of Law & Economics* 19, no. 2 (August 1976).

"Perestroika Survey." *Economist*, April 28, 1990, pp. 13–16.

"Property Wrongs." *Economist*, September 4, 1993, p. 33.

Raphael, Therese. "Unstoppable Reform in Russia." *Wall Street Journal*, January 18, 1994, p. A16.

"Russian Industry: How Not to Help Bolshevik Biscuit." *Economist*, July 17, 1993, pp. 64–65.

Schroeder, Gertrude E. "Property Rights Issues in Economic Reforms in Socialist Countries." *Studies in Comparative Communism* 21, no. 2,(Summer 1988): 175–88.

Scully, Gerald W. "The Institutional Framework and Economic Development." *Journal of Political Economy* 96, no. 3 (June 1988): 652–63.

Sirowy, Larry, and Alex Inkeles. "The Effects of Democracy on Economic Growth and Inequality: A Review." *Studies in Comparative International Development* 25, no. 1 (Spring 1990): 126–57.

Stevens, Barbara J., ed. *Delivering Municipal Services Efficiently: A Comparison of Municipals and Private Service Delivering*. A report prepared by Ecadada, Inc., for the U.S. Dept. of Housing and Urban Development (June 1984).

Stevenson, Richard W. "Czech Capitalism Gets Stock Market." *New York Times*, June 21, 1993, pp. D1 and D8.

———. "Vouchers Become Hot Tickets for Russian Bulls." *New York Times*, November 11, 1993, p. C1.

———. "The Pain of British Privatization Has Yielded a String of Successes." *New York Times*, February 22, 1994, pp. A1 and C5.

Stigler, George J. "The Theory of Economic Regulation." *Bell Journal of Economics and Management Science* 2, no. 1 (Spring 1971).

Vinton, Louisa. "Chubais: Voucher Deadline in Force." *Radio Free Europe/Radio Liberty Daily Report*, June 9, 1994, p. 1.

Whitney, Craig R. "Russia Opens up Market, but Few Have the Money." *New York Times International*, November 18, 1993, p. A3.

"World Wire: Russia Allows Land Ownership." Compiled by Richard Holman, *Wall Street Journal*, July 23, 1993, p. A3

"World Wire: Russia to Rush Sell-Offs." Compiled by Richard Holman, *Wall Street Journal*, June 9, 1993, p. A11.

"World Wire: Poland Tallies Its Sell-Offs." Compiled by Richard Holman, *Wall Street Journal*, October 21, 1993, p. A13.

5

Revenue Assignment and Intergovernmental Fiscal Relations in Russia

CHARLES E. MCLURE JR.

The assignment of revenue sources among governments in Russia has important implications for the successful transition to a market economy and the survival of the Russian Federation. This chapter examines alternative means of assigning revenues between the central and oblast governments: independent legislation and implementation by the oblasts, oblast surcharges on a tax administered by the central government, sharing such taxes on the basis of origin, and sharing revenues on some other basis. A combination of tax surcharges and revenue sharing is seen to be the instrument of choice. Surcharges preserve the fiscal autonomy of the oblasts, while avoiding administrative problems, but involve no redistribution between oblasts; revenue-sharing formulas can be designed to fill the distributional lacuna. By comparison, although independent oblast tax policy provides fiscal autonomy, it involves intolerable complexity and duplication of administrative effort. Tax sharing avoids administrative duplication but eliminates oblast fiscal autonomy. Like tax surcharges, neither addresses the need for redistribution between oblasts.

Introduction

Russia, like Australia, Brazil, Canada, Germany, and the United States, is organized as a federal system.[1] It has eighty-nine "subjects of federation," the intermediate units of government that correspond to the states of Australia, Brazil, and the United States, the provinces of Canada, and the *laender* of Germany, as well as numerous units of local government—*rayons*, cities, and villages.[2] The horizontal and vertical fiscal relations among the governments that form a federation may be as important as the political relations. (Of course, intergovernmental fiscal and political relations are generally inextricably intertwined.) Where subnational governments have few fiscal resources of their own, as in Australia, a federation may operate more like a unitary state. Conversely, where subnational jurisdictions have ample fiscal resources, as in China, a unitary system of government may function like a federation. Finally, where there is a fiscally weak central government, subnational governments may behave as in a confederation. Where intergovernmental fiscal relations are not rational, macroeconomic instability, misallocation of resources, and inequities are likely.

Included under the general rubric of intergovernmental fiscal relations are several interrelated topics: the assignment of expenditure responsibilities among the various levels of government; the assignment of revenue sources; the design of intergovernmental transfers intended to offset vertical fiscal imbalance between the central and lower levels of government and horizontal fiscal disparities among subnational jurisdictions; and the borrowing power of subnational governments. This chapter focuses on the second of these topics and to some extent discusses the third. That is, it examines the assignment of revenue sources, including intergovernmental transfers, to various levels of government in the Russian Federation, especially the assignment of revenues between the central government and the oblast level.[3]

Revenue assignment, as that term is used here, involves more than the division of public moneys—from taxes and other revenue sources—among governments and goes beyond deciding "who should tax what." After all, there are many ways of achieving a given division of revenues among jurisdictions and more than one way to implement a given decision of who should tax what. For example, revenue sharing, tax sharing, surcharges on national taxes, and taxes (and fees and user charges) legislated and administered by subnational govern-

The author wishes to thank Roy Bahl for his valuable comments on an early draft of this paper and Christine Wallich for the opportunity to work on this topic in Russia. The views expressed here should be attributed only to the author.

ments can, in principle, all be employed to implement a given division of revenues. The choices among these methods of revenue assignment (and others) have important implications for the economic behavior of taxpayers, the fiscal autonomy and behavior of subnational governments, administrative feasibility, and ultimately the fiscal viability of federalism in Russia. (Whether all these alternatives are feasible in practice depends, inter alia, on administrative realities.)

Revenue assignment is especially important in Russia at this time for several reasons. First, the potential differences in the fiscal resources available to the governments of the various regions are enormous, in part because of the geographic concentration of important natural resources. For example, the sparsely populated Siberian *okrugs* of Khanti-Mansisk (oil) and Yamal Niniets (gas) produce more than 80 percent of Russia's oil and gas, and the Republic of Sakha (Yakutia) produces 99 percent of its diamonds (25 percent of the world supply). Some resource-rich areas are demanding—and getting—a greater share in the proceeds from exploitation of "their" resources.

Geographic concentration of natural resources is not the only cause of potential fiscal disparities. Productive industrial capacity is also highly concentrated; for example, Nizhni Novgorod is relatively prosperous. By comparison, production in some cities and oblasts is so heavily concentrated in defense that the end of the cold war and the lagging conversion of the military-industrial complex are causing regional depressions and undermining fiscal bases (see also Craig and Kopits 1993).

Second, important ethnic differences are leading to calls for special fiscal treatment, if not separation, not unlike that found, for example, in Canada in French-speaking Quebec and in Spain in the Basque country and Navarre.[4] In some cases ethnic differences and concentration of natural resources combine to create especially strong centrifugal forces, as in oil-rich Tatarstan, which has claimed the right to determine how much revenue it sends to Moscow. Sakha (Yakutia) has reached an agreement with the federal government whereby it keeps all revenues raised within its borders and finances all public services in Sakha, including those provided by the federal government elsewhere. These developments have troubling implications: if the central government were to reach similar agreements with all relatively rich oblasts, it would be left with only the fiscal base of the relatively poor oblasts to finance all public services provided on their territory (and presumably outside the territory of Russia).

The inability to deal satisfactorily with problems similar to these was one reason the Soviet Union fell apart. Wallich (1992b, 108) notes that "republican transfers to the union budget dried up after the August coup attempt." The revenue shortfall resulting from "the higher-than-agreed upon retention of revenues by the republics" has been placed at an enormous 5.9 percent of GDP (Wallich 1992b, 109; see also the next section of this chapter). This fact is not lost on Russians—or on others. Craig and Kopits (1993) suggest that the "failure to establish a fair, stable, and efficient intergovernmental arrangement would tend to exacerbate political and ethnic tensions and possibly even contribute to the disintegration of the Federation."[5] In a similar vein, Litvack (1992, 1) has written that "the Russian Federation's ability to prevail, under its current borders, should not be taken for granted."

As pressures for regional independence grow, so do demands for fiscal autonomy.[6] Fiscal autonomy is a vital element of fiscal federalism; decentralization of the power to tax and spend can be an important vehicle for the practice of democracy. But ill-considered grants of taxing authority to subnational governments could have unfortunate effects. Regions might adopt tax measures that would be economically harmful to the nation or impose costly burdens of compliance and administration. For example, there is ample evidence that imposition of a value-added tax by subnational governments is extremely problematic (see the section in this chapter on the appraisal of particular taxes).

Failure to achieve a satisfactory correspondence of taxing and spending powers could seriously compromise the ability to conduct macroeconomic policy and could aggravate inflationary tendencies. Since the breakup of the Soviet Union there has been a tendency for the central government to push expenditure responsibilities down to the oblasts in an apparent attempt to eliminate its own deficit. By comparison, the oblasts have demanded increased shares of revenues, in part to compensate for these increased expenditures (see Wallich 1992b). Privatization of state enterprises, and even commercialization, will increase pressures on both levels of government, as services that previously have been provided by state enterprises, including housing, become government responsibilities (on this issue, see Alm and Sjoquist 1993).

Finally, from a technical point of view, the existing Russian system of revenue assignment is fundamentally flawed. The defects may not be apparent, or even troublesome, as long as most economic activity is conducted by large state enterprises, especially if the enterprises operate only in one oblast. But as the Russian economy becomes more like that of the West, the system of revenue assignment will become increasingly unworkable and unsatisfactory, even if centrifugal forces are overcome.

Following a brief description of recent practice in the assignment of revenues in Russia, I discuss conceptual principles of revenue assignment and alternative means of assigning revenues to various levels of government. The last section appraises alternative assignments for four important sources of tax revenues: the enterprise profits tax, the individual income tax, the value added tax (VAT), and excises. Besides drawing on the previous conceptual analyses, the appraisal takes account of administrative considerations peculiar to each of the taxes and the capacity for tax administration and compliance in Russia.

Current Practice

It is no mean feat to describe the current state of revenue assignment in Russia. The constitution that was ratified in the referendum of December 12, 1993, says nothing of substance about the topic, leaving arrangements to be worked out between the center and the oblasts in some unspecified manner. Like many others, the law on revenue assignment is in flux, and recent practice has diverged significantly from the statutory standards prescribed in the *Basic Principles of Taxation*, enacted in 1992 but not yet implemented. Moreover, administrative practices are somewhat unsettled and far from uniform. To set the stage for what follows, it will thus be appropriate to describe both the revenue assignment in the *Basic Principles* and the actual practices of revenue assignment and tax administration.[7]

THE *BASIC PRINCIPLES*

Under the *Basic Principles of Taxation*, the central government would get all the revenues from the VAT, and the oblast governments would get all revenues from the enterprise profits tax and the individual income taxes.[8] The federal government would get all revenues from the excise tax on automobiles and half those on vodka; the oblasts would get the remainder of revenues from excises (see table 5.1).

There are several taxes on the exploitation of natural resources. I focus on the production levy (a payment of 8 to 21 percent of the value of production in the case of oil). Reflecting the dual nature of the state as owner of resources and fiscal agent, this might be described alternatively as a tax or a royalty. The *Basic Principles* provides that the central government should receive either 20 percent or 40 percent of revenues from the levy on production, depending on whether production occurs in an autonomous *okrug*, and indicates how the remainder is to be divided among subnational governments.[9]

ACTUAL PRACTICE

Actual practice differs from that prescribed in the *Basic Principles* in important respects. These differences reflect practices carried over from the Soviet system.[10] Under that system, the budget of each (now independent) republic was determined by the application of budgetary "norms." In addition to purely local taxes, there were two types of shared taxes, "fixed" and "regulating." The republics

Table 5.1   Revenue Assignment in *Basic Principles*, Current Practice, and Recommended Revenue Assignment (all in percent)

Tax	BASIC PRINCIPLES		CURRENT PRACTICE		RECOMMENDATIONS	
	Central	Oblast	Central	Oblast	Central	Oblast
Value-added tax	100	0	50–76 (shared)	24–50 (shared)	100	0
Enterprise profits tax	0	100	31.25 (shared)	68.75 (shared)	100 (but perhaps surcharge)	0 (but perhaps surcharge)
Individual income tax	0	100	0	100		
Graduated rates				(shared)	100	0
Flat-rate surcharge					0	100
Excises					0	100
Automobiles	100	0	100	0	(if oblast tax	(if possible)
Vodka	50	50	50	50	is possible)	
Others	0	100	100	100		
Natural resource tax	20–40	60–80	20–40	60–80	Majority	Minority
Revenue sharing	None		None		Yes	

received a predetermined share of revenues from fixed taxes. By comparison, their shares of revenues from regulating taxes collected within their boundaries were set to allow them to cover budgetary expenditures based on norms; some republics also received subventions from Moscow. In many instances, sharing rates were set on an ad hoc basis and subventions were granted at the end of the year to cover deficits. This "system" was not really a system; it involved substantial discretion, and it encouraged negotiation over budgets, sharing rates, and subventions.[11] Moreover, unlike most systems of intergovernmental finance, revenues were shared upward, from the republics to the center.

When the Soviet Union broke up, this "system" was adopted by Russia, with the oblasts taking the place of the republics.[12] The *Basic Principles* represents an attempt—thus far unsuccessful—to get away from this system by assigning all oblasts fixed and uniform shares of each tax.[13] Although reflecting a laudable objective, this policy was not tenable for several reasons.

First, it would have produced large changes in revenues available to various oblasts. Bahl (1992, 20) concludes that the derivation-based assignment of revenues contained in the *Basic Principles* would have produced a loss of revenues for forty-one of sixty-nine oblasts studied and a gain for twenty-eight. The median loss would have been about 20 percent of revenues, and the median gain, about 18 percent of revenues.

Second, the *Basic Principles* allocated a high percentage of revenues from some taxes—most notably the enterprise tax but also the individual income tax—to subnational governments but responsibility for collecting the taxes to the State Tax Service (STS), an organ of the central government. The STS lacked incentives to devote resources and effort to collecting these taxes, instead focusing its efforts on collecting taxes that provide revenues to the federal fisc. Finally, formally assigning revenues to the subnational governments would have reduced the flexibility the central government needed to exercise macroeconomic stabilization policy.

Reflecting a retreat from the *Basic Principles*, both the enterprise profits tax and the VAT are currently being shared between the central government and the oblasts on the basis of the derivation or origin of revenues. In just over a year, the oblast share of the 32 percentage point enterprise profits tax has increased from 15 to 22 percentage points (68.75 percent of the total); the central government now gets 10 percentage points (31.25 percent).[14]

In the case of the VAT, which is levied at a basic rate of 20 percent, with a preferential rate of 10 percent on foodstuffs, the regime for sharing revenues has also not been stable. In early 1992 the sharing rate for each oblast was set in an ad hoc manner based on "needs," through negotiations between the oblasts and the Ministry of Finance. In the third quarter of 1992 the sharing rate was set at a uniform 20 percent for all oblasts. In 1993 the Ministry of Finance was again setting negotiated rates. Of the eighty-nine oblasts, twenty-four have VAT sharing rates in the range of 11 to 20 percent, another sixty have rates of 41 to 50 percent, and the remaining five have rates of 21 to 40 percent; see Bahl and Wallace (1993).

ADMINISTRATIVE ARRANGEMENTS

A system of revenue assignment such as that just described is called *tax sharing* (see the next section). The State Tax Service (STS) of the central government is responsible for administering all the taxes discussed—imposing a tax rate specified by the central government on a base also specified by the central government.[15] The central and oblast governments share revenues raised in proportions that are fixed but not necessarily identical across oblasts.[16]

This arrangement is obviously problematic. First, the STS appears to have relatively little incentive to devote its scarce administrative resources to collecting revenues that flow largely or entirely to oblast governments. Second, it allows the oblast almost no discretion in choosing its own rates for these important taxes. This limits the fiscal autonomy of the oblasts, an issue addressed at length in the next section. Third, oblasts cannot, with few exceptions, engage in "tax competition," which can be healthy, for reasons described below. Rather, taxes on business are essentially uniform throughout the country.

Even more problematic is something that is not apparent from the above description of administrative arrangements.[17] Although described as top-down sharing of central government tax revenues with the oblasts, the reality may be quite different.

In principle, officers of the STS in the various oblasts answer only to their superiors in Moscow, a common practice for local representatives of centralized tax administrations in many countries. In fact, tax-sharing arrangements probably operate in a bottom-up fashion, in part because some local STS officials appear to be heavily influenced by officials of the oblast governments where they work.[18] This is true for both historical and practical reasons.

Under the Soviet system, local tax administrators were explicitly under dual subordination to both the Ministry of Finance in Moscow and the financial authorities of the republics of the USSR (now independent members of the Commonwealth of Independent States) on whose territories they worked. This worked fairly well as long as Moscow kept the governments of the member republics of the Soviet Union on a short leash. But once control was relaxed, the republics—especially Russia—started to withhold revenues from Moscow and the union collapsed. (This is not the only reason the Soviet Union collapsed or even the primary reason, but it was certainly an important one.)

When the Soviet Union broke up, Russia inherited the institutional and organizational structure of the previous system, including dual subordination. Since then, laws on local self-government have given oblast governments greater autonomy over their budgets. Moreover, STS officials are no longer formally subordinated to oblast governments. Despite these formal changes, it may be difficult for some STS officials to stand up to their former superiors in the finance departments of the oblast governments. This is especially true because, at least in some oblasts, the oblast governments continue to provide office space, housing, and fringe benefits for STS officials; the wages that the central government pays may represent less than half the total compensation (see Wallich 1992b, 104).

Some oblast governments, especially those where mineral wealth or ethnic differences create a disposition toward separation, have been withholding part or all of the central government's share of revenues collected on their territory. Sakha's special deal with Moscow was mentioned earlier; other oblasts are making similar deals. During 1992 the oil-rich autonomous *okrug* of Khanti Mansisk sent Moscow only 1 percent of revenues from the VAT instead of the 20 percent demanded. Tatarstan, a republic that has a large non-Russian population as well as oil wealth, demanded a single channel to send only what it wanted to the central government, and as many as twenty other oblasts are following a similar course. Thus the central government of Russia is, to a large degree, being financed by more or less gratuitous transfers from the bottom up as determined by oblast governments.

The similarity of the present situation to that at the end of the Soviet era is ominous. If the Russian Federation is to survive, it must provide fiscal autonomy to the oblasts and prevent the further development of centrifugal forces that could cause the federation to disintegrate. The problem is compounded by the incipient fiscal disparities mentioned earlier, for disparities create regional tensions. But attempting to eliminate them entirely would alienate wealthy regions, which might want to withdraw from the federation. The central government has used a variety of carrots and sticks to persuade recalcitrant oblasts to honor their financial obligations to the center; these include the threat to exclude their oil from the nation's network of pipelines. Such threats, not to mention the threat of force, appear ominous.

Conceptual Foundations of Revenue Assignment

A highly centralized government will not work in a large and varied nation such as Russia. Decentralization of government is an important vehicle for the exercise of democracy, especially in such a large and diverse country. In the absence of decentralization, all decisions on public services would be made in Moscow, as they were under the Soviet system, despite the fiction of a federal system. With decentralization, the inhabitants of various regions can, at least in principle, make their own choices about the nature, quantity, and quality of the public services they receive.[19] The more decision making is decentralized, the more likely it is that people will get the public services they want.

There are, of course, limits to the feasibility or rationality of decentralization. The benefits of some services are experienced over such a wide area that excessive decentralization would lead to suboptimal provision because benefits that spill over into other jurisdictions tend to be ignored. In some cases potential economies of scale make excessive decentralization inefficient and costly.[20] To be rational, decentralization must take account of benefit spillovers *and* economies of scale. No one expects national defense to be provided by subnational governments; indeed, the idea involves a contradiction in terms. By comparison, issuing dog licenses is reasonably a local activity because it involves neither substantial economies of scale nor significant spillovers. The principle of subsidiarity requires that the lowest level of government that can effectively discharge a given activity should do so.

If government activity is decentralized only to large and diverse oblasts, there may be little benefit. To be effective, decentralization must allow those with different preferences for public activities to make decisions affecting their lives. This often requires that governments below the oblast level be decentralized.

Finally, national governments should be primarily responsible for macroeconomic stabilization and redistribution of income. This section discusses these two issues, as well as revenue assignment and efficient government, the heart of the case for fiscal decentralization, and the special case of taxes on natural resources, a question of vital interest for Russia.

REVENUE ASSIGNMENT AND EFFICIENT GOVERNMENT

If subnational governments are to make economically efficient choices, they need *autonomy* over means of finance as well as over expenditures.[21] If public officials of subnational governments are to be *responsible*, their taxpayers must (perhaps within the limits described below) pay for the public services provided by those governments, meaning that those governments must have access to revenue sources that are adequate to finance their budgets. Without adequate revenues, subnational self-government is only a mirage.

If the provision of public services is to be *efficient*, those who use the services (e.g., individuals, households, and businesses) must pay for them. For this reason, subnational governments should rely to the extent possible on taxes related to benefits received.[22] (Benefit-related taxes, fees, and charges are also commonly thought to be fair.)

Most decisions cannot be made by referendum; some form of representative government is required. There are several techniques by which preferences for public services can be expressed in a system of representative democracy. First, if citizens think that the public services being provided are not worth the taxes they pay, they can replace politicians (and perhaps bureaucrats) with others who will provide a better combination of services and taxes.

There is a chance that an effort will be made to load taxes onto business to reduce taxes on individuals. Here tax competition has an important role to play. If businesses can move between jurisdictions—or at least threaten to move—politicians, bureaucrats, and citizens who want a free ride will be limited in their rapaciousness.

In theory, if businesses are sufficiently mobile, competition between jurisdictions will help assure that business taxes reflect benefits provided to business—a requirement for economic efficiency in government. But if taxes on business are constrained to be uniform throughout the country, say because oblast governments collude in setting rates or simply because they share in revenues raised by the central government, there is nothing to guarantee that business taxes reflect benefits.[23] Thus, rather than being an undesirable feature to be condemned, tax competition has an important role in stimulating efficient government. This helps explain my strong preference for tax surcharges (oblast taxes levied on the tax base of the central government) over tax sharing (division of revenues from application of a uniform rate to the tax base). (See the next section.)

Despite the conceptual advantages of taxes and charges related to benefits, in actuality only a few forms of taxation show a close relation to benefits. Toll charges and taxes on motor fuels are perhaps the best examples of benefit-related payments.

The most important sources of revenues in most countries—the VAT, individual income taxes, and enterprise profits taxes—are not closely related to benefits of public services. Yet the reasoning of the benefit principle is instructive in assigning revenues from the VAT and the individual income tax at a conceptual level; the enterprise profits tax is a poor choice for the implementation of benefit taxation. (The next section adds administrative considerations to the equation.)

First, most public services consumed by households provide benefits where people live, not where they work.[24] This suggests that liability for income taxes should be based on residence rather than employment. In this view, payroll taxes (which are inherently related to employment) are unlikely to be closely related to most public services provided by subnational governments in the case of those who commute across boundaries of subnational jurisdictions.

Similarly, indirect taxes should be based on consumption (destination of goods and services) instead of production (origin). Retail sales taxes automatically satisfy this criterion, as does a destination-based VAT; single-stage sales taxes levied before the retail stage, origin-based VATs, and multiple-stage sales taxes do not.

Second, it seems likely, though certainty is impossible, that public services provided by subnational governments do not rise faster than income; if so, subnational taxes that impose a burden proportionate to income or consumption seem acceptable. This, plus ease of administration, suggests that it is acceptable for subnational governments to rely on flat-rate income taxes or broad-based sales taxes for much of their revenue. In this view, the use of progressive income taxes to achieve distributional objectives is reserved for the central government.

Third, taxes on enterprise profits are particularly unsuited for use as benefit taxes. There is no reason to believe that only profitable enterprises benefit from public services or that benefits increase with profits. Nor is it likely that these taxes, when levied by subnational governments, have the distributional effects— incidence on owners of enterprises or of all capital—commonly attributed to them. Through the process of threatened relocation and tax competition described above, onerous subnational business taxes that exceed provided benefits are likely to be shifted to owners of productive factors that cannot move (or can move only with great difficulty), such as labor and landowners.[25] For these reasons, enterprise profits taxes are particularly unsuited for use by subnational governments.

The situation is particularly bad in Russia. The central government continues to exert control over wages, prices—including the crucial prices of energy—and interest rates. Enterprise profits, and thus revenues from the enterprise profits tax, are subject to changes in these variables. Central government control of foreign trade and of the pace of military conversion accentuates this problem. It is inappropriate for subnational governments to rely on taxes whose revenues depend on the whim of the central government. (This is clearly only a matter of degree; as in Western economies, revenues from virtually all taxes in Russia depend to some degree on decisions of the central government.) Assigning the enterprise profits tax to subnational governments also creates or accentuates horizontal fiscal disparities,[26] with the more prosperous oblasts having relatively greater fiscal resources than the depressed ones.

Upper-level governments can generally administer any tax that a lower-level government can administer, but the converse is not true. Thus, lower-level governments should have prior claim to any tax that they can effectively administer and that is not inappropriate for them. (The last proviso deserves elaboration. The government of a port city might technically be able to administer customs duties on imports. But it would be inappropriate for it to do so because of the impediment to international trade.) This can be called subsidiarity in taxation. (See subsequent sections for a consideration of the administrative features of various taxes.)

THE SPECIAL CASE OF TAXES ON NATURAL RESOURCES

Taxing natural resources is one of the most important fiscal issues facing Russia. The oil and gas sector, the most important resource sector, is currently depressed, in part because of the failure of other sectors and the governments of consuming jurisdictions to pay for oil and gas deliveries. But it is potentially one of the brightest spots in Russia's future economic landscape. The availability of revenues from oil and gas will be crucial to the fiscal viability of the country. (It is difficult to quantify this statement because it relates to potential revenues. As long as prices are set well below world market prices and debts cannot be collected, the energy sector will continue to require subsidies instead of yielding net public revenue.)

As noted earlier, how these revenues are divided between the central and subnational governments and among the latter will determine the extent of both vertical fiscal imbalance and horizontal fiscal disparities—issues that could be crucial for the viability of the Russian Federation.[27] Those issues are the focus of this discussion.[28]

Some charges and taxes on exploitation of natural resources can be justified on benefit grounds. The most obvious are charges and taxes imposed to cover extraordinary costs of the public sector created by resource industries; for example, for roads that will carry heavy equipment to remote areas. Fees related to damage can also be justified to compensate for environmental degradation. In both cases the jurisdiction where the costs or damage occur should receive the revenues. (Because resource industries go through a natural cycle of development, maturity, and decline, it may be necessary to invest in roads and other infrastructure before tax revenues begin to flow. In some countries enterprises in the resource industry construct and maintain such roads, thereby automatically satisfying the benefit principle. Serious environmental problems sometimes become obvious only after resource extraction has declined and the enterprise responsible for the damage has ceased operations. This suggests that funds from taxes and fees related to expected environmental problems be placed in trust to cover future costs.)

Many taxes on natural resources are levied simply to raise revenue and have no relation to benefits provided by governments or to environmental degradation. Whether revenues from these taxes should accrue to the central government or to subnational governments is a controversial issue that raises fundamental questions about the nature of federalism, as well as questions of equity, economic efficiency, and stability of revenues.[29]

Where important resources are geographically concentrated, subnational taxation can create large fiscal disparities between resource-rich regions and regions that lack resources. The larger tax base of the resource-rich regions allows them to provide more public services or to levy lower nonresource taxes or both. The fiscal advantage of resource-rich regions can induce an excessive in-flow of both people and capital compared with a "level playing field" in which all regions have comparable fiscal capacities. Despite this theoretical argument, it appears that the loss of welfare resulting from such excessive location of economic activity in resource-rich regions is not large.[30]

The existence of large fiscal disparities can also be questioned on grounds of fairness. Why should access to public services depend on where within a federal system one happens to live? During the energy crisis of the late 1970s and early 1980s, fiscal disparities led to talk of blue-eyed Arabs in both the United States and Canada and a new war between the states in the United States.

Revenues from natural resources are generally unstable. Prices and quantities, and with them revenues from taxes and royalties based on the quantity or value of output, move with changes in demand and supply conditions.[31] Taxes on resource rents (the excess of revenues over costs) are even more volatile. As a result, taxes on natural resources generally are not suitable sources of revenues for subnational governments, which need stable and predictable revenues.

The economic inefficiencies, the perceived inequities of fiscal disparities, and the instability of subnational revenues can be avoided if the central government, rather than subnational governments, receives revenues from natural resources in excess of those needed to offset costs of subnational governments. But spokespeople for subnational governments of producing regions argue that those governments are "entitled" to tax natural resources located within their boundaries as their "heritage." This claim—which is circular—raises fundamental questions of the nature of federalism: are the resources the heritage of the entire nation (and therefore properly taxed by the central government) or the heritage of the subnational jurisdiction?[32]

This question is of paramount importance in Russia. If resource-rich regions are allowed large shares in public revenues from exploiting natural resources, fiscal disparities could be enormous. But if they are not, they may prefer to be independent and thus realize all the returns to their resource wealth. It may be important to walk a tightrope—allowing subnational governments enough access to resource revenues to keep them content to remain in the federation while avoiding huge fiscal disparities. This objective should be achieved through the uniform application of a given set of rules, not through special sui generis deals with individual oblasts.[33]

INCOME REDISTRIBUTION AND MACROECONOMIC STABILITY

As indicated, because of the benefits of decentralization, subnational governments can play an important role in achieving efficiency in the provision of public services. By comparison, the central government is commonly assigned primary responsibility for using taxation to reduce inequalities in the distribution of income and to avoid macroeconomic instability.[34]

Taxation and the Distribution of Income. The above discussion of the fairness of fiscal disparities raises a related issue: which level of government should be responsible for implementing tax policies that are intended to reduce inequality in the distribution of income? At a philosophical level, the answer can go either way, depending on whether the "domain of concern" about inequality is nationwide or more limited.[35] Ethnic considerations may enter in, for it would not be uncommon to find that many are most concerned about other members of the same ethnic group.

However this philosophical issue is resolved, there are likely to be practical limitations on the ability of subnational governments to use tax policy to equalize incomes. The two types of taxes commonly used for this purpose in the West are the progressive individual income tax and the corporate (enterprise) income tax.[36] As noted above, excessive taxation of enterprise income can lead to capital avoiding the taxing jurisdiction, resulting in tax incidence on workers and owners of land located where profits are subject to high taxes rather than on owners of enterprises.[37] The same general result is to be expected from excessive subnational taxation of the income of individuals. It would be counterproductive for a subnational government to encourage innovative and hardworking individuals to settle elsewhere by taxing them too heavily.

In principle, the types of pressures just described could be avoided in any of several ways. Subnational governments could agree on minimum tax rates, the central government could require a minimum oblast rate, or the central government could simply assume responsibility for redistributive tax policy. A uniform (minimum) subnational tax is equivalent in its economic effects to a national tax. All these have the disadvantage of eliminating both healthy tax competition between subnational governments and the ability of subnational governments to choose the package of benefits and taxes their constituents want.

It may appear that there is conflict between the prescriptions of progressive national taxation of individual income and flat-rate subnational taxation. This is not true. The two policies can easily coexist to meet two objectives. Of course, it may be desirable to use an administrative arrangement, such as a subnational surcharge, to avoid complexity and duplication of effort in administration and compliance. (See also the next two sections.)

Taxation and Macroeconomic Stability. The central government is also commonly assigned responsibility for macroeconomic stability, the maintenance of full employment, and price stability[38] for the following practical reasons. First, a stimulative fiscal policy commonly involves budget deficits that can only be financed by creating money or issuing debt. Subnational governments commonly lack (and should lack) the power to create money, and their ability to borrow is also commonly limited.[39] Thus their ability to engage in expansionary fiscal policy (and monetary policy) is limited.

Second, most subnational jurisdictions are relatively small and open in the sense of relying on relatively large amounts of imports from outside. This openness implies that much of the expansionary or contractionary effects of macroeconomic policies pursued by subnational governments would "leak" out into the rest of the nation or the rest of the world, making such policies relatively ineffective.

Techniques of Revenue Assignment

There are a number of ways to implement particular patterns of revenue assignment. Four are considered here: independent subnational legislation and administration of taxes, tax surcharges, tax sharing, and revenue sharing.[40] They differ in several respects, including the fiscal autonomy of subnational governments, duplication of effort, the ease of compliance and administration (especially in the case of businesses operating in more than one jurisdiction), and the potential for equalization to reduce horizontal fiscal disparities. The choice between them depends on the economic, political, and institutional realities in a particular country, including the importance placed on subnational fiscal autonomy, administrative and compliance capabilities, the existence of economic differences that could be translated into fiscal disparities, the importance of equalization, and the degree of trust between governments.

Although comments about fiscal autonomy, duplication of effort, and reducing fiscal disparities should be fairly straightforward, those about costs of compliance and administration may not be. The following section will clarify some of this section's inevitably cryptic comments about these aspects of particular taxes.

INDEPENDENT SUBNATIONAL LEGISLATION
AND ADMINISTRATION

The technique that gives subnational governments the most fiscal autonomy involves independent subnational legislation and administration of taxes. This is the technique used most commonly in the United States. Under it, subnational governments define the tax base, choose the tax rate, and administer the tax.[41] This approach gives such governments revenues that are clearly "theirs," a feature that can be especially important in environments where the rule of law is not sufficiently strong to assure that the central government will make the intergovernmental transfers of revenues inherent in the three techniques of revenue assignment discussed below.[42] This approach also avoids the risk that the fiscal authorities of the central government will not devote adequate resources to the administration of taxes from which their government does not get all the revenues.

The potential for duplicating administrative and compliance efforts is an obvious cost of this system. Inconsistencies in the tax laws of the national and subnational governments aggravate these problems, while consistency in laws and intergovernmental cooperation in administration reduce them. Under this approach there is a risk that the legislation of various subnational governments will be so different that compliance is a nightmare for businesses operating in more than one jurisdiction. That has been the experience with state taxes on corporate profits in the United States; see the appendix. The experience of Brazil shows that it is difficult to implement certain types of subnational VAT without extensive cooperation between subnational governments on both base and rates (see the next section).

To minimize duplication of effort, reduce complexity, and discourage evasion, subnational governments may cooperate with one another or with higher levels of government. Cooperation in choosing a consistent definition of the tax base (including methods of apportionment, where relevant) is especially beneficial in reducing complexity and the costs of compliance and administration. By comparison, coordination between subnational governments in the setting of tax rates has costs as well as benefits; uniformity of rates reduces distortions of the location of economic activity, but it also reduces fiscal autonomy and tax competition. (The next two parts of this section explain this in greater detail.)

Cooperation among subnational governments or between them and higher levels of government creates similarities with tax surcharges and tax sharing. As cooperation on the base increases, this approach eventually becomes almost indistinguishable from subnational surcharges on taxes of the central government. If coordination of tax rates is added to the equation, the resemblance is to tax sharing.

For some taxes, there is relatively little need for horizontal cooperation among subnational jurisdictions in defining the tax base or setting tax rates. Taxation of the production of natural resources requires little cooperation. Not much cooperation is needed to implement a retail sales tax (RST) or excise taxes, except for problems posed by cross-border shopping (inherently a difficult problem in the absence of border controls between jurisdictions) and sales made by mail order (which, in principle, can be handled rather easily); it makes little difference whether the sales tax regimes of various subnational governments are different or similar.

SUBNATIONAL SURCHARGE

Under the approach just examined, subnational governments determine both the tax base and the tax rate. Under a second approach, using subnational surcharges on taxes of the central government, subnational governments choose the rate but not the base of taxation; for administrative reasons, the base of the central government must be used, with at most minor variations.[43] This approach avoids the complexity and costs of compliance and administration caused by differences in subnational tax bases, while allowing subnational governments to choose their own tax rates.

The choice of rate is far more important than the precise definition of the tax base for subnational fiscal autonomy. Indeed, U.S. experience with both state retail sales taxes and state corporate income taxes suggests that state autonomy in the determination of tax bases is not necessarily a good thing; many states define taxable sales and taxable profits in ways that defy logic. [44]

In principle, surcharges can be administered by either the higher or the lower level of government. In fact, administration by the lower level has little to recommend it because it involves needless duplication of effort, assuming that the central government will administer its own tax in any event. Like the two alternatives that follow, using surcharges requires that the government administering the tax can be trusted to deliver the funds to the lower-level governments imposing the surcharge.

In Canada, the central government collects the individual income taxes and corporate profits taxes of most of the provinces but on condition that the province adopt the tax base of the central government. [45] Thus, the chaotic complexity that prevails in the United States (described in the appendix) is largely avoided.

In the United States, similar legislation provides for federal collection of income tax for any state that adopts the federal tax base. Thus far, no state has taken advantage of this offer; rather, each state has its own administrative apparatus. In most states the calculation of liability for individual income tax begins with the federal base; in two states the tax is simply a percentage of the federal tax. But there are commonly enough adjustments that these taxes are more appropriately described as separately legislated and administered than as surcharges. In contrast, some of the states collect local surcharges on their retail sales taxes.

Whereas some taxes lend themselves to the imposition of subnational surcharges, others do not. Thus, it is relatively easy to impose surcharges on retail sales taxes, on payroll taxes levied at the point of employment, and on the income taxes of individuals who file federal tax returns but (as explained fully in the next section) difficult to impose surcharges on the VAT; the enterprise profits tax represents an intermediate case in which surcharges are possible based on the use of formulas to allocate profits among subnational jurisdictions.

TAX SHARING

In tax sharing, each level of government takes a given share of the revenues from a particular tax that is levied at a rate determined by only one of them. [46] (By comparison, under the tax surcharge just discussed, the subnational government levies a tax rate of its choosing [within limits] on the base defined and measured by a higher-level government.) Thus, it implicitly extends national control (but not necessarily uniformity) to the aggregate tax rate, as well as the base. This approach further simplifies administration but eliminates the fiscal autonomy of subnational governments, except over the spending of a given amount of money channeled to it via tax sharing. (On the pros and cons of tax sharing, see Bahl and Linn 1992, 434–40.)

Ordinarily shared taxes are administered by the highest level of government that is to receive a substantial share of the revenues to ensure uniformity of administration. Nevertheless, administration by the lower level is clearly feasible under some circumstances, as demonstrated by the German VAT.

Tax sharing has the potential disadvantage of diluting the incentives of the tax administration. (There may be incentives to favor local business if shared taxes are administered by local governments.)

Tax sharing reduces the ability to conduct macroeconomic policy because the subnational government may spend its share of the revenues that result from a tax increase intended to restrain private spending. Conversely, a tax cut intended to stimulate the economy can cause a budgetary crisis for subnational governments. The methods discussed previously do not have this problem; they allow federal conduct of macroeconomic policy that is independent of the tax policy of subnational governments.

Implicit in tax sharing (at least as defined here) is the return of revenues to (or retention of revenues by) the subnational jurisdiction where revenues originate. Like the two techniques of revenue assignment described above, tax sharing does nothing to reduce fiscal disparities between subnational jurisdictions (unless the origin of revenues is defined in such a way as to make tax sharing indistinguishable from revenue sharing, as defined below).

Determining the origin of revenues is relatively straightforward for some taxes: for example, payroll taxes and taxes on the production of natural resources. Determining the origin of revenues from a retail sales tax is only slightly more complicated (again, subject to the difficulties caused by cross-border shopping, noted above; in principle, mail order sales from one oblast to another would be much easier to handle). For other taxes, such as those on value-added and enterprise profits, the situation, for reasons explained in the next section, is not so simple.

The administrative requirements of tax sharing are generally comparable to those of tax surcharges. In both cases it is necessary to have comparable information: for example, the geographic origin of profits in the case of a surcharge and the origin of revenues from the corporate profits tax in the case of tax sharing. This being the case, there is little reason on administrative grounds to prefer tax sharing to subnational surcharges, which provide much more subnational fiscal autonomy.

Table 5.2   Characteristics of Four Methods of Revenue Assignment

Characteristic	Separate Legislation and Administration	Subnational Surcharges	Tax Sharing	Revenue Sharing
Choice of base	Oblast	Center	Center	Center
Choice of rate	**Oblast**	**Oblast**	Center	Center
Administration	Oblast	Center	Center	Center
Revenue flows based on	Oblast tax base	Oblast tax base	Derivation	Formula

REVENUE SHARING

Revenue sharing does not attempt to return revenues to their place of origin; this differentiates it from surcharges and tax sharing. Rather, revenues are divided among subnational governments on the basis of formulas that commonly include population, measures of the need for public revenues, tax (or fiscal) capacity (intended to equalize fiscal capacities), and tax effort (the ratio of tax collections to fiscal capacity).

Provided the requisite data are available, revenue sharing is simple to implement. It does not involve administrative duplication or the need to determine the origin of revenues. Unlike the other three alternatives, it can be used to reduce fiscal disparities through proper choice of elements in the formula. It has one major drawback: it does not provide fiscal autonomy to subnational governments. Like tax sharing, revenue sharing may impede the exercise of macroeconomic policy, though this can be avoided through judicious design of the formula.

EVALUATION

I would now like to summarize the above discussion of the pros and cons of various methods of revenue assignment (see tables 5.2–5.4). The following comments are appropriate.

First, inherent in separate oblast legislation and administration is the potential for inconsistencies in legislation, duplication of effort, and increased costs of compliance and administration. Despite the advantages to oblast autonomy of separate administration, these problems should disqualify this approach from further consideration by Russia for the immediate future (say, the next five to ten years). Separate legislation and administration may, of course, be appropriate once Russia has created a large cadre of well-trained tax administrators and once taxpayers have acquired the knowledge and experience needed to deal with a dual (federal-oblast) system.

Table 5.3   Comparison of Four Methods of Revenue Assignment

Criteria	*Separate Legislation and Administration*	*Subnational Surcharges*	*Tax Sharing*	*Revenue Sharing*
Macroeconomic control	**Acceptable**	**Acceptable**	Poor	Medium
Oblast fiscal autonomy/tax competition	**Highest (good)**	**High (good)**	Low (poor)	Low (poor)
Choice of tax	**Yes (good)**	**Some (OK)**	No (poor)	No (poor)
Tax base	**Yes (good/ mixed)**	**No (OK)**	No (OK)	No (OK)
Tax rate	**Yes (good)**	**Yes (good)**	No (poor)	No (poor)
Duplication of effort	High (poor)	**Low (good)**	**Low (good)**	**Low (good)**
Costs of compliance and administration	High (poor)	**Low; depends on tax (good)**	**Low; depends on tax (good)**	**Low (good)**
Tax service incentives to collect	Not applicable	Medium; depends on central and oblast tax rates	Medium; depends on tax-sharing rates	Medium; depends on revenue-sharing rates
Reduction of fiscal disparities	None (poor)	None (poor)	None (poor)	**Possible (good)**

Second, only a separate oblast tax and an oblast surcharge allow oblasts to choose the tax rate; because this is crucial for fiscal autonomy, the entries showing it are in bold (see table 5.2). (The choice of tax base is secondary.) The lack of fiscal autonomy under tax sharing and revenue sharing is a major fault of those systems.

Third, the first three alternatives are derivation-based, in that they either tax an oblast-specific tax base or return revenues to the oblast of derivation; they provide no equalization of fiscal capacities among oblasts, and they may be counter equalizing. Only revenue sharing admits the use of formulas designed to return revenues to oblasts on a basis other than derivation; thus only revenue sharing can be used to offset horizontal disparities.

This discussion suggests that none of the four options is adequate to serve as

Table 5.4   Advantages and Disadvantages of
Four Methods of Revenue Assignment

Method of Revenue Assignment	Advantages	Disadvantages
Separate legislation and administration	Choice of tax base Choice of tax rate Control of administration	Duplication of administration Administrative/ compliance costs No equalization
Subnational surcharges	**Choice of tax rate** Uniform tax base Unified administration	No choice of tax base **No equalization**
Tax sharing	Unified administration Uniform tax base	No choice of tax base No choice of tax rate No equalization
Revenue sharing	Uniform tax base Unified administration **Equalization possible**	No choice of tax base **No choice of tax rates**

the only method of revenue assignment, but it also shows that a combination of tax surcharges and revenue sharing can achieve most of the goals of revenue assignment. In particular, surcharges can be employed to provide oblasts with a source of revenue over which they have control, through choice of the surcharge rate. Being levied by the central fiscal authorities on the tax base of the central government, surcharges minimize duplication of effort, complexity, and costs of compliance and administration. Neither tax sharing nor separate legislation and administration will suffice for this task; the former does not provide oblast fiscal autonomy, and the latter is too complicated and costly. Finally, revenue sharing is an appropriate complement to tax surcharges, as it allows funds to be directed to poorer oblasts to offset the horizontal fiscal disparities that would result from sole reliance on surcharges.

The bolded entries in table 5.3 indicate that techniques of revenue assignment receive high marks on particular criteria. Surcharges score almost as high as separate legislation and administration in terms of subnational autonomy but far better in terms of duplication of effort and costs of compliance and administration. They are similar to tax sharing in this last respect but far better in terms of fiscal autonomy. Thus they dominate both these alternatives. In contrast, revenue sharing does poorly on these criteria but is the only alternative that can reduce fiscal disparities. Table 5.4 presents the complementarity of tax surcharges and revenue sharing in a somewhat different manner.

The existing Russian system of revenue assignment is primarily one of tax sharing combined with subventions granted largely on an ad hoc basis.[47] The heavy emphasis on tax sharing is unfortunate, as is the ad hoc nature of subventions. Although tax sharing ranks high in terms of avoiding administration and compliance costs, it provides almost no fiscal autonomy for subnational governments. It also does not deal with fiscal disparities except on an ad hoc basis. In general, tax sharing is a poor choice. It would require no more effort to impose a surcharge than to implement tax sharing.

Appraising Particular Taxes

If the reasoning of the previous section is accepted, there remains the question of which taxes can be subjected to oblast surcharges. This depends largely on technical administrative considerations, as well as political questions and the conceptual issues discussed in the first section. In both the *Basic Principles* and in actual practice, Russia seems to have paid little attention to the practical realities of assigning various revenue sources (or to conceptual considerations, for that matter). This section describes some of those practical realities.

INDIVIDUAL INCOME TAX

It can be argued that people consume public services primarily where they live. If this is true, liabilities for a flat-rate, residence-based income tax would be reasonably closely related to benefits of public services. The individual income tax would be an excellent source of revenue for subnational governments, provided that most people either work where they live or file tax declarations.[48]

In fact, neither of these provisos is fulfilled in reality, especially when one considers large metropolitan areas and intraoblast assignment of revenues. Many workers commute to work across oblast boundaries or between smaller jurisdictions within a single oblast. (Some two million persons commute between Moscow oblast and Moscow City each day.)

As noted previously, it is relatively simple to collect a subnational individual income tax where labor income is earned; such a tax can be administered separately or as a surcharge on a tax of the central government. It is also simple to share revenues from a national tax with jurisdictions where employment occurs.

Whether it is equally simple to collect a residence-based individual income tax (perhaps as a surcharge on the tax of the central government) or to direct tax-sharing payments to the jurisdiction of residence depends in part on whether taxpayers file tax returns; if they file returns showing their residential address, levying a residence-based tax or sharing revenues on the basis of residence is relatively simple. But in Russia most taxpayers are not required to file tax returns and, for administrative reasons, should not be.[49] This makes it difficult to collect a residence-based subnational income tax or to share revenues on the basis of residence.

In principle, it should be possible to obtain the information needed for residence-based tax sharing from the records of state enterprises. (It might be too much to expect similar information from private enterprises, except those that previously were state enterprises. Small firms and the self-employed presently escape tax for the most part.) In fact, records seem to be inadequate for this purpose.

It would seem to be fairly simple to rectify this problem: employers need only ask their employees where they live. (Presumably this would be mandated by the central government; it would probably be impossible for an oblast acting alone to obtain the information needed to impose a residence-based income tax from enterprises located in other oblasts.) But if tax rates differ greatly between subnational jurisdictions, to minimize taxation, there will be an incentive to misstate place of residence. This may place an undesirable limit on the ability to use residence-based individual income taxes to finance the services people want and are willing to pay for.

The upshot is that subnational governments will not soon be able to implement residence-based taxation of individual income. Although residence-based sharing of a tax collected by the central government is also not feasible at present, this capacity might develop relatively quickly. In the meantime, taxation by the jurisdiction of employment is likely to be the only practical alternative. This is likely to be satisfactory in most cases but not in all.

ENTERPRISE PROFITS TAX

I argued earlier that, for conceptual reasons, the enterprise profits tax is not appropriate for subnational governments. Administrative considerations accentuate that conclusion.

In modern market economies, enterprises commonly operate in more than one subnational jurisdiction; indeed, many large enterprises operate in dozens of countries through branches or subsidiaries. This implies that it is highly problematic to assign the enterprise profits tax entirely, or even largely, to the oblasts, as Russia has done. At the very least, there are questions of determining the origin of profits; in addition, oblasts may interfere with economic activity to maximize their revenues from the tax on enterprise profits.

If enterprises operate in more than one jurisdiction, it is necessary to determine the geographic source of profits.[50] Russia appears to handle this problem in two ways. In the case of enterprises using separate legal entities to operate in different oblasts, it relies on the breakdown of profits reported in the books of account of the enterprises. By comparison, it divides the profits of a single legal entity operating in several oblasts in proportion to employment in the various oblasts.

It is generally not satisfactory to try to isolate the profits occurring in various oblasts through the use of separate accounting, even if these activities are conducted by different legal entities. In many cases economic activities are interdependent, and it is thus impossible, even as a theoretical matter, to use separate accounting to determine the geographic source of profits. Moreover, if tax rates are not the same in all oblasts, there will be incentives to manipulate transfer prices on transactions between affiliated firms so as to place profits in oblasts with the lowest tax rates. (Of course, oblasts should be allowed to have different rates, in the interest of fiscal autonomy.) Even if there is no attempt to manipulate transfer prices, there may not be enough third-party transactions to form a valid base for calculating transfer prices.

These considerations suggest that the best idea is to use a formula to divide (or apportion) the nationwide profits of multioblast enterprises among the oblasts where they operate. What is being recommended is a tax surcharge, not tax sharing; although there would a uniform determination of profits and their apportionment among the oblasts, oblasts would retain control of the tax rate that would apply to their shares of profits.

It is important that all oblasts use the same definition of taxable income, the same apportionment formula, and the same definition of the taxable entity. Otherwise, there will be gaps and overlaps in the tax base and problems of both compliance and administration. (The appendix indicates how unimpeded state legislation in this area has created chaos in the United States.) The only sensible way to administer such a uniform system is to entrust administration to the central government.

The apportionment formula now being used in Russia, which is based on payrolls alone, is defective. It would be valid only if one ignored the influence of both markets and capital in determining profitability. Although it may be defensible to ignore sales, capital should not be ignored.[51] Production in Russia is very capital-intensive; the apportionment formula should recognize capital's contribution to profits. Moreover, payroll figures do not have the same meaning they have in the West; they are distorted by the extraordinary but far from uniform enterprise provision of fringe benefits such as housing.

Adding property to the apportionment formula would not be easy. Much of Russia's capital is not productive, and much of its industry is not profitable. The central government of Russia does not have good data on the value of business property in the various oblasts. Even if it has data on the original cost of investment, by oblasts, converting such data to current values would be an enormous task, and undertaking such a task only to implement a system of tax sharing or surcharges on the profits tax does not appear to be a good use of the resources of the government or taxpayers.[52] All things taken into account, Russia might want to consider using a three-factor (payroll, property, and sales) formula, which is common in the United States or—if reliable data on the value of capital are not available—a two-factor (payroll and sales) formula such as that employed in Canada.

Like an origin-based VAT, the enterprise income tax can distort locational decisions if it is not levied at uniform rates throughout the nation because enterprise profits are not a good measure of benefits received by enterprises. For this reason, as well as the administrative problems just described, the enterprise profits tax is not a good subnational tax base. Yet it is one of the few taxes on which surcharges can be imposed, thus avoiding a situation of horizontal fiscal imbalance in which subnational governments are starved for revenue. There is thus a conflict between fiscal autonomy, on the one hand, and locational neutrality and administrative considerations, on the other.

VALUE-ADDED TAX

The central government of Russia has been sharing revenues from the VAT with the oblast governments on a derivation basis. Determining the oblast of derivation of VAT revenues, however, raises problems similar to those encountered under the subnational imposition of a VAT. The experience of Brazil—the only country to have adopted a subnational VAT—and the European Union (EU, formerly the European Community)[53] suggests that Russia is making a mistake by sharing VAT revenues. An oblast surcharge would not be any better because it raises similar issues. On these issues, Bahl (1992, 21, 27) writes, "VAT is not appropriate for assignment to the subnational level. . . . Moreover, an unmitigated disaster would result if subnational governments were given the power to make discretionary changes in VAT. The VAT is not an appropriate subject for a surtax."

Interoblast Trade.   There are two ways to deal with domestic trade between oblasts; each has problems. Under the *destination principle,* tax is not collected on trade flowing to another oblast (or is rebated through the use of zero rating), but the importing oblast collects the tax; this is the system commonly employed for international trade. It results in tax being collected by the jurisdiction where consumption occurs.

Implementating the destination principle has commonly been thought to require border controls, which would interfere with the free flow of internal trade. It may be possible to avoid this problem by basing tax liability solely on the enterprises' books of account. Under one scheme, the central government would collect both its own VAT and the VAT of the oblast of destination; purchasers of business inputs would take credit for both taxes as shown on invoices. The central government would serve as a clearinghouse, sending funds to the proper oblast.[54] As yet no country has had the confidence to attempt such a scheme. Given the state of Russian accounting and tax administration (including the computing capacity of the fiscal authorities, which is crucial to the success of such a scheme), it seems unlikely that Russia should do so soon.

Under the *origin principle*, tax is collected by the jurisdiction where production occurs. Thus, if 60 percent of the value of a good is added in one jurisdiction and 40 percent in another, the two jurisdictions would tax those percentages of the total value of the final product. (Under the destination principle, the jurisdiction where consumption occurs would collect all the tax; in the case of exports there would be no Russian tax.) To achieve this result in international trade, all products being imported and exported must be valued. This, along with the apparent disadvantage suffered by domestic producers, helps explain why this system is rarely used.

The origin principle can be implemented on domestic (interoblast) trade if one oblast allows credits for taxes paid to other oblasts.[55] But this approach works satisfactorily only in the context of uniform tax rates. If tax rates are not uniform, the border controls required to implement the origin principle must be more stringent than those under the destination principle because of the incentive to misstate where value added occurs in order to minimize taxes. If rates are not uniform, an origin-based VAT will also distort the location of economic activity in favor of low-tax jurisdictions. Finally, if rates are not uniform, tax is not truly levied on value added in a given jurisdiction. Brazil has encountered all these problems because it levies different rates on interstate and intrastate trade. Of course, the requirement of uniform rates would vitiate one of the primary reasons for wanting to assign VAT revenues to subnational governments, fiscal autonomy.

It is worth noting that in the early 1960s the European Common Market (ECM, now the European Union) decided to adopt the origin principle for trade within the ECM (but not for trade external to the ECM, hence the term *restricted origin principle*). But because of the need for uniform tax rates, this decision has never been implemented.

Triangular Trade.   Brazil, which uses the restricted origin principle, has a particular pattern of trade that creates another problem that appears to have its counterpart in Russia. In Brazil, a disproportionate share of imports come in through the relatively prosperous South and exports leave through the poverty-stricken Northeast. As a result of the workings of the restricted origin principle, the southern states, on balance, collect VAT on imports and the northeastern states rebate taxes on exports. For years, Brazil has used a controversial system of interstate payments to compensate for this unsatisfactory arrangement.

By assigning a portion of revenues to its oblasts and municipalities on the basis of derivation of revenues, Russia has created the same problem. Oblasts and cities where the export terminals of oil pipelines are located may be asked, in effect, to rebate some of the tax collected by other oblasts. Similarly, oblasts and cities through which imports flow may be able to siphon off a share of the tax paid on goods consumed elsewhere. Such a system makes no sense.

Moreover, the law, which is somewhat murky, and the way it is interpreted provide opportunities for manipulation, disputes, and abuse. It appears that the contractual terms under which imports and exports occur determine which oblast and city are obligated to rebate VAT on exports and which are entitled to collect tax on imports. This is also not satisfactory.

The Russian Situation. Russia has deviated from the standard destination principle, consumption-based, credit method VAT in several ways.[56] First, imports are exempt from VAT. Second, it employs a form of subtraction method tax in the case of wholesalers and retailers (that is, tax is levied on the difference between purchases and sales; under the credit method, tax paid on purchases is subtracted from the tax on sales). Third, it does not allow immediate credits or deductions for all business purchases; this is true for goods added to inventory as well as for capital investments. Fourth, in the case of trade with other members of the former Soviet Union, it employs a hybrid system that contains elements of an origin principle tax.[57]

All these deviations complicate the Russian VAT and make sharing its revenues even less appropriate than the description above suggests. I will mention a few of the problems. Using subtraction for wholesalers and retailers implies a need to value goods moving between oblasts to prevent understatement of exports and overstatement of imports.

Wholesalers and retailers are allowed to take deductions for purchases only when goods are sold, not when they are bought, as under the standard consumption-based tax. This requirement is implemented by tracking particular products, where possible. In principle, this tracking makes it possible to determine the oblast where value added occurs; in fact, tracking and thus implementing the system is not feasible.

The combination of exempting imports and applying the subtraction method to wholesale transactions implies that the preimport value of imported finished goods automatically escapes tax. (By comparison, exempting imports of products undergoing further processing before sale is irrelevant because of the mechanics of the credit method.) By treaty manufacturers are allowed credit for VAT paid to other republics of the former Soviet Union; the credit depends on the tax rate in the exporting republic. These features further complicate assigning value-added revenues to particular oblasts.

Summary Assessment. In principle, some of these problems could be overcome by adopting a standard VAT and carefully drafting laws and regulations. But not all problems can be overcome in this way; some are inherent in the decision to share revenues from the VAT. Thus, the VAT should be reserved for financing the central government. If it is desirable to channel VAT revenues to subnational governments, it should be via revenue sharing, with no pretense at sharing on the basis of derivation of revenues, not via tax sharing (or a subnational surcharge).

EXCISES

In principle, excise taxes can be excellent sources of revenues for subnational governments, which can vary their tax rates to reflect their preferences for public services. They can reasonably be used to finance such public services as roads and highways and the care of those suffering from the effects of smoking and the abuse of alcohol. To do so, they must be assigned to the jurisdictions where consumption occurs; it makes no sense to assign revenues to the jurisdiction where excisable goods are manufactured or imported, as they are in Russia. (Excises related to environmental degradation represent an exception; they should be assigned to the polluted area.) The problem is achieving consumption-based taxation.

Motor vehicle registration fees are an ideal source of revenue for subnational governments because they are relatively easy to administer and they reflect benefits received. (They can be justified on the grounds of vertical equity, but that is primarily a national concern.) They are superior to excises on vehicle purchases in a country where both smuggling and automobile theft are problems. (If a car is stolen, the posttheft owner must pay the registration fee and the original owner does not lose the value of the unamortized excise tax.) Substantial uniformity of rates is needed to prevent improper registration in low-tax oblasts.

Motor fuel taxes can serve as surrogates for benefit charges for the use of roads and highways. Whether they can be levied by oblasts where consumption occurs depends on the technology of distribution. Differential subnational taxation is feasible if pumps at retail outlets have sealed meters. Failing this, taxes could be collected at the refinery (or point of importation) and divided among oblasts on the basis of the records of distributors and pipelines. This is likely to be workable in the relatively densely populated western part of Russia, where there are many relatively small oblasts, only if tax rates are essentially uniform. Otherwise, records will be falsified and drivers will buy fuels in low-tax jurisdictions.

Taxing alcoholic beverages and tobacco products in the jurisdiction of consumption is problematic, unless tax rates are uniform, because of the ease of transporting these commodities from one place to another. In some countries tax stamps are used to indicate whether tax has been paid to the appropriate subnational jurisdiction.

NATURAL RESOURCES

In addition to the crucial philosophical and political issues raised earlier, there are important practical questions of tax administration and economics in the assignment of taxes on natural resources.

Economic efficiency in the taxation of natural resources requires that a tax be levied on economic rents—the difference in revenues and costs of production. (This statement sets aside those taxes required to cover costs of public services to the extractive sector and environmental degradation.) Relatively few governments have tried to tax resource rents, especially subnational governments, which have generally been content to tax the volume or value of output or (in the United States, where natural resources generally are not publicly owned) the value of mineral property. Such taxes are likely to induce suboptimal decisions.

EVALUATION

This discussion does not lead to great optimism. There are few taxes that can easily be subject to surcharges levied by subnational governments. (The problem would be no less daunting for tax sharing.) The VAT clearly should not be subject to a subnational surcharge or tax sharing with subnational governments.

Similar conclusions apply to the enterprise profits tax but not so strongly; necessity may require that there be subnational surcharges on profits deemed to be earned in particular oblasts, despite the disadvantages and difficulties of doing so. It is important that the system that implements such a policy be carefully designed; the present approach is not viable in the long run. Although some variation in tax rates can be tolerated, excessive variation could cause distortions of the location of economic activity and manipulation of the location of profits for tax purposes.

Individual income appears to be the best of the four alternatives for subnational governments. Unfortunately, revenue from a surcharge on individual income cannot easily be attributed to jurisdictions of residence. Attribution based on information supplied by workers may be inaccurate if there are substantial differences in tax rates across subnational jurisdictions. This is, of course, important in only a few oblasts.

To implement consumption-based excises (or subnational surcharges) on motor fuels, alcoholic beverages, and tobacco products, it would probably be necessary to rely on information on the destination of shipments from refineries, distilleries, breweries, factories, and ports. This might work satisfactorily in the case of motor fuels. But, given the ease of transporting alcoholic beverages and tobacco products, this may work for them only if differences in tax rates are small enough that there is little incentive for abuse.

Summary and Conclusions

THE BASIC PROPOSAL

A consideration of conceptual and administrative features of various methods of assigning revenues to subnational governments in the Russian Federation leads to several basic conclusions. First, to provide subnational governments with the independent sources of revenue needed for fiscal autonomy, Russia should shift from tax sharing to tax surcharges. Tax sharing does not provide fiscal autonomy because subnational governments have no control over tax rates. Although subnational tax rates might be constrained to fall within a certain (wide) range, there is no reason to expect them to be uniform across taxes or jurisdictions. Although separately legislating and administering subnational taxes would provide far more local autonomy, the costs of duplication and potential complexity are unacceptable. Surcharges provide a feasible and attractive middle ground between a system based on separate legislation and administration and one based on tax sharing.

The most important source of surcharge revenue would be the individual income tax. Beyond this, the choice of taxes on which surcharges might be imposed is limited by administrative realities. Indeed, given the difficulty of imposing surcharges on some tax bases, subnational governments should probably continue to receive all the revenue from the individual income tax, except that from graduated rates intended to reduce inequalities in the distribution of income.

Surcharges on the VAT should not be attempted for reasons stated earlier. Excises, with revenues flowing to the subnational government where consumption occurs, form a conceptually attractive base for surcharges and should be used to the extent possible. But administrative problems may stymie this approach for the foreseeable future. Excise revenues should not be assigned to the places where production and importation occur.

The individual income tax and excises are unlikely to provide adequate revenues for subnational governments for the foreseeable future. (The sum total of 100 percent of individual income tax revenues, 100 percent of revenues from excises, and the subnational part of "all other taxes" in table 5.5 is less than half the amount subnational governments received from these sources, the VAT, and the enterprise profits tax in 1992.) It seems inevitable that the enterprise profits tax will provide a substantial amount of revenues for subnational governments for the foreseeable future.[58] Surcharges should be imposed using a common definition of profits (not subject to subnational discretion) and a formula that recognizes the contribution to the profits of multijurisdictional enterprises of economic activity located in various jurisdictions; the current method of

Table 5.5   Revenue Assignment, 1992 and 1993 (projected)
             (collections in billions of rubles)

| Tax | 1992 COLLECTIONS | | PERCENT SUBNATIONAL | |
	Total	Subnational Share	1992	1993 Budget
Individual income tax	431.3	431.3	100.0	100.0
Enterprise income tax	1,566.8	920.9	58.8	66.7
Value-added tax (VAT)	1,998.9	498.7	24.9	30.4
Excises	211.5	110.8	52.3	61.5
Foreign trade taxes	467.4	8.0	1.7	NA[1]
All other taxes	1,566.1	374.3	23.9	NA[1]
Total taxes	5,313.7	2,529.5	47.6	43.4
Individual/enterprise income taxes, VAT, and excises	4,205.5	1,960.9	46.6	63.2

[1] NA = not applicable

SOURCE: Ministry of Finance data, reported in Bahl, Martinez-Vazquez, and Wallace (1993).

determining the geographic derivation of profits should be abandoned at the earliest opportunity.

Second, Russia almost certainly needs to utilize some form of revenue sharing to prevent vertical fiscal imbalance, to equalize the fiscal capacities of subnational governments, and perhaps to reflect differences in need.[59] Relying solely on derivation-based assignment of revenues (whether via separate subnational legislation and administration, surcharges, or tax sharing) would produce unacceptable horizontal disparities in the fiscal capacities of subnational governments. Moreover, if subnational governments were to receive all the revenues from the individual income tax, excises, and half the enterprise profits tax, they would still not have enough revenues. (See the data on 1992 and 1993 collections in table 5.5. In 1993, subnational governments were budgeted to receive 30 percent of revenues from the VAT in addition to all revenues from the individual income tax, 67 percent of revenues from the enterprise profits tax, and more than 60 percent of revenues from excises.) Presumably, shared revenues would come from the central government's portion of the most important taxes (enterprise profits, individual income, VAT, and excises), plus others. The present system of subventions, based on discretion and negotiation, should be eliminated.

Third, one of the most important issues of fiscal federalism—the assignment of revenues from taxes on natural resources—has no easy answer. There are strong conceptual arguments for substantial centralization of revenues but equally strong political arguments against it.

Fourth, to prevent the Russian Federation's dying a fiscal death similar to that of the Soviet Union, reforms must be undertaken to increase the accountability of regional tax authorities to the central government and to assure the upward flow of revenues due the central government. Although a full discussion is beyond the scope of this chapter, it is clear that these tax authorities should not depend on subnational governments for their office space, housing, and fringe benefits. Also, geographic rotation of tax officials will help prevent their becoming clients of subnational governments (see also Bahl 1992). Banks should be under strict obligation to channel tax revenues to the proper levels of government. The adoption of surcharges may facilitate this by fixing distinct liabilities to the various levels of government.

Fifth, the opposite problems—the tax service's lack of incentives to collect taxes that flow largely to subnational governments and the risk that subnational governments will not actually receive revenues collected on their behalf—must also be addressed. Again, those issues cannot be addressed in depth here, but two observations can be offered. First, clear instructions to banks and using surcharges, instead of tax sharing, may benefit subnational governments, as well as the central government. Second, consideration might be given to having representatives of subnational governments sit on oversight committees charged with supervising the work of the tax service to give them a voice in the allocation of the service's resources and to ensure that the tax service is conducting its activities in strict compliance with the law.

This proposal for revenue assignment stands in marked contrast to both current practice and the *Basic Principles*; see table 5.1 for a comparison. The *Basic Principles* makes assignments that are questionable (the enterprise tax entirely to the oblast level) or undesirable if the alternative is feasible (certain excises to the central level). Current practice is almost as bad (31.25 percent of the enterprise tax shared with the oblasts), as bad (excises), or worse (24 to 50 percent of the VAT shared with the oblasts). Because both systems channel revenues to the place of economic activity or the origin of revenues, they lack the equalizing features provided by revenue sharing and cry out for the use of subventions, which in actuality are made on a discretionary basis, to deal with the revenue shortfalls, especially in the poorest regions.

COMPARISON WITH WORLD BANK PROPOSALS

The proposals made above differ somewhat from those of a World Bank study (Bahl 1992) that proposed sharing a pool of revenues from the four major taxes (enterprise profits, individual income, VAT, and excises). Under the World Bank proposal, part of the pool would be shared on the basis of the derivation of particular taxes and part would be shared on the basis of a formula that reflects need and fiscal capacity. For reasons similar to those stated above, the VAT would be excluded from the pool to be shared on the basis of derivation. In the terminology of this chapter, this proposal might be described as a having two components: (1) tax sharing (on a derivation basis) for part of the revenues from the individual income tax, corporate profits tax, and excises and (2) revenue sharing for part of these revenues, plus the VAT.

Leaving aside certain procedural differences (e.g., determination of the overall size of the pool to be shared in the World Bank study but not here), the proposals differ primarily in the choice of tax surcharges here and tax sharing in the World Bank study. This does not appear to be an insurmountable difference. As Bahl (1992) notes with regard to surcharges on the individual income tax, "The added administrative burden imposed by this system is surprisingly small." It appears that the same can be said for surcharges on the enterprise profits tax and excises. It is true that it is not possible to impose surcharges on either of these in the refined manner that is ideal because of lack of information (for example, on the consumption of excisable products and the location of property and the destination of sales). But those defects are equally troubling to efforts to share revenues on the basis of derivation.

POLITICAL PROSPECTS

The present system is not working well. It denies subnational governments needed fiscal autonomy. Moreover, it gets too little money to the subnational jurisdictions that need it most even when one factors in ad hoc grants made as a result of negotiation and the exercise of discretion. This helps explain demands to replace tax sharing with *tax assignment*—a term that is not always clear. The proposed system deals explicitly with both these problems. Tax surcharges are a form of tax assignment.

It is far from clear whether Russia is likely to adopt any system that involves a substantial amount of revenue sharing intended to equalize fiscal capacity. Commenting on the political viability of a system of equalizing grants, Craig and Kopits suggest that "at first glance, the design and implementation of the scheme looks like a pipe dream, in view of the weak sense of solidarity among regions following the collapse of the totalitarian unitary system." It is unclear whether equalizing revenue sharing would be the glue that holds the federation together or the wedge that drives it apart. Of course, a common feature of both the present proposals and those of the World Bank is that the weight placed on equalization can be varied by changing the revenue-sharing formula.

It may be appropriate to conclude with the following quotation from the World Bank study:

The importance of developing a framework such as this, built on consensus, and in the context of an institutional process to which all oblasts and the central government adhere cannot be overstated. An intergovernmental system which is perceived to be fair and equitable in a country such as Russia, has the potential to defuse other difficult resource allocation issues in the federation, such as the sharing of natural resources, and the demands for autonomy on parts of oblasts with ethnic populations. A transparent and fair system—where all agree on the rules—means that oblasts do not need to hold on to the few bargaining chips— natural resources, their revenue share—they feel they have. In sum, at a time when nation building is paramount, a well designed intergovernmental fiscal system has a contribution to make to this end. (Bahl 1992, 28.)

Appendix
Formula Apportionment in the United States: Chaos to Be Avoided

If one writes the formula for tax liability under an apportioned state profits tax, as it is commonly applied in the United States, one finds that virtually everything is up for grabs.[*] Thus,

$$T_i = \frac{t_i \times P\,[f_w(W_i/W) + f_a(A_i/A) + f_s(S_i/S)]}{f_w + f_a + f_s},$$

where,
T_i is tax liability in state i,
t_i is the tax rate in state i,
P is the company's taxable profits,
W_i, P_i, and S_i are payroll, property, and sales in state *i*,
W, A, and S are the company's total payroll, property, and sales, and
f_w, f_a, and f_s are the weights given payroll, property, and sales.

In the United States the tax rate and the ratio of in-state to out-of-state payroll are the only parts of the right-hand side of this formula that have not been subject to considerable controversy. (The law determining the location of employment for purposes of unemployment compensation is commonly used to define the latter; this is not required.)

Within extremely broad limits, each state can adopt its own definition of taxable profits; there is no requirement of conformity with the federal definition

---

[*]This appendix appears, with slight modifications, in McLure (1993b; 1993c; 1994a).

or the laws of other states. Similarly, states need not treat sales in the same way. Most measure sales at destination, but others measure them at origin. Some (an increasing number) depart from the typical formula by double weighting sales. Some states that generally measure sales at destination apply a "throw-back" rule, whereby they also include sales originating within their boundaries that are made to a state that does not tax corporate profits or in which the firm does not have taxable nexus (one of the few issues on which the law is relatively clear, thanks to a 1959 decision of the Supreme Court). No effort is made to distinguish between sales made to final consumers and sales to business; thus the tax on the portion of profits apportioned by the sales factor resembles a turnover tax. Double weighting sales increases this tendency.

Nor is there agreement about the entity to which the formula is to be applied. Some states adopt a strict legal entity approach. This opens the door for abuse through manipulation of transfer prices, as well as failing to recognize difficulties inherent in isolating the income of related enterprises. Others combine related companies deemed to be engaged in a "unitary business," but there is no accepted definition of what a unitary business is. Some states apply the unitary combination on a worldwide basis, whereas others restrict the use of combination to "the water's edge," apportioning only profits deemed to be earned in the United States.

The treatment of intercorporate dividends is particularly troublesome. Dividends flowing between firms filing combined reports are eliminated from the calculation. Some other dividends are taxed, but others are exempt; this varies from state to state.

The result of this chaotic situation is inequity, distortion of economic choices, excessive costs of compliance and administration, protracted litigation, annoyance of the trading partners of the United States, and taxpayer uncertainty. The constitutionality of certain features of the system are under review by the Supreme Court—and have been for over a decade. *

Much of the problem could be eliminated by choosing a common definition of profits (ideally the definition used by the federal government), a common apportionment formula, common ways to measure the factors in the formula, a common definition of the taxable entity, and uniform treatment of dividends. Given all this uniformity, it would make no sense to have a totally decentralized administration.

These problems are essentially avoided in Canada because the taxes of most of the provinces are administered by the central government, using a uniform definition of the tax base and a single formula based on sales and payroll. The Canadian approach (though not necessarily the Canadian apportionment for-

---

*This stands in marked contrast to the situation at the federal level, where there are few constitutional challenges to the income taxes.

mula) is the only one Russia should consider. Even this approach is not without problems, however.

In addition to administrative problems, formula apportionment creates economic distortions. Basing apportionment on payrolls and property (and on sales of capital goods and intermediate products) attributes most corporate profits to states where production occurs, rather than to states where consumption occurs. The inclusion of sales in the apportionment formula, although it has the apparent advantage of giving some weight to the consuming jurisdiction, introduces an element of turnover tax into the formula; this is undesirable.

Notes

1. Rikker (1964, 11) defines a federal system as having three characteristics: a hierarchy of governments, a delineated scope of authority, and institutionalized autonomy at each level of government; see also Weingast (1993). Many more countries are, of course, formally organized as federations. Bird (1993b) notes that only about seven developed countries (the four listed, plus Austria, Belgium, and Switzerland) and three developing countries (Brazil, India, and Nigeria) actually function as federations. The rest, while legally organized as federations, operate more like unitary systems. Most of the examples in this chapter are drawn from the five countries listed, plus China and Ukraine (which are not federations) and, of course, Russia itself.

2. Autonomous republics, *krais, okrugs*, and cities having the status of oblasts, as well as the more numerous oblasts, are subjects of federation. For expositional convenience, this chapter uses the term *oblast* in generic collective references to all these.

3. Although necessary to make the analysis manageable, limiting the focus of the chapter in this way is somewhat artificial. Revenue assignment cannot be fully divorced from the other three topics (expenditure assignment, intergovernmental transfers, and borrowing authority of subnational governments). Indeed, as Bahl (1992, 1994) notes, assigning revenues before assigning expenditures puts the horse before the cart. Moreover, intraoblast assignment of revenues is also important; see Bahl and Wallace (1994) and Bahl et al. (1993a, 62–70). By implication the chapter does address the assignment of revenues from taxes on natural resources to local governments—one of the most crucial questions in this area.

4. For other examples of special fiscal regimes, see Litvack (1992) and "Russian Federation: TACIS—Policy Advice" (1993).

5. Craig and Kopits (1993) note that in a meeting with regional leaders in Petrozavodak on October 13, 1993, President Boris Yeltsin threatened to use force, if necessary, to suppress separatist tendencies.

6. Regions that supported Yeltsin in his confrontation with the parliament in October 1993 demanded greater independence and fiscal autonomy as their reward. Access to sales and income taxation were mentioned as important components of fiscal autonomy.

7. The description, which focuses on major taxes, is based on Bahl (1992, 1994) and Bahl et al. (1993), as well as the *Basic Principles*.

8. To avoid possible confusion, this chapter uses the term *profits tax* to refer to what, in the West, might be called either an income tax or a profits tax. Readers should be aware, however, that in Russia these last two terms have quite different meanings. In Russian terminology, an income tax does not allow the deduction of payments to labor in calculating the tax base, but a profits tax does. Russia (like some other members of the former Soviet Union) has used the income tax in an effort to hold down wages paid by state enterprises. It has vacillated between the two in its recent taxation of enterprises; it is now using the profits tax but is imposing an extra tax on wages in excess of a certain amount. The defects of an income tax, including its lack of credibility in capital-exporting countries, are troublesome, but they are not the topic of this chapter, which focuses on intergovernmental fiscal relations, rather than structural tax policy. For this reason, the remainder of this chapter deals only with assigning the profits tax, which one hopes will ultimately replace the income tax. For further discussion of this issue, see McLure (1994a).

9. The *Basic Principles* prescribes the following division of revenues from the production levy in these two cases (production in and not in an *okrug*):

Level of government	Okrug	Nonokrug
Central government	20%	40%
Oblast	20%	30%
Okrug	30%	—
Rayon or city	30%	30%

The first column is especially important because, as noted earlier, the Siberian *okrugs* of Khanti-Mansisk (oil) and Yamal (gas) produce more than 80 percent of Russia's oil. For a further description and discussion of Russia's taxation of oil, focusing on questions of revenue assignment, see McLure (1992a, 1994b).

10. This discussion draws on Wallich (1994).

11. In correspondence with the author, Roy Bahl made the following comment about the Russian system that is equally pertinent to the Soviet system it supplanted:

> The formal Russian system of subnational finance is a veil anyway. Variable VAT sharing (ad hoc determination); CIT, PIT and excise derivation based sharing; subventions (ad hoc); expenditure assignment (ad hoc); budget approval. Change any one of these . . . to make it more transparent, and [they] will just alter something else. In the end they will make it come out the way they want. You need to see the whole picture to see the folly of, for example, changing the method of VAT sharing as they did in 1993.

12. One is reminded of the fractiles that apparently characterize much of the physical world; see Gleick (1993).

13. It might be said that the *Basic Principles* would have abolished the concept of regulating taxes, leaving only fixed taxes.

14. In early 1992 the oblasts received revenues from only 15 percentage points of the

profits tax. The oblast rate was increased to 19 percent in the third quarter of 1992 and to 22 percent for 1993. Oblasts are allowed to reduce their share of the aggregate tax rate by 2 percentage points (i.e., to 20 percent).

15. In actuality, the oblasts have severely limited discretion in varying their part of the tax rate applied to enterprise profits (they can reduce their rate from 22 to 20 percent and thus the aggregate rate from 32 to 30 percent) and in providing tax exemptions for profits from certain activities occurring within their jurisdictions. To the extent that oblasts can choose their own tax rates, the system of revenue assignment applied to the enterprise profits tax might better be described as an oblast surcharge. I address this issue in a subsequent section.

16. This terminology (*tax sharing*) seems appropriate even in the case of the individual income tax, with its oblast share of 100 percent, because the tax rate and base are determined centrally, oblasts do not have the authority to choose their own tax rates, and the tax is administered by the central government.

17. This description draws on Wallich (1992a, 1992b, 1994).

18. The mechanics of converting a top-down system to a bottom-up system are more complicated than described here. Oblast control of local banks has presumably also been involved. While recognizing this problem, "Russian Federation: TACIS—Policy Advice" (1993, 8) suggests that this may have changed, at least in some places: "We were also told, however, that the tax return contains separate sections in relation to Federal and regional obligations; and that the banks are required to make separate credit transfers of the relevant sums."

19. Implicit in this discussion is the view that most important "public services" will eventually be provided by governments—or at least financed by them—rather than being provided by enterprises, as under the Soviet system. This does not necessarily mean that the services will be produced by governments; they could be produced privately under government contracts, or individuals or households could purchase them from private firms using vouchers provided by the government. These important issues are well beyond the scope of this chapter.

20. Economies of scale exist if it is not necessary to increase all inputs proportionately to get a given increase in output. They result in a decline in the average cost of production as output increases.

21. This is not intended to be a complete discussion of the attributes of efficient government. At most these are necessary conditions for efficiency; they are not sufficient. It is also necessary to have a locally elected legislative body, a locally selected chief administrative officer, and local power to determine the budget. This does not describe the situation in Russia. See also Bahl and Linn (1992, chap. 12).

22. There is also a strong case for benefit financing of services provided by national governments. But benefit financing is generally more feasible in the case of services provided by subnational governments. Moreover, national governments, not subnational ones, are commonly thought to have important responsibilities for redistribution of income; redistribution requires resorting to taxes not related to benefits.

23. In this regard it is useful to distinguish between the convergence of tax systems that is induced by tax competition and the convergence that occurs when jurisdictions agree

not to compete. The analogy to the determination of prices in a cartel and under competitive conditions is instructive. Cartels attempt to maintain uniform prices at a level that exceeds costs by suppressing competition. By comparison, in a competitive industry prices tend toward uniformity at a level approximating costs. Just as consumers benefit from competition in the market sector, users of public services fare better when governments compete.

24. Bahl (1992, 158) writes of the intraoblast division of revenues from the individual income tax, "the assignment of all individual income tax revenues to the rayon of work seems unfair because the rayon of *residence* provides basic services (education, health) to the workers and is not compensated. In border cities, even the oblast of residence will receive no revenue." Bahl notes in correspondence with the author that oblasts can alter intraoblast sharing rates for the VAT to compensate for the effects of commuting within the oblast.

Like the statement in the text, this discussion is based on an implicit assumption that many services now provided by enterprises will be provided by governments. As long as services are provided by enterprises, it makes little sense to speak of benefit-related taxes.

25. See McLure (1980a, 1981). For purposes of this discussion, factors of production are labor, capital, and land.

26. Bahl (1992, 20) concludes from his analysis of the effects of implementing the *Basic Principles*, "These changes will go against the poorer oblasts."

27. The movement of domestic oil prices to world prices would increase revenues oil-rich oblasts receive from production taxes, while perhaps reducing the amounts the central government receives from export taxes, which have been used to equalize the net returns from domestic and export sales. In addition, by depressing production in energy-intensive industries, higher energy prices would reduce revenues in energy-consuming oblasts. I am indebted to Craig and Kopits (1993) for these observations. It is worth noting that energy taxes would not be exported to consumers of energy (and energy-intensive products) via higher prices. The increase in energy prices would burden consumers; higher taxes would shift part of the potential increase in resource rents from energy companies to governments.

28. It is important that resource taxes be designed carefully, so that they will not distort decisions. (This statement is based on the admittedly heroic assumption that other impediments to efficiency have been reduced to the point that one can be confident that neutral tax policy is a defensible objective.) See McLure (1992a) for a discussion of taxes on resource rents, which do not distort many decisions.

29. This discussion draws on McLure (1992a, 1994a, 1994b) and McLure and Wallich (forthcoming), which discuss several topics not covered here, including techniques for the taxation of resource rents, the claims of indigenous groups and others to income from exploitation of natural resources, alternative use of revenues from natural resources, and the potential role of "trust funds" in converting resource wealth into financial capital.

30. On this, see Mieszkowski (1983), Mieszkowski and Toder (1983), and Watson (1986). I am grateful to David Sewell for the last reference.

31. Subnational governments commonly tax the quantity or the value of output of natural resources. This is true partly as a matter of expediency. Whereas subnational

governments have access to the information needed to tax the quantity or value of output, they lack some of the information needed to tax economic rents. Yet from the point of view of economic efficiency, economic rent is the far superior tax base. Consuming jurisdictions use formula apportionment to divide the income of multijurisdictional firms. Subnational taxation of rents and formula apportionment generally produce inconsistent results. These are further reasons to favor taxation of natural resources by the central government.

32. McLure (1992a, 1994b) asks whether the "domain of concern" is the nation or the subnational jurisdiction. Stated differently, who are "we" and who are "they"?

33. The suggestion in "Russian Federation: TACIS—Policy Advice" that, given the situation in which "the Federal government has reached agreements with some regions whereby the region receives a proportion of natural resource tax revenues, . . . the best way forward would be for the Federal government to reach individual agreements with the affected regions on the proportion of tax revenues from natural resource exploitation to be retained by the region" is unsettling. This seems to be a recipe for disaster. But going back on deals already made is also problematic.

34. It is worth noting that under the Soviet system a variety of tools were used to prevent the emergence of inequalities in the distribution of income; these included guaranteed employment, equalization of wages, price controls, and social benefits, many of which were provided by state enterprises. The budgetary procedures described earlier may also have contributed to the achievement of this objective. The problems associated with cyclical instability in the West, unemployment and inflation, were avoided by fiat, by guaranteeing full employment and stable prices—but not without the cost of disguised unemployment and shortages.

35. As in note 32, who are "we" and who are "they"?

36. A few countries have taxes on net wealth. For administrative reasons, it is unlikely that these will merit consideration in Russia for the foreseeable future. It might, however, be reasonable to use some forms of visible wealth as a presumptive measure of income.

37. This discussion assumes privatization of enterprises. In the absence of privatization it makes little sense to discuss using enterprise taxation to reduce inequalities in the distribution of income.

38. Some would argue that governments cannot do much to affect macroeconomic variables, except in the short run. This chapter does not address that issue. The question at hand is which level of government, if any, should be responsible for macroeconomic stability?

39. In market economies, limits on the ability of subnational governments to issue debt take three forms: bondholder reluctance to hold the debt, constraints imposed by higher-level governments, and constitutional and legal limits contained in the constitution of the subnational government itself. The first of these operates in Russia, making it virtually impossible for any level of government to issue debt, except to multinational organizations, foreign governments, and the banking sector.

The second deserves special mention. It would be a serious mistake for the central government of Russia to guarantee the debt of subnational governments or to allow those governments to issue debt to the banking sector, especially to banks they control. Either could undermine macroeconomic policy. In fact, the January 1993 law on local budgets, while laudably absolving the central government of responsibility for financing the budgetary shortfalls of subnational governments, gives these governments the authority to issue bonds and borrow from banks. Moreover, state enterprises owned by subnational governments also borrow from banks, which are often captive organizations. This contributes to the problem of excessive credit that threatens the economic stability of Russia.

40. There is no commonly accepted terminology in this area. This is unfortunate because different persons use the same terms to mean different things. Bahl (1992, 2) uses the term *tax assignment* to describe separate (and sole) legislation and administration of a tax by a subnational government, calls tax surcharges *tax base sharing*, and treats what is here called revenue sharing as a variant of tax sharing. By comparison, "Russian Federation: TACIS" says the present Russian system is based on tax assignment (not tax sharing) and advocates a surcharge, calling it a form of tax assignment. For another attempt at a taxonomy, see Bahl and Linn (1992, 432–33). The terms adopted here have the advantage of describing each approach accurately, if not completely, in a few words. Separation of taxing powers—the unique assignment of particular taxes to specific levels of government—has little to recommend it; see McLure (1993).

41. For expositional parsimony, the discussion that follows refers only to choosing "the tax rate," even though more than one rate or a schedule of rates may be involved.

42. This sentence assumes that taxes are collected by the central government, which may or may not pass funds on to subnational governments. As the earlier discussion indicates, the opposite problem—subnational retention of federal funds—has plagued Russia (and the Soviet Union before it).

43. In principle, the central government could levy a surcharge on a subnational tax. Although this approach is sometimes advocated by those who do not think through the consequences and is even used occasionally, it has little to recommend it and is not considered further.

44. For example, some states impose retail sales taxes on sales to business but exempt services utilized primarily by households. Some states tax dividends received by one corporation from another and, via the "throw-back" rule, count sales made to states that have no corporate income taxes as in-state sales in calculating the ratio of in-state to total sales for the apportionment formulas used to divide the profits of multistate firms between states; see also the appendix. This is not to say that the tax bases would be any more sensible if defined by the federal government.

45. The provinces that do not take advantage of this offer apparently prefer to retain the option of using their tax systems to attract economic activity.

46. It seems useful to include, under the rubric of tax sharing, cases where one level of government receives all the revenue from a tax if a different level of government sets the tax rate, as well as defining the tax base, as in the case of the Russian tax on individual income.

47. As noted earlier, the oblasts of Russia can, within narrow limits, vary the rate of enterprise profits tax from which they obtain revenue (but not the part going to the central government). Formally this arrangement could be described as an oblast surcharge that is subject to a lower limit. But oblast latitude is so severely limited that it may be better to

describe it as tax sharing. On the other hand, as Roy Bahl has noted in personal correspondence with the author, "if you take tax administration into account, you get some local autonomy . . . , in the form of discretional administration."

Bahl has also expressed some concern with the classification of the VAT as a shared tax because the VAT sharing rates for the various oblasts are set on an ad hoc basis, instead of being uniform. Bahl and Linn (1992, 432–33) distinguish between determination of the size of the pool of funds to be shared (a matter of vertical fiscal relations) and the way that pool is distributed among subnational governments (a matter of horizontal fiscal relations).

48. For the most part, the discussion that follows involves only labor income. In the case of source-based taxation of business income of individuals, administrative questions are similar to those for the enterprise profits tax.

It is important to coordinate the individual income tax and the enterprise profits tax. If business income of individuals is subject only to the tax of the central government, but labor income is taxed by both levels, the tax rate applied to business income should be high enough to discourage artificial conversion of labor income to business income.

Subnational taxation by the jurisdiction where interest and dividends are earned is problematic because it might be thought appropriate to ask the geographic source of income underlying the payment in question. This question is not considered further here, as it is not likely to be important in Russia for the foreseeable future.

49. For this argument, see McLure (1992b).

50. This is the only sensible interpretation of the objective of assigning revenues on a derivation basis. China and Ukraine have chosen other alternatives, both of which are even more problematic. In China the jurisdiction that owns an enterprise taxes it. This makes administration simple but creates undesirable incentives to favor local enterprises over others. This can be avoided only by distinguishing (a) the ownership link between governments and enterprises and (b) the fiscal (taxation) link; in its latter role governments should treat all enterprises alike, regardless of their ownership. See also Wong et al. (1993).

In Ukraine enterprises are taxed by the oblasts in which they are chartered even if they operate in other oblasts. Besides being manifestly unfair (and violating sensible standards for assignment of revenues), if rates are not uniform across the country, this practice creates incentives for the existence of "tax haven" oblasts—oblasts that enact low enterprise tax rates in order to attract the fiscal headquarters of enterprises. This practice could be avoided if the central government sets tax rates but only at the sacrifice of fiscal autonomy. One would expect oblasts to discriminate against enterprises chartered elsewhere and perhaps to require that any enterprise operating within their boundaries be chartered there. This would interfere with the rational choice of business structures, and taxation of separate entities would leave unaddressed the need to determine the source of income. See also McLure (1994a, 110–14).

51. For a discussion of apportionment formulas, see Peggy Musgrave (1984).

52. Moreover, it should be noted that there are several flaws in the American way of calculating property values for use in the formula. Property is valued at its historical cost, not its value. This can be important in some cases (e.g., mineral properties). Moreover,

no adjustment is generally made for either depreciation or inflation. This can be important if the pace and composition of investment have not been uniform throughout the country.

53. This discussion draws heavily on McLure (1993b).

54. See Poddar (1990).

55. This system is being used for trade between members of the CIS.

56. This discussion has benefited substantially from conversations with Satya Poddar.

57. This presumably reflects, at least in part, the reluctance to treat these republics as truly foreign.

58. The focus on the tax side of the budget equation in this discussion should not be allowed to obscure a fundamental fact—that governments at both the national and subnational levels must eliminate all inappropriate public expenditures and reduce to the minimum even those that could be classified as generally appropriate.

59. The system currently in effect does not equalize fiscal positions of the oblasts; see Bahl and Wallace (1993).

References

Alm, James, and David L. Sjoquist. "Enterprise Expenditures on Social Services and the Privatization Process." In Roy Bahl, James Alm, Henry M. Huckaby, Jorge Martinez-Vazquez, Charles McLure, David Sjoquist, Sally Wallace, and Joan M. Youngman (Bahl et al.), "Intergovernmental Fiscal Relations in Russia," Final Report to the NIS Task Force, USAID, November 1993, pp. 107–47.

Bahl, Roy. "Revenues and Revenue Assignment." In Christine Wallich, ed., *Intergovernmental Fiscal Relations in the Russian Federation*. Washington: World Bank, 1992, annex 2.

———. "Revenues and Revenue Assignment: Intergovernmental Fiscal Relations in the Russian Federation." In Christine Wallich, ed., *Russia and the Challenge of Fiscal Federalism*. Washington: World Bank, 1994, pp. 129–80.

Bahl, Roy, James Alm, Henry M. Huckaby, Jorge Martinez-Vazquez, Charles McLure, David Sjoquist, Sally Wallace, and Joan M. Youngman (Bahl et al.). "Intergovernmental Fiscal Relations in Russia," Draft Report to the NIS Task Force, USAID, September 1993a.

Bahl, Roy, James Alm, Henry M. Huckaby, Jorge Martinez-Vazquez, Charles McLure, David Sjoquist, Sally Wallace, and Joan M. Youngman (Bahl et al.). "Intergovernmental Fiscal Relations in Russia," Final Report to the NIS Task Force, USAID, November 1993b.

Bahl, Roy W., and Johannes F. Linn. *Urban Public Finance in Developing Countries* (New York: Oxford University Press, 1992).

Bahl, Roy, Jorge Martinez-Vazquez, and Sally Wallace. "Intergovernmental Fiscal Relations in Russia." In the Proceedings of the National Tax Association, Saint Paul, Minn., November 9, 1993, pp. 78–86.

Bahl, Roy, and Sally Wallace. "Revenue Sharing in Russia." Paper presented at the TRED conference on Intergovernmental Finance in Transition Economies, Cambridge, Mass., October 15–16, 1993; in *Environment and Planning C: Government and Policy C*, Vol. 12 (1994).

Bird, Richard M. "Threading the Fiscal Labyrinth: Some Issues in Fiscal Decentralization." *National Tax Journal* 66, no. 2 (June 1993a): 207–27.

———. "Aspects of Federal Finance: A Comparative Perspective." Paper prepared for the International Symposium on Fiscal Reform, Sao Paulo, September 9, 1993b.

Cnossen, Sijbren. "Interjurisdictional Coordination of Sales Taxes." In Malcolm Gillis, Carl S. Shoup, and Gerardo P. Sicat, eds., *Value Added Taxation in Developing Countries*. Washington: World Bank, 1990, pp. 43–57.

Craig, Jon, and George Kopits. "Intergovernmental Fiscal Relations in Transition: The Case of Russia." Paper prepared for the TRED conference on Intergovernmental Finance in Transition Economies, Cambridge, Mass., October 15–16, 1993.

Fisher, Ronald C. "Macroeconomic Implications of Subnational Fiscal Policy: The Overseas Experience." In D.J. Collins, ed., *Vertical Fiscal Imbalance and the Allocation of Taxing Powers*. Sydney: Australian Tax Research Foundation, 1993, pp. 125–52.

Gramlich, Edward M. "Subnational Fiscal Policy." *Perspectives on Local Public Finance and Public Policy*" 3 (1987): 3–27.

———. "A Policymaker's Guide to Fiscal Decentralization." *National Tax Journal* 66, no. 2 (June 1993): 229–35.

Kopits, George, and D. Mihaljek. "Fiscal Federalism and the New Independent States." In Vito Tanzi, ed., *Transition to Market: Studies in Fiscal Reform*. Washington: International Monetary Fund, 1993, pp. 155–76.

Litvack, Jennie. "Accommodating Regional Demands through Fiscal Federalism: International Experience." In Christine Wallich, ed., *Intergovernmental Fiscal Relations in the Russian Federation*. Washington: World Bank, 1992, annex 4.

Longo, Carlos. "Restricted Origin Principle under Triangular Trade: Implications for Trade and Tax Revenues." *Journal of Development Economics* 10, no. 1 (1982): 103–12.

McLure, Charles E., Jr. "The State Corporate Income Tax: Lambs in Wolves' Clothing." In Henry J. Aaron and Michael J. Boskin, eds., *The Economics of Taxation*. Washington: Brookings Institution, 1980a, pp. 327–46.

———. "State-Federal Relations in the Taxation of the Value Added." *Journal of Corporation Law* 6, no. 1 (Fall 1980b): 127–39.

———. "The Elusive Incidence of the Corporate Income Tax: The State Case." *Public Finance Quarterly* 9, no. 4 (October 1981): 395–413.

———. "Assignment of Corporate Income Taxes in a Federal System." In McLure, ed., *Tax Assignment in Federal Countries*, pp. 101–24; also in *Canadian Tax Journal* 30, no. 6 (November–December 1982): 840–59.

———. "Fiscal Federalism and the Taxation of Economic Rents." In George Break, ed.,

State and Local Finance: The Pressure of the 80's. Madison: University of Wisconsin Press, 1984a, pp. 133–60.

———. "Defining a Unitary Business: An Economist's View." In McLure, ed., *The State Corporation Income Tax: Issues in Worldwide Unitary Combination.* Stanford: Hoover Institution Press, 1984b, pp. 89–124.

———. "Tax Competition: Is What's Good for the Private Goose also Good for the Public Gander?" *National Tax Journal* 39, no. 3 (September 1986): 341–48.

———. "The Intergovernmental Division of Natural Resource Tax Revenues in the Russian Federation." In Christine Wallich, ed., *Intergovernmental Fiscal Relations in the Russian Federation.* Washington: World Bank, 1992a, annex 3.

———. "Income Tax Policy for the Russian Republic." *Communist Economies and Economic Transformation* 4, no. 3 (September 1992b): 425–36.

———. "A North American View of Vertical Fiscal Imbalance and the Assignment of Taxing Powers." In D. J. Collins, ed., *Vertical Fiscal Imbalance and the Allocation of Taxing Powers.* Sydney: Australian Tax Research Foundation, 1993, pp. 239—63; also published as *Vertical Fiscal Imbalance and the Assignment of Taxing Powers in Australia.* Essays in Public Policy series. Stanford: Hoover Institution, 1993a.

———. "The Brazilian Tax Assignment Problem: Ends, Means, and Constraints." Forthcoming in the Proceedings of the International Symposium on Fiscal Reform, Sao Paulo, Brazil, September 6–10, 1993b.

———. "Intergovernmental Fiscal Relations in South Africa: The Assignment of Expenditure Functions and Revenue Sources and the Design of Intergovernmental Grants and Transfers." World Bank, 1993c.

———. "The Assignment of Revenue Sources and the Design of Intergovernmental Transfers." In Jorge Martinez-Vazquez, Eileen Browne, Malcolm G. Lane, Charles McLure, Dale McComber, Andrew D. Pike, and Sally Wallace, "Intergovernmental Finances, Budgeting, and Tax Administration in Ukraine," Final Report to the NIS Task Force, USAID, January 1994a, pp. 63–150.

———. "The Sharing of Taxes on Natural Resources and the Future of the Russian Federation." In Christine Wallich, ed., *Russia and the Challenge of Fiscal Federalism.* Washington: World Bank, 1994b, pp. 181–217.

———. "The Taxation of Natural Resources and the Future of the Russian Federation." Proceedings of the National Tax Association, Saint Paul, Minn., November 9, 1993, pp. 87–91; also in *Environment and Planning C: Government and Policy C,* Vol. 12 (1994c), pp. 309–18.

McLure, Charles E., Jr., ed. *Tax Assignment in Federal Countries.* Canberra, Australia: Centre for Research on Federal Financial Relations, ANU Press, 1983a.

McLure, Charles E., and Christine Wallich. "Special Issues in Russian Federal Finance: Separatism and Natural Resources." In Robert D. Ebel, Richard M. Bird, and Christine I. Wallich, eds., *Fiscal Decentralization from Command to Market.* Washington: World Bank, forthcoming.

Martinez-Vazquez, Jorge, Eileen Browne, Malcolm G. Lane, Charles McLure, Dale McComber, Andrew D. Pike, and Sally Wallace. "Intergovernmental Finances, Budgeting, and Tax Administration in Ukraine," Draft Report to the NIS Task Force, USAID, November 1993.

Messere, Ken. "A Defence of Present Border Tax Adjustment Practices." *National Tax Journal* 32, no. 4 (December 1979): 481–92.

Mieszkowski, Peter. "Energy Policy, Taxation of Natural Resources, and Fiscal Federalism." In McLure, ed., *Tax Assignment in Federal Countries.* Canberra: Centre for Research on Federal Financial Relations, 1983, pp. 129–45.

Mieszkowski, Peter, and Eric Toder. "Taxation of Energy Resources." In McLure and Mieszkowski, eds., *Fiscal Federalism and the Taxation of Natural Resources.* Cambridge: Lexington Books, 1983, pp. 65–91.

Musgrave, Peggy B. "Principles for Dividing the State Corporate Tax Base." In McLure, ed., *The State Corporation Income Tax: Issues in Worldwide Unitary Combination.* Stanford: Hoover Institution Press, 1984, pp. 228–46.

Musgrave, Richard A. *The Theory of Public Finance.* New York: McGraw-Hill, 1959.

———. "Who Should Tax, Where, and What?" In McLure, ed., *Tax Assignment in Federal Countries.* Canberra: Centre for Research on Federal Financial Relations, 1983, pp. 2–19.

Oates, Wallace E. "The Theory of Public Finance in a Federal System." *Canadian Journal of Economics,* February 1968, pp. 37–54.

———. *Fiscal Federalism.* New York: Harcourt Brace Jovanovich, 1972.

Pauly, Mark V. "Income Redistribution as a Local Public Good." *Journal of Public Economics* 2, no. 1 (February 1973): 35–58.

Poddar, Satya. "Value-Added Tax at the State Level." In Malcolm Gillis, Carl S. Shoup, and Gerardo P. Sicat, eds., *Value Added Taxation in Developing Countries.* Washington: World Bank, 1990, pp. 104–12.

Rikker, William H. *Federalism: Origin, Operation, and Significance.* Boston: Little Brown, 1964.

"Russian Federation: TACIS—Policy Advice," Project Number 1/103, Budgeting Policy, October 1993.

Shah, Anwar. "Perspective on the Design of Intergovernmental Fiscal Relations." Paper prepared for the International Symposium on Fiscal Reform, Sao Paulo, September 9, 1993.

Thirsk, Wayne R. "Tax Assignment and Revenue Sharing in Canada." In McLure, ed., *Tax Assignment in Federal Countries.* Canberra: Centre for Research on Federal Financial Relations, 1983, pp. 234–50.

Wallich, Christine. "Subnational Finance in the Context of Stabilization and Reforms: Macroeconomic Dimensions of Subnational Finance and Privatization." In Wallich, ed., *Intergovernmental Fiscal Relations in the Russian Federation.* Washington: World Bank, 1992a, chap. 2.

———. "Intergovernmental Finances: Past and Present." In Wallich, ed., *Intergovernmental Fiscal Relations in the Russian Federation.* Washington: World Bank, 1992b, annex 1.

————. "Intergovernmental Fiscal Relations: Setting the Stage." In Wallich, ed., *Russia and the Challenge of Fiscal Federalism*. Washington: World Bank, 1994, pp. 19–63.

Watson, William G. "An Estimate of the Welfare Gain from Fiscal Equalization." *Canadian Journal of Economics* 29, no. 2 (May 1986): 298–308.

Weingast, Barry. "The Economic Role of Political Institutions." Photocopy, January 1993.

————. "Federalism, Chinese Style: The Political Basis for Economic Reform in China." Paper presented to the IPR/AID Workshop on Structural Reform, Washington, D.C., November 5, 1993.

Wong, Christine, et al. "Economic Reform and Fiscal Management in China." Asian Development Bank, 1993.

6

Credibility, Commitment, and Soviet Economic Reform

PETER J. BOETTKE

The former Soviet Union has been in a state of perpetual economic crisis since 1917. One reform measure after another was introduced only to be reversed within a few years. The liberal market reforms of the 1920s, 1950s, 1960s, and 1980s were "one big lie." In each case the government failed to establish a credible commitment to liberal reform. Unfortunately, the Yeltsin reforms of the 1990s have followed suit, and they too have failed to transform the Russian economy.

Introduction

The former Soviet Union has been in a state of economic crisis since 1917. One reform measure after another (whether inspired by socialism or liberalism) has been introduced only to be reversed within a few years. The

Financial assistance from the Austrian Economics Program at New York University and the Sarah Scaife Foundation in addition to support from the Earhart Foundation and the National Fellows Program at the Hoover Institution on War, Revolution and Peace, Stanford University, is gratefully acknowledged.

original socialist construction project, embarked on following the November revolution in 1917, had to be abandoned in the early spring of 1921. Introduced in 1921, the New Economic Policy, which represented the first Soviet-era perestroika (but not glasnost, as all dissension within the party was outlawed by V. I. Lenin's simultaneous decree), lasted for seven years until it was drastically reversed by Joseph Stalin's revolution from above. The Stalin years (1928–1953) represented a political and economic buzz saw. Collectivization of agriculture, industrialization, political purges, mass terror, labor camps, wartime emergencies, and so forth characterized Stalin's twenty-five-year reign of power. The Nikita Khrushchev years, especially the period immediately following his 1956 speech denouncing Stalin's "cult of personality," represented the second Soviet-era perestroika and a limited period of glasnost, as Stalin's crimes against humanity were partially unmasked. The "thaw generation," however, had to wait another twenty years before glasnost was to have any lasting meaning. Khrushchev's ill-conceived economic policies generated lackluster results and bolstered the political challenge to his leadership.

The ensuing Leonid Brezhnev years were a mix of halfhearted attempts to improve the economic mechanism and political corruption. From the Khrushchev years through the entire eighteen-year reign of Brezhnev, Soviet leaders embarked on a "continuous process of reforming the reforms" (Linz 1987, 150). The oil shock of the early 1970s gave the regime a short reprieve and hid from immediate view the deterioration of the economic situation. But by the late 1970s it was evident to many observers that the Brezhnev era had nothing to show but economic deprivation and political cynicism. Neither Yuri Andropov (who may have wanted to change things) nor Konstantin Chernenko (who did not) had enough time in office to effect a change in Brezhnev's legacy. Mikhail Gorbachev, however, did have the time and the political will.

The Gorbachev period of political and economic reform, though, must be judged a failure.[1] After six years in power, the Gorbachev government left the official Soviet economy worse off, and the Soviet Union as a political entity no longer existed. Perestroika simply did not deliver the goods, and democratic political reform was much too limited. Andres Aslund, for example, even before the attempted August coup, concluded that "looking back at Soviet economic policy during the second half of the 1980s, it is difficult to avoid the impression that virtually every possible mistake has been made. Perestroika has proved to be an utter economic failure" (1991, 225).

The perestroika period (1985–1991), along with previous attempts at economic reform such as the New Economic Policy (1921–1928), Khrushchev's sovnarkhoz reforms (1957), and the Brezhnev–Aleksey Kosygin reforms (1965), can now be safely treated as history. These reform efforts were all heralded in their time as liberalization policies, and they all came to an end less than a decade after they were initiated. These reform packages were simply not sustainable economic policies.[2]

Understanding why these reform attempts failed is important, not only for antiquarian interests but also for what it can tell us about the general theory of social organization and public policy. An examination of previous failed reform efforts may offer invaluable insights into how to construct a workable postperestroika constitution of economic policy in the former Soviet Union—the task that has now been left to Boris Yeltsin's government.

A Basic Problem in Policy Design

Public policy must be constructed in a manner that recognizes the obstacles presented by *information* and *incentives*. Policy must first and foremost be compatible with basic economic incentives. Policies that are based on notions of public-spiritedness and humanitarian goals but that disregard economic motivations are most likely doomed to failure. Moreover, even if public policies offer rewards to those who perform as expected, economic actors must possess the relevant information to act appropriately. If actors have the motivation to "do the right thing," they must also have access to information about what the right thing to do would be in their present context.

Unfortunately, the problem of constructing an optimal governmental policy that intervenes properly without distorting incentives and the flow of information is compounded by the passage of time. For one, the relevant economic data are contextual and not abstract. Information gathered yesterday may be irrelevant for decisions today because of changing conditions. The price system overcomes this problem by alerting individuals to these changes through the adjustment of relative prices. Political coordination, in contrast, does not have access to a similar register of changing conditions.

Even in cases where discretionary political intervention might be desired to correct for perceived market failures, the problem remains as to how to acquire the requisite knowledge to intervene properly. Ignorant or haphazard intervention will simply lead to further destablization and exacerbate the problem it sought to correct originally.

The dynamics of change associated with the passage of time also present a timing problem for public policy, as Milton Friedman pointed out a long time ago. A long and variable lag exists between (1) the need for action and the recognition of this need, (2) the recognition of a problem and the design and implementation of a policy response, and (3) the implementation of the policy and the effect of the policy (Friedman 1953, 145). Because of these lags, Friedman argued that discretionary public policy will often be destabilizing. For this reason, he argued the case for rules rather than discretionary public policy.

Finally, the passage of time introduces strategic problems for policy makers. Policies that seemed appropriate at t_1 may not be deemed appropriate at t_2. In fact, a basic presupposition of the argument for discretion is exactly that policies accepted for one period may prove to be inappropriate for another and, therefore, that policy makers must possess the ability to shift as circumstances change. Such shifts in public policy (coupled with the impact these shifts have on the expectations of economic actors), however, may prove destabilizing to the overall economic environment.

The Issues of Credibility and Commitment

Recognizing the temporal dimensionality of choice is fundamental in establishing viable economic policy. Our concern here is with the public choice problem that follows from the strategic interaction between rulers and citizens. A fundamental problem faces public choosers when a policy that seemed optimal when introduced appears less so as time passes. Without a binding commitment to the policy, the government will change policy to what now appears to be optimal. The problem is that economic actors who realize this will anticipate the policy change and act in a counterproductive manner from the perspective of the policy maker.

Optimal intervention, by definition, requires that a large degree of discretionary control be entrusted to government decision makers. The expectational problems of discretion, however, generate difficulties for government planning in general (see Kydland and Prescott 1977). One reason discretionary control does not work as optimally as desired is that current decisions by economic actors depend on expectations concerning future policy; those expectations are not invariant of the policies chosen. For example, if, for whatever reason (either an increase in demand or reduction in supply), market conditions produced a windfall profit for the oil industry, the government could respond by proposing to tax away those profits with the argument that this will not affect the current supply of oil because it is the result of a past decision. But such a policy would lead oil companies to anticipate that similar expropriations will occur again in the future, and they will make their investment decisions so as to reduce the future supply of oil. Policy decisions and social rules create expectations, and expectations guide actions.[3] A decision tree illustrates the basic policy dilemma (see figure 6.1).

In figure 6.1, player 2 is the representative citizen, player 1 is the government

Figure 6.1   Basic Commitment Game

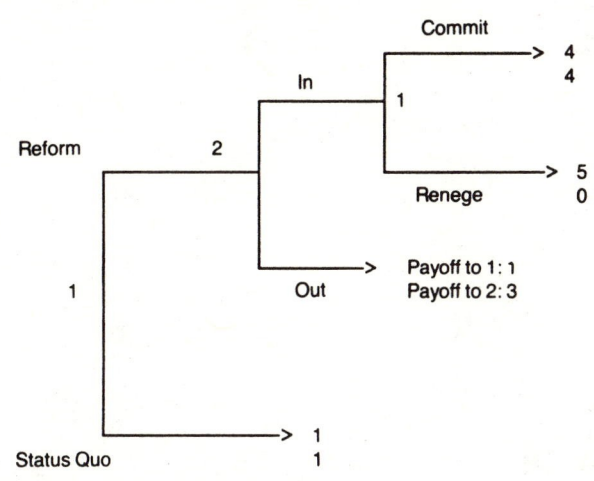

decision maker. The government announces an economic reform that liberalizes trade. Player 2 must choose to enter the game or stay out. The problem is that, once player 2 enters the game, player 1 can benefit from confiscating the wealth of player 2. Knowing the sequentially rational moves of player 1, player 2 will choose the only viable equilibrium, Out, and reforms will stall unless player 1 can successfully tie his own hands.

This is the basic commitment game. But the actual commitment game is more complicated. In fact, the problem is one of information. The citizens do not really know who they are playing with (see figure 6.2).

The logic and structure of the game are basically the same as in figure 6.1, except in figure 6.2 the informational difficulties are highlighted. The ruling regime (player 1), which can be either sincere or insincere, announces a plan to introduce an economic liberalization policy. The citizen (player 2) now must decide to enter the market or stay out. A major problem confronting the citizen, however, is that she or he does not know whether the regime is sincere or insincere. The citizen's only prior information concerning the regime is policy history, but the reform announcement was presumably intended to signal a break from the old way of doing things. If the citizen decides to enter the official market in expectation of continued liberalization, then the regime must decide to either continue the liberalization policy that was announced or renege on the announcement and tighten political control in the second round by cracking down

Figure 6.2   Sophisticated Commitment Game

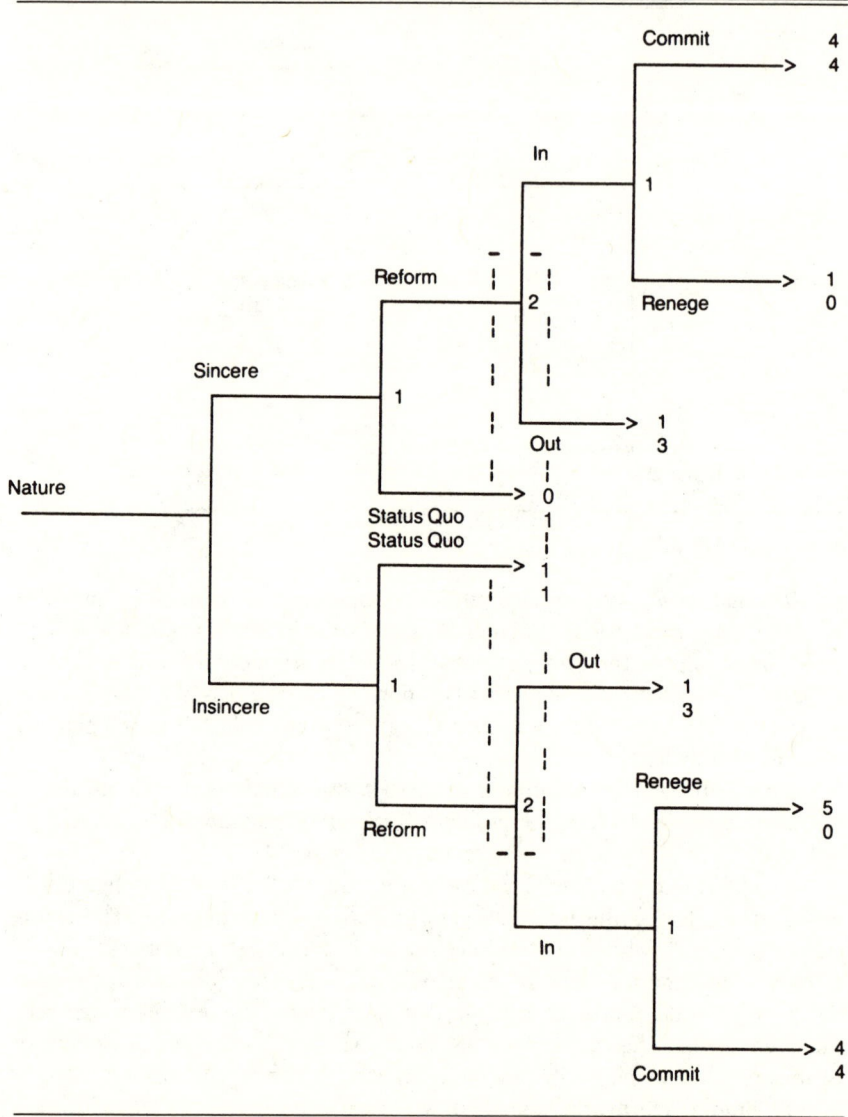

on individual economic activity and confiscating the wealth created in the previous period.

If the ruler is following a discretionary policy, then the citizen will foresee that the ruler may likely renege in the second period of this game and therefore will choose to stay out. But if the ruler can convey a credible commitment, he or she would announce liberalization and the citizen would choose to come into the official market. The ruler's payoff, independent of whether the regime is sincere or insincere, will be higher with commitment conveyance than it would be without it, but the insincere ruler would be better off, once the announcement of liberalization elicited citizen market participation, to renege and crack down on private economic activity in the form of increased taxation, regulation, or confiscation. The sincere reform regime, however, will not crack down and will continue to pursue liberalization policies.

In such situations, though, because the citizens are uninformed about the sincerity of the ruling regime, and given certain probabilities that are derived from their previous experience with the regime's efforts at reform, it may be rational for them to expect that the ruler will go back on her or his announcement to pursue economic liberalization. If this is the case, citizens will choose to stay out of the economic game and thus defeat both the short-term and long-term goals of the ruler. The only way out of this policy impasse is to establish a binding and credible commitment to economic reform.

The reform regime's problem, however, is even more difficult than solving the basic paradox of governance—establishing constraints on its activities that do not deter its positive ability to govern. To get economic reform off the ground, the regime has to simultaneously establish binding constraints on its behavior and signal a sincere commitment to reform to the citizenry. During war, for example, if the commanding officer's troops crossed over a large river to do battle with opposing forces, he may order the bridge burned—thus precommitting his troops to the battle ahead by eliminating the only possible escape. At the same time, however, opposing troops witnessing the smoke have received a signal that the other side will fight a hard battle. The reforming regime must do something similar to establish trust and bind itself to the reform policy.[4]

This simple illustration of the basic problem of policy design and the failure to solve the dilemma goes a long way toward explaining the failures of the various reform cycles in the former Soviet Union. Marshall Goldman (1991, 37–38), for example, emphasizes that all previous efforts at reform within the Soviet Union were viewed as a "big lie" by the citizens of the former Soviet Union. The suppression of the kulaks in the 1920s and 1930s and Khrushchev's agricultural policies in the early 1960s had not been forgotten by the population, which explains why individuals were reluctant to invest private income on economic ventures during the Gorbachev era. Hardly a family in the former Soviet Union did not have a member that was directly affected by Stalin's terror, and this served as part of a historical memory that each citizen possessed concerning the nature of the Communist Party of the Soviet Union. Obviously other issues were involved in the complex history of the design and implementation of Soviet reform, but focusing on the credibility and commitment problem allows us to highlight a key reason for the recurring failure of reform efforts.

Illustrations of the Problem

THE POLICY GAME UNDER THE NEW ECONOMIC POLICY (NEP)

The introduction of NEP in the early spring of 1921 represented a drastic reversal from the previous policies pursued by the Bolsheviks. During war communism the Bolshevik regime had pursued policies of extreme centralization that sought to eliminate market exchange and production completely and establish a centrally planned economy.[5] The war communism policies had to be reversed, for they resulted in a drastic reduction in production and threatened the political alliance between the peasant and the proletariat. NEP represented, in large part, a policy of economic liberalization that was intended to restore partial economic freedom to the peasants to appease political unrest and spur the farm production that was necessary to feed the emerging industrial strata of society.

On May 24, 1921, a decree from Sovnarkom (Council of People's Commissars) permitted not only the sale of surplus food by peasants in farmer markets but also trade by others of goods produced by small-scale private manufacturers. Whereas private trade during war communism was basically outlawed—though it did continue in the form of black-market bazaars—under NEP sales could now be conducted from permanent facilities. Decrees concerning hired labor of not more than ten or twenty, leasing factories, and so forth followed throughout 1921 and 1922. "The property rights and legalized spheres of business activity that had been granted to Soviet citizens during the first two years of NEP were collected and set down in the Civil Code of the RSFSR [Russian Soviet Federated Socialist Republic], which went into effect on January 1, 1923. Although not a dramatic extension of the rights of private businessmen, the Civil Code . . . represented a clear reversal of the policies of War Communism."[6]

This policy shift to partial liberalization was meant to induce private economic initiative, and it worked to an extent. But the policy signal was not unambiguous. *Nepmen*, a term used to describe private businessmen in the 1920s, were subject to many taxes and fees, including business and income taxes. The most substantial of these was the fee for the use of business facilities. In fact, this fee accounted for twice as much revenue from private traders as did the business tax in 1922. In January 1923, it was announced that the fee would be increased. At this time, applications to rent facilities for private business declined 20 percent (see Ball 1987, 30).

The legal ambiguity of the Nepmen was highlighted in the laws against speculation and price controls. In 1924, as a result, there was a marked decline in the economic activity of private traders. The government tried to reverse this downward trend by providing more favorable treatment—for example, easy state credit—to the Nepmen. But this policy was reversed in 1926–1927. State credit to private business, for example, was cut by 25 percent in 1926. The administrative tool that proved most devastating in the war against the Nepmen was taxation. There was a 50 percent rate increase in the tax on profits of urban private traders from 1925 to 1927 (12.9 percent to 18.8 percent). In the Sokol'nicheski quarter of Moscow, for example, in 1929–1930 private traders and manufacturers represented 1.7 percent of the region's income taxpayers, with 8.2 percent of the total taxable income, but accounted for 55 percent of the region's income tax receipts (see Ball 1987, 75). The tax burden, in combination with their political status as *lishentsy* (the deprived), assured that Nepmen were most vulnerable.[7] By 1928, as Aleksandr Solzhenitsyn points out, "it was time to call to a reckoning those late stragglers after the bourgeoisie—the NEPmen. The usual practice was to impose on them ever-increasing and finally totally intolerable taxes. At a certain point they could no longer pay; they were immediately arrested for bankruptcy, and their property was confiscated" (1973, 1: 52).

The cumulative effect of these policies was to discourage individuals from investing in the official market even though liberalization policies had been announced by the regime with the introduction of NEP. Economic actors chose to withdraw from the economic game, despite pleas from the Bolsheviks for them to invest in profitable aboveground activities (see, for example, Bukharin 1925). Ambiguity in the economic rules of the game, Bukharin argued to his fellow Bolshevik comrades, would produce nothing but contradictory expectations, which would deter economic progress. Sizing up the situation, he stated,

> Consider the fact that the well-to-do upper stratum of the peasantry, along with the middle peasant, who is also striving to join the well-to-do, are both afraid at present to accumulate. A situation has been created in which the peasant is afraid to buy an iron roof and apprehensive that he will be declared a kulak; if he buys a machine, he makes certain that the communists are not watching. Advanced technology has become a conspiracy. . . . The result is that the middle peasant is afraid to improve his farm and lay himself open to forceful administrative pressure; and the poor peasant complains that we are preventing him from selling his labor power to the wealthy peasants, etc.

In response, Bukharin argued that "in general and on the whole, we must say to the entire peasantry, to all its different strata: enrich yourselves, accumulate, develop your farms" (1925, 196–97).

Price controls on grain provide another example of the contradictory expectations on the part of economic actors (alluded to by Bukharin) that were generated by discretionary Soviet policies. After the initial announcement of price liberalization in the agricultural sector, the government reversed course. In 1924, the People's Commissariat of Internal Trade attempted to fix a maximum price for grain. But over the years peasants had learned that grain was a good hedge against inflation, so they withheld grain from the market. Tax pressures to enforce sales were enacted, but peasants went to great lengths to pay the tax in anything but grain. A private illegal market developed wherein grain sold above the maximum price, creating parallel markets—one with state-regulated prices, another with free prices.

In response regional authorities attempted to issue orders declaring it obligatory to deliver 25 percent of all flour milled in a region to the state-purchasing authority at the fixed price, but this merely led to a cessation of aboveground milling operations. By December 1924 the state had collected less than half its projected amount of grain (118 million *pods* [Russian unit of weight equal to 36.11 pounds] out of 380 million). Moreover, the grain stocks of the state declined, from 214 million *pods* on January 1, 1924, to 145 million *pods* on January 1, 1925. The price-fixing policy of the Soviet state had been defeated (see Carr 1958, 1: 208–9).

Foreign economic relations provide another example of the regime's inability to bind itself to a credible commitment undermining the reform effort, despite the announcement of liberalization. At the Genoa Conference (April–May 1922), for example, the Soviet delegation refused to conclude an agreement with Western powers on the question of Russia's debts (see Carr 1953, 3: 377). In addition, at the end of 1922 a proposal for relaxing the foreign trade monopoly was rejected. Prospects for the expansion of foreign economic relations were, therefore, reduced considerably. Without such ties, long-term economic development was unlikely. Foreign governments simply had no reason to trust the Bolsheviks in economic deals.

The exchange rate policy also hindered economic development and ran counter to the intentions of NEP. The hard currency reforms in the beginning of NEP—the *chervonets* reforms—were a major accomplishment. But the hard currency reforms did not even last two years. The low levels of gold reserves, the unrealistic exchange rate, and the small volume of Soviet exports all undermined the monetary reform. Moreover, beginning in 1928, Gosbank refused to exchange Soviet money for foreign currency (see Khanin 1989, 21, 24).

The general policy of grain procurement under NEP clearly illustrates the problem. The cornerstone of NEP was the substitution of the tax in kind for the grain requisitioning of war communism. Peasants, though, with the war communism period still fresh in their memories, had to be convinced that arbitrary requisitioning was not a policy option, that is, the government had to make a credible commitment to maintain NEP. As we have seen, however, the Bolsheviks did not commit to any such binding constraint. As a result, by the end of 1928 peasants no longer had an incentive to market grain surplus. From the peasants' point of view, the market was simply not a secure outlet.[8]

Thus, NEP was abandoned in 1928, and Stalin ruled over the Soviet system until his death in 1953. The reversal from the quasi liberalization of NEP to the authoritarian measures of collectivization is one of the most drastic and fateful turn of events in the twentieth century. The abandonment of NEP, though, did possess both an economic and a political logic: NEP's failure was due neither to the inability of market institutions to provide the basis for economic development nor to the peculiarities of Stalin's personality, which thrived on political authoritarianism; rather, the internal contradictions of NEP led to an ever-increasing reliance on the substitution of political rationales for economic rationales in setting economic policy. The shifting policies produced an expectational regime that worked against the goals of policy makers. Because the Bolsheviks were not willing to construct a binding commitment to economic liberalization, the only way out of the policy impasse was complete authoritarianism. Stalinism was the unintended consequence of the failure of the discretionary regime of the 1920s to cope with the obstacles that information and incentives present to political economies.

THE POLICY GAME UNDER KHRUSHCHEV

After Stalin's death in 1953, Soviet leaders had to face some cold facts about economic life. Collectivization, war, and political terror had taken their toll on the economic system. The post-Stalin triumvirate of Georgy Malenkov, Vyacheslav Molotov, and Lavrenty Beria could not simply continue along the path laid out by Stalin. Out of the political shakeout that followed the succession struggle, Khrushchev emerged as a major post-Stalin political figure. Khrushchev's Central Committee speech on agriculture in 1953 detailed the results of collectivization. Productivity was down, livestock did not compare favorably with either 1928 or even 1916 figures. Peasants received low wages, and the level of investment by the collective farms was too low. Taxes levied on private plots were too high and discouraged production. All these negative policies, Khrushchev insisted, must be reversed.[9]

Malenkov, in contrast, was accused by economic planners and military leaders of overconcentrating on the consumer goods sector and thus distorting the Soviet economy by shifting priority away from heavy industry. The preoccupation with consumer material well-being associated with Malenkov did not sit well with leaders of heavy industry and the military. After Malenkov's fall, Khrushchev emerged as the dominant political figure. As first secretary from 1955 to 1964, however, Khrushchev never achieved the dominant status that Stalin had, and political maneuvering was an omnipresent part of policy decisions. Nevertheless, Khrushchev initiated the major policies during that period.

Most of Khrushchev's reforms were directed at changing the incentives within the agricultural sector to improve the efficiency of production and improve the plight of peasants.[10] One of his most ambitious initiatives, though, was attempting to improve the economic mechanism within the Soviet system—the *sovnarkhoz* reforms of 1957.[11] In response to a political strategy on the part of his opponents to consolidate a power base in the economic planning system and establish a superministry that would coordinate the activities of all the subordinate economic ministries, Khrushchev reorganized the planning system by decentralizing power to regional economic councils (*sovnarkhozy*). This decentralization of the planning system was supposed to combat ministerial empire building and reduce the coordination problems that plagued the state-ministerial hierarchy.[12] The industrial ministries were abolished, and the regional council system (coordinated by Gosplan) was established. State enterprises were now subordinate to the 105 regional councils rather than to a ministry.

The danger of this policy was that localism would replace ministerial empire building as the main threat to efficient economic management. Regional councils favored their enterprises over all others, as would be expected, and economic performance suffered.[13] That Khrushchev's initiatives would substitute localism for departmentalism lends credence, Joseph Berliner argues, to the interpretation that political maneuvering rather than economic considerations provided the rationale for the 1957 reforms (Berliner 1983, 352). Unfortunately for Khrushchev, the reforms were correlated with a decline in the measured rates of economic growth along with reports of the excesses of localism. As a result, even though Khrushchev reversed the 1957 reforms in March 1963, his political rivals used the failed reforms to discredit him. Khrushchev's fall in October 1964 was soon followed by a full reinstatement of the ministerial system.

The Khrushchev era, then, did nothing to convey to state enterprise managers, agricultural workers, or urban citizens that economic activity would be insulated from political manipulation. The so-called liberalization policies of decentralization were part of a larger political ploy to divest power from Khrushchev's rivals. The 1957 reforms were not only ill-conceived but reinforced the adverse reputation Soviet reform efforts possessed and thus compounded the difficulty of signaling a credible commitment to economic liberalization in the future.

THE POLICY GAME UNDER KOSYGIN AND BREZHNEV

The failure of the Khrushchev reforms did not squelch debate over the problems with the Soviet economic mechanism. The *sovnarkhoz* reform did not get at the fundamental problem of incentives but was instead limited to a question of supervision of state enterprises. Decision making within the state enterprises was not addressed, though this was an aspect of Soviet planning that was seriously in need of reform. The gross output target of enterprise success (and the corresponding bonus system) provided incentives to the state enterprise managers (who responded rationally) that generated perverse consequences in terms of input use and output quality.

Late in the Khrushchev era, Evsei Liberman proposed a reform of the incentive system for state enterprises.[14] Liberman thought that if the state enterprise manager's reward was tied to the "profitability" of the enterprise—defined as the ratio of profit to the stock of capital—then the enterprise manager would possess the incentive to minimize costs. Under the appropriate incentive system, Liberman argued, managers would be induced to operate their enterprises at full productivity, improve the quality of goods produced, and seek out least-cost production techniques.

With Khrushchev's ouster the debate over enterprise incentives did not wane. In September 1965, Kosygin announced the restructuring of the economic mechanism. The ministerial system was to be fully reconstituted, the basic incentive system in enterprises was to be overhauled, and a price reform was to be implemented. The ministerial system constituted a recentralization of economic decision making away from the regional authorities and back to Moscow. As Hewett points out, this is important because many interpreters confused the incentive reform with regard to enterprises with a net decentralization of decision-making power within the economy. This was not the case in either the design or the result of the 1965 reforms.

The incentive scheme limited the number of planned targets that supervisory ministries were authorized to issue to firms. Where obligatory targets had once ranged from thirty-five to forty, they were now limited to eight: physical output, sales volume, total profit and the rate of profit on capital, total wage fund, level of payment to state budget, capital investment, introduction of new technology, and allocation of vital resources. Moreover, the sales volume target replaced the gross output target as the basis for bonuses. These new rules were supposed to give more autonomy to the enterprises, but as we will see this was not the effect owing to the ambiguity in implementation.

As a complement to the recentralization of economic power, the 1965 reforms also entailed a centralization of price setting with the formation of Goskomtsen—which coordinated all price setting and price revision. The price "reform," however, did not intend to improve the ability of prices to convey information concerning the relative scarcities of resources in the Soviet economy. For example, prices were not to interfere with the central planning directives— they were to remain merely convenient tools for accounting purposes. As a result, prices that were set in a fashion that had little to do with the actual cost of resource use continued to distort the structure of production in the Soviet economy.

The effect of the 1965 reforms was largely limited to expanding the Soviet economic bureaucracy.[15] In terms of improving the economic mechanism, the reforms were both ill conceived and unimplemented. In other words, they were incentive incompatible and not credible. The policy schemes to improve incentives within the enterprises, according to Nove (1992, 383), were ineffective for a variety of reasons. Notably, the rules of the game were arbitrarily and frequently altered so that there was no stability in the environment even within a single planning period. Interviews with former enterprise managers concur with this interpretation of the 1965 effort to change the incentive system. "We didn't really have a reform," one former head of a planning department stated. "We were preparing for it, but it was never ratified." Another former manager summed up the enterprise reforms in the following manner: "They only poured water from one bottle to another. . . . In practice nothing changed. . . . One time they tried to give more rights to the enterprise . . . but they became afraid of private enterprise and stopped it." Another former manager had this to say: "Liberman . . . created a whole system in which the enterprise would have an incentive to make a profit. They introduced it almost everywhere, but then they changed it so much that it didn't even resemble itself."[16]

Again, the announcement of radical reform merely represented tinkering with the mechanism. There were no good reasons for enterprise managers or private citizens to expect a change in the situation. The only stable political economy rule in effect was that the planning bureaucracy could arbitrarily change the rules any time it desired. The expectation of arbitrary action on the part of the bureaucracy reinforced the incentives that were generated by a system of state control over the economy. Resource use was systemically wasteful, and the future was completely disregarded. The economic system generated no incentives to conserve scarce resources or employ these resources in valued uses, let alone discover better ways to allocate resources among the alternatives (i.e., to find the least-cost production techniques). As Hewett (1988, 240) put it: "If a 'death certificate' were issued for the 1965 reforms, it would read 'ministerial interference, aided by the lack of attention by the obstetrician (L. Brezhnev).'"

THE POLICY GAME UNDER PERESTROIKA

The key legal components of perestroika included the law on individual economic activity (1986), the law on state enterprise (1987), and the law on cooperatives (1988). Despite the rhetoric and promise of these laws, they contained contradictions and ambiguities that prevented them from achieving the objectives of economic reform. Furthermore, they failed to convey any binding commitment on the part of the Gorbachev regime to true market reform. From 1985 to 1991, Gorbachev introduced at least ten major policy packages for economic reform under the banner of perestroika, but not a single one was fully implemented.

The law on state enterprise, for example, was supposed to introduce self-accounting, self-financing, and self-management. But, unwilling to move too quickly with the reform of state enterprises, the government decided to stagger conformity to the law. Some enterprises would operate under the new guidelines as of January 1, 1988; others would do so the following year, January 1989 (see Goldman 1991, 140).

In addition, given the commitment to full employment by the regime, there was no way to introduce self-financing in a manner consistent with a "hard budget constraint" (see Kornai 1986). Enterprise managers and employees knew that, despite whatever announcement was made concerning self-financing, as long as the regime was committed to full employment, enterprises would possess a "soft budget constraint" with all the corresponding inefficiencies.[17] Bankruptcy would not be tolerated, and state subsidies would continue as before.

Not only did the law on state enterprises fail to aid the move to the market economy, it contributed to the economic problems of the already struggling official industrial sector. Managers—in an effort to return the favor to workers to whom they owed their jobs and because they did not face hard budget constraints—readily approved wage increases. Average wages rose by 8 percent in 1988 and 13 percent in 1989 (see Goldman 1991, 141–42). Thus, state enterprise costs increased and with them the demand for increased state subsidies from the enterprises. This, in turn, put an increased strain on the state budget and, consequently, the monetary system as the printing press was employed to monetize the debt. The persistence of microeconomic inefficiency bred increased macroeconomic destabilization as economic agents responded rationally to the contradictory rule changes.

The law on private economic activity was passed in November 1986 and became effective in May 1987. This law allowed individuals to engage in activities that had previously been deemed illegal. Despite several restrictions—such as the length of time that state employees could devote to individual enterprise—the intent of the law was to encourage individual economic enterprise and market experimentation. Family members of state employees or individuals such as students, housewives, and pensioners were allowed to work full time if they desired. To do so, though, individuals had to apply for a license from local authorities and pay either an annual income tax or a fee. The fee applied particularly to cases where it was difficult to monitor income, such as taxi driving.

In 1987, the fee for a private taxi was 560 rubles, which meant that a worker who was moonlighting as a taxi driver had to earn the equivalent of three months' wages before driving the taxi would cover its costs (see Hewett 1988, 340n. 60). The perverse consequence of this policy in terms of the persistence of a black market in taxis is described by William Taubman and Jane Taubman in their book *Moscow Spring*. The law on individual enterprise, in this case, amounted to simply regulating and taxing an activity (the private market for taxi services), which had gone on "unofficially" for years. As a consequence, few if any of the Moscow *chastniki* (private taxis) they encountered were registered and, therefore, official. "Registration," they point out, "required burdensome medical exams, payment of a fee, and of course heavy taxes. . . . But most burdensome was the requirement that all individual labor activity be moonlighting; the workers must have primary jobs in the state sector" (1989, 46).

An even more fundamental problem with the law on private economic activity was the campaign against unearned income, which required individuals to have appropriate documentation explaining how they made their money (see Belkindas 1989). A natural market response to this was the emergence of an illicit market in documentation and a decline in economic well-being as the informal networks, which historically filled the gaps caused by the inefficient official system, were disturbed.[18] The attitude of the regime as conveyed by the campaign reinforced citizens' lack of trust concerning the government's commitment to reform. Without a credible conveyance of commitment to market reform, farmers, workers, and others had no incentive to invest in the aboveground market.

This is seen in the way in which cooperatives developed in the Soviet Union under Gorbachev.[19] The law on individual enterprise (adopted November 1986) provided the legal foundation for the cooperative movement because it permitted family members who lived together to form businesses. Formal recognition of cooperatives came with the Law on Cooperation in the USSR, adopted May 26, 1988. Whereas the number of cooperatives was 8,000 employing 88,000 on October 1, 1987, by July 1, 1989, there were more than 133,000 employing 2,900,000. The output of cooperatives amounted to an estimated 350 million rubles for 1987, 6 billion rubles in 1988, and was estimated to be 12.9 billion rubles by June 1989. Despite this explosion in cooperatives, hostility from both the public and the government toward the economic success of cooperatives threatened their long-term viability.[20] Because this hostility resulted in accusations that cooperatives' financial gains were made without any real effort—just exploiting the shortage situation—the threat of the campaign on unearned income was very real. Often, state shortages got blamed on the cooperatives. A state shortage of buns and sausages translates into a cooperative sandwich with a corresponding high price—at least that is how some described the situation.

The precarious position of cooperatives was compounded because they had to rely almost exclusively on the state sector for supplies, even though they were not officially hooked up to the central supply network. Thus, cooperatives had to rely on illicit transactions, such as bribes and agreements with state enterprises, to obtain resources, which increased their vulnerability to blackmail both by officials and by criminals. In fact, cooperatives were often assumed to be fronts for criminal activity.

In addition, the legal status of cooperatives and the tax policy to which they would be subject have changed often. Even before the end of 1988, a resolution was passed that sought to restrict the activities of cooperatives. In February 1989, republican authorities were given the authority over taxation policy toward cooperatives and were encouraged to set differential rates based on the type of cooperative, its pricing policy, and so forth. The "speculative tendencies" of cooperatives were subject to criticism, and authorities were encouraged to take steps to bring cooperative pricing in line with state pricing. Cooperatives were subject to taxes ranging from 25 to 60 percent of their income, depending on their pricing policy. The August 1989 law on cooperative taxation, for example, established new regulations on cooperatives and tied their taxation to the relationship between state and cooperative prices.

By constraining the freedom of cooperative and private market experimentation, the Gorbachev government prevented the market from serving one of its most vital functions—inducing an increase in the supply of goods in response to excess consumer demand. The demand side of the market bid up the price of goods in short supply, but the supply side was not free to respond. When supplies failed to increase, it was inevitable that cooperative prices would rise. Consumers, therefore, could either wait in long lines at the state store and attempt to purchase goods that were becoming increasingly nonexistent at the fixed state prices, or they could go to the cooperative market and purchase goods at high market prices until the shelves in those private stores were emptied. Either way, expectations of a better future were dashed, and the credibility of the reforms and perestroika was irreversibly damaged.

The undesirable effects of the policies adopted under perestroika were not limited to their incentive incompatibility with entrepreneurial activity but went much deeper, undermining the basic constitution of economic policy. The continual flux in the legal environment for the cooperatives conveyed a lack of commitment on the part of the regime to private sector experimentation. But without such a commitment, there was no way to induce the investment and hard work that were needed to develop the Soviet economy.[21] So, in addition to incentive incompatibility, there was the debilitating problem of adverse reputation that results from policy reversals and the failure to commit.

That inability to convey any kind of commitment to reform sealed perestroika's fate. The reforms could not get the economy going, and the consumer crisis grew more acute (see Schroeder 1991a, 1991b; Noren 1991). The political instability of failed reforms, alongside deflated expectations on the part of the population, produced a highly troublesome situation for the Gorbachev regime. "As Gorbachev moved back and forth from one comprehensive reform to another," Marshall Goldman argues, "he became more and more uncertain about subjecting the Soviet Union to the type of shock therapy such reforms would inevitably necessitate. He also concluded that unless reined in, the reform process would ultimately shrink his powers and those of the Soviet Union over central economic control, thus reducing the Soviet Union to an ineffective economic entity" (1991, 222).

Gorbachev's economic zigging and zagging was not the only credibility issue at hand. The politics of discretionary power was also an issue of concern with liberal intellectuals, who were not certain that the zigs permitted today would not be superseded by repressive zags tomorrow. "Today," Andrey Sakharov warned, "it is Gorbachev, but tomorrow it could be somebody else. There are no guarantees that some Stalinist will not succeed him" (as quoted in Kaiser 1991, 245).

In the fall of 1990, when Gorbachev backed out of his commitment to the radical Shatalin Plan and moved to the right, he lost credibility with his liberal allies. But perestroika had already cost him his credibility with communist conservatives, so the winter zig to the right did not gain Gorbachev much. As he tried to zag to the left in the spring of 1991, especially with the April compromise with Yeltsin, the conservative forces in the former Soviet Union prepared for one last effort to regain control.

First, they sought to regain control through "constitutional" means; when that failed, they resorted to the August 1991 coup. Even though the coup failed, the failure certainly cannot be attributed to the policies of perestroika. Rather, it was the failure of perestroika that resulted in the coup attempt. As the regime kept introducing liberalization policies only to go back on them, the official economy sank into an abyss. The bureaucracy, which was threatened by reform, knew that more and more radical measures would be necessary to get out of the abyss. Those measures, however, would be undesirable from its point of view.

The unraveling of the Soviet Union as a political entity, however, was the *unintended* by-product of Gorbachev's policy of perestroika. The regime's failure to convey the commitment to economic liberalization that was necessary to reform the Soviet system proved to be perestroika's undoing.

THE POLICY GAME UNDER YELTSIN

In January 1992 the government of Boris Yeltsin, under the orchestration of Yegor Gaidar, embarked on a liberalization program that was far more ambitious than anything introduced during Gorbachev's reign. Most consumer prices were to be liberalized overnight, mass privatization programs were to be forthcoming, a tight monetary policy was to be pursued, and a sound fiscal policy was to be instituted. This "shock therapy" program, however, was never implemented as originally announced.

Price regulations, for example, were maintained on essential consumer products, such as sugar, salt, vodka, bread, and dairy products. The authority for price regulation was delegated to local authorities. This partial liberalization produced unintended consequences that undermined the reform effort.

The price control on milk provides a perfect example of the perverse consequences of partial price reform. Milk prices were not liberalized, but sour cream prices were; in response, dairy producers shifted production out of milk and into sour cream. An abundance of sour cream and a shortage of milk resulted, as predicted by standard economic theory. Local authorities began trying to alter the perverse consequences of one set of controls with additional controls. Whereas in January 1992 only fourteen food products were under price and output controls, by the summer of 1992 that figure had risen to twenty-four. In addition to food, a wide variety of other products were under state controls, not the least being energy. The official situation was one of continued state control over the economy.

It is important to stress the word *official* because the de facto market escaped state controls. The continued existence of the black market during a period of economic liberalization demonstrates that liberalization has in fact not taken place. The dichotomy between the official and the de facto economy is a source of trouble for government leaders, especially because it represents the leakage of a source of state revenue. Victor Chernomyrdin's first decree as the new prime minister was an attempt to bring the de facto economy under government control by regulating prices and monitoring profits. The decree was issued on December 31, 1992, but revoked on January 18, 1993, because it was not credible.[22]

The economic situation in Russia since January 1992 has been one of continued consumer subsidies while tax revenue continued to escape into the black market. The industrial sector of the economy tells a similar story of poor policy design. Enterprise reform was supposed to establish hard budget constraints in the state enterprises. The consequence of enterprise reform, however, was the ballooning of debt between state firms. The interenterprise debt reached 3.2 trillion rubles in the summer of 1992, and many enterprises were threatened with bankruptcy.[23] The Russian parliament resisted the bankruptcy and engineered the Central Bank's issuing rubles to eliminate the debt crisis. The Central Bank remained under parliament's, not the president's, control.[24] The issuance of state credits to resolve the interenterprise debt crisis eliminated the impact of a hard budget constraint, and enterprise reform was stalled. Microeconomic inefficiencies at the enterprise level generated macroeconomic imbalances in the economy.

The link between microeconomic inefficiency and macroeconomic imbal-

Table 6.1   Percentage Increase in Prices on Average for 1992–1993
              as Shown by Monthly Rates of Change in the
              Consumer Price Index

| | 1992 | 1993 |
Month	Rate of change	Rate of change
January	245.0	26.5
February	38.3	25.7
March	29.8	21.4
April	21.6	24.7
May	12.0	19.3
June	18.6	19.9
July	11.0	22.0
August	9.0	26.0
September	12.0	21.0
October	23.0	21.0
November	26.0	21.0
December	25.0	19.0

SOURCE: *PlanEcon Report*, December 19, 1993, p. 26.

ance is a holdover from the Soviet system. The Soviet system of banking involved
a cash sector and a noncash sector. The noncash sector involved an internal
accounting system that linked state enterprises. The Soviet banking system provided enterprises with the financial assets to settle accounts with one another.
Unfortunately, this meant that microeconomic inefficiencies automatically translated into macroeconomic imbalances: deficits and monetization. During the
Soviet era, macroeconomic imbalances were hidden from immediate view by
false accounting or repressed inflation.[25] Reform would bring these imbalances
into the open; partial reform adds to them.

From July 1992 to October 1992 alone the money supply more than doubled,
from 1.4 trillion rubles to 3.4 trillion rubles. In November an additional 18.7
billion rubles, and in December another 61.5 billion rubles, were issued. This
had a dramatic effect on the purchasing power of the ruble in the first year of
reform under the Yeltsin government, as would be expected (see table 6.1).

The "dollarization" of the Russian market economy reflects the unwillingness
to hold rubles for market exchange and as such is perhaps a slightly better indicator
of the real status of the currency than movements in the average price level. In
the first months of the Yeltsin reforms, the ruble gained against the dollar in the

Table 6.2   Ruble/Dollar Exchange Rate at the Interbank Market Rate

Month	1992 Exchange rate	1993 Exchange rate
January	204	489
February	176	570
March	152	664
April	153	767
May	122	917
June	125	1036
July	144	1025
August	170	986
September	225	1059
October	353	1188
November	427	1194
December	415	1245

SOURCE: *PlanEcon Report*, December 19, 1993, p. 37.

currency market. But beginning in June 1992, the ruble fell steadily (see table 6.2).

Continued consumer and producer subsidies, in contrast, swelled the fiscal responsibilities of the Russian state at the same time that reliable sources of tax revenue continued to slip into the unofficial economy.[26] The central government of Russia is faced with an acute fiscal crisis.[27] Not the least of Russia's problems is the military budget. If glasnost-era data are accurate, then the Soviet Union spent around 25 percent of the state budget on defense. With the breakup of the Soviet Union, however, Russia has assumed that burden at the same time that its sources of revenue have been reduced. The burden of the defense sector has thus increased during the Yeltsin period.[28] Fiscal crises are usually "eliminated" through monetization. Inflationary environments, however, destroy the ability to calculate alternative investments rationally and as such deter economic development.

The Yeltsin shock therapy was ill conceived and contradictory from the beginning.[29] Moreover, without the appropriate political changes, the economic reforms could not get implemented as the situation dictated. In combination with the economic environment, the political crisis increased the uncertainty of the situation. The "war of decrees" between parliament and the president was not the only problem; many of Yeltsin's decrees were inconsistent with basic economic incentives. Tax rates and other business fees, for example, are inconsistent with the goal of attracting business investment. Foreign investment has been deterred by both economic and political uncertainty.[30]

Often the message is mixed from the government, which adds to the confusion. In addition, the vacuum of power in the central government and the fiscal crisis the center is experiencing have led regional authorities to claim more autonomy. Effective governmental power in Russia by the spring of 1993 had already shifted to the regional leaders.[31] As the events of late September and early October 1993 demonstrated, the uncertainty of the transition policy has not been overcome. And in the wake of the unexpected election results of December 1993, the Yeltsin government appears to have decided to move toward a more cautious reform program with major concessions to state enterprises and state farms.[32] For now, at least, it appears that the rhetoric of the Yeltsin regime has shifted from one of liberalization to conservative management.[33]

A historical perspective suggests that the troubling uncertainty in Russia is natural during a time of regime change and that there is no spontaneous mechanism that guarantees a benign outcome.[34] It took more than sixty years of turmoil in England, for example, until the political bargain of the Glorious Revolution was struck in 1688 and economic productivity increased markedly.[35]

That history offers us no easy and fixed rules for moving from an autocratic government and state-run economies to liberal political and economic arrangements does not change the basic message of the argument presented in this chapter: political rules must be established that effectively constrain discretionary behavior, and a clear and well-defined (i.e., transparent) legal system must be constructed *before* private sector economic experimentation can be expected to yield the promised welfare gains.

Conclusion

One of the most basic insights of political economy is the need for rules to govern economic activity. Modern political economy is a research program that focuses our inquiry on the working properties of rules and the processes of social interaction that take place within rules. By examining both the rules of social interaction and their impact on social processes, scholars can begin to develop ideas about workable constitutions of economic policy.

In developing a workable constitution of economic policy, it must be recognized that the obstacles that incentives and information present to discretionary behavior are formidable. The Soviet experience shows that without effectively signaling and establishing a binding and credible commitment to broad liberalization, the behavior of the government simply destabilizes the situation.

The argument against government intervention in the free-market process does not amount to asserting that government intervention must necessarily lead to totalitarianism. That was a misunderstanding of the argument on the critics' part. Rather, the argument suggests that interventionism produces unintended results that will be viewed as undesirable from the government's own point of view. Thus, interventionist policy constantly forces on government officials the choice of either rejecting their previous policy or intervening even more in the attempt to correct past failings. The argument is a stability argument. Intervention is just not stable as an economic and political system. The discretionary behavior of the government results in situations that undermine its own initiatives.

Whereas the instability of the 1920s in the Soviet Union led to Stalinism, the instability of the late 1980s has led to the dissolution of the Soviet Union. The efforts in the 1950s and 1960s at liberalization failed and were quickly reversed. Even under Yeltsin's post-Soviet experiment in free-market shock therapy, the new government failed to establish the sort of binding political and legal commitments required. Each of these experiences illustrates the basic point: discretionary behavior on the part of the government fails to produce the stable environment that is necessary for economic prosperity. The insights that the Soviet and post-Soviet experience offer should become basic material in developing a workable constitution of economic policy in the postperestroika era.

Notes

1. See Boettke (1993) for an examination of perestroika. This chapter draws freely from that earlier treatment.

2. I will not directly address the problems associated with socialist reform attempts, such as Lenin's war communism or Stalin's collectivization, in this chapter but instead concentrate on the difficulties of liberalization within a socialist regime. On the difficulties associated with socialist reforms, see Boettke (1993, 46–56) and the literature cited therein.

3. See Klein (1990), Klein and O'Flaherty (1993), and Roderik (1989) for components of the theoretical argument that follows.

4. Roderik (1989) argues that policy overshooting can reduce informational confusion. The more severe the credibility gap, however, the more drastic the policy overshooting must be in order to send the appropriate signal.

5. For an examination of the policies of war communism, see Boettke (1990, 63–111).

6. Alan Ball (1987, 23). Also see N. Gubsky (1927) for a contemporary account of the Civil Code.

7. The Soviet constitution barred from voting or holding office (1) people using hired

labor to make profits, (2) people living on "unearned income," which included income from private enterprises and property, and (3) private traders and middlemen. The *lishentsy* could not have careers in the military or join cooperatives or trade unions or publish newspapers or organize gatherings. In addition, they had to pay higher fees for utilities, rent, medical care, school, and all public services.

8. As Robert Conquest explains: "When the market mechanism had failed to give satisfaction, requisition made up the shortfall, and the government then went back to the market. *But from the peasant point of view, the market was no longer a reasonably secure outlet, but one that might be superseded at any moment by requisition.* And in the further deterioration of market relations thus produced, the government remembered the success it had had with forced requisition, and did not reflect that it was the requisition of grain produced with the incentive of the market, and that in the new circumstances this was certain to shrink in quantity" (1986, 93).

9. See the discussion of Khrushchev's speech in Nove (1992, 336ff).

10. As Nove points out, however, Khrushchev's agricultural policies crowded out the only remaining sphere of autonomy left to the peasants after collectivization—the private plot. As such, Khrushchev's agricultural policies were counterproductive. See Nove (1992, 372–77).

11. See the discussion in Hewett (1988, 223–27), Nove (1992, 351–54), and Gregory and Stuart (1990, 143).

12. Coordination problems included duplication of supply arrangements, components manufacturing and that all decisions (minor as well as major) required approval from Moscow.

13. See Hewett (1988, 226, table 5-1) for an examination of the growth rates during this period.

14. Liberman's original article was published in *Pravda*, September 9, 1962. See Hewett (1988, 227–45). Also see Pejovich (1969) for a critical examination of the divergence between "announcement" of a reform, the content of a reform proposal, and the implementation of a reform proposal. In the language of this chapter, it is precisely the discrepancy between the announcement and the content and implementation that generates the credibility gap that must be closed before economic reform can be expected to generate positive results.

15. For a discussion of the Soviet bureaucracy and the difficulties this system presented for reform, see Gregory (1990). Also see Rutland (1993) for the involvement of local party organs in the economic management bureaucracy.

16. See Linz (1987, 156) for the report of these interviews.

17. As John Litwack explains: "A Soviet manager . . . is often averse to expending resources for improving the performance of his or her firm. But this is not because of a well-defined progressive tax scheme that requires sharing future benefits with the government. The problem is that the tax scheme tomorrow is at the discretion of superiors in the hierarchy. They will determine conditions only after observing the performance of the firm today. In the absence of long-run commitment, these superiors naturally attempt to

extract surpluses from those subordinate organizations that reveal themselves to be more productive. In addition, poorly performing enterprises are typically 'bailed out.' . . . The expectation of discretionary extraction and bailouts creates an incentive problem at lower levels" (1991a, 257).

18. As Belkindas (1989) points out, opportunities for unearned income originate because of the shortage economy. Illegal housing transactions, medical care, admission to an institution of higher education, and so forth are just some examples of how illicit transactions can "correct" for the failings of the official economy.

19. See Belkindas (1989, 37–97) for an overview of the development of private cooperatives in the Soviet Union. In addition, see Jones and Moskoff (1991).

20. See Jones and Moskoff (1989). With regard to the hostility toward the emerging cooperatives, they state that "cooperative activity has . . . engendered a great deal of hostility from two groups: the consuming public, which it is supposed to serve, and the bureaucracy, which it threatens" (1989, 32). Also see the discussion of the economic environment within which cooperatives had to operate and the array of official responses in terms of restrictions, interference, and taxation that stifled the development of cooperatives in Jones and Moskoff (1991, 34–77). In addition, see Goldman (1991, 113). "The halfhearted toleration of cooperative and private trade," Goldman states, "was guaranteed to sabotage the whole effort."

21. The evolution of working capital markets, for example, depends on the ability of the state to be bound by commitments that it will not confiscate assets. "The shackling of arbitrary behavior of rulers and the development of impersonal rules" that successfully bind the state are key components of institutional transformation. See North (1990, 129) and Litwack (1991b).

22. See *Radio Free Europe/Radio Liberty (RFE/RL) Research Bulletin*, February 3, 1993, pp. 2–3.

23. For an examination of the interenterprise debt, see Ickes and Ryterman (1992).

24. Thus, it was ironic when Western critics of "shock therapy" blamed the poor results on "monetarism." The monetarist policy prescription is predicated on control of the money supply—the Central Bank of Russia (under parliament's direction) pursued a loose monetary policy to bail out the failing state enterprises. The struggle between the government policy makers and the Central Bank guaranteed that a uniform monetary policy would not emerge. On September 21, 1993—along with disbanding the parliament—Yeltsin transferred control of the Central Bank to his government.

25. See, for example, Shelton (1989). Shelton, building on the work of Soviet émigré economist Igor Birman, challenges Soviet budget records, pointing out, for example, that there was a gap between claimed revenues and identified sources of revenue in the budget figures in 1987 of around 146.4 billion rubles. This gap, she says, was persistent from 1970 on and ranges from a 20 percent gap in 1970 to a 36 percent gap in 1987. Shelton concludes that the internal budget mess in the Soviet Union was severe even before Gorbachev.

26. The debate over bread price decontrol is illustrative of the problem with the Russian reform package. Complete decontrol of bread prices was first scheduled for October 1,

1993, but postponed until October 15, 1993. On October 12, Chernomyrdin announced that the government was reconsidering the decision to decontrol bread prices. Bread allowances subsidize consumption to low-income citizens at an estimated 1,400 rubles per month. See *RFE/RL*, October 13, 1993.

27. The 1993 budget approved by parliament, for example, included a 22.4 trillion-ruble deficit that amounted to about 25 percent of gross national product (see *RFE/RL*, August 26, 1993). As pointed out in an *Izvestiya* article, each liberalization of the Russian economy has been accompanied by promised subsidization, so the fiscal strains on the Russian budget continue to grow (see *RFE/RL*, August 30, 1993). Moreover, because Russia lacks a well-developed securities market, deficit financing translates immediately into pressure to monetize, that is, the government cannot borrow and, therefore, must finance its affairs either through taxation or inflation.

28. Interview with Professor Gennadi Zoteev, vice director of the Economic Research Institute, Ministry of Economics of the Russian Federation, in his Moscow office on January 25, 1993.

29. See Boettke (1993, 138–44) for a discussion of some of the opposition, both from conservative and liberal reformist factions, to Yeltsin's policy design.

30. See *RFE/RL*, August 3, 1993, where it is reported that *Izvestiya* announced that an insurance fund had been established by the State Investment Corporation and the European Agency for Export Guarantees to protect foreign investment from political uncertainty in Russia. The fund's founding capital consisted of gold and precious metals to the value of about $100 million and would be deposited in a West European country.

31. See Burke (1993). Also note that thirty of the eighty-nine republics and regions of the Russian Federation are withholding taxes from Moscow. Some, for example Checheno-Ingush, are simply refusing to pay any taxes to the center. Others, such as Bashkir and Tatar, have declared "fiscal sovereignty"—a unilateral decision on their part as to how much tax revenue will be sent to Moscow.

32. See *The Economist*, January 22, 1994, pp. 52–53.

33. It is important to stress that one cannot legitimately conclude that shock therapy failed in Russia because it was never tried. Thus, it is particularly ridiculous when Chernomyrdin argues that the Russian government has already tried to guide the process of transition with monetary controls and failed and that now it is time to shift to nonmonetary means of control (i.e., wage and price controls) to guide the transition. What shock therapy amounted to was a reform announcement followed by partial steps toward implementation and then reversal of the policy. Yeltsin simply repeated the general pattern of the Soviet reformer that I have tried to document.

34. The evolution of liberal institutions of governance are in no sense guaranteed. Instead, effective liberal revolutions result from a peculiar mix of indigenous institutions and cultural practices combined with careful design of liberal rules that can tap into these indigenous traditions and cultivate a sustainable liberal order.

35. See the discussion of the evolution of institutions of public choice in seventeenth-century England in North and Weingast 1989.

References

Aslund, A. *Gorbachev's Struggle for Economic Reform*. 2d edition. Ithaca, N.Y.: Cornell University Press, 1991.

Ball, A. *Russia's Last Capitalists: The Nepmen, 1921–1929*. Berkeley: University of California Press, 1987.

Belkindas, M. *Privatization of the Soviet Economy under Gorbachev, II*. Berkeley-Duke Occasional Papers on the Second Economy of the USSR, no. 14. April 1989.

Berliner, J. "Planning and Management." In Abram Bergson and Herbert Levine, eds., *The Soviet Economy: Toward the Year 2000*. London: Allen and Unwin, 1983.

Boettke, P. *The Political Economy of Soviet Socialism: The Formative Years, 1918–1928*. Boston: Kluwer Academic Publishers, 1990.

———. *Why Perestroika Failed: The Politics and Economics of Socialist Transformation*. London: Routledge, 1993.

Bukharin, N. "Concerning the New Economic Policy and Our Tasks (1925)." In N. I. Bukharin, *Selected Writings on the State and the Transition to Socialism*, ed. Richard Day. New York: M.E. Sharpe, 1982.

Burke, J. "Russia's Regions Emerge as Key Power Brokers." *Christian Science Monitor*, March 15, 1993, p. 6.

Carr, E. H. *The Bolshevik Revolution, 1917-1923*. 3 vols. New York: Norton, 1981 (1953).

———. *Socialism in One Country, 1924–1926*. 2 vols. Baltimore: Penguin Books, 1958.

Conquest, R. *The Harvest of Sorrow*. New York: Oxford University Press, 1986.

Friedman, M. "A Monetary and Fiscal Framework for Economic Stability." In Friedman, *Essays in Positive Economics*. Chicago: University of Chicago Press, 1953.

Goldman, Marshall. *What Went Wrong with Perestroika*. New York: Norton, 1991.

Gregory, P. *Restructuring the Soviet Economic Bureaucracy*. New York: Cambridge University Press, 1990.

Gregory, P., and Stuart, R. *Soviet Economic Structure and Performance*. 4th edition. New York: Harper and Row, 1990.

Gubsky, N. "Economic Law in Soviet Russia." *Economic Journal* 37 (June 1927).

Hewett, E. *Reforming the Soviet Economy*. Washington, D.C.: Brookings Institution, 1988.

Ickes, B., and R. Ryterman. "The Interenterprise Arrear Crisis in Russia." *Post-Soviet Affairs* 8 (1992).

Jones, A., and W. Moskoff. "New Cooperatives in the USSR." *Problems of Communism*, November–December 1989, pp. 27–39.

———. *Ko-ops: The Rebirth of Entrepreneurship in the Soviet Union*. Bloomington: Indiana University Press, 1991.

Kaiser, R. *Why Gorbachev Happened?* New York: Simon and Schuster, 1991.

Khanin, G. I. "Why and When Did NEP Die?" *EKO*, no. 10 (1989); translated in *Problems of Economics* 33 (August 1990).

Klein, D. "The Microeconomic Foundations of Rules versus Discretion." *Constitutional Political Economy* 1, no. 3 (Fall 1990).

Klein, D., and B. O'Flaherty. "A Game-Theoretic Rendering of Promises and Threats." *Journal of Economic Behavior and Organization* 21 (1993).

Kornai, J. "The Soft Budget Constraint." *Kyklos* 39, no. 1 (1986).

Kydland, F., and E. Prescott. "Rules Rather than Discretion: The Inconsistency of Optimal Plans." *Journal of Political Economy* 85, no. 3 (1977); 473–91.

The Law on Individual Enterprise. *Pravda*, November 21, 1986; translated in *Current Digest of the Soviet Press* 38, no. 46 (1986).

The Law on State Enterprises. *Pravda*, July 1, 1987: translated in *Current Digest of the Soviet Press* 39, nos. 30–31 (1987).

The Law on Cooperatives. In J. L. Black, ed., *USSR Document Annual*. Gulf Breeze, Fla.: Academic International Press, 1988.

Linz, S. "The Impact of Soviet Economic Reform: Evidence from the Interview Project." *Comparative Economic Studies* 29, no. 4 (Winter 1987).

Litwack, J. "Discretionary Behavior and Soviet Economic Reform." *Soviet Studies* 43, no. 2 (1991a).

————. "Legality and Market Reform in Soviet-Type Economies." *Journal of Economic Perspectives* 5, no. 4 (Fall 1991b).

Noren, J. "The Economic Crisis: Another Perspective." In Ed Hewett and Victor Winston, eds., *Milestones in Glasnost and Perestroika: The Economy*. Washington, D.C.: Brookings Institution, 1991.

North, D. *Institutions, Institutional Change and Economic Performance*. New York: Cambridge University Press, 1990.

North, D. and B. Weingast. "Constitutions and Commitment: The Evolution of Institutions Governing Public Choice in Seventeenth-Century England." *Journal of Economic History*, December 1989.

Nove, A. *An Economic History of the USSR, 1917–1991*. New York: Penguin, 1992.

Pejovich, S. "Liberman's Reforms and Property Rights in the Soviet Union." *Journal of Law and Economics* 12 (April 1969).

Rodrik, D. "Promises, Promises: Credible Policy Reform via Signalling." *Economic Journal* 99 (September 1989).

Rutland, P. *The Politics of Economic Stagnation in the Soviet Union*. New York: Cambridge University Press, 1993.

Schroeder, G. "The Soviet Economy on a Treadmill of Perestroika: Gorbachev's First Five Years." In Harley D. Balzer, ed., *Five Years That Shook the World*. Boulder, Colo.: Westview Press, 1991a.

———. "'Crisis' in the Consumer Sector: A Comment." In Ed Hewett and Victor Winston, eds., *Milestones in Glasnost and Perestroika: The Economy*. Washington, D.C.: Brookings Institution, 1991b.

Shelton, J. *The Coming Soviet Crash*. New York: The Free Press, 1989.

Solzhenitsyn, A. *The Gulag Archipelago*. 3 vols. New York: Harper and Row, 1973.

7

Gradual versus Rapid Liberalization in Socialist Foreign Trade

RONALD I. MCKINNON

In transitional socialist economies, the pace of liberalizing foreign trade must be carefully geared to the pace of price decontrol, existing tax mechanisms, and the degree of financial liberalization in domestic commerce. These initial conditions are important in determining whether a move to current-account convertibility between domestic and foreign monies should be rapid—as in Chile after 1973 or in Poland after 1989—or more gradual, as in China and Vietnam in the 1980s into the 1990s. Otherwise, a debacle like the ill-fated Russian liberalization of 1992 cannot be ruled out.

THIS ESSAY CONSIDERS two highly stylized but logically consistent approaches to liberalizing socialist foreign trade. The first is rapid, on the *Chilean model,* and presumes that domestic markets and price decontrol are virtually complete when the trade reforms begin and that individuals and enterprises have commercial contacts with foreigners and some familiarity with international markets. Chile's move to freer trade and full currency convertibility on current account, after the fall of the socialist Salvador Allende regime in 1973, is briefly laid out in an idealized format—consolidating and summarizing the previous analyses of Chile in McKinnon (1991, 1993).[1]

The second approach is more gradual liberalization on the *Chinese model,* which presumes that domestic markets and price decontrol are still incomplete. At the outset of the trade reforms, a dualistic system of financial and price controls treats the state and nonstate sectors differently—extensively analyzed in McKinnon (1991, 1993, and 1994). Initially, this financial dualism is important for maintaining the economy's monetary equilibrium and generating revenue for the government (i.e., monopoly profits in the state-owned sector). Thus any rapid move to full current-account currency convertibility and world relative prices must be ruled out. Yet other measures for encouraging foreign trade—special economic zones, broad foreign exchange retentions by exporters, and delimited interenterprise swap markets in foreign exchange—can still be effective in gradually opening the economy. To illustrate this more gradual approach, this essay draws on the Chinese experience after 1978—again in an idealized format that omits many details and missteps along the way.

Which of these two paradigms of trade liberalization is more appropriate depends on the initial economic conditions facing a new reform government.

The Chilean Model of Rapid Trade Liberalization

First, let us briefly review the chaotic situation the new Chilean government faced in 1974. From 1970 to 1973, the previous populist government had intervened to reduce prices relative to wages. Most enterprises were thus forced to operate with severe losses, which were covered by borrowing from the nationalized banking system. Together with huge central government fiscal deficits also covered by the banks, this enterprise borrowing caused the Chilean money supply to spiral out of control with price inflation that was only partly suppressed. As shops were emptied of goods at the controlled prices, a cash overhang developed. But the underlying monetary system was still unified; Chile's experience with socialism was too short for the government to develop dual monetary circuits where "soft" enterprise deposit money was separated from "hard" household cash. Thus, to get control over the unified money supply, rapid price decontrol was a feasible method of eliminating enterprises' current deficits, on the one hand, with the subsequent one-time high inflation eliminating the excess stocks of cash balances, on the other. Similar to Poland in 1990 but unlike China in 1978, immediate price decontrol—where prices rose relative to wages—was necessary for establishing monetary and fiscal balance. (Using the value-added tax [VAT] as the centerpiece of its revenue-raising effort, Chile also successfully restructured the public finances in parallel with the freeing of domestic prices.)

From 1970 to 1973, interventions in foreign trade paralleled those in domestic trade. Multiple exchange rates had proliferated, with the peso cost of foreign exchange being ten or more times as high in some categories as in others—with widespread foreign exchange rationing. Similarly, tariffs were extremely high in some categories with the import of many goods "prohibited"; yet a few favored importers received blanket exemption from these trade restrictions.

Parallel with the decontrol of domestic prices, the new government completely unified the exchange rate system by 1975 and rationalized commercial policy with full current-account convertibility by 1976. All previous quantitative restrictions on imports and exports were replaced by "equivalent" ad valorem tariffs, which cascaded from relatively high rates on finished consumer goods to moderate rates on finished producer goods to a basic 10 percent rate on industrial raw materials. From the government's perspective, this immediately increased revenue. Then, in 1977, it was announced that the highest tariffs in the cascade would be reduced step by step to a uniform 10 percent by the end of 1979. Provided that the real exchange rate was not allowed to become overvalued (unlike what happened in Chile in 1980–81), this relatively rapid liberalization of foreign trade was intended to remove the bias against exporting from the old regime's heavy protection for import-substituting industries. This intention was eventually realized in the late 1980s and early 1990s, when a major export boom developed. Protectionism had been eliminated, and import tariffs were confined to a low uniform level of 10 to 15 percent for purposes of raising revenue. (Into the early 1990s, however, Chile has had to retain various exchange controls on capital accounts—mainly on capital inflows—to prevent the exchange rate from once more becoming overvalued.)

In summary, the initial economic conditions in Chile favored rapid commodity price decontrol and currency convertibility on current accounts as a means of securing financial equilibrium. Because an appropriate system of commodity and income taxation had been relatively quickly (re)established, both measures tended to improve the government's revenue position. The rapid privatization of nationalized industries—in part by simply returning them to their original owners—virtually eliminated the syndrome of the soft budget constraint affecting the core of Chilean industry. Because budget constraints on enterprises were hardened,[2] Chile could move quickly to full current-account convertibility. To import, enterprises could bid freely for foreign exchange at a unified exchange rate. But even Chile did not resort to "shock therapy" (i.e., completely free trade) at the outset. Quantitative restrictions on imports were converted into temporarily cascaded tariffs to give domestic producers a few years to adjust before being fully exposed to world relative prices.

The Chinese Model of Gradual Liberalization

Detailed descriptions of the evolution of Chinese foreign trade practices before and after liberalization began in 1978 are now available (Cheng

1991; Lardy 1992; Wong 1992; Panagaryia 1993). Here, I shall take a different tack.

First, let us identify the Chinese trade and payment regime's key facets that supported classical central planning before 1978. To maintain domestic monetary and fiscal balance under centralized price controls and output allocations, financial insulation from the rest of the world was necessary.

Second, domestic liberalization after 1978 took the form of industrial and financial dualism: soft budget constraints on the old state-owned enterprises, which could borrow from the state banking system, and hard budget constraints on agriculture and "nonstate" enterprises, which were much more limited in their access to bank finance. In a somewhat idealized fashion, the main facets of this financial dualism are summarized in table 7.1 to reflect earlier analyses by the author (McKinnon 1991, 1993). As the Chinese economy became progressively more open, what evolutionary path of relaxing restraints on foreign trade was consistent with maintaining macroeconomic equilibrium? (Unlike Chile or Poland, China had no monetary overhang or other serious macroeconomic disequilibria at the outset of its liberalization.)

CENTRAL PLANNING AND COMMODITY INCONVERTIBILITY

Within the industrial sector of a centrally planned economy, the current output of producer goods and services is centrally allocated by administrative fiat. Instead of being determined by the market, prices serve only a passive role in accounting for cash flows when goods pass from one enterprise to another. Nominal prices often remain unchanged for years. To generate cash surpluses in state-owned manufacturing enterprises, however, the prices of raw materials and intermediate inputs are generally kept low relative to the prices of finished (consumer) goods. Relative to world market prices, the prices of agricultural goods are kept similarly low to set nominal wages low and further increase the cash surpluses in enterprises.

Because these controlled prices do not reflect relative scarcity either domestically or internationally, any attempt to open a market—with free bidding for goods at these prices—could well lead to a perverse allocation of resources. But this potential problem is suppressed by having goods allocated by central planning and by blocking the cash balance holdings of the enterprises so they cannot bid freely for scarce inputs. In effect, the money of domestic enterprises is not freely convertible into domestic commodities (i.e., there is *commodity inconvertibility*).

Because prices are not used to allocate goods domestically, it is inconceivable that foreigners be permitted to do what domestic enterprises cannot do (i.e., freely exercise domestic monetary claims to buy whatever goods seem attractive at prevailing prices). Not only would centrally administered materials be upset, but low price tags on on some potentially exportable goods—like industrial raw

Table 7.1   Alternative Financial Arrangements for Enterprises
in a Model Transitional Economy

| | TRADITIONAL ENTERPRISES[a] (STATE SECTOR) | LIBERALIZED ENTERPRISES (NONSTATE SECTOR) | |
		Collective[b]	*Private*
Taxation	Expropriation of surpluses[c]	Uniform value-added tax	Uniform value-added tax
Deposit money; domestic commodity convertibility[d]	Restricted	Unrestricted interest-bearing	Unrestricted interest-bearing
Credit eligibility	State bank	Nonbank capital market	Nonbank capital market
Wages	Government determined	Collectively determined	Market determined
Residual profits	Accrue to government	Dividends to collective, retained earnings for reinvestment	Dividends to owners,[e] retained earnings for reinvestment or lending to other private enterprises
Foreign exchange convertibility	Restricted	Current account only (swap market)	Current account only (swap market)
Producer prices	Pegged with intramarginal delivery quotas[f]	Market determined	Market determined

[a] Traditional enterprises are those whose output and pricing decisions are still largely determined by a central government authority or planning bureau with centrally allocated inputs and credits from the state bank to cover (possible) negative cash flows. In China, traditional enterprises would be in the so-called state sector, while new entities outside these traditional controls would be in the nonstate sector.

[b] Collective can refer to any level of government ownership or sponsorship, as with Chinese township and village enterprises. For example, the VAT administered by the central government would apply equally to liberalized enterprises owned or registered in different local jurisdictions.

[c] Although residual profits revert to the state, they could include a shadow VAT levy in order to better understand the true profitability of traditional enterprises.

[d] Commodity convertibility here means the freedom to spend for domestic goods and services or to buy and hold domestic coin and currency but need not imply convertibility into foreign exchange.

[e] Dividends would be subject to the personal income tax when paid out to private owners, but retained earnings would not be taxed.

[f] After satisfying delivery commitments to other traditional enterprises, marginal output can be sold at free-market prices.

materials—may well conceal the fact that they are very costly in real resources or are in actual shortage. Formal accounting prices need bear no systematic relationship to their value in use as seen by the planners. Thus commodity inconvertibility also prevented nonresident foreign enterprises from freely purchasing domestic goods or services should they be unlucky enough to build up domestic deposits with the state bank.

Nor were foreign-owned domestic balances freely convertible into foreign exchange. Commodity and foreign exchange inconvertibility went hand in hand.

A natural concomitant of commodity convertibility, therefore, is the concentration of all import and and export activity in a state trading agency or agencies for purchasing foreign goods to be sold domestically or domestic goods that are to be sold abroad. Centralized state trading agencies act as necessary buffers between foreign and domestic relative prices. At the official exchange rate(s), they ignore any profits or losses from selling or buying domestic goods abroad—all of which are mandated by the central plan. These purchases and sales are insensitive to how the official exchange rate is set.

For China, we have Christine Wong's description:

> The prereform trade system was characterized by centralized planning and management under the Ministry of Foreign Trade (MFT). All foreign trade was dictated from the center, which specified the products and quantities to be imported and exported. Trading was undertaken by 12 Foreign Trade Corporations (FTCs) under MFT, each specializing in a different product line. The FTCs had headquarters in Beijing and branch offices in the provinces. The system was highly centralized—only the FTC head offices had the right to sign contracts for exports and imports, although fulfillment of the contracts was often assigned to provincial bureaus and branches.
>
> All procurement for export was done by the FTCs and assigned to enterprises as part of their production and delivery plans. With the procurement conducted at domestic prices, enterprises were indifferent between selling on the domestic or export markets. On the import side, FTCs were given an allocation of foreign exchange to fulfill their import plans for sale at domestic prices. In this way, the FTCs acted as sole contact points for external trade, completely insulating Chinese enterprises from the world market and its prices—a role that has been described as "air lock." Since Chinese prices for manufactures were higher than world prices, FTCs engaged in importing were generally profitable, and their profits subsidized the losses of the exporting FTCs (except those in raw material products, which were also profitable)." (Wong 1992, 50)

This air lock system was strongly biased against foreign trade. Domestic enterprises did not become familiar with foreign selling or buying opportunities— and had no economic incentive to exploit them should they appear. In particular, exporting was not at all commercialized. Because the central planning authorities first determined import needs by domestic demand and supply conditions—or, more accurately, unanticipated gaps between planned supplies and planned usage—a list of exports would be more or less arbitrarily identified to generate the needed foreign exchange. However inefficient it might have been in an allocative sense, the air lock system preserved the government's ability to collect revenue domestically by rigging the domestic relative prices to generate "monopoly" profits in state-owned manufacturing enterprises. The 1970s were generally a period in which the Chinese central government's revenues rose quite strongly as a share of gross national product (GNP) (Wong 1992)—undergirding the price stability of that period by avoiding the buildup of a monetary overhang.

THE REFORM PROBLEM

After 1978, the philosophy governing China's foreign trade policies shifted dramatically from repression to expansion—although the policies themselves did not change all at once. Starting from a situation of highly repressed foreign trade and a very small foreign trade sector (a little more than 5 percent of GNP in 1979), in a rapidly growing economy exports had risen even more rapidly, reaching 20 percent of GNP by 1992.[3]

To accomplish this great feat, China first had to end the commercial isolation of its domestic manufacturing industries from world markets and improve the allocative efficiency of its exporting and importing. Second, this liberalization had to be accomplished at the margin so as not to undermine the commercial viability of the old state-owned enterprises (SOEs)—many of which would have exhibited negative or very low value added at world market prices (McKinnon 1991, chap. 12)—or to undermine the government's ability to collect revenue from these SOEs even faster than it declined in practice. Third, in the more liberalized setting, the Chinese could not afford to let the foreign exchange regime itself become an engine of inflation by, say, engineering a deep discrete devaluation when the economy became more open, as did Poland in January 1990, or simply by losing control of the foreign exchange market altogether with an even deeper ongoing devaluation cum inflation, as did Russia in 1992. Without any access to foreign aid or financial support from abroad in the late 1970s and early 1980s, China depended heavily on the willingness of domestic households and nonstate enterprises to build up financial claims on the state banking system (denominated in the domestic currency) voluntarily to finance the government and the SOEs (McKinnon, 1994). Thus an inflationary policy of loosening foreign exchange constraints too rapidly so as to allow domestic nationals to switch into foreign monies, or precipitately opening the whole economy to free importing and exporting while simultaneously protecting domestic tradable goods industries by a deep devaluation, would have undermined the incentives for high real financial growth (i.e., for domestic financial deepening).[4]

CHINESE TRADE LIBERALIZATION AT THE MARGIN

Gradual trade liberalization in China had complementary foreign exchange and commercial policy aspects after 1978. But both were geared to giving potential exporters of manufactured goods strong incentives to begin breaking out of the air lock imposed on them by the FTCs. Instead of import needs arbitrarily determining exports as in the old regime, the idea was to develop new exports on a commercial basis (i.e., where exporters could begin to see more or less correct relative prices in world market terms). Although imports would remain restricted by the FTCs themselves or by new licensing procedures, the scope for importing would gradually be liberalized more or less in line with any increase in export earnings. (And China has, from 1978 through 1992, achieved a rough balance between cumulative export earnings and cumulative expenditures for imports; net foreign debt remains very small for the size of the economy.) So what were the principal measures for promoting exports at the liberalizing margins of the economy?

Special Economic Zones (SEZs). To begin an open-door policy outside the ambit of domestic relative prices, the policy of creating SEZs was begun in 1978, first with Guangdong and Fujian and then by many others. In these quasi–free trade zones, exporters were allowed to keep 100 percent of their foreign exchange earnings for purposes of importing needed inputs of raw materials or capital goods into the zone. Joint ventures with foreigners were given preferentially low tax rates on profits or gross output in these zones. Within these SEZs, the relative prices facing exporters more closely reflected those prevailing in world markets; the low taxes were a kind of subsidy toward developing normal commercial contacts, which had been unnaturally repressed, with the outside world. This strategy, using Hong Kong as a commercial contact point and entrepôt, was enormously successful in promoting explosive growth in manufactured exports from these areas.

Decentralization of the FTCs. Much decision making in the FTCs themselves was transferred to provincial and local governments, which resulted in a tremendous proliferation in their number, from twelve in 1978 to one thousand in 1984 to five thousand in 1990 (Wong 1992). These trading agencies were still constrained in a general sense; import and export licensing was introduced in 1984 to replace direct centralized controls. Concomitantly, the number of products whose quantities of imports or exports were centrally planned fell from about three thousand on the eve of reform in 1978 to about one hundred thirty by 1988

(Lardy 1992). Export licenses had to be retained on those raw materials and agricultural goods still kept below world prices.

Export Retentions and Foreign Exchange Contracting.   Instead of confining the export retentions to the SEZs, in 1979 the government further increased incentives for export promotion by allowing local governments—perhaps represented by their own FTCs—to retain a portion of their foreign exchange earnings, typically 25 percent. By the late 1980s, this culminated in an export-contracting system whereby exporters retained a fixed proportion of their basic quota earnings for the year but then could retain a much higher proportion of export earnings, typically 80 percent, for exports beyond the negotiated basis. Again, this was a very substantial incentive for increasing exports at the margin throughout China—whether in an SEZ or not.

Swap Markets for Foreign Exchange.   To prevent exporting enterprises from holding foreign exchange outright (a form of capital outflow), however, the retained foreign exchange had to be deposited with the People's Bank of China and only drawn on when the enterprise wanted to make approved imports. Initially these entitlements were not transferable, and the holder would bear substantial exchange risk should the renminbi be officially devalued before the right to import was exercised. Moreover, the holder might have no need to import in the immediate future. To break this logjam,

> The first swap market for foreign exchange opened in 1985 in Shenzhen, followed by a second in Shanghai in 1986. By 1988, there were 39 centers, and by 1989 over 90. Total volume reached $6.3 billion in 1988, and $8.57 billion in 1989. To date, participation in the markets has been limited to organizations and enterprises which have foreign exchange earnings. Individual and enterprises without other access to foreign exchange cannot participate. The main form of trading is bilateral: enterprises have to find buyers/sellers on their own, and then use the swap market to actualize the exchange. (Wong 1992, 49)

The development of foreign exchange swap markets, albeit limited and imperfectly arbitraged geographically, was a major step forward in liberalization. It increased the incentives for exporting because exporters could immediately get cash for their quota rights on the one hand and increase their allocative efficiency on the other. A wider range of enterprises and organizations could bid for foreign exchange at the free swap rate. Nevertheless, the government still retained substantial control over who could participate in the market on current-account and international capital flows.

The Foreign Exchange Rate and the Swap Rate.   Although China began with an apparently overvalued exchange rate of 1.49 yuan per U.S. dollar in 1979, it made little difference because most trade had to be filtered through the FTCs. But as decision making became decentralized down to the enterprise level, getting the foreign exchange rate right became progressively more important. The official exchange rate has been devalued several times; in 1992 it was 5.8 yuan per U.S. dollar, with the swap rate varying between 7.0 and 9.0 yuan to the dollar. In 1993, the concern may well be that the renminbi is undervalued (i.e., the exchange rate is above the level that would yield purchasing power parity with the outside world).

PROJECTING THE CHINESE EXPERIENCE

Because the overall economy is now much more open, and the foreign trade sector is now large, this undervaluation seems to be a factor in generating too much inflationary pressure in the economy in 1993. Subsequently, the exchange rate should be set with more of an eye to controlling domestic price inflation rather than simply stimulating exports. In this perspective, the distinction between the free swap rate and pegged official rate should soon be abandoned. Once exports become large and the economy open, further subsidizing some exporters through a dual exchange rate system is counterproductive.

China's step-by-step liberalization of its foreign exchange and foreign trade regime has been successful in building up a manufactured export base, which has incorporated best-practice technologies from the rest of the world. Up to 1993 at least, no major mishaps in the foreign exchanges upset the domestic economies' macroeconomic equilibrium. Foreign trade truly has been a major engine of growth in the remarkable increase in per capita GNP in China since 1978.

However, the use of special economic zones has caused this development to be seriously unbalanced. Coastal provinces are getting rich, while those in the interior languish by comparison. To some extent, the Chinese government is recognizing this. In 1991, export retentions, whether in an SEZ or not, were made more uniform throughout the country.

In the long run, tax concessions to SEZs and foreign joint ventures tend to further undermine the government's revenue position as well as worsening regional imbalances. For raising revenue, China's foreign trade may now be undertaxed relative to the rest of the economy. Given the pre-1978 policy of severe repression of foreign trade, providing tax relief for a substantial learning period can hardly be faulted—particularly when the foreign trade sector is still small. But once the infant becomes large and the air lock is effectively dismantled, taxing foreign trade in line with the rest of the economy becomes urgent. Having a uniform VAT, administered by a centralized internal revenue service (McKinnon 1991), fits in naturally because the tax is most easily collected at border crossings.

At this point, our Chinese model begins to dovetail with the Chilean one. Much earlier in its liberalization process, Chile managed to impose a uniform VAT and dismantle all trade restrictions except for a low, uniform revenue tariff. And Chile never had to resort to establishing special economic zones whose privileges would later have to be rescinded or to a dual exchange rate system that would later have to be unified. Needless to say, neither Chile nor China resorted to "shock therapy" (i.e., suddenly throwing the previously cosseted economy open to unrestricted foreign trade), in the mode of some of the economies of Eastern Europe and the former Soviet Union after 1989.

Notes

1. Chile's major mistakes in financial policy led to exchange rate overvaluation and a financial crash in 1982–83 (Edwards and Edwards 1987). But trade policy per se was sound and appropriate for others with similar initial conditions to follow.

2. In practice, the budget constraints facing the recently privatized firms were not hard enough. The failure of the Chilean monetary authorities to supervise the lending practices of the newly liberalized commercial banks adequately from 1974 to 1980 led to excessive lending to insider business groups that controlled both banks and enterprises. I am simply treating this unfortunate event as being outside our Chilean paradigm of trade liberalization.

3. One has to be careful with exchange rate valuations because the renminbi may well have become undervalued in the latter part of the period—thus exaggerating export growth in the GNP accounts. By any alternative standard, however, real export growth was enormous from 1978 to 1992.

4. Indeed, undue credit expansion in China in early 1993, coupled with undue depreciation of the renminbi in the interenterprise swap market for foreign exchange, seems to be resulting in higher domestic inflation, which is violating these historical guidelines.

References

Cheng, H. S. "China's Foreign Trade Reform, 1979–90," Working Paper PB92-01. Federal Reserve Bank of San Francisco, February 1992.

Edwards, Sebastian, and Alejandra Cox Edwards. *Monetarism and Liberalization: The Chilean Experiment*. Chicago: University of Chicago Press, 1991.

Lardy, Nicholas R. *Foreign Trade and Economic Reform in China, 1978–1990*. Cambridge: Cambridge University Press, 1992.

McKinnon, Ronald I. *The Order of Economic Liberalization: Financial Control in the*

Transition to Market Economy. 2d ed. Baltimore, Md.: Johns Hopkins University Press, 1993.

———. "Macroeconomic Control in Liberalizing Socialist Economies: Asian and European Parallels." In A. Giovannini, ed., *Finance and Development: Issues and Experience.* Cambridge: Cambridge University Press, 1993, pp. 223–60.

———. "Financial Growth and Macroeconomic Stability in China, 1978–92: Implications for Russia and Other Transitional Economies." *Journal of Comparative Economics*, forthcoming.

Panagariya, Arvind. "Unravelling the Mysteries of China's Foreign Trade Regime." *The World Economy* 16, no. 1, (January 1993): 51–68.

Wong, Christine. *Economic Reform in China.* Manila: Asian Development Bank, 1992.

PART THREE

SPECIFIC PROBLEMS IN REFORM

8

Contract Enforcement Institutions: Historical Perspective and Current Status in Russia

AVNER GREIF and
EUGENE KANDEL

The policy analysis of transforming Russia to a market economy has ignored the nature, evolution, and economic implications of contract enforcement institutions. This chapter presents a theoretical and historical perspective on the role of contract enforcement institutions in economic systems. It presents the nature and examines the role of legal contract enforcement institutions as well as of "private-order" institutions, which are based on reputation and the coercive power of organizations other than the state. The informational needs and the function of arbitration in each of these types of institutions are discussed. This examination will enable the study of the historical development of contract enforcement institutions in the USSR and the implications of the recent political and economic events on the development and functioning of such institutions in Russia. The conclusions of this analysis illuminate the economic deficiencies of the current Russian system of contract enforcement and the need for appropriate policy.

Introduction

Recently a Russian plant manager signed a multimillion-dollar contract with a Western company to supply equipment for his plant. Several days later the company officials found out to their astonishment that he had signed an identical contract with their competitor. When asked how he could do such a thing, the Russian executive answered, absolutely seriously, "These days we have a market economy and competition. So I let them compete: whoever supplies the best equipment will get paid."

This anecdote illustrates two points. First, some Russian managers still do not understand the workings of the market economy and completely misinterpret some of its concepts. Second, and more significant for this chapter, is the manager's complete disregard of a signed and supposedly legally binding contract. Understanding the behavior of decision makers in the Russian economy, and hence the economy itself, requires the examination of institutions that determine which contracts are considered binding and which are not.[1]

This chapter provides a theoretical framework for understanding contract enforcement institutions and elaborates on the mechanisms developed throughout history to ensure enforcement. This elaboration serves as a background for examining contract enforcement and the related institutions in the USSR and contemporary Russia (with special emphasis on the latter). We call attention to the similarity in the historical development of contract enforcement and the developments in Russia and to various factors that determine the degree of usage of various institutions, namely, the historical path of development, cost-effectiveness, and control over the use of coercive power. Most important, we hope that, although the scope of this chapter precludes a detailed examination of each institution we discuss, we will draw attention to the importance of contract enforcement institutions in Russia's transition to a market economy and that this awareness will provoke additional research.

The authors would like to thank Sergei Smirnov for his help and comments. Eugene Kandel gratefully acknowledges the support of the Olin Foundation. Avner Greif gratefully acknowledges the support of NSF grant #9223974 and research support provided by the Institutional Reform and the Informal Sector at the University of Maryland at College Park. This paper was written while he was a national fellow at the Hoover Institution, Stanford University, whose kind hospitality greatly facilitated this study. Comments from Izyaslav Darakhovsky and seminar participants at CEMI (Moscow) were also helpful.

Contract Enforcement Institutions in Historical Perspective

Theoretically, a good is characterized by its physical attributes as well as by its location in time and space. An exchange transaction, or a contract, is an agreement among individuals with specific identities on property rights to goods. Note that, unlike the casual way of defining contracts as legally binding, there is nothing in the economic definition above that requires or implies legal enforceability of the contract. The study of contracts in economics is, to a large extent, a study of the various institutions used to ensure contract enforceability. By *institution* (or *mechanism*), economists mean any constraint that restricts the transacting parties and is not a technologically determined feature of the exchange.

When a person has to decide whether or not to enter into a specific exchange transaction, he or she takes into account the physical attributes of the goods to be exchanged, the distance in time and space between the *quid* and the *quo*, and the identity of the other party. In the theoretical world of perfect markets, where contract enforceability is assured, the identity of the parties and the distance in time and place between the *quid* and the *quo* do not impose any restrictions on the decision about whether or not to assume an exchange transaction. Hence any mutually beneficial exchange is feasible.[2]

In reality, however, the institutions that support the exchange by ensuring compliance determine the feasible set of mutually beneficial exchange transactions. In other words, the nature of the contract enforcement institution determines the set of exchange transactions an individual is ready to assume, and hence it determines the feasible gains from exchange in the economy. The institutions that support exchange determine how close the economy is to a perfect market, in which contract enforceability does not hinder trade and any mutually beneficial exchange can take place independently of the parties' identities and the distance in time and place between the *quid* and the *quo*. To illustrate the effect of contract enforcement institutions on the ability to exchange, consider, for example, an economy in which exchange is supported only by social ties within a small community. Any distance between the *quid* and the *quo* is feasible in exchanges among members of that community, but any gains from transacting with members of other communities are foregone. Markets for goods exchanged between members of different communities cannot function.

Within a modern capitalist economy the visible hand of the state, the legal system, provides an institution for contract enforcement that contributes greatly to the operation of the invisible hand of the market. Yet the visible hand of the state can support market exchange only up to a limit. Incompleteness of contracts, asymmetric information, the boundaries of the state's judicial power, and litigation costs limit the state's ability to support exchange. Nevertheless, the extent of the market is not determined solely by the state's ability to support exchange because private-order institutions support exchange as well. Like the legal system, private-order institutions facilitate exchange by securing property rights. They secure these rights, however, without relying on the authority of the state.

Various studies have traced how private-order institutions facilitate exchange without explicitly relying on the legal system in modern capitalist economies. For example, Williamson (1983, 1985) elaborated on the role of "hostages" in supporting an exchange between a firm and its suppliers when the transaction is characterized by nonverifiability and assets specific to the relations. The firm will retain property rights over the assets used by its suppliers in the production process to curtail their ability to act opportunistically. Klein (1989) demonstrated the important role of credit bureaus in the U.S. economy, enabling credit transactions despite the existence of a priori asymmetric information. Bernstein (1992) examined how extralegal contractual relations supported by commercial sanctions enable low-cost exchanges to flourish in the international diamond industry. Macaulay (1963) documented that American businesspeople are reluctant to use the legal system to mitigate their disputes because of the high cost of legal proceedings.

The coexistence of private-order institutions and a legal mechanism for contract enforcement is not surprising. After all, the legal systems of capitalist economies such as England and the United States are outgrowths of the interactions between the state-enforced legal codes and private-order institutions.[3] At the same time, the nature of the private-order institutions is shaped by the nature of the state and its legal system.[4] Hence both private-order and legal institutions for contract enforcement are products of a complex, path-dependent dynamic process through which the institutional structure of an economy evolves.[5] Different economies are likely to develop different institutional infrastructures as a function of their histories.[6]

Yet there are common elements in various institutional infrastructures due to three factors. First, various institutional infrastructures are products of a common motivation, labeled by Adam Smith as the desire of human beings to barter and exchange. Second, they are aimed at mitigating the same problems. Finally, they are based on the same set of principles. In other words, institutional infrastructures are constructed by applying some combination of the same set of basic contract enforcement mechanisms. An examination of this set of basic mechanisms and how they transpired in various historical episodes is a useful preface to the study of the particularities of the evolution of the Russian contract enforcement institutional infrastructure.

For an economic agent to enter a contract, he should expect *ex ante* that the best the other party can do *ex post* is to follow the explicit contract agreed on. For contract enforceability to be effective, those expectations should be fulfilled. The better certain informational preconditions are achieved, the more likely the expectations are to be fulfilled (although various contract enforcement institutions differ in the information necessary for their operation). By and large, information should be available regarding possible future contingencies, the identity of the parties involved, the actions available to each of them, and the return to each from taking a specific action at each possible contingency. An important role of institutions is to generate, collect, provide, and disseminate such information.

Although appropriate information is necessary for contract enforceability, it is far from sufficient. For enforceability, information not only must be generated but also must be used in a manner that makes it known, beforehand, that each party's best option is to follow the contract. Throughout human history this has been achieved by institutions that link current and future transactions. To illustrate this general principle, consider a credit transaction. If it is commonly known that not paying a debt implies future inability to borrow, a potential borrower may be able *ex ante* to commit himself to pay his debt *ex post* and thus receive the loan. He will be able to commit himself if the present value of the foregone future borrowing is higher than the gain from not paying the current debt because the best a borrower can do is pay his debt. Linking a current credit transaction with future credit transactions enables exchange. Clearly, linking credit transactions is not the only linkage that can be used to ensure contract enforceability. For example, failing to pay the debt may imply being thrown in jail. Linking the credit transaction to the exchange relations among the borrower, the lender, and the state ensures debt repayment as well.

As the above examples illustrate, the study of contract enforcement institutions requires an analysis of not only how information is generated but also how this information is used to link transactions. The mechanisms linking transactions can be categorized by the nature of the punishment and reward administered and by who administers the remuneration. To limit the scope of this chapter, we ignore mechanisms based on ethics and social pressure and elaborate only on mechanisms in which the nature of the remuneration is either physical (that is, entailing the use of coercive power) or pecuniary.[7]

The use of coercive force to enforce contracts associates economic transactions with the relations between individuals and their rulers, that is, those who can use coercion to alter payoffs. The ruler is what we identify either as the state or as other individuals or groups with relatively high coercive ability, such as the warlords of the past or the infamous mafia of the present. Historically, the distinction between the former and the latter was often vague. The state and its legal enforcement organizations may have evolved from the desire of individuals or groups with relatively high coercive ability to increase their income by providing contract enforceability. As a matter of fact, Olson (1993) has claimed that the modern state evolved from groups of roving bandits who settled down and provided legal enforcement to their subjects in exchange for taxes. Those sedentary bandits developed an autocratic state that, in some cases, evolved to democracy. The incentive for all these changes was the incentive of the rulers to provide legal enforceability of contracts and thus increase their tax base.

That rulers established legal systems to advance contract enforceability and hence their revenue is reflected, for example, in the historical records of England. In the *carta mercatoria* of 1303, for example, Edward I, the king of England, assured all alien merchants "that every contract entered into by [them] . . . shall be firm and stable," that is, will be enforced by the English legal system. The alien merchants paid for this protection: "The above-mentioned merchants, every one of them, . . . have . . . granted us . . . by way of custom" specific amounts to be paid in the English ports.[8] Similarly, to encourage foreign merchants to provide local traders with credit despite the slow litigation procedure of the local borough courts, some English boroughs during the thirteenth century took an extraordinary step: They paid foreign creditors with out-of-town funds and later took a double indemnity from the local debtor.[9]

When contract enforcement is supported by a legal system, the incentives of that system are important in determining economic efficiency. Because many modern legal systems are financed by the state and thus provide legal services subject to budget constraints, they will not necessarily minimize cost. Historically, legal systems were usually financed by their litigants and attempted to maximize their profit by controlling the volume of trials and their operation costs subject to the constraints imposed by technology and state regulations. The economic implications of such attempts depended on the nature of the particular institution and the extent of competition for legal services. For example, in France before the Revolution, local courts were paid by the litigants and faced little or no competition. In sharp contrast, the English legal system of that period was characterized by a multiplicity of jurisdictions and a high level of legal competition. The result was economically devastating for France because the high cost of litigation prevented economic development. Profitable projects not undertaken in France because of high litigation costs were carried out in England.[10]

Legal systems with the incentive to minimize their costs and facilitate contract enforceability would announce in advance a set of rules or laws to be used in determining who was at fault and how compensation would be determined. Such rules enable the parties to better evaluate the costs and benefits of their exchange under various contingencies, including the case in which one party cannot follow its contractual obligations. In that way, the legal system creates expectations regarding the likely outcome of trials, thereby reducing the need for actually using the legal system.

Another method often used by legal systems to facilitate exchange is to create an auxiliary arbitration organization. Applying for the assistance of a coercive institution may be costly in time, fees, delays, and expenses associated with familiarizing the court with the details of that economic transaction, the costs that may arise because a court is committed to certain procedures in evaluating evidence, and so on. Hence the parties may prefer to seek arbitration by impartial experts who can discreetly provide quick decisions at low cost. Legal systems motivated to advance economic efficiency are likely to find it efficient to make the decision of the arbitrators legally binding. Indeed, in many historical cases arbitration emerged to facilitate exchange. For example, Argenti (1958), who investigated the operation of the legal system in Chios from 1346 to 1566, noted that "the high proportion of extant notarial deeds which record the appointment of arbitrators [in civil cases], to whom disputes were referred for legally binding settlements, proves that this method of 'settling out of court' was generally preferred to going to law, perhaps because justice was slow and expensive, perhaps because it was unreliable" (ibid., 464).

A legal system, like any other contract enforcement system based on coercive power, cannot support all beneficial exchange transactions. As discussed above, the operation of such systems is restricted by the extent to which information is available and by the system's incentives. Indeed, by and large, institutions based on linking economic transactions over time or across economic agents or both are at least as important in ensuring contract enforceability as institutions based on coercive power.

To illustrate the operation of such institutions, consider an economy consisting of two individuals who can gain from cooperation in every period but of whom at least one can gain from cheating if the other cooperates.[11] Cooperation can be sustained if future cooperation is made conditional on past conduct and if the present value of future gains from cooperation is higher than the one-period gain from cheating. Because this mechanism enables contract enforcement by the fear of losing future gains, it is also referred to as the *reputation mechanism*. In a variant of this mechanism, past behavior is used by economic agents to form beliefs regarding unobserved characteristics of other agents.[12] In particular, observing honest past behavior that is not induced by coercive power may foster trust among the agents in the sense that it strengthens belief in future honest behavior. Hence it enables, over time, a higher level of cooperation. Furthermore, as demonstrated by Boot et al. (1993), economic agents may choose to contract outside the realm of law, even in transactions that can be supported by the legal system, in order to acquire reputation and hence facilitate cooperation in transactions that cannot be supported by the legal system.

The ability of reputation to support exchange depends on the details of the situation. In particular, it will fail to support cooperation if the economic agents are not patient and hence do not value the future much, if the agents are risk averse and there is high uncertainty with respect to future payoffs, if agents have outside options that are more attractive than the future gains from cooperation, or if there is high probability that, for exogenous reasons, the parties will have to cease cooperating although none has cheated. To mitigate these types of problems, the basic mechanism above can be supplemented by the threat of retaliation from individuals who were not cheated in the past (that is, a third-party enforcement). The credibility of the threat depends on the availability of information and the incentives for economic agents to participate in collective punishment. To illustrate the variety of institutional forms that can provide this information and incentives, several historical examples are discussed below.

During the twelfth and thirteenth centuries, the Champagne Fairs were the main center for international trade in Northern Europe. Milgrom et al. (1990) have argued that impersonal contract enforceability among traders from various countries at the Champagne Fairs was achieved by a Law Merchant system based on a multilateral reputation mechanism. This system enabled merchants to trade, although there was no court that could force a merchant to meet his contractual obligations once he left the fair, and each merchant was not expected to interact with any specific merchant frequently enough that a bilateral reputation mechanism would ensure contract enforceability. To understand the operation of the Law Merchant system, suppose that each pair of traders is matched only once and that each trader knows only his own experience. Because the fairs' court lacked the ability to enforce judgment once a trader left the fairs, assume that the court is only capable of verifying past actions and keeping records of traders who cheated in the past. Acquiring information and appealing to the court are costly for each merchant. Despite those costs, an equilibrium exists in which cheating does not occur and in which merchants are induced to provide information to the court and acquire information from it. The court's ability to activate a multilateral reputation mechanism by controlling information enables exchange and the provision and acquisition of information. By transmitting information only to merchants who had never cheated and who provided information to and acquired information from the Law Merchant system, merchants were motivated to take those costly actions and to be honest. If a trader cheated, he was unable to trade again. Hence a local court ensured contract enforcement through time, although it could not use coercive power against cheaters.

Greif (1993b) has examined how exchange was supported in the eleventh-century Mediterranean trade between merchants and their overseas agents who handled the merchants' goods abroad. Because of the international nature of these agency relations, they could not be supported by the legal system. Furthermore, no individual merchant was able to commit himself to future agency relations with any specific agent. Yet, at least among the group of traders examined, that of the Maghribi traders, agents were honest because the traders arranged agency relations through a peer organization that we would call a coalition. Members of the Maghribi traders' coalition provided one another with agency services, thus increasing the value of a member's capital. Each trader benefited from being a coalition member more than from establishing agency relations based on a reputation mechanism outside the coalition. Obtaining the benefits of coalition membership depended on proper conduct in the past, and the short-run gain from cheating was less than the long-run benefit an honest coalition member could obtain. Because this situation was common knowledge, the merchants perceived that the agents could not do better by cheating. In short, the traders used a *perpetuum mobile,* which reduced the transaction cost associated with agency relations through contractual relations among them and thus motivated each coalition member to honor those contractual relations.[13]

Once a group has generated enough rent from its contractual relations, it can, under certain conditions, use this rent to assure contract enforcement between itself and others. To illustrate this point, suppose that in each period a member of a coalition was matched with a nonmember with whom he could beneficially cooperate were he able to commit himself to respect the contractual relations between them. Yet because the relations between these two particular people are not expected to repeat, simple reputation mechanisms can not support cooperation. Cooperation can be supported, however, if members of the coalition threaten to punish any member who cheats an outsider. The group would be motivated to do so because otherwise none of them could benefit from cooperation. Recognizing that, the outsiders will willingly cooperate with an insider.

The operation of multilateral reputation mechanisms such as those described above requires that the same action be considered as cheating by various participants. For example, a coalition such as that of the Maghribi traders is based on uncoordinated responses of merchants at different trade centers. For the threat of collective punishment to be credible, cheating must be defined so that it ensures a collective response. If some merchants consider specific actions to constitute cheating but others do not, the effectiveness of the collective threat is undermined. Various institutions based on collective punishments coordinate interpretations of actions differently. In the Maghribi traders' coalition, a set of cultural rules of behavior accepted by all the merchants provided coordination. In the Champagne Fairs, the *ex post* decree of the local court determined what constituted cheating. In other cases, arbitrators, after examining the evidence, declared whether a specific action constituted cheating or not.

The discussion so far has treated institutions based on coercive power and institutions based on reputation as substitutes. The relations between these two types of institutions, however, are more complex. In some situations contract enforcement may be achieved only when a reputation-based institution is supplemented by an organization with coercive power. Furthermore, the reputation mechanism can restrain an organization with coercive power from abusing its power or reneging on its contractual obligations.

To illustrate these two points, consider institutions that governed the relations between rulers and alien merchants in premodern trade. During this period, a ruler had a monopoly over the coercive power in his territory. Hence, in the absence of an institution that enabled a ruler to *ex ante* secure the property rights of alien merchants, those merchants were not likely to frequent that ruler's territory, thereby depriving its population, the ruler, and the merchants of the benefits of trade.[14] In particular, when there are many merchants who, as far as the ruler is concerned, are perfect substitutes for one another, a simple bilateral reputation mechanism fails to constrain the ruler from using his coercive power to abuse merchants' rights at the *efficient* level of trade. At that level, the benefit to the ruler from the future trade of the marginal trader (owing to customs payments) is zero. Hence the ruler can profit from abusing that trader's rights. In a level of trade lower than the efficient one, however, the value to the ruler of the future trade of the marginal trader may be high enough that the ruler will respect the trader's rights. Commerce would expand not to its efficient level but to a lower one. The extent of trade is then a function of the ruler's ability to commit.

If the merchants can collectively and credibly threaten to cease trading if any merchant is abused, the ruler can commit to the efficient level of trade. Hence the operation of the reputation mechanism can constrain the use of coercive power. Nonetheless, the threat of collective retaliation is usually not credible; it entails a complete boycott, during which trade would shrink below the level at which, for example, a simple reputation mechanism effectively supports some trade. Hence some merchants would renegotiate with the ruler to resume trading.

To support the efficient level of trade by having a multilateral reputation mechanism constrain the ruler's coercive power, the merchants must establish an organization that will not only enable them to coordinate their actions but ensure traders' compliance to boycott decisions. In many cases during the premodern period, this was achieved by having the merchants take advantage of a political system outside the realm of the ruler to whose territory they traveled to trade. This political system provided the merchants with the coercive power required to ensure compliance with their embargo decisions.

Summary

This section presented two basic types of institutions that ensure contract enforcement: those using coercive power and those linking current and future economic transactions. Both types of institutions alter the payoffs of the contracting parties in a way that makes compliance optimal. The use of coercive power can come from the state or from rulers with sufficient physical force behind them. Institutions based on linking current and future economic transactions do not require the threat of coercive power, relying instead on the threat of the foregone economic gains for the reneging party. Information gathering and dissemination play a crucial role in both types of institutions, and although arbitration may be used in either, it is used for different reasons; in the first, it is used to reduce cost, while in the second it is used to coordinate responses.

The historical examples discussed above indicate that, at any given moment, the ability to exchange is constrained by existing institutions. Furthermore, history suggests that those institutions do not have an inherent tendency to converge to an optimal institutional structure.[15] This is true of institutions based on coercive power and institutions based on reputation. For example, the inefficient French legal system prevailed for centuries until it was demolished by the French Revolution. Similarly, the ability of the Maghribi traders to employ agents was constrained by the size of their group, which was determined by social rather than economic factors. In other words, although gains from trade gave rise to institutions that supported some contract enforceability, these institutions were not able to exhaust all gains from trade.

The next sections of this chapter demonstrate that the existing mechanisms used in Russia to ensure contract enforceability bear a remarkable resemblance to the historical examples above and to modern Western institutions and that contract enforcement institutions in Russia are a product of Russia's historical development. As such they are neither optimal nor have any inherent tendency to converge to an efficient institutional structure in response to market incentives. Institutional structure seems to be constraining Russia's economic development, and appropriate policy measures should be taken to relax this constraint.

The History of Contracts and Their Enforcement in Russia

THE USSR BEFORE PERESTROIKA

The main attribute of the Soviet economy until the late 1980s was its planned nature. The state central planning agency, Gosplan, which was essentially in charge of all economic activity in the country, constructed the production-consumption tables for most major industries, allocated resources, and set production quotas. Five-year plans were prepared by Gosplan and approved by the Central Committee of the Communist Party. Actual planning and resource allocation were performed annually, whereas monitoring took place yearly, quarterly, and monthly. Gosplan allocated resources directly to important enterprises and municipalities, passing the rest on to Gossnab, the agency responsible for allocating clients to suppliers. Regional and republican-level branches of

Gossnab, as well as various ministries, finalized the allocation of clients to suppliers within their areas of responsibility. The allocations would specify quantities, prices (which were set by yet another agency, Goscomzen—"the visible hand"), and delivery dates. When this process was completed, each enterprise had a list of entities it had to supply and a list of its suppliers.

As a mechanism for resource allocation, the plan was supposed to render obsolete problems associated with contract enforcement. All contractual obligations were dictated by the state, and their enforcement was supported by the state's authority. In reality, however, because of ideology, informational asymmetry, and managerial incentives, this was not the case. Contracts dictated by Gosplan were only partially followed or enforced, and other contracts were initiated by the parties and enforced through alternative mechanisms. Describing the contract-enforcing institutions in Russia requires some elaboration.

The five-year plan specified by Gosplan was ideologically motivated to demonstrate the growth of the Soviet economy as proof of the communist system's superiority. Officially, production was supposed to increase steadily from one five-year plan to the next,[16] which meant that, more often than not, the total output plan exceeded the actual production capability of the economy. The magnitude of the discrepancies is seen in the ratio of actual production to planned production for the last twenty years of the former USSR (see table 8.1).[17]

The legal mechanism established to enforce contracts and resolve disputes among enterprises was theoretically well suited to the planned system. The State Arbitration Committee, under the auspices of the Counsel of Ministers, could order a particular distribution within the state allocation system. It was a government agency (not an independent judicial system) that resolved disputes between state enterprises and enforced contracts. Individuals and small semiprivate enterprises were not allowed to submit claims. In case of a dispute, the original contract was basically irrelevant, and final decisions were dictated by the plan and the current needs. There was little incentive to use the system to enforce contracts and resolve disputes for two reasons: First, to avoid responsibility for a production delay, the manager of an undersupplied enterprise had only to obtain written confirmation from his superiors that failure to produce the quota was not his fault. Second, even if the undersupplied enterprise actually needed more supplies, its managers were reluctant to bring a formal claim because the plan dictated future interactions between them and the supplier; thus the latter could retaliate.

The Civil Code of the USSR, enforced by the state court system, governed contracts involving small transactions between individuals, but the contracts themselves were subject to many other rules and regulations. In particular, contracts consistent with the law but inconsistent with the "rules of socialist coexistence" could be nullified.[18] The courts were used, but their impact on the economy was minuscule.

If an enterprise fulfilled 100 percent of its planned production, its managers

Table 8.1   Percentage of Planned Quota Fulfilled during the
Last Year of Successive Five-Year Plans (by industry)

Industry/Year	1970	1975	1980	1985	1990
Electricity	89	101	97	100	94
Oil	102	101	97	96	91
Natural gas	88	96	109	107	98
Coal	94	102	91	94	90
Rolled steel	97	98	90	92	97
Fertilizers	89	100	71	92	77
Plastics	80	82	67	84	81
Fibers	80	91	81	87	80
Presses	83	84	99	N/A	N/A
Trucks	87	89	98	N/A	N/A
Cellulose	61	81	77	90	78
Cardboard	60	74	89	90	81
Paper	84	94	88	94	88

SOURCES: Planned quotas are from the statistics of the 23d to 27th party conferences (1966, 1971, 1976, 1981, 1986). Actual production is from *Narodnoye Hozyaystvo SSSR*, years 1975, 1985, and 1990.

and workers were eligible for a bonus, which could be as high as half their annual salary. Other benefits, such as additional housing construction and a better supply of consumer goods, also depended on 100 percent plan fulfillment; the marginal incentive in excess of that was negligible. Clearly, the managers had strong incentives either to bring their production up to the level of the plan or to bargain with the authorities to bring the plan down to the level of current production. The quota was assigned by Gosplan, which had to rely on the data supplied by the enterprise itself to evaluate its needs and capacities. Within certain limits, the managers were able to manipulate the data; in particular they could overstate the resources required and understate the production capacity, increasing their chances for the bonus. Despite strict reporting guidelines from Gosplan, hoarding was common because nobody could be sure that the next year's allocation and delivery would be sufficient for that year's quota. Gosplan officials in Moscow, who had no way of closely watching over forty-five thousand large and medium-sized enterprises in the USSR, tried to guesstimate this bias by allocating fewer resources and increasing the quota. This adjustment increased the incentives to misrepresent data; as a result, the collected data could not be trusted, and individual enterprises frequently ended up with either more or fewer resources than were required to fulfill their quotas.

Hence, the right to an allocated amount was a necessary but not sufficient condition for actually obtaining some product. The directions to the supplier did not specify what to do in case of deficits, and hence the supplier had some degree of freedom in choosing whom to supply. Enterprises within the military-industrial complex had enough clout to obtain full allocations, implying that all the other claimants were even less likely to receive their allocated products. Everybody thus understood that if one waited passively for supplies, they would not be likely to arrive. There was a powerful incentive to spend resources to obtain the largest possible allocation.

The combination of ideology, asymmetric information, and managerial incentives created potentially large discrepancies between planned and actual resource allocation at the enterprise level. To support the actual resource allocation, there was a need for contract enforcement mechanisms other than those provided by the state. The implicit contracts used to support actual allocation were a priority of the enterprise managers and the main task of the *snabjenets*, salespeople in reverse who were employed by almost every enterprise of a reasonable size and whose goal was to make sure that their enterprise got most of its allocation. *Snabjenets* did not have an official title because the position was not supposed to exist. Hired under the pretense that they were highly skilled (and hence relatively highly paid) production workers, *snabjenets* were the lowest level in an undereconomy of resource allocation. The nonprice competition for the fixed supply of scarce resources included enterprises' general managers, deputy ministers, and even ministers on the republican level who frequently paid visits to the suppliers of the most crucial commodities or to their bosses in Moscow ministries and the Central Committee of the party.

The actual allocation of scarce resources in many cases was influenced by side payments, either monetary or in-kind. In either case the transaction was entirely illegal, which meant that the official of the various enterprises were potentially able to incriminate one another. The threat of calling in the state was thus the major mechanism of contract enforcement. Because trust was important, long-term relations were cultivated and maintained.

Similar types of informal institutions for contract enforcement evolved in the parallel (or shadow) economy, another by-product of the planned economy. Imperfect information implied that there was an excess of some products and a chronic shortage of others. There were always entrepreneurs who realized the opportunities created by the discrepancies and produced goods (and occasionally services) for which demand was not satisfied. They either organized small-scale production or entered into an agreement with a state enterprise to soak up its excess capacity and then distribute the products through official stores and the black market. Their activities—obtaining raw materials, renting production capacity, and distributing the products—constituted criminal offenses. Not surprisingly, the contracts governing this underground economy could not be enforced in a court of law, but had to rely on long-term relationships and mutual trust, backed by the threat to all of them from the state.

It is alleged that hard-core criminals in the USSR were collecting protection money from the underground entrepreneurs. Because the entrepreneurs' actions were illegal, the latter could not seek state protection from racketeering. It also may have been, however, that in exchange for protection money they got some real protection, both from rival criminals and from partners reneging on contracts. In any case, the criminal forces (racketeers) traditionally played a significant role in the underground economy.

The market voluntary exchange system, which is based on contracts and mechanisms for their enforcement, did not officially exist in the economy of the Soviet Union. Planning substituted for contracting, and disputes were resolved within the planned framework. But the nature of the official economy gave rise to an underground economy that relied on self-enforcing contracts based on long-term personal relations, informal codes of behavior, and criminal forces. The judicial system did not develop the expertise to deal with complex contracts and dispute resolution because these were not legal matters at that time. Inadequate laws and unprepared personnel could not cope with the later breakup of the established order.

AFTER PERESTROIKA

The main goal of perestroika was to promote economic growth by inducing initiatives at the local level and by relaxing Moscow officials' regulatory control. Not surprisingly, perestroika eroded the central government's power and the rigidity of the centralized contract system. Initially, enterprises were given the freedom to sell part of their above-quota output to clients of their choice, which led to a new type of large-scale transaction among enterprises outside the control of the planning agency.

To understand these transactions, suppose A is a sheet metal plant, B is a refrigeration equipment plant, and C is a meat-processing plant. Before 1986, A would have been assigned to supply sheet metal to B, who in turn would have to supply C with refrigeration equipment. But C's list of clients would not necessarily (or likely) include A or B (see figure 8.1a, with arrows representing the direction of supplies). Because one of the enterprises' responsibilities (especially in remote areas) was to ensure the supply of foodstuffs to their workers, managers of both A and B needed meat. Yet they could not officially use their contractual relations with C to obtain it. Instead, they had to depend on allocations from the meat-processing plant they had been assigned to.

After 1986 other transactions could take place officially using the government set prices because now all three plants had a certain degree of freedom in allocating their output. A and B could exchange metal for refrigeration equipment; B and

Figure 8.1   Officially Permitted, Large-Scale Transactions
               among State Enterprises

Figure 8.1a   Figure 8.1b
Before 1986   After 1986

C could exchange refrigeration equipment for meat. More-complex transactions were common: A would supply B with sheet metal on the condition that C supply A with meat (see figure 8.1b, with arrows representing the flow of goods). In the latter case it was B's task to ensure contract enforcement, which was supported by their repeated business with each other. Even more complicated transactions involving several stages of barter exchange took place as well. In most cases the contracts were not written, signed, or legally binding. Yet because of their repeated business, as imposed by the official authorities, no legal mechanism was required to enforce those contracts. The individuals who were previously engaged in the shadow economy frequently helped arrange the flow of products among the enterprises, using the contacts, expertise, and reputation they had built over the years.

In 1988, it became legal to establish private cooperatives for the purpose of economic activity, but they had to be sponsored by a state enterprise or organization. (Later, private small enterprises were permitted as well.) The new cooperatives fell into three main categories: first, small establishments providing services in areas not adequately covered by state enterprises, such as restaurants, tailor and repair shops, and so forth; second, cooperatives that imported electronics and personal computers for resale to state organizations, enterprises, and individuals, realizing large profit opportunities from price discrepancies; third, cooperatives engaged in manufacturing and services in affiliation with the state enterprises and using state-owned resources.

The third type of cooperative manufactured products for which there was an excess demand and sold them at a price higher than or equal to the official one. Those cooperatives paid token fees for the use of equipment, the raw materials, and the infrastructure of their sponsoring state enterprise while, in many cases, selling their products to the same enterprises. State enterprises entered into such arrangements because it enabled them to convert the "noncash" (budgetary) rubles to cash: receiving cash from the cooperatives while paying them with state funds that could not officially be used to compensate an enterprise's workers or managers. In many cases, the cooperatives' managers were also the managers of the state enterprise.

The parallel economy veterans were among the first to identify and exploit those opportunities because they had the capital, the expertise, and the right state of mind for the newly permitted activity. The newly established cooperatives had to look for sources of supply and distribution channels, thereby increasing the number of transactions among enterprises with no previous relations. Those transactions would have been facilitated by a legal contract enforcement mechanism, but no such mechanism existed.

In that environment the existing legal system provided poor mechanisms for contract enforcement and dispute resolution. The complex transactions meant complex contracts that could not be dealt with under the then-current laws and personnel. The legislative body was under pressure to modify the Civil Code to accommodate the new reality. But because the issues of contract enforcement were inevitably linked to the question of property rights, which had yet to be resolved by the parliament, the change was slow. There was a pressing need for alternative mechanisms.

Legal contracts were used to only a small extent because more and more regulations were put in place to slow the surge in private activity. Many transactions involved the export of raw materials, the prices of which in the USSR were sometimes as low as 10 percent of the world level. Exporting raw materials was under particularly tight restrictions that most companies attempted to circumvent. The contracts that were used were almost never enforceable in the courts, and the plaintiffs would not seek legal redress even had enforcement been ensured. An alternative contract enforcement system developed because the deals were too profitable to pass up. Certain practices reduced the possibility of reneging by, for example, using the asymmetry of the ability to use the legal system between the state enterprises and the private firms. The state enterprise paid up front, expecting the private company or the cooperative to deliver the product. In case of default, the state organization could always file a civil (and sometimes a criminal) suit because it had a much better chance of winning than the private company.

The criminal elements followed the underground economy when it began to surface. Because there were many opportunities for extortion, racketeering became a widespread problem. Many former athletes and security personnel extorted money from anybody they could identify as a potential victim: street vendors, small shop owners, restaurateurs, and other proprietors of small businesses. Owing to the government and racketeering, the costs of doing business were extremely high. Gangs established territories of influence and branched out into additional activities, such as establishing "debt collection" agencies and security firms. The collectors' fee was a percentage of the collected amount, as in the West, but the methods used in Russia were allegedly much more violent.

There is no evidence that gangs actively enforced contracts except in those cases that directly concerned their interests. The police could not cope with the rising tide of illegal activity for several reasons: First, while the gangs were multiplying, the police ranks did not increase sufficiently to match the new challenge. Second, widespread bribery induced police officers to protect gang members, not arrest them. Finally, the police had trouble adjusting their methods to the new era of openness. This period marks the beginning of the deterioration of law and order in the USSR.

The perestroika was followed by a dramatic increase in business uncertainty resulting from the disintegration of the planning system, political uncertainty, and rapid inflation. As the central power declined the authority of local governments increased. More than ever before, enterprise managers had to be attentive to the demands of regional authorities. In a famous incident in the summer of 1990, the head of Ryasan' Region, near Moscow, refused to supply the capital with meat because the Moscow City Council had introduced a rationing policy in the retail stores that excluded nonresidents. Despite their obligations under the plan, the enterprises in this region chose to obey the local official. The increase in local power, coupled with various nationalistic considerations, led to a more fragmented and uncertain supply system. Occasionally, enterprises had to start looking for entirely new sources of supplies and new clients.

After the breakup of the USSR, political fighting between the former republics led to tariffs, boycotts, export and import restrictions, and outright seizure of assets. The immediate result was that many long-term relationships among large state enterprises were broken up, as their suppliers and clients suddenly "moved" to another country. The magnitude of these changes is illustrated by the degree to which the enterprises were concentrated in various republics of the Soviet Union before the breakup (see table 8.2). It should be noted that the table underreflects one problem: in many cases the parts were manufactured all over the USSR, while the assembly was done in one location. In particular, although Russia had a dominant position in almost all industries, in many cases crucial suppliers or customers were located in other republics. New suppliers and clients had to be identified and their credibility established. In addition, the reduction in the importance of central planning increased the number of independent transactions; thus the number of contracts needing enforcement increased dramatically.

Yegor Gaidar's government, formed in the beginning of 1992, proceeded with rapid price liberalization, the costs and benefits of which were widely disputed. One effect of this policy was inflation reaching between 3 and 9 percent a week, which introduced new incentives to renege on contracts. The managers of state enterprises, who were used to operating in a stable price environment, did not immediately change their ways of doing business and many of them suffered large losses in real terms. The potential for reneging prevailed on either side of any transaction: When goods were delivered, payments were postponed.

Table 8.2   Market Share of Enterprises in the Five Largest Republics, 1990, by Industry

Industry	Russia	Ukraine	Belarus	Uzbekistan	Kazakhstan
Electricity	62.7	17.3	2.3	3.3	5.1
Oil	90.4	1.0	0.4	0.5	4.5
Natural gas	78.6	3.5	—	5.0	0.9
Coal	56.2	23.5	—	0.9	18.7
Rolled steel	57.0	34.5	0.6	0.8	4.4
Electric motors	22.7	36.9	12.8	1.6	—
Presses	64.7	25.7	2.7	1.4	2.8
Tools (metal cutting)	47.2	23.6	9.8	—	1.6
Bricks	53.5	22.9	5.1	4.7	5.0
Cotton fibers	—	—	—	62.4	3.8
Paper	85.2	6.0	3.2	0.4	0.1

SOURCE: *Narodnoye Hozyaystvo SSSR*, 1990.

When prepayment was arranged or demanded, sellers charged the list price on the day of delivery because contracts usually did not fix the price on the day of prepayment. An additional amount would be requested, or the amount of goods delivered would be reduced. The banks, which also benefited from the float, took up to two months to transfer the money, causing loses of 30 to 40 percent in real terms.

Overall, this period was characterized by a decline in central economic and political power and, as reflected in table 8.1, a decline in the degree of quota fulfillment. Uncertainty, contractual complexity, and inflation increased, while security of property rights deteriorated, and many long-term commercial relations were terminated because of political reasons. The legal contract enforcement system was inadequate, while incentives for reneging on contracts increased as uncertainty and inflation eroded the ability of reputation-based mechanisms to support exchange.

The Current Status of Contract Enforcement in Russia

The historical structure of contract enforcement institutions in the USSR and the political and economic changes outlined above determine the current nature and efficiency of contract enforcement institutions in Russia. There is an immense demand for inexpensive, quick, and unbiased contract enforcement and dispute resolution mechanisms. Although institutional responses can be observed in Russia, so far they are wholly inadequate in this respect.

THE NATURE OF THE LEGAL CONTRACT ENFORCEMENT SYSTEM IN RUSSIA

As we indicated earlier, contract law in the former Soviet Union, which was mostly concerned with small transactions between private citizens and not suitable for handling the large volume of complicated transactions in the uncertain environment of early 1992, was based on the 1964 Civil Code, the 1977 Soviet constitution, and several modifying and generalizing amendments. The reformers of the Russian economy, recognizing the limitations of this body of law, put in two new Russian laws that addressed contract enforcement: a December 1990 law on enterprises and entrepreneurial activity and a July 1991 law on arbitration courts. These were steps in the right direction, but they were far from sufficient.[19] Required is a comprehensive set of Russian laws governing contracts and their legal enforcement.

That need was to have been addressed in part by the Arbitration Procedural Code (APC), which enabled the operation of the arbitration courts. The APC was approved by the Russian parliament in March and became law in April 1992. The arbitration courts in Russia deal with economic issues, and the APC enabled the establishment of an entire structure of arbitration courts, consisting of the High Arbitration Court of the Russian Federation, the High Arbitration Courts of the republics in the Russian Federation, and regional and even municipal arbitration courts in large cities. The APC also provided guidelines for dispute resolution via binding arbitration and the enforcement of those resolutions by the arbitration courts. The following cases were put exclusively under the jurisdiction of the arbitration courts: recognition of property rights and their enforcement, contract enforcement and imposition of damages, as well as economic interactions between the state or a state organization and a commercial entity, including all the disputes resulting from privatization, land allocation, registration of enterprises, and other activities involving central and local governments.

The passage of the APC was a breakthrough in three major aspects:

1. The law was specifically designed to govern the procedure for resolving disputes arising from economic activity. The APC presented the arbitration courts with clear procedural guidelines and forced them to use appropriate laws to support their decisions.

2. The arbitration system was transformed from being a government agency, where the decisions were dictated by a bureaucrat, to a judicial

entity, mostly independent of the state and basing its judgments on the law.

3. Private citizens engaged in economic activity were given equal rights to petition the court with the largest state and private organizations. They could hire representatives and rely on expert witnesses to advance their cases. This was a major change from the time when the Arbitration Committee would accept claims only from the state enterprises.

Although the APC represents a tremendous advance in the Russian legislative effort, it suffered serious problems in its implementation. First, there are few qualified legal professionals with expertise in economic affairs in a market economy and a highly uncertain environment. This situation is especially grave in the remote areas, where insufficient resource allocation to the judicial system makes the operation of courts and the enforcement of their decisions all but impossible. Second, despite the procedural clarity, the legal basis for court actions is the modified 1964 Civil Code and peripheral laws, which are still inadequate. For the APC to be effective, the procedures must be complemented by a set of comprehensive and internally consistent statutes governing property rights, contracts, and other aspects of economic activity. In Russia, the passage of such laws is blocked by the conservative parliament, which opposes many of the needed changes for political reasons.[20] Third, the local authorities, which are in many cases antagonistic to entrepreneurial activity, openly defy certain laws, such as privatization and land allocation, and renege on the contracts that these courts are supposed to enforce. Because the courts depend on the local governments, legal contract enforcement in those areas does not exist. Finally, legal market participants have not yet developed a set of behavioral norms required for stable economic relations that could be used instead of or alongside the formal laws.

These difficulties are finally being recognized, and changes leading to remedies are under way. The Russian Legal Academy and the Bar Association offer courses for judges and prosecutors to familiarize them with the statutes and guide them in their implementation. A new lobby, the Association of Private and Privatized Enterprises, headed by former Prime Minister Yegor Gaidar, is demanding a comprehensive set of laws on property rights and contracts. The association holds the lack of such laws to be one of the main concerns of its constituents. Finally, norms of accepted behavior are gradually developing in the Russian business community, especially among the larger participants.

The design of the State Arbitration Court system has several drawbacks that reduce its usefulness to private companies and individuals. One is that the procedure is costly: in a case involving a monetary claim, the parties are expected to pay 10 percent of the claim as a court fee, splitting it in proportion to the allocation of the claim between the plaintiff and the defendant. Another drawback is that, although the court is supposed to pass judgment within a month, it often takes up to six months to arrive at a verdict. This is potentially ruinous for the plaintiff in inflationary times. Finally, the court hearings are open to the public unless state secrets are involved, meaning that sensitive proprietary information may be released to competitors or to the authorities. Given that the frequently inconsistent rules and regulations on the federal and the local levels make full compliance with the law all but impossible, the majority of contracts may not be entirely "kosher." Companies are thus reluctant to use the arbitration courts because of high costs, long waits, and publicity, resorting to them only if other, more convenient methods of dispute resolution and contract enforcement are not available. This creates a demand for alternative systems of contract enforcement.

THE NATURE OF INFORMAL CONTRACT ENFORCEMENT IN RUSSIA

As outlined in the first section, there are three major avenues through which contract enforcement can be achieved without directly relying on the legal system: self-enforcing contracts in which contract enforcement is achieved by linking economic transactions, binding arbitration in which contract enforcement is indirectly supported by the legal system, and enforcement based on the coercive power of parties other than the state. All these strategies, of which there are numerous historical examples, can be found in Russia today. Their exact form and nature reflect, to a large extent, the nature of the informal contract enforcement institutions that evolved in the USSR. Yet the political and economic changes in Russia undermined the operation of some of these institutions and gave rise to some new institutional forms as well.

Self-Enforcing Contracts.   Large industrial enterprises in Russia remain monopolies in their respective industries. Despite losing some of their older suppliers and customers, the sheer size and influence of those enterprises allow them to rely on the self-interest of their new suppliers and customers to abide by their contracts and fulfill their obligations. Withholding future business is a significant threat when it comes from your only customer or supplier. Several private conglomerates, that possess similar power, grew out of smaller entities established earlier in the reform process, mainly by people who had informal or formal business relations in previous periods and hence have a long common history and mutual trust. Formal conglomerates, such as Menatep Group, control banks, trading houses, retailing operations, and manufacturing. A company reneging on a contract with such a conglomerate may anticipate legal action but can be certain that it will never do business with any of the conglomerate's companies again. At the same time, both large state enterprises and conglomerates value the reputation that draws business to them. Thus the contracts seem to be honored, making legal actions rare.

Reputation-based institutions also provide contract enforceability among smaller business enterprises by forming an interesting organizational structure in which business partners are not connected by any formal organizational ties. For a lack of a better name, we will call these structures *business groups*, which are combinations of individuals engaged in various business activities within the former USSR and in the international market. Each venture is done separately, requiring a separate set of people to put it together. Each person is responsible for solving a particular problem such as obtaining credits and export licenses, arranging transportation, providing distribution channels, or ensuring security, creating a "virtual corporation" for each deal. The contracts are informal; legal documents are prepared, frequently after the transaction has been accomplished, for the sole purpose of satisfying the numerous regulatory requirements. The group may consist of more people than are required for any given deal, and every individual is involved in several deals. If a group member reneges on a contract or if there is a dispute, legal action is never considered. Instead the other members (the "elders") pass judgment, which is final. Noncompliance results in the termination of "membership," meaning that no new deals will be offered to the transgressor. Because belonging to a business group is lucrative, contract enforcement is rarely a problem.

Notice the similarity of these business groups to the Maghribi traders' coalition described earlier. The similarity is hardly surprising, as similarities in the environments led to similarities in the solutions to common problems. The business groups described above should not be confused with the mafia-type organizations we discuss below, which are involved in various illegal activities alongside their legitimate businesses. The methods used, the identities of the leaders, and the types of businesses make the two completely different. Yet reliance on a self-enforcement mechanism is common to both. In the case of the mafia, however, along with the withdrawal of future business, the physical penalty for reneging on a contract can be severe. Disputes are allegedly resolved by people with authority in the criminal world, and the verdict cannot be appealed. Clearly matters are never brought before a court of law.

When a deal involves separate entities with no previous contacts who are not likely to engage in future transactions, multilateral reputation mechanisms can become important. Similar to the situation in the Champagne Fairs, semipublic organizations provide crucial information. The Russian Chamber of Commerce and Industry compiles a list of large companies (private and state-owned) that provides financial data and records alleged contract violations and legal actions brought against a company. This is similar to the activities of the Better Business Bureaus and Chambers of Commerce in the United States and the services of Dunn and Bradstreet worldwide.

Despite the effectiveness of these mechanisms, they constitute *barriers to entry* because there is no information on newly established firms or small enterprises. In such cases self-enforcement of contracts based on expected future gains (or past behavior) is not feasible. Although small individually, the enterprises in this category compose the majority of all new business ventures in Russia today. Hence lack of contract enforceability, which restricts the development of this sector, has a profound impact on the economy.

Binding Arbitration.   Even when large enterprises rely on self-enforcing contracts, disputes are inevitable, especially when the norms of business conduct have not yet been firmly established. When two companies have contractual disputes, each can resort to legal action through the arbitration courts, but for practical reasons they often prefer to resolve their disputes more cheaply, quickly, and quietly. Binding arbitration has been for a long time a solution to similar problems in the West.

The APC specifically addresses binding arbitration. Various organizations are allowed to set up permanent arbitration committees (called *tertiary courts* in Russian) for dispute resolution. Arbitration committees were established by the commodities exchanges to resolve disputes among the brokers, buyers, and sellers using the exchange (similar to the arbitration common in the U.S. exchanges) and by banking associations to speed up disputes between member banks. The Bar Association has a permanent arbitration committee that can be used by everyone. The two main aspects on which these committees concentrate are the speed of conflict resolution (the Intrabank Credit House arbitration committee resolves all disputes within one business day) and the low cost of arbitration, usually between 1 and 3 percent of the disputed amount. The decision to apply for arbitration must be mutual, but the decision is binding and cannot be appealed to the arbitration court. If the defendant refuses to comply with the decision, however, the plaintiff can petition that the arbitration court issue a ruling forcing the plaintiff to comply. The APC specifies that such a ruling should always be upheld unless the arbitration committee has violated the APC statutes.

The need for dispute resolution and contract enforcement is so great that in June 1993 more than a hundred companies (Russian and foreign), including more than thirty banks and insurance companies, paid a membership fee to establish the Moscow Commercial Court, an unaffiliated permanent arbitration committee. Its decisions are to be enforced by the Moscow Arbitration Court. By luring highly skilled professional jurists to high-paying positions on this "private court," the organizers commit to resolve disputes in less than a month, charging less than 1 percent of the disputed amount, which is only 10 percent of the arbitration court fee. Companies based in Saint Petersburg plan to follow the example of their Moscow colleagues.

Permanent arbitration committees are usually set up by large organizations, but a provision in the APC allows for the establishment of special ad hoc arbitration committees to resolve disputes. Participation is voluntary; the number of committee members is usually three, one appointed from each side and the third appointed by the two sides. The decisions are binding, and the rules of enforcement are the same as for the permanent committees. Use of ad hoc arbitration committees is reported to be fairly high. The basic advantages were outlined above: speed, cost-effectiveness, and no sensitive information leakage.

The particular importance of the APC is that there is no attempt by the state to monopolize the dispute resolution mechanism. The difference between the English and French systems, described above, comes to mind: lack of competition in the dispute resolution services tends to increase the transaction costs and thus slow down economic development. Fortunately, the Russian system encourages competition in this area.

Private Enforcement by Force.   The surge of racketeering and other criminal activity surrounding business transactions that started in the late 1980s continues to increase. The criminal elements quickly understood that it is much more profitable to engage in business activity than to extort money from people who engage in it. In early 1990, gangsters were allegedly already moving into legitimate businesses such as trade, entertainment, construction, and even banking. The use of coercive power has not been abandoned but appears in the form of security personnel who defend the firm from extortion attempts from other criminal groups and who enforce contracts with other parties.[21]

In a business world where one competitor has the ability and the will to use coercive power, other competitors must acquire matching coercive ability or get out of business. Unless it relies on physical force, an enterprise cannot withstand the pressure of extortion and cannot enforce contracts with other entities who use force. Not surprisingly, then, most banks and many large private companies maintain large security departments. Bank security people fend off attempts to extort cheap credits or collect delinquent debts. An acquaintance in Russia told the story of an executive in a commercial bank whose husband was approached by a group of people requesting that he help them obtain a loan. When he refused, they threatened him. The executive went to the extortionists' hotel room and told them that, if they ever spoke to her husband again, she would report them to her bank's security department. The extortionists were never heard from again. When we asked whether the security department would have done anything, our acquaintance assured us that the bank had no choice but to use physical force to prevent such attempts; otherwise the owners would lose their bank to the extortionists. Western countries long ago adopted a more efficient system, wherein the state acts as the primary defender and deterrent against extortion and enforces contracts, thus eliminating the need for costly duplication of efforts by many market participants.

Collection agencies still exist, but it has now become more lucrative to provide security services. Rather than maintaining a sufficient security force, a company hires a security firm to perform the same functions for a fee. In some cases, large security firms are taken on as partners. On one hand, this is an efficient use of resources because of the economies of scale in protection services; on the other, there is always the danger of a firm being taken over by the security firm that was supposed to protect it. Some businesses use these firms despite the danger of being drawn into the criminal world, but others choose to forgo potentially profitable transactions because enforcement costs are too high. Although there is no hard evidence on contract enforcement by the security firms because they tend to keep their dealings secret, contract enforcement on their part would be natural. Certain areas of business in Russia today are based on feudal relations, wherein the "rulers" collect taxes from their "subjects," making it optimal for the rulers to protect their subjects from other rulers so that the tax amount will be maximized. One form of protection is contract enforcement. If somebody owes money to the ruler's subject, the ruler has an incentive to collect it because part of it will become his.

As stated earlier, some companies that would prefer to use legal mechanisms are forced to use private enforcers by the abundance of laws prohibiting certain transactions, imposing high taxes, and limiting market functions. Many businesses are pushed into the semilegal world when many authorities issue conflicting decrees, as is happening in Russia.

Large companies use their own security departments as private enforcement systems, which forces their smaller counterparts to use other forms of contract enforcement to level the playing field, thus driving up their costs of doing business. Because small businesses are crucial for the growth of the Russian economy, the consequences are dramatic. The system is wasteful because it does not exploit the economies of scale in protection and contract enforcement. Also, disputes are frequently resolved by people with little or no understanding of the issues involved. Moreover, the decisions are made on the basis of the force standing behind each of the parties. These forces make the process unpredictable and thus costly because the relative strength of the parties can change. New forces will attempt to emerge to take their place; the ability to use violence will be a substitute for law school diplomas. Decision making in such unpredictable conditions requires a high risk premium, so many potentially profitable projects are not undertaken. For the projects that are undertaken, the required rate of return is very high, and prices will reflect that. Another danger of using the private enforcement mechanism is how to break ties with the enforcers because one criminal activity is often related to other criminal activities. Private contract enforcement may lead to racketeering the same way that racketeering leads to private enforcement.

Conclusion

We conducted an informal experiment by comparing the responses of American Master of Business Administration students with the responses of Russian students in Economics to the following question: "What is the role of the state in the marketplace?" According to the Russian students, contract enforcement was the most important task. In sharp contrast, the American students mentioned contract enforceability only after extensive prodding by the instructor. Those responses illustrate the differences between the two economies in their present state of development. The American students did not mention contract enforcement because it is taken for granted in a system committed to that task. Russian students, however, have experienced the problems stemming from the state's inability to enforce legal contracts and thus attached high priority to this task.

As we have shown above, the current contract enforcement institutions in Russia are insufficient. The legal system, burdened by its past, lacks appropriate rules, tradition, and trained experts. At the same time, the political and economic uncertainties undermine the reputation mechanisms' ability to provide contract enforceability. Some features of the previous period—the existence of large conglomerates and networks of informal relations—support some reputation-based institutions. Adapted to the new situation, these institutions ensure contract enforcement to some degree but at the cost of forestalling the entry of new firms and hence the emergence of a competitive economy. New reputation-based institutions seem to be emerging, as well as institutions that involve the use of coercive force by organizations other than the state.

The overall institutional structure is far from being efficient and does not seem to be converging toward being efficient. In particular, small and new businesses are unable to commit themselves to honoring their contracts. The resulting barriers to entry forestall the growth of a market economy in the short run and are likely to lead to uneven income distribution and underutilization of entrepreneurship in the long run. Contract enforcement institutions based on coercive power promote growth by enabling contract enforcement; they forestall growth by increasing the transaction costs of doing business relative to the situation in which the government has a monopoly over coercive power and is restricted to use it for the provision of impartial justice through a "competitive" court system.

In Russia today, the absence of an appropriate institutional infrastructure for contract enforcement is producing severe economic problems. There has been a relative lack of attention to contract enforcement on the part of Russian economists and politicians as reflected in a book titled *The Difficult Transition to Market* (July 1990), edited by academician Leonid Abalkin, who was President Gorbachev's economic adviser. It is a collection of thoughts and prescriptions by all the leading Russian (and several Western) economists about what is required to accomplish the transition to a market economy. Although it raises many important points, it does not once mention that the lack of legal or extralegal contract enforcement is an impediment to the development of a market economy.

Addressing aspects of contract enforcement is mandatory for facilitating economic growth in Russia. In particular, legislation for improving the operation of the legal system is needed as soon as possible. In addition, market participants and legal personnel should be apprised of the nature of property rights and contracts in a free-exchange economy as well as of the basic principles the legal system uses to resolve disputes. Furthermore, policy should take into account the interrelations among institutions based on the legal system and extralegal institutions. Economic growth in market economies is fundamentally based on the ability to exchange, which is limited by the ability to enforce contracts. Fostering economic growth requires policy aimed at enhancing contract enforcement.

Notes

1. Although our chapter explicitly relates to Russia, similar situations prevail in other former Soviet Union states.

2. For ease of presentation, we ignore budget constraints.

3. For Europe, see van Caenegem (1992). For the United States, see Auerbach (1983).

4. See Greif (1993a).

5. The theory of path dependence is presented by David (1988, 1992a).

6. At the same time, institutional infrastructures are among the society's "carriers of history"; see David (1992b).

7. Throughout history social norms and customs have served as mechanisms for the reduction of transaction costs, in particular as contract enforcement mechanisms. Ben-Porath (1980) discussed the importance of the family and close social surroundings as transaction facilitators. Analysis of peer pressure and social norms as incentive devices in small groups can be found in Kandel and Lazear (1992) and Kandori (1992).

8. See Douglas (1975), pp. 515–16.

9. Plucknett (1949, 137).

10. For discussion, see Rosenthal (1991).

11. The discussion implicitly assumes an infinite horizon. It holds, however, for cases where the horizon is finite but where there is uncertainty when termination will occur or

where there are multiple Pareto ranking equilibria in the stage game. For discussion, see Pearce (1992).

12. The operation of reputation mechanisms was originally studied by Kreps et al. (1982).

13. For the operation of a coalition in Mexican California during the nineteenth century, see Clay (1993).

14. The following discussion is based on Greif et al. 1994.

15. For additional elaboration on this point, see Greif (1993a).

16. Bergson (1989) indicates that from 1966 to 1985 the average quota increased 6 percent relative to the earlier year.

17. The numbers in the table actually underestimate the problem for many enterprises because the military-industrial complex would get its full allocation, forcing the others to divide the remains.

18. The same situation prevailed in most other Eastern European countries as documented by Gray et al. (1992).

19. At the time of their passage, Russia was not yet an independent state.

20. The old parliament was dispersed by presidential decree, but it remains to be seen whether the newly elected one is more willing to pass the required legislation.

21. This is not to say that criminal activity has been completely abandoned. Other groups now control drugs, prostitution, theft, extortion, and murder. But even they are becoming more businesslike; the current most popular form of extortion is forcing property owners to sell cheaply.

References

Abalkin, Leonid. *Trudniy Povorot k Rinku (Difficult Transition to Market)*. Moscow: Economica, 1990.

Auerbach, Jerold S. *Justice without Law?* New York: Oxford University Press, 1983.

Argenti, P. *The Occupation of Chios by the Genoese, 1346–1566*. Cambridge, Eng.: Cambridge University Press, 1958.

Ben-Porath, Yoram. "The F-Connection: Families, Friends, and Firms and the Organization of Exchange." *Population and Development Review* 6 (1980): 1–30.

Bergson, Abram. *Planning and Performance in Socialist Economies: The USSR and Eastern Europe*. New York: Unwin Hyman, 1989.

Bernstein, Lisa. "Opting Out of the Legal System: Extralegal Contractual Relations in the Diamond Industry." *Journal of Legal Studies* 21 (January 1992): 115–57.

Boot, Arnoud W., Stuart I. Greenbaum, and Anjan V. Thakor. "Reputation and Discretion in Financial Contracting." *American Economic Review*, forthcoming.

Bull, Clive. "The Existence of Self-Enforcing Implicit Contracts." *Quarterly Journal of Economics*. February 1987, pp. 147–59.

Clay, Karen. "Trade Institutions and Law: The Experience of Mexican California." Working paper. Stanford University, 1993.

David, Paul A. "Path-Dependence: Putting the Past into the Future of Economics." Technical Report no. 533. IMSSS. Stanford University, 1988.

————. "Path Dependence and the Predictability in Dynamic Systems with Local Network Externalities: A Paradigm for Historical Economics." In *Technology and the Wealth of Nations*, ed. C. Freeman and D. Foray. London: Pinter Publishers, 1992a.

————. "Why Are Institutions the 'Carriers of History'?" Stanford Institute for Theoretical Economics working paper, Stanford University, July 15, 1992b.

Douglas, David C., ed. *English Historical Documents*. Vol. 3. New York: Oxford University Press, 1975.

Gray, Cheryl, et al. World Bank Publications Series on the Legal Systems in the Eastern European Countries, 1992.

Greif, Avner. "Institutional Infrastructure and Economic Development: Reflections from the Commercial Revolution." In Proceedings of the Tenth World Congress of the International Economic Association, ed. Michael Kaser. London: Macmillan, 1993.

————. "Contract Enforceability and Economic Institutions in Early Trade: The Maghribi Traders' Coalition." *American Economic Review* 83, no. 3 (June 1993b): 525–48.

Greif, Avner, Paul Milgrom, and Barry Weingast. "Merchant Gilds as a Nexus of Contracts." *Journal of Political Economy*, August 1994.

Kandel, Eugene, and Edward P. Lazear. "Peer Pressure and Partnerships." *Journal of Political Economy*, 1992, p. 100.

Kandori, Michihiro. "Social Norms and Community Enforcement." *Review of Economic Studies*, 1992.

Klein, Daniel. "Cooperation through Collective Enforcement: A Model of Credit Bureaus." Working paper. University of California at Irvine, 1989.

Kreps, D., P. Milgrom, J. Roberts, and R. Wilson. "Rational Cooperation in the Finitely-Repeated Prisoners' Dilemma." *Journal of Economic Theory* 27 (1982): 245–52.

Macaulay, S. "Noncontractual Relations in Business: A Preliminary Study." *American Sociological Review* 23 (1963): 55–70.

Milgrom, Paul R., Douglass North, and Barry R. Weingast. "The Role of Institutions in the Revival of Trade: The Medieval Law Merchant, Private Judges, and the Champagne Fairs." *Economics and Politics* 1 (1990): 1–23.

Narodnoye Hozyaysvto SSSR. Years 1975, 1985, 1990.

North, Douglass C. *Institutions, Institutional Change and Economic Performance*. Cambridge, Eng.: Cambridge University Press, 1990.

Olson, Mancur. "Dictatorship, Democracy, and Development." *American Political Science Review* 87, no. 3 (1993): 567–76.

Pearce, David G. "Repeated Games: Cooperation and Rationality." In *Advances in Economic Theory, Sixth World Congress*, ed. Jean-Jacques Laffont. Vol. 1. Cambridge, Eng: Cambridge University Press, 1992.

Plucknett, Theodore Frank Thomas. *Legislation of Edward I*. Oxford, Eng.: Clarendon, 1949.

Rosenthal, J. L. *The Fruits of Revolution*. Cambridge, Eng.: Cambridge University Press, 1991.

van Caenegem, R. C. *An Historical Introduction to Private Law*. Cambridge, Eng.: Cambridge University Press, 1992.

Williamson, O. E. "Credible Commitments: Using Hostages to Support Exchange." *American Economic Review* 73 (1983): 519–40.

———. *The Economic Institutions of Capitalism*. New York: The Free Press, 1985.

9

Publicly Provided Goods and Services in a Transition Economy

EDWARD P. LAZEAR and
SHERWIN ROSEN

In the former Soviet Union, many social services were tied to the enterprise. The provision of housing, medical care, child care, food, vacation privileges, and other goods and services were frequently provided through the state enterprises. As the proportion of the economy that is in private hands grows, those goods and services will tend to be provided by the market sector. But some firms remain under state control and continue to provide social goods to their workers.

In this chapter, previous practices are discussed. The way in which the provision of social goods and services has changed during the past few years is documented. We consider the implications for social welfare.

There are two main points. First, under the old system, consumer sovereignty was neither present nor desired. Certain goods and services were viewed as more important by the general society and were provided. In a market economy, consumer sovereignty reigns and ensures that individuals get the most satisfaction out of their incomes. Second, labor mobility is restricted when goods and services are provided by the employer on the basis of seniority. Workers tend not to move to their most valuable activity because they will lose their places in the queue for valuable and scarce goods and services. Thus, untying goods and services from employment is both a natural and a socially desirable consequence of reform.

Introduction

In command economies, the enterprise, as an arm of the state, often serves as the natural administrative unit through which consumption goods are allocated. As these economies reduce their reliance on exclusive state control of production, they must reorganize the distribution of goods and services previously provided by state enterprises to their employees. Should these goods and services continue to be provided by the state but in some other form? Do particular agencies of the state have comparative advantage in administering their distribution? As firms become privatized in the transition to market structures, what obligations do the new private enterprises have to previous employees? What kinds of job security or severance pay should replace the lifetime employment guarantees workers had before? Many families previously received a significant portion of their income through in-kind payments from their state enterprise, such as housing services, child care, sometimes medical care, vacation homes, and many consumption goods at reduced prices. How should these distributions be factored into the picture in assessing future financial claims on those firms?

We focus attention on Russia here, but much of what follows is relevant to other economies that are in transition from command to market structures. The discussion is organized around two basic economic principles. One is the role of consumer sovereignty. Another is that labor and other resources must move to their highest-valued uses to maximize production efficiency. Labor mobility is essential in any well-functioning market economy. The in-kind provision of goods and services by the firm can affect labor mobility.

Some specific information about Russia was obtained from a questionnaire sent to Natalia K. Erokhina, the deputy minister of social protection. The informal questionnaire, completed in September 1993, requested information about the provision of goods and services by state enterprises under the Soviet system. She was asked to describe the kinds of goods and services that were provided in this manner and for details on how they were distributed. We asked how the allocations had changed over time, to assess the current situation compared to the past, and about the nature of available alternative sources of supply. Inquiries were made about the differences in the provision of the goods between firms. For example, was it only very large state enterprises that provided housing or was it smaller ones as well? In addition to social services provided by firms, we also asked about those provided directly by the state, such as pensions and

This work was supported in part by the National Science Foundation.

education. We also requested information about how state enterprises had previously affected the distribution of services provided by other governmental agencies through influence or bribes and for supplementary information on possible illegal sources of supply; this information was necessarily more impressionistic, when it could be supplied at all.

The Role of the Firm in Providing Private Goods

In the United States approximately a quarter of total compensation takes the form of fringe benefits and pension payments provided by firms. In the former Soviet Union, the proportion was much greater. A substantial amount of housing was provided at subsidized rates, as were public utilities, child care, and large subsidies implicit in low prices for food and other goods distributed through the firm. A study by Spitz and Vinokurova (1994) claims that pecuniary compensation is almost a trivial fraction of total compensation in Russian firms today and that workers care so little about it that most of them don't even know what their pecuniary compensation is.[1] Before the breakup of the Soviet Union, party members had access to distinctly superior goods and services compared with what was available to the general public. The implicit value of all those goods and services, as distributed either through the party or through the state enterprises where ordinary citizens worked, would have increased the value of fringes and nonpecuniary compensation to total compensation to much higher proportions than in the United States or elsewhere.

Why were so many goods and services tied to and distributed through the firm under the old system? After all, it was possible simply to increase the amount of monetary compensation paid to employees and allow them to buy the goods and services from state stores or to rent housing from a state-operated independent housing market. This of course occurred in practice, but still a large fraction of total compensation apparently was distributed in kind rather than in rubles. There were two principal reasons for this division of labor in the Soviet distribution system; one was theoretical and one was practical.

One reason is that the state and society in general were not indifferent as to how workers spent their earnings. The socialist structure was inherently paternalistic, preferring that particular kinds of goods were favored over other kinds. Conspicuous consumption always had a stigma associated with it, whereas the purchase of housing, education, food, and health services was viewed as a more productive kind of consumption. Consumer sovereignty was suppressed in the interest of common consumption goals.

The theoretical rationale for the state imposing common consumption standards relies on externalities. For example, if particular individuals in a society do not take appropriate care of themselves or of their families, then distributing goods in kind, rather than in money, might prevent some of these undesired transactions from occurring.[2] This is often given as the reason for public education, public housing, and public health care, even in Western societies. Another potential rationale is political and related to communist ideology. Certain goods were considered valuable for society and others were not. The same was true of certain kinds of labor activity. Farming and manufacturing were highly valued, whereas commerce and finance were considered to be subversive. Extra consumption of goods produced by the favored sectors was considered as a positive force in society, whereas consumption of goods from less-favored sectors was viewed as socially destructive.

There is a related theoretical rationale for firms to influence the consumption of their workers and to act paternalistically toward them, independent of state activities. Suppose some personal consumption activities of workers, such as drinking, are detrimental to the productivity of the enterprise. Not only may intoxication render workers less productive, but the lack of productivity may interfere with the productivity of workmates.

If workers could be held fully accountable for their acts, they would internalize all these side effects and act in a socially efficient manner. For example, if the workers had to compensate the firm and their coworkers for the secondary negative repercussions of their consumption on others or if the firm subsidized positive repercussions on others, then the personal benefits of unproductive consumption would be weighed against their full costs to others, and everyone would be induced, as if by an invisible hand, to consume at socially efficient levels. For a variety of reasons related to transactions costs and the establishment of a quasi-market system, it is not always possible to assign full property rights in these externalities. Workers then do not necessarily take the full consequences into account unless they are directed to do so by their employer. It can be economically efficient for firms to provide some of these goods in kind rather than in cash.

Finally, there is a practical reason why firms act as consumption agents for workers in command economies: When the price system is not allowed to ration goods among buyers and sellers, surpluses and shortages inevitably become a chronic condition of life. Other, less-efficient social institutions arise to allocate goods. Queues are the most familiar manifestation; however, there are others. In a command economy, clout, political connections, and barter often substitute for generalized purchasing power that is essential to a price mechanism. Of course, connections and clout are not without value even in market economies. These things get greatly magnified in centrally planned societies.[3]

To carry out production plans, the central Soviet had to restrict the mobility of workers. In addition, more goods were made available in cities such as Moscow than in other places. An elaborate system of passport control was established to ensure that workers stayed more or less where the plan allocated them. State control of housing was also necessary for these purposes. After all, a free housing market would have made it difficult, if not impossible, to enforce passport restrictions. Tying housing to one's job has apparent virtues for the state in these circumstances. To get the workers they wanted, perquisites such as better-quality houses, access to otherwise unattainable consumption, and the like must of necessity serve as important substitutes for cash wages in such societies. To be sure, perquisites have great value in market economies. Their value becomes much greater in centrally directed economies because the desires of citizens must be coordinated with the desires of the state. It is impossible to judge how these incentive alignment forces affected the structure of labor relations and consumption in the former Soviet Union, but the forces must have been considerable. Substituting markets for direct allocations will reduce firms' taking such paternalistic attitudes toward their workers. The rate at which they disappear will depend on the speed and certainty with which economic reforms move toward a truly decentralized system.

Summary of Specific Benefits

HOUSING

The general picture is that enterprises with a thousand workers or more providing housing to said workers. Although those enterprises did not generally construct the housing, they did secure it from other state agencies and make it available to their employees. (Some firms with workforces exceeding three thousand employees did engage in housing construction.) In addition to what was provided through firms, housing could be obtained through municipal authorities, the typical method for persons who worked in smaller enterprises. Another alternative was to obtain housing through housing construction cooperatives that were either municipally owned or enterprise owned. The cooperatives enabled individuals to become housing owners. The general pattern was for the person to put 30 percent down and to pay off the rest of the capital expense over a fifteen-year period.

Specific housing units were allocated lists of individuals and families desiring housing. A particular family could be on many lists at the same time. For example, because men and women were generally both employed, the husband could be on a list at his enterprise, the wife could be on a list at her enterprise, and a grandparent could be on a list through the pension authority for municipal housing. This family would wait for housing to come up on the various lists and then select the highest-quality unit they could. Urgency was a factor in determining places on these lists. Invalids received priority, as did people with diseases such as tuberculosis. Families with large numbers of children were ranked higher than those with smaller families. And of course party members received special privileges; their housing allocation mechanism was distinct from that of nonparty members.

Although we are somewhat unclear on the nature of work and social discipline in state enterprises, one penalty imposed on workers whose behavior deviated from the norm was to be moved to a lower place on the housing list. This is important because the value of housing was well above the price that workers paid for it, and a substantial part of workers' welfare depended on their rank in the housing list. Disciplining them by changing priority in the queue could have a major impact on their wealth.

In theory, housing maintenance was done by the authority who managed it. So in the case of enterprise-supplied housing, the enterprise was responsible for repair. For municipally supplied housing, the municipality was responsible for repair. Whether in practice the enterprise or municipality was effective in maintaining the building or had much interest in upkeep is uncertain. What is clear is that, even when the enterprise and municipality neglected these tasks, individual residents had great incentives to maintain the dwellings in which they resided because economic rents to possession were so large.

CHILD CARE

A recent study by Alm and Sjoquist (1993) found that the bulk of expenditures by state enterprises on social services are allocated to either housing or to child care. Child care consists primarily of enterprise-provided kindergartens or preschool centers. Kindergartens in the work establishment allow children to be cared for near the workplace of their parents. In addition, municipalities provided child care for workers employed by firms that did not supply it and for other individuals. One major difficulty associated with workplace-provided child care is that workers' housing tended to be located throughout the city but that child care tended to be located at work. As a result, families traded slots to accommodate their children in day care centers that were close to home rather than close to the workplace. Apparently, this kind of trading was widespread; a barter network existed that allowed people to allocate their children to day care centers in a more efficient manner than that dictated by individual employment patterns. This kind of "resale" is often observed when goods are provided in kind.

HEALTH CARE

For the most part, medical services were provided by local municipalities. In addition, some enterprises had their own medical clinics, hospitals, and sanitoriums, which generally were of higher quality than those attached to the cities. Enterprises were able to obtain better equipment and attract more capable physicians. Only individuals who were ineligible for enterprise-provided medical care voluntarily chose to go to the municipally provided health care facilities.

OTHER ITEMS

In addition to the main categories of housing and child care and some subsidized health care, firms often provided cultural and sports facilities that frequently were made available to other local residents as well as to employees. We have not been able to obtain specific data, but our impression is that a number of consumer goods were also distributed through the enterprise. For example, most employees received some of their meals at the firm in canteens and cafeterias. In addition, enterprises served as intermediaries for the distribution of some basic food supplies to employees for preparation at home. Some workers were given access to agricultural plots to grow their own vegetables. Goods that were unavailable or that had to be obtained in lengthy queues in state stores could be made more accessible to workers through enterprise connections. For example, automobiles, which were extremely difficult to buy and had very long waiting lists, might occasionally be obtained through employment at particular enterprises. Other goods available through firms included access to sanitoriums, country cottages, vacation resorts, hotels and sports camps, furniture, refrigerators, and summer camps.

EDUCATION

Although day care and kindergartens were provided through the enterprises, elementary and secondary education was and still is almost exclusively provided and controlled by the municipalities. Even so, state enterprises sometimes make payments to secondary schools as compensation for training their employees, and some enterprises subsidize schools and teachers to get better facilities in their particular localities. Some enterprises provide direct technical education through formal vocational schools, but available data indicate that this is a small fraction of the total expenditures made by state enterprises on social services.

PENSIONS

Unlike the United States, the entire pension payment in Russia is administrated by the central government, not by enterprises or private pensions. There is ambiguity here, however, because some benefits carried over into retirement. For example, enterprise-provided housing often was occupied by older individuals who were no longer associated with the enterprise. This may have reflected an implicit retirement benefit.[4]

JOB SECURITY

Until 1994, layoffs were extremely rare; essentially, workers had ownership rights to their jobs. Although some forms of worker discipline, such as changing queue priorities for goods and services, could be used by an enterprise, for the most part workers were entitled to their jobs for their entire working careers at state-determined wages. That has changed somewhat in the past couple of years, as firms have attempted to become more efficient and have reduced their workforces, especially the firms that have become privatized. Now private organizations have the right to choose the size of their workforce as long as they comply with the statutes associated with the privatization.

Job security under the old system was so great that there was virtually no reason for unemployment compensation. Workers spent very little time in transition between jobs, and those periods were covered either by disability insurance or by other forms of payments. Unemployment insurance as we know it in the West was not a feature of the economy.

The Current Situation

The current situation differs somewhat, but not greatly, from the past. Despite all the talk and accounts in the popular press, Russia has not undertaken major steps to change its economy's structure. Most workers are still employed in state enterprises, most people still live in state- or enterprise-owned housing, and most medical services, education, and other public services are still provided through the state.

One significant change is the privatization of not only small enterprises but also housing. In 1991, only 1 percent of the dwellings were privately owned. By 1992 that number had risen to 10 percent (Alm and Sjoquist 1993). Enterprise provision of housing has also changed. First, many enterprises have stopped providing housing, although prosperous enterprises are still engaged in their own construction businesses. Additionally, municipal flats are now sold at market prices. In Moscow it is claimed that approximately 25 percent of the municipal flats are for sale in a private market. The housing construction cooperatives that existed under the previous system are probably being replaced by the development of a private housing market.

The absence of well-defined financial institutions to smooth consumption over the life cycle requires that many private firms engage in constructing and financing housing for their workers. Housing is provided in exchange for a loan to be repaid over some period of time, usually related to employment. Under the current structure, enterprise influence is used primarily to affect the distribution of materials used for housing. Because construction materials are now much more expensive in real terms than they were previously, enterprises attempt and often succeed in obtaining these materials at below-market prices.

In the Soviet era, enterprise-associated medical services were provided primarily to employees. That system has changed dramatically; now the enterprise makes available all its medical services at market prices to anyone who is willing to pay for them. This changes somewhat the allocation of medical services. If, as is reported, the best medical facilities are associated with the enterprises, then better-quality medical care is now available to a larger proportion of the population than was previously the case.

Pensions are financed somewhat differently than they were previously. Before, enterprises contributed 9–10 percent of the production cost to support pension funds and social insurance. At this point, firms are responsible for contributing 27 percent of the wage bill to pension funds. Personal pension benefits seem unrelated to the amount or method of previous contribution.

COMPARISONS BETWEEN PAST AND FUTURE PROVISION OF SOCIAL SERVICES

Individual consumer choice was not only unimportant under the Soviet system, it was downright discouraged. The Soviets placed a premium on uniform consumption across individuals in terms both of absolute levels and in the composition of goods consumed. This was especially true of goods associated with social welfare, particularly housing, education, and health care. In a decentralized market economy, consumer sovereignty is supreme. Individuals are not only permitted but encouraged to choose their own consumption baskets. Economists generally think that allowing individuals to choose their own goods is superior to direct allocations of goods by others. Consumers possess superior information about their own preferences, and the costs of acquiring information about the personal preferences of others and the related transactions costs are avoided when people choose for themselves. Increasing individual control over consumption choices is an idea making its way into the current system throughout Eastern Europe and elsewhere. As goods become less tied to enterprises, this will happen to an even greater extent.

Even in the West, education is viewed as a good that should be publicly provided because some common level of education is considered socially desirable. There are a number of justifications for the goal of similar educational attainment levels, perhaps the most important of which is equality. The same kind of argument is extended to housing and pensions as well. In most societies, it is felt that children particularly need to be assured of a minimum standard of living.

There are a number of ways to achieve these goals in a market economy, but we must take care to distinguish carefully between means and ends. If the state wants to ensure that a minimum housing standard applies to every citizen, the state need not be in the business of either constructing or choosing housing for individuals. Less-interventionist policies, such as vouchers, allow the exercise of private choice even when expenditure levels are targeted. Vouchers restrict consumer sovereignty because exchanging vouchers for money is prohibited: individuals are required to spend them only on the particular good in question. For example, recent voucher proposals for public schools prohibit their being used to consume additional housing, even if housing is viewed as socially desirable. But vouchers allow more freedom of choice because individuals can choose the school they consider best.

In an economy where consumer freedom is not particularly valued and sometimes discouraged, it is not difficult to tie the provision of goods and services to the enterprise at which people work. When choice is restricted, firms do not have to produce the entire range of goods and services that are feasible for the economy. If, for example, it is deemed appropriate for individuals to have a particular kind of housing, then a firm can simply construct that kind of housing and make it available to all employees. Even if this type does not suit the precise needs of particular workers, it may maximize the greater social good under the old view of what society is supposed to accomplish, especially if scale economies are achieved thereby. Once consumer sovereignty becomes an important consideration, however, tying the consumption of goods and services to employment presents difficulties. In order for workers to obtain the precise kind of goods they desire, the firm has to produce a vast array of alternatives or give workers income and allow them to purchase on their own. Payments in cash—generalized purchasing power—untie the provision of goods and services from the job.

If individual tastes and preferences are to be respected, then tying social services to the firm is likely to result in an inferior allocation of resources. Services directly provided by the firm are likely to constrain the worker to more-limited choices than would be available in a decentralized environment. Consider housing, for example. The firm necessarily offers a limited number of housing types to its workers, and their choice is restricted to a relatively small number of alternatives. Workers who match up with the firm primarily on the basis of their talents as workers are forced to buy a job and housing at the same time. They might choose quite differently if the whole deal were not presented as a package. Some socially productive employment opportunities might go unfulfilled in these circumstances.

Perhaps the major difficulty in tying consumption to employment is that goods and services are provided in a way unrelated to their true social costs of production. The key informational role of market prices in a decentralized system fails to operate, and goods are not consumed in their socially optimal proportions. Furthermore, the nonpecuniary methods needed for allocation impede other socially useful exchanges. Being in the queue for a long time is a valuable asset

Table 9.1   The Allocation of Housing

Worker/Family	Housing
A	best
B	middle
C	worst

(workers listed by seniority)

Firm 1 *allocates middle housing to*	Firm 2 *allocates best and worst housing to*
Family A's male	Family A's female
Family C's female	Family B's male
	Family B's female
	Family C's male

that workers are reluctant to give away, which can adversely affect worker mobility. For example, suppose a worker employed at a particular state enterprise for sixteen years has worked his way up to obtaining a one-bedroom flat in central Moscow. If he were to take a superior job in another enterprise in Moscow, he might have to give up his hard-earned housing opportunity and start anew at the low end of the housing list of the new enterprise. One's place on the enterprise's list is a valuable asset that only has value as long as employment continues with that particular firm and is thus destroyed by mobility. That firm-specific asset, then, imposes private costs on workers by hindering their mobility and imposes social costs on society as a whole by restricting the gains from trade.

Another problem with tying consumption to employment is that, for many consumption decisions, the family is the relevant unit of analysis, whereas for employment, the individual is the relevant unit of analysis. Resources are allocated inefficiently when a family is on multiple lists. If a central agency were allocating housing, it might do so in an efficient manner. But if two firms are allocating resources, there is coordination failure because those firms do not take into consideration the actions of one another and distortions result (see table 9.1).

In table 9.1 there are three houses, best, middle, and worst, and three families, A, B, and C. Social preferences rank Family A over Family B and Family B over Family C, which may correspond to different family sizes and different relative demands for housing services. The socially best allocation is when A gets the best house, B gets the middle house, and C gets the worst house. Suppose, however, that workers are allocated between two firms, Firm 1 and Firm 2, and that the male in Family A and the female in Family C work at Firm

1, while the female in Family A, the male and female in Family B, and the male in Family C work in Firm 2. Suppose that the best and the worst houses are controlled by Firm 2 and that the middle-quality house is controlled by Firm 1.

Firm 2 would allocate the first choice to the female in Family A because she has the most seniority. Firm 2 would allocate the second choice to Family B's male. The third choice then goes to Family C's male (because Family B prefers the second to the third choice at Firm 2). Firm 1 would give the option to choose its only house, middle, to Family A. But the family chooses between its allocation by *either* Firm 1 or Firm 2. Because the female in Firm 2 is allocated the top-quality house, she prefers that over the middle-quality house allocated to her husband in Firm 1. As result, the female in Firm 2 chooses the top-quality house, which is socially appropriate. But now Firm 1 must allocate the middle-quality house to its other employee, in this case the female in Family C. She will choose to live in that house because middle is better than what her husband is offered by Firm 2, which now has only worst left to allocate. The final allocation, then, is that Family A lives in best, Family C lives in middle, and Family B lives in worst.

This allocation is inefficient and could easily have been avoided had it been completely centrally determined or completely decentralized by a market. The conflicts that result from two independently competing allocation mechanisms cause inefficiency.

Two general points: free labor mobility is necessary for a well-functioning labor market, and market economy allocations of goods and services are the best way society has found to distribute things that individuals want to buy. Goods and services should be tied to a firm only if the firm is a more efficient provider than an independent market institution would be. Providing lunch at the workplace is a trivial but obvious example of a good that might be efficiently provided within an organization; having a cafeteria at the plant conserves on transaction costs that workers would otherwise have to bear. Even here, however, there are offsetting factors to consider. Workers can bring their most preferred food from home for a cost that may not be much higher than the one associated with having food provided at the organization.

A productive efficiency case can be made for supplying some goods at the workplace. If exercise improves worker productivity, it may be beneficial for the firm to provide exercise facilities to its workers. Here, too, a decentralized solution is possible if workers' outputs are fully observable. If firms paid workers directly on the basis of their output, then workers would have the appropriate private incentives to efficiently choose their diets, exercise, or other things. Firm provision of complementary inputs is important only when output is not easily observed or measured. Under those circumstances workers' wages are more rigidly tied to their jobs than to individual performance, and the firm has incentives to provide efficiency-enhancing goods along with the job. Certainly, goods of this kind would be the exception and not the rule.

In market economies such as the United States, many fringe benefits are tied to the firm to avoid taxes. Private firms supply health care because income in the form of health care services is not taxed. This artifact of the particular tax structure promotes excess use and is not a desirable property of a market economy. Obviously, firms should only supply those goods and services where they have a technical comparative advantage. Is a firm a more natural supplier of day care services than an organization that specializes in day care? Perhaps day care is efficiently provided at the workplace if parents prefer to have their children close to where they work. But, in fact, the reverse is also true in Russia because we know that families trade slots to acquire day care positions near their homes rather than near their workplace. And if it is desirable to supply cafeterias at workplaces, meals need not be provided free. Instead, as in many firms, food services could be contracted out to a firm that specializes in providing food and sells at market prices.

Housing is the most interesting good to consider because so much of it has been supplied by firms in the past. A new system must be put in place now that is likely to take the form of privatization to current residents of existing dwellings. In fact, this is already happening in many transition economies and in Russia. The main issue involves financing. Because capital markets are extremely undeveloped in these economies, substitutes for implicit firm-based financing of housing must be found. One possibility is allowing municipalities and other government agencies to issue mortgage debt to residents. It is undesirable, however, for the government to be involved in real estate lending. In the West, government loans have notoriously high default rates when made to individuals. Private institutions are generally better at handling default risk, except when they are insured by the state and the private institution does not bear the full cost of loan defaults.

Capital market imperfections do not dictate that housing must be tied to the enterprise. If housing continues to be supplied by or financed through the state, there is no need for state enterprises to be the administrative agency. Unbundling housing from the state enterprise is appropriate to minimize distortions that are caused by any particular system of social service provision. Every state property and state-financed housing system creates some type of distortion. An institution that minimizes these distortions should be selected.

Financial constraints are particularly important in the high-inflation environment that former Soviet Union republics are encountering. High inflation rapidly transferred ownership claims from some individuals to others. Still, a large portion of the population is unable to borrow the necessary resources to privatize its housing. Unless a stable banking sector that ties interest payments to a stable currency is created, there is little hope of developing a private financial structure that will support housing markets. Rather than tie housing to the firm, the appropriate solution is to ensure the efficient functioning of financial intermediaries who at present face high rates of inflation and are sharply constrained on the interest that they can pay. Interest rates are lower than the rate of inflation, so principal is given up as a result of saving activity, which obviously has adverse incentive consequences on the willingness of people to save and invest in future consumption.

Housing and other social expenditure obligations of firms can be transferred to local governments. So far, the complaint has been that the municipalities cannot afford those responsibilities because of lack of funds. But this argument is superficial. The purchase price for a private enterprise reflects whether those liabilities are attached to the firm or transferred to the municipality. If social goods continue to be the obligations of firms, the price that any prospective owner would be willing to pay for a particular enterprise would be significantly lower. A private purchaser of a state enterprise might be willing to pay a higher price to eliminate the obligation, but his ability to do so depends on financial considerations. If capital markets are constrained, some beneficial transactions do not take place. Purchasers of firms may be unable to buy out their tied social responsibility. If so, they retain the obligation to provide social services to their workers regardless of whether it is efficient.

Fiscal Federalism and the Provision of Services

As stated above, it has been argued that municipalities do not have the money available to finance desirable social services. A number of points are involved in this claim, beyond that just made, that refer to the issue of fiscal federalism.[5] What is the extent to which municipalities have the authority and power to raise revenue through taxation? Suppose municipalities are as effective at providing these services as the firms that previously were responsible for them. The municipality picks up the obligations and their expense, and the firm pays the municipality to handle them. There would be no net effect if the municipality or other agencies were better able to distribute the services than the enterprise itself; there are gains from trade, and firms need not be taxed to the full extent of the previous cost of delivering those services. Everyone is better off.

Of course, many of these services need not be provided by the state at all. Private housing can be purchased or rented in the market. Wages can be adjusted upward by the per-worker amounts firms were previously spending on housing. Firms would be no worse off because the additional amount that they paid in wages would exactly offset the amount that they were previously spending on housing. But workers, who now have the money in rubles rather than in housing services, are then free to choose the kind of housing they prefer and how much of their income to spend on it.

Coordination failures at different levels of government complicate things. Suppose that the central government is taking too large a share of revenues and not providing services previously distributed by the enterprise. Then municipalities would balk at taking over these services because cities would know that they were not in a position to obtain enough revenue to support them. As a result, firms would be obligated to continue to provide them, not because they were more efficient providers but because of difficulties between various levels of government. This is related to problems associated with the lack of financial institutions discussed earlier. Although it might otherwise be efficient for housing to be provided through the market, the inability of individuals to borrow directly makes firm- or enterprise-provided housing desirable, even if enterprises are inefficient in these activities. Similarly, state-provided services that were more efficiently located at the municipality rather than in enterprises might not be transferred to municipalities because of their inability to raise the requisite revenue.

Job Security

Labor markets with individual choice and free mobility have much more turnover and less job security than those dominated by central resource allocation. Along with freedom to move from job to job comes additional personal responsibility. Enterprise-based employment tied to social services encourages workers to view job security as one of their primary rights. In a mobile economy, job security is no longer a right. How does an economy go from a situation where workers essentially own their jobs to one in which employers determine work schedules? One possibility is for the firm to buy out of its previous obligation to provide job security. The firm might be obligated to make severance payments to workers to facilitate their transitions from one job to another.

Severance pay serves as short-term unemployment insurance. However, it also has some adverse consequences. If employers know that additional severance pay costs are associated with reductions in employment, then fewer workers are likely to be hired in the first place. Thus, a system of severance pay in exchange for job security provides some but not complete mobility. Of course, a severance pay provision must be at least as attractive to the firm as provisions guaranteeing workers' rights to jobs because employers can always choose to continue employment and forgo the severance payment. Instituting a system of severance pay could facilitate privatization to the extent that some payment is either required or permitted. Worker opposition to privatization would be reduced.

Alternatively, severance pay can be made by the state rather than by the individual enterprises. This is what unemployment insurance does. A state-controlled unemployment insurance system has the disadvantage that firms sometimes are induced to lay off workers excessively. It has the advantage of not reducing initial hiring rates.[6]

The specific form of unemployment insurance affects the allocation of resources. Below we describe some of the relevant issues associated with unemployment insurance:

1. Unemployment insurance is supposed to cover larger risks to individuals who suffer significant hardship from unemployment. Deductibles are desirable for this, so unemployment insurance should not be paid to individuals who are out of work for only short periods of time. Payment should begin after some amount of time has elapsed so that the system is not exploited by workers or firms to finance planned transitions from one job to another.

2. For an individual to qualify for unemployment compensation, it is generally necessary that the worker be employed with an organization for some significant period of time, like six months or more. Otherwise, workers can come in, work for a short period of time, quit, and then extract money from the system. Similarly, it is desirable that covered workers be employed for some minimum number of hours per week so that they are truly attached to the labor market and are not merely secondary employees who use unemployment insurance to finance tastes for leisure.

3. Unemployment compensation formulas vary, but they generally replace significantly less income than the previous wage. If they replaced the entire wage, workers would have little incentive to work or to seek new jobs. There is a trade-off between insurance and incentives. Although society would like to insure people so that they do not suffer during periods of unemployment, it also does not want to encourage them to become unemployed simply to take advantage of unemployment benefits.

4. The duration of time that unemployment compensation can be received should be limited, depending on general unemployment conditions in the economy. When many people are unemployed, it is more difficult for workers to obtain jobs quickly, and unemployment compensation should be available for a longer period of time. During normal conditions, the length of eligibility for unemployment compensation is reduced. Those who exhaust their benefits apply for welfare, which has more conditions attached to it. Welfare can be made sufficiently unattractive so that few people want to remain on welfare, but it covers basic minimum needs for individuals who are unable to find work in the system.

Unemployment compensation is not the primary method of support for individuals who are disabled or for the elderly. Those individuals receive disability or retirement pensions that are more generous than unemployment compensation. Russia, like most other countries, has a state-supported pension benefit system, but its pension benefits have become extremely low in the recent inflationary environment. The reason is that wages have been adjusted more closely to price increases than have pension payments. However, pensions can be indexed to inflation, tying payment amounts to some cost-of-living index.

Private Pensions and State Pensions

Most countries have large state-administered pensions and small private pensions, but this is not a necessity. The United States, for example, has a large private pension sector, and other countries, such as Chile, have recently fully privatized their formerly public pension systems. Pensions are generally tied to the enterprise to a greater extent in Western market economies than they are in command economies. One reason for this is tax avoidance, but it is certainly feasible for private pensions to be independent of firms. In fact, it might be better that way. Then pensions would be fully portable and would not have any adverse effects on labor mobility.

Conclusion

We wanted to emphasize two things in this essay: First, much of the efficiency of market economies rests on decentralization and consumer sovereignty. The desire for consumer sovereignty means that providing social goods and services should not be tied to the firm. Second, labor mobility can be adversely affected by tying goods and services to employment because the tie-ins increase the personal costs of moving. Goods and services provided by agencies other than the firm enhance efficiency.

Notes

1. An alternative explanation for this phenomenon is that the data were collected during a period of rapidly changing prices and wages, which produced great uncertainty about wage levels.

2. The role of altruism as described in Becker (1991) may have extended directly to

nonfamily members. The Soviets replaced the implicit altruistic linkages to nonfamily members by explicit ones, Bernheim and Bagwell (1988) notwithstanding.

3. See Murphy, Shleifer, and Vishny (1992) and Shleifer and Vishny (1992) for a discussion of partial reform and the effects of corruption. Also, see Greif and Kandel (this volume) and Anderson (this volume).

4. See Alm and Sjoquist (1993).

5. See McLure (this volume).

6. In Lazear (1990), it is shown that a severance pay requirement can be completely undone by an efficient labor contract so that no distortions result. Necessary for this is that the state does not intervene in the contract either by providing unemployment insurance or by taxing the firm based on either the number of workers it has or on the amount of unemployment compensation that the state pays out.

References

Alm, James, and David L. Sjoquist. "Enterprise Expenditures on Social Services and the Privatization Process." In *Intergovernmental Fiscal Relations in Russia*, Bureau for Private Enterprise, U.S. Agency for International Development. September 1993.

Becker, Gary S. *A Treatise on the Family.* Enlarged edition. Cambridge: Harvard University Press, 1991.

Bernheim, B. Douglas, and Kyle Bagwell. "Is Everything Neutral?" *Journal of Political Economy* 96 (April 1988): 308–38.

Erokhina, Natalia K. "Questionnaire of September 1993." Moscow, December 1993.

Lazear, Edward P. "Job Security Provisions and Employment." *Quarterly Journal of Economics* 105, no. 3 (August 1990): 699–726.

Murphy, Kevin, Andre Shleifer, and Robert Vishny. "The Transition to a Market Economy: Pitfalls of Partial Reform." *Quarterly Journal of Economics* 107, no. 3 (August 1992): 889–906.

Shleifer, Andre, and Robert Vishny. "Pervasive Shortages under Socialism." *Rand Journal of Economics* 9 (Summer 1992).

Spitz, Janet, and Natalia Vinokurova. "Labor, Wages, and Productivity in the Transition Russian Enterprise: The Inheritance of a Centrally Planned Compensation Scheme." Troy, N.Y.: Rensselaer Polytechnic Institute, January 1994. Mimeographed.

10

The Red Mafia: A Legacy of Communism

ANNELISE ANDERSON

The mafia is a major feature of Russia's making the transition to a market economy. This article inquires into the nature and origin of this phenomenon. The evidence suggests that the Russian mafia phenomenon is a direct outgrowth of the informal economy and the related corruption that were a significant part of the economy of the Soviet Union. Economists have usually concluded that the informal economy improved efficiency and consumer satisfaction in the Soviet economy. As aspects of this informal economy have developed into mafia activity, however, it has become less benign and is a possible threat to the success of the market economy in Russia because it threatens to defeat competition and thus the major benefit of a market economy.

Introduction

This chapter inquires into the mafia phenomenon in Russia to evaluate its potential for threatening the success of economic reform. The first section considers the term *mafia* in popular parlance and in the economic literature. The second section looks at the historical conditions associated with the development of mafias. The third section addresses the underground economy in the latter years of the Soviet Union as the framework from which the current Russian mafia, the subject of the fourth section, developed. The claim that

Russia's problems with crime are merely an early stage of capitalism is addressed in the fifth section. A final section considers public policy approaches.

Mafias and Organized Crime

Economists are uncomfortable with the term *mafia*, preferring to talk and theorize about *organized crime* and *the criminal firm*. The resulting speculations or models are sometimes intended to characterize the entities known to the public and the press as mafia organizations. At other times they are more general, intending to cover all organizations engaged in criminal activity, with the assumption that mafia organizations fall in this more general category.

The term *mafia* arose in Italy around 1865 to characterize some powerful Sicilians or Sicilian families engaged in violent and criminal activity who also achieved considerable control of local economic activity. (The term encompasses similar activity by Neopolitan and Calabrian organizations.) In the United States the term was adopted to describe organized criminal groups engaged initially in gambling and loan-sharking and later, during Prohibition, in illegal liquor traffic. As early as the 1970s in the Soviet Union mafia described the combination of underground economic enterprises and the officials involved with those underground enterprises as protectors and beneficiaries. Today it is used to describe a wide range of criminal activity in Russia.

In Italy and the United States *mafia* has a more specific meaning than is implied by *organized crime*, even though the the two are often considered to be synonymous. Many crimes are undertaken by gangs or groups with some division of labor, a hierarchical structure, and a distribution of the spoils. (Even small criminal groups, such as a gang that robs banks, have some organizational structure: someone drives the getaway car and someone else rides shotgun; positions in the structure may be vacant and need to be filled.) A gang that robs banks, however, is not a mafia, nor is a terrorist group, despite its use of violence. Neither organization nor violence associated with criminal activity is sufficient to define a mafia.

The term *mafia* is more often associated with illegal market enterprises providing drugs, illegal liquor, or gambling. These are usually ongoing enterprises in which arrangements and agreements that are not legal contracts are made among participants. To go beyond personal relationships in which deals are completed at face-to-face meetings, participants may need a larger organizational structure to enforce agreements among members of the group and outsiders and to punish or redress violations thereof. Indeed, the successful groups in such enterprises may be those who succeed in establishing such organizational structures. Such structures may greatly increase the size of the deals they can undertake, expand the scope of their market (the distance over which they can do business and the number of people with whom they can deal), and entail the use of violence or the threat of violence. An organization able to enforce agreements and punish violators is also likely to decide which agreements it will enforce. It may come to control entry into various lines of criminal activity and the behavior (at least to some extent) of those who come under its protection. Thus a characteristic of a mafia is that it performs governmental functions—law enforcement and criminal justice—in spheres where the legal judicial system refuses to exercise power or is unable to do so.

Another characteristic of mafias is their influence in the legal law enforcement and criminal justice systems. Leaders of the mafia may succeed in bribing individuals anywhere in the criminal justice system—police, courts, corrections. Cases may be dismissed, juries bribed, sentences reduced, parole lifted. The mafia may agree in some cases to use its powers on behalf of others who are not generally under its protection. It may also use its law enforcement connections against rival groups; the police crack a case, and the mafia eliminates a competitor.

T. C. Schelling of Harvard University, perhaps the first economist to address the mafia phenomenon analytically, defines *organized crime* as "large-scale continuing firms with the internal organization of a large enterprise, and with a conscious effort to control the market" (1967, 115). Schelling considers the suppression of rivals, possibly in collusion with the police, one of the basic skills of organized criminal groups and argues that their basic business is extortion from the criminal enterprises that actually supply illegal goods and services to the public (Schelling 1971).

Economist William Jennings agrees that organized crime is carried out for profit by groups but rejects monopoly as its defining characteristic. Instead, he says that "organized crime is distinguished from other group-based crime by the degree to which organized crime employs resources to insure that its members do not aid the police" by requiring oaths of loyalty and silence (Jennings 1984, 317). Jennings developed a model that incorporates profitability and the costs of administering and enforcing oaths of noncooperation with the police, given probabilities of apprehension and conviction, to predict what kinds of crime will be undertaken by organized criminal groups. From the model he predicts that mafias will avoid offenses such as shoplifting, where direct observation is the basis of apprehension, and specialize in activities where oaths are of greater relative advantage. Becker and Stigler (1974, 4) suggest another reason mafias are found in ongoing illegal markets: "It is difficult to bribe or even intimidate the enforcers who would be involved in a nonrepetitive violation."

In Jennings's model the cost of enforcing the oath of noncooperation with the police is a function of the probability of arrest and of time in jail, but the cost is also a function of the authorities' efforts to develop informants among the criminal group and the vulnerability of members to such efforts. One cost of enforcing noncooperation is punishing violators of the oath; in the American and

Sicilian mafias the punishment is death. There are also the costs of preventing cooperation by offering, in return for taking the oath, the benefits of membership in the organization: the opportunity to participate in profitable businesses and financial aid and the influence the group leaders wield over the criminal justice system for those arrested

The groups that fulfill Jennings's definition of organized crime, including specifically the American and Italian mafias, have one other characteristic: they devote resources not only to ensuring that members do not cooperate with the police but also to corrupting the legal and regulatory authorities. It is this last characteristic—the corruption of legitimate government authority—that warrants the term *mafia* in popular parlance around the world, and it is in this sense that the term was first used in the Soviet Union. A *mafia*, then, is a group that is characterized by profit-oriented criminal activity, that uses violence or the threat of violence, that expends resources to discourage cooperation of its members with the police, and that corrupts legitimate governmental authority.

When legitimate governmental authority becomes corrupted, the government may lose, if it ever had, the power to protect citizens and legitimate businesses from criminal activity. For example, theft and fencing become more attractive than other crimes when those who fence stolen goods are not prosecuted. But worse, the subversion of the criminal justice system allows the mafia to run protection rackets, that is, to extract payments from, control entry into, and mandate conditions of operation of legitimate business enterprises. Under these circumstances the mafia uses its influence in the criminal justice system to perform activities comparable to the taxing and regulating powers of legitimate government. The corruption of the government may extend beyond the criminal justice system to other regulatory agencies or agencies that award contracts or grants.

A full-fledged mafia can therefore have serious consequences for the economic growth of the legitimate economy. The mafia may create monopolies in local enterprises, control entry, and maximize revenue by extracting monopoly profits as protection payments. New investment may be discouraged and old investment driven out. Risk-averse investors are likely to seek localities less arbitrary and dangerous.

Pino Arlacchi (1986, 229–30), a sociologist and leading expert on the Sicilian mafia, points out that in the 1970s and early 1980s the areas of southern Italy with the highest growth rates were those with the lowest levels of both organized and conventional crime, whereas those areas with the greatest mafia presence were the only economically stagnant regions of Italy. In a survey designed by Arlacchi of young Italian industrialists, almost 27 percent of respondents in the three regions of Italy where organized crime is the most established claimed to have decided not to invest in their area because of criminal pressure (the average for the country was less than 3 percent). In the same three regions 58 percent claimed that they had withdrawn tenders for public contracts as a consequence of criminal threats or political pressure (*The Economist* 1994, 53–54).

This relationship leaves open the possibility that a common factor is involved in both the mafia presence and the poor economic performance. Political scientist Robert Putnam (1987), who studied representative regions in Italy in the 1860–1920 period and in the 1970s, suggests that the weakness of civic associational culture could be responsible for both. Putnam found that civic participatory culture in the earlier period was a strong determinant not only of civic culture but also of economic development (e.g., the percentage of the labor force in industry) in the later period, indeed a stronger determinant than the level of economic development in the earlier period.

The American and Sicilian mafias admit members, socialize them to their responsibilities, enforce the oath of noncooperation, and deliver the benefits of their influence over the criminal justice system. They may control entry into illegal and legal markets as well. But those organizations are not themselves the economic entities that undertake criminal enterprise. The criminal activity—the businesses operated by the members of the group that bring in the revenue—is undertaken by enterprises far less permanent than the group itself and often involving outsiders. The economic structure is not the same as the governing structure.[1] For particular illegal markets the organization may function like a cartel, a franchiser, or a trade association, with the significant difference that it does not leave the monopoly of violence to the state.

Why Mafias Develop

Historically, three major conditions are associated with the origins and development of mafias: (1) an abdication of legitimate government power, possibly encouraged by the population's rejection of government authority, (2) excessive bureaucratic power, and (3) the financial potential of illegal markets. These conditions may interact, each providing growth opportunities to a mafia originating for one of the other reasons.

ABDICATION OF POWER

The island of Sicily, with a long tradition of resistance to outside domination, saw the rise of the Sicilian mafia in the second half of the nineteenth century, especially after the unification of Italy in 1870. Raimondo Catanzaro, an Italian scholar, notes that both "before and after unification, people tended to use new systems of private protection for securing their land and property" (1992, 6). The Sicilian case is thus an example of the rise of a mafia in a vacuum of power or of the inability or unwillingness of the state to ensure public order in a society that had turned, over hundreds of years, away from state power to private means of protecting property and ensuring order (Catanzaro 1992, 20). The state implicitly let local powers control peasant unrest. Catanzaro concludes that "in contrast to what had happened in the past, [violence] occurred within the framework of the weak authority of a state that formally held, but failed to exercise, the legitimate monopoly over violence. It therefore compelled the state to come to terms with those who exercised de facto power at a local level and to delegate to them the functions of exercising that monopoly. Indeed, in practice, the state deferred to their authority, for although it officially prohibited private violence, it nevertheless granted the power to govern on behalf of the central government to that same local ruling class that made use of it" (Catanzaro 1992, 76).

Owners of large estates hired *gabelloti* (custodians) to run the estates in their owners' absence. The mafia put many of its men in *gabelloti* positions and thus achieved control over products and manufactured goods going to market as well as control of the peasants. Thus the mafioso played critical roles of mediation among peasants, landowners, and the state and between the countryside and the outside world (Chubb 1989, 9).

Between 1925 and 1929 the Italian Fascists made a concerted effort to eliminate the mafia and reestablish government control of the use of violence, but Prefect Cesare Mori—the man implementing this effort—was dismissed when he targeted powerful people supporting the Fascist regime. Mori's effort did replace mafia control of the relationship between peasants and landowners with state control, but it did not eliminate the problem. The mafia reestablished itself when fascism fell and was given a further boost when the Allied occupation in 1943 turned to local powers for assistance in governing (Catanzaro 1992, 110, 113–114).

The Italian government is not the only government that has turned to nonstate violence to accomplish what it was unwilling to do for itself. The U.S. Navy turned to Lucky Luciano, the imprisoned leader of the American mafia, to protect the New York docks from Nazi sabotage during World War II (Sterling 1990, 56). They were indeed protected, and it is reasonable to assume that the methods used were not ones the U.S. government would have been willing to employ.

Two U.S. economists, Stergios Skaperdas and Constantinos Syropoulos, provide a theoretical model of how gangs, which they interpret as primitive states, develop in situations of anarchy. They define *gangs* as long-lived organizations involved primarily in economic activity and having a near-monopoly of violence in a defined territory and a symbiotic relationship with the authorities. "Gangs emerge," they say, "out of situations in which there is a power vacuum that the State is unable to fill" (1994, 4, 5). One reason may be geographic isolation (as in nineteenth century Sicily), but the inability to govern does not require such geographic distance—for example, the inner cities in the United States. Illegal markets are another source of anarchy. When a government makes a product or service illegal, it also ceases to enforces some laws, such as contract law, in the illegal market.

In the Skaperdas-Syropoulos model, primitive states arise not out of cooperation but out of coercion. Initial endowments of resources are important in determining which people become the rulers, as is relative efficiency in producing the means of coercion (e.g., guns) rather than consumer goods: "the agents with the comparative advantage in unproductive activities and a greater number of resources become the rulers of the anarchic territory or, in another interpretation, those agents have higher rank within the organization emerging out of anarchy" (1994, 15). In the resulting primitive state people more efficient at producing consumer goods will seek to migrate to less arbitrary and coercive states.

Excessive Bureaucratic Power

In general, excessive bureaucratic power and discretion provide the basis for corruption—for bribery, shakedowns, and extortion—especially when the criteria for bureaucratic decisions are unclear and difficult to monitor and evaluate. The corruption of a bureaucratic agency may begin with the clients of the agency, such as the members of a regulated industry. Thus building contractors may seek to speed up the work of the agencies that give building permits. More often, however, the bureaucrats originate the corruption by demanding payment. Getting a government contract may require a kickback; tips or bribes may be necessary to secure a wide variety of government services. In the Soviet Union bribes were necessary to secure everything from drivers' licenses to medical care and even higher education, as well as goods.

This sort of corruption is worldwide and does not necessarily lead to the development of full-fledged mafias. Rather, corruption may be sporadic and action to correct it possible, or a standard pattern of paying government bureaucrats for their services may emerge. Government positions may be awarded to favored people to give them access to a share of the political spoils—a form of bureaucratic mercantilism. Bureaucratic corruption takes on a mafia character when violence or threats of violence are used to exclude competitors and thus to control market entry or access to contracts. At this point the efficiency benefits sometimes attributed to bribing government officials to do faster or better what they ought to do anyway collapse. Corrupt bureaucrats in collusion with criminal gangs—"the mafia"—may monopolize industries, award inflated contracts, and operate outside public safety standards. The activity may be extraordinarily persistent, defying repeated investigation and prosecution, as has been the case in New York City's construction industry (Rowan 1988, 129–138).

ILLEGAL MARKETS

In the United States, Prohibition created the potential for a major illegal market in alcohol, and America can trace the growth in scope and power of its mafias to the Prohibition years. Illegal market enterprises generate a good deal of cash that can be used for bribes and investment in other industries. It is easier for legal authorities to overlook voluntary trade among consenting adults, even if illegal, than it is to take bribes to permit crimes that involve victims. Law enforcement agencies may be able to meet their quotas for arrests more easily if they cooperate with the market leaders in illegal industry. The police may exclude new entrants or drive out competition by enforcing the law in cooperation with the dominant criminal group. Illegal drug markets have been a major factor in the virulence of the Sicilian mafia in the last several decades.

The Mafia Phenomenon in the Soviet Union

Two of the three conditions historically related to the development and growth of mafias—excessive bureaucratic power and illegal markets—were characteristic of the Soviet Union before its breakup at the end of 1991. The literature on the underground economy in the Soviet Union paints the following picture:

1. A substantial underground economy—"off the books" of the state-owned enterprises—operating within and in association with the legal or planned economy. This was in addition to legal private enterprise, such as the private agricultural plot.

2. Bribery and extortion as systematic features of economic transactions throughout the economy. From retail outlets to large manufacturing enterprises to medical care and education, bribery was standard in state-operated enterprises and private businesses, both for private gain and to achieve the goals of state enterprises.

3. Monitoring and control by the Communist Party and other bureaucrats of all aspects of economic activity at all levels of the economy.

4. Knowledge by those in positions of authority of the underground economy and the bribery and extortion. Selective enforcement of the variety of laws, rules, and regulations governing conduct and selective use of other powers (for example, the approval of job assignments) enabled the

authorities to control or manipulate underground economic activity for their own political purposes.

Joseph Berliner's study (1957) of management methods and factory operations in the USSR between 1938 and 1957 demonstrated that, even for factory managers whose goals were consistent with the incentive structure of the planned economy, "only by engaging in irregular practices can the manager run a successful enterprise" (324). To meet plan targets (and receive bonuses and promotions) under conditions of continual shortages, the effective factory manager used influence (*blat*) for a variety of purposes. The factory position of *tolkach* developed to obtain "all manner of scarce commodities through a combination of influence and gifts" (319). In return the factory manager or the *tolkach* provided supplies or services to others through various illegal methods, such as labeling good products as rejects.

In the mid-1970s a number of studies demonstrated that the irregular economic activity in the USSR went beyond the pursuit of goals and rewards defined by the state. In a 1977 article, Gregory Grossman of the University of California at Berkeley describes the major forms of illegal economic activity in the Soviet Union. He drew on a variety of sources including extensive Soviet press reports and accounts of emigrants. Stealing from state enterprises including collective farms was practiced "by virtually everyone," providing extra income to employees and "an important, often indispensable, basis for the second economy" (29). Grossman cites peasants stealing fodder, workers stealing tools and materials, physicians stealing medicines, drivers stealing gasoline, truck drivers diverting freight, and enterprise managers diverting goods either to the black market or into barter channels for needed supplies (29–30).

In the Soviet economy shortages of consumer and producer goods provided the opportunity for additional income at all stages in the process of exchange. Goods arriving at retail stores were often set aside for preferred customers who paid extra, the extra funds—not entered on the books—going into the pockets of employees and management. Those who controlled the distribution of producer goods, housing, and consumer durables were often in a position to extract additional payments from consumers (Grossman 1977, 30). Speculation in a variety of goods was another form of illegal economic activity.

Illegal production was also a feature of the Soviet economy in construction gangs, household and automotive repair, tailoring, and other services (Grossman 1977). Some underground firms, often operating under the cover of state-owned enterprises, produced goods. These underground firms "are privately bought and sold at capitalized values that presumably reflect their expected profitability discounted for risk." Such activity had gone on since at least 1952 (30–31).

All this illegal market activity was accompanied by gifts or bribes to "highly placed authorities, ranging up to the ministerial level; local government chiefs;

and, not least, provincial and possibly higher party secretaries and first secretaries" (Grossman 1977, 32). Reporting the sale of a variety of official positions for relatively large sums of money, Grossman finds that the process of bribery and graft was institutionalized. "Very probably there is a close organic connection between political administrative authority, on the one hand, and a highly developed world of illegal economic activity on the other. In sum the concept of kleptocracy . . . does not seem inapplicable" (33). In Georgia, underground entrepreneurs were reported to have "significant control" over major party appointments in the republic. "Illegal private economic activities," Grossman concludes, "are a major and extremely widespread phenomenon that for a very large part of the population is, in one form or another, a regular, almost daily, experience" (36). Grossman also notes that laundering illegally earned cash was a major problem, often accomplished by purchasing winning lottery tickets from the winner (37n. 44).

Konstantin Simis was a Soviet defense attorney who had many clients involved in the underground economy. He considers bribery and corruption fundamental to the nature of the Soviet regime—"the most prominent characteristic of which is the concentration of a monopoly of power in the hands of the Party hierarchy. . . unfettered either by the law or by public opinion" (Simis 1977, 35). Those involved in the corruption include "secretaries and heads of departments within the district committees of the Communist Party, district-level KGB and militia commanders, the chairmen of district executive councils, their deputies and departments heads, as well as the heads of district inspectorates (the fire, public health, sanitation, and veterinary services) and, in districts not forming part of a large town or city, the district prosecutors" (36). In general, "the entire senior staff of a district—from the Party secretary to the public prosecutor and the militia chief—provide protection for the very same directors of state farms and shops and chairmen of collective farms who are engaged in criminal activity (embezzlement, deception of customers and fraudulent stock-keeping) . . . any attempt to combat such organized crime is doomed to failure. Even when the criminal activities of a local mafia are reported to higher authority, there is as a rule no attempt to crack down on them, and the mafia then has a chance to round on those who tried to have their crimes exposed" (38).

Simis's use of the term *mafia*, an early one in writing about the Soviet economic system, whether journalistic or academic, is consistent with conventional use—criminal activity protected by the authorities, against which the ordinary recourse of going to the police proves unproductive. Simis tells many stories about defending people involved in the underground economy in the Soviet Union, several of which involve people who reported criminal activity and corruption to the authorities and, as a result, were forced to leave town or were themselves prosecuted. Thus the extensive rules and regulations were selectively enforced to meet the objectives of those in power (Simis 1982, 68–72). As a junior Soviet official said, "The government knows exactly who is dealing in what—arrests are made only when there is some larger political reason" (O'Hearn 1980, 219).

Simis's description of how underground business enterprises function in the absence of legally enforceable contracts resembles the privately adjudicated Law Merchant in Europe in the early Middle Ages, whereby a community of traders was able to ostracize those of unreliable reputation (Milgrom, North, and Weingast 1990). Disputes in the Soviet underground economy were heard by arbitrators who had a reputation for fairness and impartiality. The parties to the dispute agreed to be bound by the results, with which they usually complied. Cheating and misrepresentation were dealt with by ostracism from a community that had some solidarity. Regional communities doing underground business were relatively small, and regions were linked; word of unreliability spread rapidly. In Georgia and Azerbaijan there were, Simis reports, people murdered for "nonfulfillment of commercial obligations," but he knows of no such instances in the Baltic republics, Ukraine, or central Russia (1982, 155–56).

Simis (1982) also reports that since the 1950s private enterprise has often been entered by buying an existing businesses operating within a state-owned enterprise. The purchaser acquired the right to the equipment and labor the previous owner had used "off the books," as well as the previous owner's connections within the state-owned enterprise and with outsiders. Sometimes even a private escrow arrangement was used (159). Simis describes a business that he claims is typical, one of whose principals he defended. The three brothers who owned the business, which produced leather products, made decisions jointly or by majority vote. The day-to-day managers were employees of the state-owned Moscow enterprise within which the business operated. The directors of the state-owned enterprise were paid by the brothers for useful connections, but they did not exercise control over the private enterprise activities. The twenty-eight codefendants in the case, even those who had admitted guilt, gave little information about the main defendant or the violations of others—because the three brothers were committed to continuing their off-book salaries and paying their legal expenses provided they did not betray others or be "overly frank" with the authorities (162). The code here is similar to that of a mafia family.

These three brothers maintained good contacts with ministry officials and bribed "people in laboratories or research institutes" to inflate raw material requirements and allowable waste for state production. Thus more would be left over for off-book production. Relations with other factories producing related inputs were good (Simis 1982, 164). In time the output of this privately owned business became large enough to establish a traveling sales force selling to sixty-four regions and towns (165). (The brothers falsified or counterfeited the bills of lading required for transporting the goods.)

Aron Katsenelinboigen (a Soviet emigrant) and Herbert Levine (1977) categorize the various market relationships in the Soviet economy and describe practices such as bribery and obtaining cash through paying phantom employees. Two articles by Gerald Mars and Yochanan Altman (1987a, 1987b), case studies of firms in the underground economy of Soviet Georgia, describe in detail how supplies are obtained for production, how goods are transported, bookkeeping and documentation problems, and bribery.

A paper by Peter Boettke and Gary M. Anderson (1992) provides an overview of legal and illegal private economic activity in the Soviet Union and recounts a variety of instances of bribe taking and the sale of important positions, concluding that they are "not isolated cases, but *endemic* to the Soviet system. Moreover, positions of political authority or influence allow for the holders to extract rents from individuals throughout the economy. . . .Protection from legal sanction and regulation was a lucrative source of revenue for strategically placed officials" (24).

Boettke and Gary Anderson (1992) interpret the Soviet economic system as a form of mercantilism—"an economy where the central government sells strategic rent-generating positions within the economy for the purpose of raising revenue" (6). The function of the central plan was, they propose, "to protect the value of mercantilist monopoly rights" and was thus an important device for monitoring competition within and among cartels (15, 30). The controlling organization was the Communist Party, which determined important appointments and supervised enterprises. Loyalty was rewarded, but rewards—especially the nonmonetary rewards of access to better housing, medical care, food, recreation, and so forth—could be withdrawn if an individual fell out of favor with the party.

Economists Hillman and Schnytzer (1986) apply the concept of rent seeking[2] to the information provided by Simis, Grossman, and others, noting that "the evidence reveals that the illegal economy is not marginal to the official and officially-sanctioned systems" (88). They consider rent seeking an alternative to and better analytic framework than Grossman's kleptocracy. They note that the rents received by officials in the hierarchy were not capitalized—loss of a job meant not only loss of income, legal and illegal, but also loss of special privileges. They suggest that this situation leads to an economic theory of the purge. Purges undertaken from above are rent protecting, eliminating competition from below; purges undertaken from lower levels are part of the process of competing for rents (93–94). Like Boettke and Anderson, they find vested interests a substantial problem for reform. "To the extent that a centrally-planned economy generates rents . . . it is rational for individuals to engage in rent-seeking and, consequently, rent-protecting activity. . . . The uncertainties of the market remain, while the bureaucratization of society and the illegality of most market operations give rise to a plethora of rents" (97).

In the Gorbachev era (1985–1991) two pieces of legislation, the Law on

Individual Labor Activity, which went into effect in May 1987, and the Law on Cooperatives of 1988, significantly affected the underground economy. These laws legalized private business (albeit with a variety of restrictions); by January 1, 1990, about 200,000 cooperatives were in operation (Jones and Moskoff 1991, (16, 17). Some of the cooperatives were former underground enterprises that became legal; others, according to Jones and Moskoff's book on the cooperatives of the Gorbachev era, were fronts for racketeers. Some were spontaneous new business ventures; some were created by local governments; but the largest number were created within state-owned enterprises, often by the managers. Like their underground predecessors and the state-owned enterprises, they had supply problems and used various illegal sources and methods of supply. They also found bribery essential to survival; for example, bribes were necessary to obtain office space in Moscow (36–38, 78–85). In summary, "there were crimes committed by cooperators themselves, crimes perpetrated against the cooperatives, and wholesale extortion committed from top to bottom in the state government" (92).

The cooperatives came under attack for high prices (often on goods diverted from the state sector) and, in general, their profit orientation, which conflicted with the socialist mentality. The government regularly changed the rules—on licenses, lines of business, prices, hiring, taxation—for cooperatives and brought a variety of law enforcement actions against them, at the same time failing to protect the cooperatives from criminal activity, especially protection rackets. Cooperatives responded by paying protection (75 percent of the cooperatives in Moscow and 90 percent of those in Leningrad made protection payments) and establishing their own protection services (Jones and Moskoff 1991, 85–86). Jones and Moskoff also state that violence against cooperatives during the Gorbachev era was "occasional," but threats may have been more common. In the words of former Yekaterinburg police official Yuri Mizum, "When cooperatives were permitted in the mid-80's . . . authorities saw no need to provide them with any special protection. We were all taught to regard private property as somehow illegitimate anyway. The police stayed away from these businesses like the plague, and offered them no help, so of course when they were threatened by black marketeers, they had no alternative but to go along. Now, it's too late" (Handelman 1993, 30).

Under the cooperative legislation many new banks were also created. Although some were independent, some of them were created by associations of cooperatives and made loans to their owners, thus providing the funds the state-owned banks were unwilling to lend. Another group was created by state-owned enterprises (often with partial ownership by government ministries) and made loans to state-owned enterprises.

The Russian Mafia

In the 1960s and 1970s—and on into the 1980s—the Soviet economy was characterized by extensive illegal market activity involving systematic bribery of people in positions of power, which was primarily in the hands of the Communist Party. The close association between illegal market enterprises and the authorities marked this system as *mafia*,[3] although it differed in one important respect from the classic mafias of Italy and the United States: violence appears in almost all cases to have been exercised not by the underworld but by those in positions of power, through the purge in Hillman and Schnytzer's interpretation or, from Boettke and Anderson's viewpoint, the government structures enforcing state mercantilism. As far as can be judged from available accounts, it was individuals or groups in the official sector who competed for the monopoly rents, not underground operators.

During the late 1980s, however, violence or threats of violence began to come from gangs, who had a vulnerable target (the new cooperatives) and, increasingly, the means—firearms and other weapons. By the time of the Soviet breakup in 1991, Soviet officials had identified more than seven hundred gangs or clans operating in the Soviet Union. Organized along ethnic or family lines, each gang was headed by a boss called the *thief-in-law* (Handelman 1993, 40). By the late 1980s identifiable gangs based on ethnic ties were operating in Moscow. For example, the Chechens controlled black market car sales; the Azerbaijanis had the fruit and flower concessions (*Newsweek* 1993, 38).

Since the breakup of the Soviet Union and the demise of the Communist Party, many more gangs have formed that compete with one another for control of illegal markets and the territories for protection rackets. They began using violence extensively in that competition and against uncooperative legitimate entrepreneurs in early 1992. In Moscow and other major cities murders have increased substantially (many of them associated with gangland-style shoot-outs), as have crimes such as burglary, mugging, car theft, and robbery (Bohlen 1993, A1; *Newsweek* 1993, 38). Russian authorities have provided various estimates of the number of crime groups now operating in Russia, ranging from 2,600, of which 300 are "large syndicates" (Handelman 1993, 15), up to 3,000, of which 150 have become "well-organized fraternities" (Bohlen 1993). Nine or ten large gangs from other regions of Russia operate in Moscow (Bohlen 1993, A1).

Banking and finance are especially targeted by the mafia in postcommunist Russia. Between December 1992 and August 1993, there were eleven violent attacks against bankers, some of which were fatal (Bohlen 1993, A1). One reason for blackmailing and threatening bankers is to gain access to their books to determine which enterprises to target and how much to extort (Bohlen 1994, 6).

In Yekaterinburg an investment broker whose business and influence had, police think, grown to the point where it was threatening the local mafia was gunned down in September 1992, the fourth such murder in six months. Five gangs, at least one headed by a respected person in the community, are believed to be involved in export-import operations, banking and finance, and construction, as well as the Uralmash machine-producing complex. A Yekaterinburg Internal Affairs spokesman is quoted as saying, "No honest businessman can do anything in this city unless he pays unofficial taxes to crime groups, who in turn control many of our officials through bribes." He believes that "corruption has already penetrated some of the highest levels of the Government and security forces" (Handelman 1993, 32).

The Uralmash mafia, named after the state enterprise where it originated, is especially interesting because it was active in black markets in the days of the Soviet Union, selling goods and materials from Uralmash plants in return for needed supplies. With the state enterprise in financial difficulty in 1991, Handelman reports that, according to the police, the group "virtually moved inside the factory door." It "set up subsidiaries to purchase directly from the factory's assembly line, took over the factory's former Soviet-style youth club and established [its] own soccer team, restaurant, sportswear outlet and, reputedly, brokerage house" (Handelman 1993, 40). Handelman presents no information on what, if anything, this group is now doing that is illegal; this story thus illustrates the problem of sorting out the legitimate from the criminal. The brothers who ran the Soviet-era underground operation have, it would seem, brought their business aboveground and made it legitimate; if they must still proffer bribes to local officials, are they mafia or are the police overeager to so identify them?

One mafia source in Moscow provided writer Andrew Solomon with a description suggesting that Russia's gangs are developing the characteristics of classic mafia families—recruiting members and helping them with law enforcement problems. The source claimed that more and more young people are interested in joining the mafia. "When I get in trouble," he said, "the family helps; I was in prison in Finland, and they got me out" (Solomon 1993, 38–39).

Another kind of story about the Russian mafias is the direction of violence by the state agencies themselves. According to Handelman, "assumptions are widespread that the crime groups are not only protected, but also in some cases instructed by Government officials and the police" (1993, 32). A government report prepared for President Boris Yeltsin noted that police officers tip off gangs about vehicles carrying valuable cargo in the city of Tver. The same report noted that 70 to 80 percent of private businesses and commercial banks in major cities make payoffs of 10 to 20 percent of their turnover to organized crime (Bohlen 1994, 1).

Today major illegal activity involves selling or trading raw materials (including oil) at below-market prices. The raw materials are then sold in the West at market prices, and the difference is pocketed by the individuals, sometimes by deposit in a foreign bank account. The security ministry (formerly the KGB) is evidently involved in some export businesses, and other companies involved have been "set up by the Communist Party to get funds out of the country" (Erlanger 1993, A5). A commodity trading firm based in Switzerland, headed by Marc Rich, was trading grain, sugar, alumina, and machinery to Russia in exchange for oil and refined aluminum ingot, making profits by "skinning" the Russians. "Has Rich bribed influential pols and bureaucrats in the former Soviet Union?" *Forbes* asked. "Probably" (Klebnikov 1992, 41–42).

The accounts of the mafia in Russia are not nearly as detailed as the information that has been gathered over the years about the American and Sicilian mafias by journalists, through court records and the publication of wiretaps, and through testimony before legislative committees. Nevertheless, a fairly clear picture of the current situation is beginning to emerge.

With the failed coup of August 1991 and the demise of the Communist Party, neither local officials nor those in central government agencies now seem to be constrained in their corrupt activities by any high-level authority. Viktor Shchekochikhin, the president of the Union of Russian Entrepreneurs, puts it this way: "Before, officials took money in a more or less orderly way, because they knew that people could continue to come back to them. They behaved properly, if one can say that. With the arrival of the democrats came temporaries, who know that in the next elections they will be thrown out. They have to assure their future now" (Bohlen 1992, 4).

Government officials have thus become free to compete within their own spheres of authority using their economic powers and their connections with criminal groups. Their economic influence is buttressed by the continued existence of monopoly production in many sectors of the economy, as well as state control of most output in the major industries (power, communications, transportation). This continuing legacy of the old Soviet economy ensures that connections will continue to be important in obtaining supplies and services.

Criminal organizations are now willing to use violence. Some of these gangs are new; others existed before the breakup of the Soviet Union. Private protection agencies, often formed by or employing former KGB and army people, may do battle with criminal gangs or front for them. Some larger criminal organizations are absorbing smaller ones and taking their businesses. A small-time hood noted that his gang now supplies muscle for a larger group that controls his gang's old markets. It is widely believed that criminal gangs using violence may at times be operating under the direction and protection of government officials at central or local levels.

The government's efforts to combat corruption, violence, and business fraud are severely hampered for several reasons. The law itself is unclear, incomplete, and sometimes internally contradictory, as are property rights. More fundamental is the lack of consensus on what is legitimate, moral, and acceptable versus what is not and thus ought to be illegal and subject to criminal prosecution. The Soviet press vilified participants in the private underground economy and was used to attack cooperatives. Like the purges of the Soviet era, anticorruption efforts may be as much attacks on political opponents as genuine efforts to reform the system. The extent of corruption, and its acceptance and institutionalization as a reward to those loyal to the communist regime in the Soviet era, makes it difficult to attack. The political forces who support an anticorruption campaign place their supporters as well as their opponents in jeopardy. Even legitimate law enforcement efforts against gang violence and protection rackets may affect the corrupt interests of government officials.

An Early Stage of Capitalism?

Some Russians and Americans hold the view that crime in Russia, especially organized crime, is simply an "early stage" of capitalism, implying that conditions in Russia today are like those in some earlier era in the United States, perhaps the era of the frontier West or that of the so-called robber barons. "Some Russians argue," Handelman (1993, 50) says, "that a period of lawlessness is part of the price every society pays for radical economic change. Pointing to examples as disparate as the development of the American West and the transformation of Latin American economies, they suggest that without a certain amount of robber-baron-style entrepreneurship, the consumer goods in most Russian cities would disappear."

"Russia right now is a bit like America west of Dodge City in the mid-1800s," according to George Melloan (1992, A9). "Today's corruption," writes Michael Scammell, a professor of Russian literature at Cornell, "seems to be characteristic of a period of profound change and upheaval, when Russian society is in the stage (to paraphrase Marx) of the primitive accumulation of capital." A Russian friend told Scammell that "the situation should be compared not with profit-making in today's America but with the rough-and-tumble of America of a century ago, and the new entrepreneurs should be compared with the robber barons of those days" (Scammell 1993, 11E).

But the Russian mafia phenomenon and other peculiarities of economic life in Russia have little similarity to conditions in the nineteenth-century United States or to any "early" stages of capitalism.

THE RULE OF LAW, NOT GANGS

An important characteristic of the United States from its formation (and before) was a respect for the rule of law. "For eighteenth-century Americans, like the English writers they admired, liberty demanded the rule of law," writes historian Pauline Maier (1978, 80). Furthermore, property law and contract law had been developing in Great Britain for centuries, and the legal system of the United States drew heavily on British common law. William E. Nelson (1975, 145–64), in a study of the legal system in Massachusetts between 1760 and 1830, found substantial changes in the law on relationships between debtors and creditors and in contract and property law, generally in the direction of facilitating commerce and competition as Massachusetts became less agrarian and more industrialized. But these developments proceeded in an orderly way through legislation and court cases on the basis of colonial and common law.

As the settlers moved West they sought to adopt the legal codes established in other states and create legal institutions in the new territories and states. Nevertheless, law enforcement was stretched thin on the frontier and the Western states. Sometimes local officials could not handle the problems confronting them, and help from the statewide law enforcement authorities, depending as it did on the state's priorities, was not always available. There were interstate criminal gangs as early as the eighteenth century and, especially in frontier areas, horse theft and counterfeiting of private bank notes; after the Civil War gangs robbed trains and banks (Brown 1969, 44).

The response to this "absence of effective law and order in a frontier region" was not the gang as a primitive state but a uniquely American response: the vigilante group of citizens who took the law into their own hands. Brown notes that members of these groups were leading citizens in their communities and often well-known public figures. He sees their purpose as establishing in frontier regions the community structure of older areas "along with the values of property, law, and order" (Brown 1969, 63, 64). Some of these groups functioned well; others did not.

Brown differentiates the vigilante group from the lynch mob—"an unorganized, spontaneous, ephemeral mob which comes together briefly to do its fatal work and then breaks up" (1969, 63). In fact it was not until the mid–nineteenth century that lynch mob came to imply illegal hanging or killing. Before that, from its origin in the late 1760s, it had meant whipping or other physical punishment for real or alleged crimes without due process of law. Nevertheless, like the vigilante groups, the motivation of lynch mobs was anticrime and supportive of what was understood to be the law except in the South, where it was racially motivated and the black victims had often committed no offense.

Thus there was no mafia phenomenon in the early United States. No "gangs as primitive states" emerged. Scholars are also beginning to question the popular assumption that the Western frontier was violent and lawless. A study of two typical frontier mining towns (Bodie, California, in the 1870s and 1880s and Aurora, Nevada, in the 1860s) by Roger McGrath 1989 found that robbery, theft, and burglary were rare and that bank robbery, rape, racial violence, and serious juvenile crime were nonexistent (123). A considerable number of homicides occurred, but most were the result of fights between willing combatants—men who were "brave, strong, reckless, and violent" (123, 142).

It was not until the early twentieth century that "centralized, city-wide criminal operations under the control of a single 'syndicate' or 'organization' began to take shape in New York." Urban criminal gangs appeared in the decades before the Civil War but were "limited in significance and restricted to ethnic 'slum' neighborhoods" (Brown 1969, 45).

BRIBERY AND GOVERNMENT CORRUPTION

Bribery was not an institutionalized practice in the early United States, but neither was it rare. The Constitution identified bribery as one of the reasons for impeachment (the others being treason and the catchall, other high crimes and misdemeanors). Revelations of bribery brought forth public outrage, and laws were passed relating to conflict of interest and bribery. Noonan (1984) recounts the history of bribery and antibribery legislation in the United States as well as the writings of journalists and novelists about bribery, the general thrust of which is that the public found bribery and corruption severely objectionable. By the 1960s the United States, "unlike any previous society," had "statutes comprehensively extending the criminal law of bribery to almost every class and occupation" (579). With the Foreign Corrupt Practices Act of 1977, the United States "for the first time in the history of the world . . . made it criminal to corrupt the officials of another country" (680).

It is possible to compare the extent of antibribery legislation in Russia with that in the United States at different times in history, but quantifying the extent of bribery is another matter. Certainly bribery was extensive in the United States in the era of big-city machine politics. "Where the voters, the legislature, or the newspapers of New York needed to be won, Tweed was a bribegiver. Where the city had a say, Tweed took. . . . Bribery is central," says Noonan (1984, 525).

But any comparison or any attempts at quantification is overwhelmed by the fact that in the early United States and even until the Second World War, government expenditures—at all levels—were small relative to the size of the economy (see table 10.1), and regulatory controls minor, so that whatever the level of corruption, its effect on the economy was limited. Most of the economy proceeded unhindered by authorities at either the federal, state, or local levels.

Table 10.1   U.S. Federal, State, and Local Expenditures
              as a Percentage of Net National Product

Year	Percent
1902	7.5
1913	8.7
1922	13.6
1927	12.7
1938	22.8
1940	22.0

SOURCE: U.S. Bureau of the Census, *Historical Statistics of the United States: Colonial Times to 1957* (Washington, D.C.: U.S. Government Printing Office, 1960), Series Y401–411, p. 722, and Series F6-9, p. 139.

BUSINESS FRAUD

Changing technology and economic growth provided opportunities for business fraud and dishonesty in the nineteenth and early twentieth centuries. Changing technology is always a source of new kinds of crime, but law enforcement and legislation continually adapt to changing technology. Today the challenge comes from computers and electronic property. The question is not a "stage" of capitalism but the ability to respond to change with appropriate legislation and law enforcement—and appropriate judicial decisions—by building on existing concepts of contract, property, and commercial law. Again, commitment to the rule of law and substantial consensus on what the law should accomplish have characterized the United States since its founding. It is also far easier to deal with business fraud if the authorities are not themselves involved in corrupt practices.

OTHER POINTS OF CONTRAST

The early United States differed from Russia today in a number of other important ways.

The Banking System.   The banking system of the early United States had its ups and downs but on the whole served developing farming and commercial interests well. Banks were privately owned, although regulated by state legislatures. In Russia, by contrast, few banks are truly privately owned. Most are partially or entirely owned by state-owned enterprises, the central bank, or ministries, which have powers left over from their role in the communist era. Writing about how things work, Bill Thomas and Charles Sutherland (1992) say this about Russian banks: "Bankers control business assets by approving (or disapproving) quarterly budgets that have to be sent in long before any withdrawal. And even then, getting them to okay a request often has less to do with the soundness of the budget than the size of the accompanying bribe" (104). Other sources of financing—the capital markets—developed in the early United States as well, and thus the dependence of business on government as a source of funds was minimal.

The Interstate Commerce Clause.   For the economy, one of the unique aspects of the U.S. Constitution was the combination of decentralization of authority—the central government was relatively weak—and the limitations it placed on the powers of state authorities through the interstate commerce clause. The result was a considerable limitation on the influence of government in the economy and a check on the powers of state governments through people and businesses' ability to move to competing jurisdictions.

Taxation.   Taxes were low by today's standards, reflecting the low level of government spending. There was no income tax until 1913. Businesses paid no payroll taxes. The federal government collected only customs duties and excise taxes on tobacco and alcoholic beverages (Webber and Wildavsky 1986, 342). The low level of taxation for much of the nation's history may be responsible for the tradition of voluntary compliance and for the low level of corruption of tax authorities.

In addition, the nineteenth-century United States was a country with a low median age, a minimum bureaucracy, few regulations, virtually no welfare state, a weak central government, capital inflows rather than capital flight, and courts that could draw on the common law to deal with economic change.

In sum, there is little support for the view that the fraud, violence, and development of mafias in Russia are simply an early stage of capitalism. They have no counterpart in the early history of the United States and have arisen instead from the legacy of the communist era: excessive bureaucratic regulation, massive illegal markets, and, with the demise of the Communist Party, a vacuum of power engendered by confusion in the legal code and unsureness about what should and should not be legal.

These conditions are not an early stage of capitalism but an early stage of organized crime, when gangs abound, compete for territories and markets, and are especially violent. As some competitors are eliminated (often with the complicity of law enforcement), spheres of influence are established, and future gang wars arise primarily when there are new markets to contest.

An appealing feature of the early stage of capitalism argument is that time and the normal course of development will provide the cure. Unfortunately this is not the case. Mafias tend to be extraordinarily persistent, probably because the governments that control law enforcement are themselves beneficiaries of the underworld through corruption or other benefits provided by the mafia organizations. In Sicily the mafia controlled peasant unrest in its early years and delivered the vote in more recent times. So unwilling were the politicians to support any definitive strategy against the mafia that law enforcement agencies were unable to counter threats to their own people or other government officials, and the murder of prosecutors and public officials became characteristic of Italian life. By contrast, in the United States law enforcement officials have rarely been at risk from the mafia.

Public Policy Implications

The greatest risk of the mafia phenomenon in Russia is that an entrenched alliance between central or local officials and mafia groups will prevent competition in many markets and reduce the benefits of the fledgling market economy.[4] Theft from state-owned enterprises and export for personal gain will continue and perhaps accelerate. More serious is control over market entry in legitimate businesses to create competition with state-owned enterprises or other private enterprises. The means to limit entry is extensive, ranging from demands for excessive bribes to control of permits and licenses, enforcement of detailed regulations, and violence. Significant in this mix is control of the banking system and thus enterprises through the banking system. The primary objective of law enforcement in the economic arena should therefore be the encouragement and protection of genuine competition.

To deal effectively with the mafia phenomenon in Russia, it will be necessary to eliminate its causes by reducing anarchy, reducing the size and influence of the government bureaucracy, and eliminating most illegal markets.

REDUCING ANARCHY

It will be difficult for the government of Boris Yeltsin, given the December 12, 1993, parliamentary elections, to pursue reform at the pace his supporters would prefer. Clear legislation on property rights, contract law, and a commercial code may be slow in coming.

Nevertheless, the executive branch does control law enforcement and can set policy objectives and priorities. If the objective is to encourage competition, law enforcement agencies must target practices that are designed to prevent or drive out competition. By this standard, for example, violence and threats of violence would be more serious than a protection racket that extracts a modest sum from retailers but makes no effort to prevent new businesses from entering the market.

One former police chief considers the failure of the police to protect legitimate private businesses a key problem, one that began in the Gorbachev era. The new cooperatives had no alternative but to comply with gangs running protection rackets (Handelman 1993, 30). Defending legitimate private enterprise against violence and threats of violence would greatly reduce the scope of mafia activities.

The courts are a potential source of clarifying the law through its application to specific cases. Unlike the early United States, Russia has no common law tradition on which to draw, but it does have a new constitution that provides a framework for interpreting the statutes. A series of consistent decisions on commercial relationships, contracts, and property, free from political influence, would help reduce confusion.

REDUCING BUREAUCRACY AND THE POWER OF CENTRAL AND LOCAL GOVERNMENT OFFICIALS

One method to reduce the powers of government officials is to reduce their discretion. For example, businesses could be required to register (if necessary) rather than obtain a license requiring official approval. Also, routine small bribes are less damaging than anticompetitive practices that prevent entry. Anticorruption efforts directed toward public officials should be targeted at those who employ the services of groups willing to use violence in pursuit of their objectives.

Continued privatization will gradually reduce government power and enterprise theft as private owners become residual claimants to profits. The continued privatization of the banking system and the commercialization of banking as a service rather than a device for controlling enterprises will also further competition.

In the area of taxation, a tax code that eliminates negotiated privileges (tax holidays and the like) reduces discretion and opportunities for corruption. Without special privileges, lower tax rates could collect the same amount of government revenue and sharply reduce the benefits of bribing the tax negotiator or collector and the potential for extortion by government officials.

REDUCING ILLEGAL MARKETS

The communist economy created a vast array of illegal markets in products and services that are accepted as legal in market economies. Some prices are still controlled in Russia, providing opportunities for illegal gain in what should be legal enterprise, such as exporting oil rather than selling it internally.

Russia's new constitution, accepted by referendum on December 12, 1993, includes, in Article 8, a clause that empowers the government to pursue policies that favor competition and limit the powers of local officials to obstruct markets: "In the Russian Federation the unity of the economic area, the free movement of goods, services, and financial resources, support for competition, and freedom of economic activity are guaranteed." A clause in Article 71 places within the jurisdiction of the Russian Federation "the establishment of the legal foundations of the single market; financial, currency, credit, and customs regulation, monetary emission, and the foundations of pricing policy; federal economic services, including federal banks." Article 4 (as well as other clauses) gives primacy to federal over local law (*Foreign Broadcast Information Service* 1993, 19, 26).

Thus the central government of Russia now seems to have the basic tools it needs to encourage competition and prevent lower-level governments from defeating the market economy. In fact the greatest potential for the future may lie in competition among regions and cities. If the central government succeeds in establishing and enforcing basic property rights, a commercial code, and contract law, the cities or regions that manage to elect honest politicians committed to making their jurisdictions attractive to new enterprises and foreign investment are likely to surpass those that do not.

Notes

1. See Anderson (1979, 1994) for a more extensive discussion of the functions of mafia families in the United States and Italy.

2. Rent seeking is competition for economic privilege allocated by the government in the form of licenses, grants, and the like. The resources used in seeking rents are an economic waste. The term was invented by Anne O. Krueger. See Bates and Krueger (1993) for the application of the concept to several reforming economies and Buchanan, Tollison, and Tullock (1980) for theoretical analyses.

3. Indeed, the Soviet system as a criminal enterprise is the thrust of a book by Arkady Vaksberg (1991), who as a Soviet journalist had published accounts of official corruption.

4. A related danger is that politicians will turn to mafia violence to deliver the vote.

References

Anderson, Annelise G. *The Business of Organized Crime: A Cosa Nostra Family*. Stanford: Hoover Institution Press, 1979.

———. "Organized Crime, Mafia, and Governments." In Gianluca Fiorentini and Sam Peltzman, eds. *The Economics of Organized Crime*. Cambridge, Eng.: Cambridge University Press, 1994.

Arlacchi, Pino. *Mafia Business: The Mafia Ethic and the Spirit of Capitalism.* Trans. Martin Ryle. London, Eng.: Verso, 1986.

Bates, Robert H., and Anne O. Krueger. *Political and Economic Interactions in Economic Policy Reform: Evidence from Eight Countries.* Cambridge, Eng.: Basil Blackwell Limited, 1993.

Becker, Gary S., and George J. Stigler. "Law Enforcement, Malfeasance, and Compensation of Enforcers." *Journal of Legal Studies* 3, no. 1 (January 1974): 1–18.

Berliner, Joseph S. *Factory and Manager in the USSR.* Cambridge, Mass.: Harvard University Press, 1957.

Boettke, Peter J., and Gary M. Anderson. "Socialist Venality: A Rent-Seeking Model of the Mature Soviet-Style Economy." Hoover Institution Working Papers, Stanford, 1992.

Bohlen, Celestine. "Corruption Grows in Greedy Russia." *New York Times*, March 14, 1992, p. 4.

———. "Russia Mobsters Grow More Violent and Pervasive." *New York Times*, August 16, 1993, p. A1.

———. "Graft and Gangsterism in Russia Blight the Entrepreneurial Spirit." *New York Times*, January 30, 1994.

Brown, Richard Maxwell. "Historical Patterns of Violence in America." In Hugh Davis Graham and Ted Robert Gurr, eds. *Violence in America: Historical and Comparative Perspectives: A Report to the National Commission on the Causes and Prevention of Violence.* New York: New American Library, 1969, pp. 43–80.

Buchanan, James M., Robert D. Tollison, and Gordon Tullock, eds. *Toward a Theory of the Rent-Seeking Society.* College Station, Tex.: A&M University Press, 1980.

Catanzaro, Raimondo. *Men of Respect: A Social History of the Sicilian Mafia.* Trans. Raymond Rosenthal. New York: Free Press, 1992.

Chubb, Judith. "The Mafia and Politics: The Italian State under Siege." Western Societies Program Occasional Paper No. 23, Center for International Studies, Cornell University, 1989.

Erlanger, Steven. "In Kremlin, Hints and Allegations: Corruption, Real or Not, Has Paralyzed Russia's Government." *New York Times*, August 25, 1993, p. A5.

Foreign Broadcast Information Service–Soviet Union (FBIS–SOV). "Draft Constitution Published." *FBIS-SOV-93-216*, November 10, 1993, pp. 18–37.

Grossman, Gregory. "The 'Second Economy' of the USSR." *Problems of Communism.* 26 (September–October 1977): 25–40.

Handelman, Stephen. "Why Capitalism and the Mafiya Mean Business." *New York Times Magazine*, January 24, 1993, pp. 12–50.

Hillman, A.L., and A. Schnytzer. "Illegal Economic Activities and Purges in a Soviet-Type Economy: A Rent-Seeking Perspective." *International Review of Law and Economics* 6, no. 1 (June 1986): 87–99.

"Italy: Still Crooked." *The Economist*, February 5, 1994, pp. 53–54.

Jennings, William P. "The Economics of Organized Crime." *Eastern Economic Journal* 10, no. 3 (July–September 1984): 315–21.

Jones, Anthony, and William Moskoff. *Ko-ops: The Rebirth of Entrepreneurship in the Soviet Union*. Bloomington: Indiana University Press, 1991.

Katsenelinboigen, Aron, and Herbert S. Levine. "Market and Plan, Plan and Market: The Soviet Case." In Morris Bornstein, ed., *The Soviet Economy: Continuity and Change*. Boulder, Colo.: Westview Press, 1981, pp. 61-70. Reprinted from *American Economic Review* 67, no. 1 (February 1977): 61–66.

Klebnikov, Paul. "How Rich Got Rich." *Forbes*, June 22, 1992, pp. 41–43.

McGrath, Roger D. "Violence and Lawlessness on the Western Frontier." In Ted Robert Gurr, ed., *Violence in America*, vol. 1, *The History of Crime*. Newbury Park, Calif.: Sage Publications, 1989, pp. 122–45.

Maier, Pauline. "Popular Uprisings and Civil Authority in Eighteenth-Century America." In Lawrence M. Friedman and Harry N. Scheiber, eds., *American Law and the Constitution Order: Historical Perspectives*. Cambridge, Mass.: Harvard University Press, 1978, pp. 69–84.

Mars, Gerald, and Yochanan Altman. "Case Studies in Second Economy Production and Transportation in Soviet Georgia" and "Case Studies in Second Economy Distribution in Soviet Georgia." In Sergio Alessandrini and Bruno Dallago, eds., *The Unofficial Economy: Consequences and Perspectives in Different Economic Systems*. Hants, Eng.: Gower Publishing Company, 1987, pp. 197–245, 219–45.

Melloan, George. "Steering Clear of Russia's Mafias." *Wall Street Journal*, March 16, 1992, p. A9.

Milgrom, Paul R., Douglass C. North, and Barry R. Weingast. "The Role of Institutions in the Revival of Trade: The Law Merchant, Private Judges, and the Champagne Fairs." *Economics and Politics* 2, no. 1 (March 1990): 1–23.

Nelson, William E. *Americanization of the Common Law: The Impact of Legal Change on Massachusetts Society, 1760–1830*. Cambridge, Mass.: Harvard University Press, 1975.

Newsweek. "A Long, Bloody Summer," August 30, 1993, pp. 38–39.

Noonan, John T., Jr. *Bribes*. New York: Macmillan Publishing Company, 1984.

O'Hearn, Dennis. "The Consumer Second Economy: Size and Effects." *Soviet Studies* 32, no. 2 (April 1980): 218–34.

Putnam, Robert D. "Institutional Performance and Political Culture in Italy: Some Puzzles about the Power of the Past." Harvard University Center for European Studies Working Paper Series, 1987.

Rowan, Roy. "The Mafia's Bite of the Big Apple." *Fortune*, June 6, 1988, pp. 129–38.

Scammell, Michael. "What's Good for the Mafia Is Good for Russia." *New York Times*, December 26, 1993, p. 11E.

Schelling, Thomas C. "Economic Analysis and Organized Crime." Appendix D of President's Commission on Law Enforcement and Criminal Justice, *Task Force Report: Organized Crime*. Washington, D.C.: U.S. Government Printing Office, 1967, pp. 114–26.

———. "What Is the Business of Organized Crime?" *American Scholar* 40, no. 4 (Autumn 1971): 643–52.

Simis, Konstantin. "The Machinery of Corruption in the Soviet Union." *Survey: A Journal of East & West Studies* 23, no. 4 (105) (Autumn 1977–78): 35–55.

———. *USSR: The Corrupt Society*. New York: Simon and Schuster, 1982.

Skaperdas, Stergios, and Constantinos Syropoulos. "Gangs as Primitive States." In Gianluca Fiorentini and Sam Peltzman, eds., *The Economics of Organized Crime*. Cambridge, Eng.: Cambridge University Press, 1994.

Solomon, Andrew. "Young Russia's Defiant Decadence." *New York Times Magazine*, July 18, 1993, pp. 16–51.

Sterling, Claire. *Octopus: The Long Reach of the International Sicilian Mafia*. New York: W. W. Norton & Company, 1990.

Thomas, Bill, and Charles Sutherland. *Red Rape: Adventure Capitalism in the New Russia*. New York: Dutton, 1992.

Vaksberg, Arkady. *The Soviet Mafia*. New York: St. Martin's Press, 1991.

Webber, Carolyn, and Aaron Wildavsky. *A History of Taxation and Expenditure in the Western World*. New York: Simon and Schuster, 1986.

11

Defense Conversion and Economic Reform in Russia

SUSAN GATES

The size and nature of the Russian defense industry make it impossible to consider the problem of economic reform apart from the issue of defense conversion. In implementing an economic reform strategy, the government must acknowledge the relationship that exists between economic reform strategy, defense conversion strategy, and economic outcomes. A reasonable economic reform strategy must include an explicit policy toward the defense industry as a whole. Defense conversion strategies can vary along two principal dimensions: the centralization of decision making (administrative or economic conversion) and the nature of resource transfer from defense to civilian uses (direct or indirect conversion). The centralized, direct conversion strategy of the Soviet government under Mikhail Gorbachev proved difficult to implement. The current Russian government has distanced itself from this strategy to follow a more economic and indirect defense conversion policy. The success of the new program will depend on the government's ability to adequately establish the "rules of the game" by creating the economic institutions necessary to support this type of conversion.

DEFENSE CONVERSION has been an important item on the Soviet, and now Russian, political and economic agenda since December 1988, when Mikhail Gorbachev, in a speech to the United Nations General Assembly, announced Soviet plans to reduce military expenditures and begin the process of converting defense industry resources to civilian uses. Since that time, both the aim of conversion as well as the method of achieving it have changed dramatically. During the communist-led attempts at economic reform of the late 1980s, defense conversion was viewed as the cornerstone of Soviet economic revitalization. At that juncture, it implied a direct transfer of the country's best technological and managerial talents from the defense sector to the civilian sector. As a result of this process, the high-quality production standards and efficiency of the defense sector would be achieved in the civilian sector as well. In this way, defense conversion was central to and synonymous with economic reform. As governments changed, and economic reform plans became more broad and radical, defense conversion began to take a backseat to more-general economic reform. The current market reform program of Boris Yeltsin's government devotes little direct attention to defense conversion. Instead, it focuses on the details of economic reform, such as mass privatization, and hopes that defense conversion will follow naturally from the overall process of economic restructuring. Military and defense industry leaders argue that the current economic reform program is in danger of failure precisely because it fails to articulate a reasonable plan for restructuring the defense industry. The defense industrialists do not necessarily want a centrally directed conversion plan but rather increased state support in the form of financial credits for restructuring, social security for defense industry workers, and the continuation of defense orders during the transition.

In Russia, defense conversion *is* economic reform and economic reform *is* defense conversion. Each process is crucial to and heavily influenced by the other. The sheer magnitude of the Russian military-industrial complex suggests that defense conversion of some sort will be an important part of Russia's transition from a centrally planned to a market economy, regardless of whether the government institutes an overt defense conversion program. The success of defense conversion and economic reform ultimately depends on conversion activities that take place at the firm level. Defense firms are economic actors, and the behavior of those firms during the economic transition from communism will have a significant impact on the progress of reform. The decisions that those firms make regarding defense conversion are significantly influenced by the political and economic environment, which is in turn influenced by government action (as well as government inaction). In implementing an economic reform strategy, the government must acknowledge the relationship that exists among the economic reform strategy, the defense conversion strategy, and economic outcomes. A reasonable economic reform strategy must include an explicit policy toward the defense industry as a whole. This policy need not involve a centralized defense conversion program. It should, however, clearly establish the economic rules of the game to allow managers of defense firms to make reasonable decisions. The Soviet government under Gorbachev, although realizing that defense conversion could play a significant role in economic reform, failed to acknowledge that economic reform would significantly influence the process of defense conversion. The Yeltsin government is in danger of making the opposite mistake—failing to realize the significant impact that defense conversion, or lack of it, has on the overall process of economic reform.

The Russian Defense Industry

To appreciate the link between economic reform and defense conversion in Russia, it is necessary to understand the nature of the Russian defense industry. There are three aspects of the Russian defense industry that complicate the process of defense conversion and render it crucial to economic reform. The most striking aspect is its enormous size. Although it is difficult to determine the level of Soviet defense spending during the cold war, there is little doubt that the Soviet government spent a greater portion of gross national product (GNP) on defense than did the United States. Western experts on the Soviet defense industry estimate that the Soviet Union allocated somewhere between 15 and 25 percent of GNP for defense during the cold war;[1] some Soviet economists suggest that the figure may have been as high as 30 percent.[2] Because the defense industry was such a large part of the Soviet economy, a great number of Soviet citizens worked in defense firms. In 1985, approximately 12 percent of the former Soviet Union and nearly 25 percent of the Russian industrial workforce were employed in the military-industrial complex.[3] Moreover, about 75 percent of the Soviet national research and development (R&D) budget was directed for military use.[4] In contrast, the United States spent 6.3 percent of GNP on defense, and only 5.5 percent of the U.S. labor force was involved in either defense production or direct military service in 1986. At the peak of cold war spending, nearly 70 percent of U.S. federal R&D funds were supporting defense-related activities; however, federal R&D funding comprised only about half the total national spending on R&D.[5] It is evident that the defense industry played a much more significant role in the the Soviet economy than it did in the U.S. economy. The fact that a greater fraction of national resources was being devoted to defense implies that a smaller fraction was being used for commercial production, provision of services, infrastructural maintenance and development, and investment.

The second important aspect of the Soviet military-industrial complex is the curious institutional isolation of the defense industry, coupled with the proliferation of civilian production within defense firms. Under the communist system, defense firms were part of the Ministry of Defense and fell under a different organizational hierarchy than civilian firms, which were part of the Ministry of Industry. Of particular importance is the fact that the two sectors had different supply and distribution networks. Despite this institutional separation, a significant number of civilian products, particularly ones involving more-complex technology, were produced by defense firms. For example, in 1985, all Soviet televisions, radios, cameras, and videotapes, as well as 90 percent of Soviet personal computers, were produced in defense industry enterprises.[6] Because defense firms had access to the best resources, even for their nonmilitary production, they generally produced higher-quality civilian products than did the civilian sector. This led many Soviet leaders to conclude that defense firms were more efficient than their civilian counterparts; however, the success of defense firms was in effect engineered by the government at the expense of the civilian sector. By isolating the defense sector from the civilian sector, the government was able to ensure that the best resources, both human and capital, were allocated to defense firms.

Although by 1985 about 40 percent of defense industry output consisted of civilian products, defense production continued to maintain its prominent position within defense firms. Spare capacity was devoted to civilian production, but civilian production was not designed to respond to consumer needs or achieve high levels of efficiency. It was structured so as to be compatible with the firm's military product mix and allow for rapid conversion in the event of an emergency.[7] Although such organization of production may have been appropriate in a command economy, in which firms need only respond to government production orders, it is not likely to be an efficient organizational form in a market economy, where producers must respond to and satisfy consumer demand and eventually compete with more-specialized producers of a given civilian product. As a result, a significant amount of both inter- and intrafirm restructuring will be part of the defense conversion process.

The final distinguishing feature of the Soviet military-industrial complex is that it is highly concentrated in two major respects. First, it is highly concentrated geographically. About half of Moscow's and three-quarters of Saint Petersburg's industrial workers were employed by the defense industry.[8] Almquist reports that "there are seventy-four cities in Russia where over 80% of all workers are employed by defense-sector enterprises."[9] Many of those cities were once so-called closed cities involved in the development of sensitive (often nuclear) weaponry, which were isolated from other parts of the country. Second, in addition to being concentrated geographically, the defense industry is also highly concentrated in the sense that the enterprises themselves tend to be large conglomerates with tens of thousands of employees. For example, 1992 employment at Vympel (Moscow) was nearly sixty thousand; Svetlana (Saint Petersburg) employed thirty thousand; Saratov Aviation Plant (Saratov) had eighteen thousand workers in 1992.[10] The size of these firms is sure to complicate the privatization, restructuring, and conversion process.

What Is Defense Conversion?

The peculiar nature of the Russian defense industry indicates that any economic reform is likely to have a significant impact on the defense industry and that defense conversion will remain an important issue in Russia. The term *defense conversion* is a flexible one and can be used to describe a variety of policies and processes. There are two essential aspects of defense conversion: the locus of decision-making authority during conversion and the mechanism through which conversion, broadly defined as an increase in the relative importance of civilian over military production in the overall economy, occurs.

Decision-making power during defense conversion can be concentrated in the hands of a small group of people, such as government officials, or it can be delegated to the countless economic entities, such as enterprise managers, whose actions are ultimately governed by market forces. Malleret defines the first process as *administrative conversion* and the second as *economic conversion*.[11] Administrative conversion is a top-down method of defense conversion consistent with central planning and state ownership of the defense industry. Under this type of conversion program, the government, or other central authorities responsible for defense conversion, articulates an overall plan that includes both general production targets as well as detailed recommendations regarding the product mix of all firms. In the extreme, the central authorities determine which production lines will be retooled or converted and provide the resources for these activities. Although, in theory, the government recommendations or mandates could be based on market needs, under administrative conversion, firms are not responding to market incentives but to the mandates of the central authorities in charge of the conversion process.

Economic conversion, in contrast, is a decentralized, market-driven process. Firms make their own decisions regarding what to produce based on their technological capabilities and market opportunities. There is no central authority dictating what will be produced by whom. The logic of economic conversion is that market forces induce economic decision makers to reallocate existing defense industry resources in the most efficient manner. Some resources are maintained in the their current use, others are "converted," and some are simply retired. In addition, markets guide structural changes such as mergers and spin-offs. An absence of centralized control over the conversion process as a whole, however, need not imply a lack of government action with respect to defense conversion. Indeed, the need for defense conversion ultimately stems from an identifiable government "action"—a decline in demand for military goods. The government, as the major purchaser of defense industry output, inevitably plays an important role in the market for defense goods.

To the extent that economic conversion is driven by market forces, any market failures can create problems for the conversion process. Even in well-developed market economies, it is frequently argued that the defense industry inevitably suffers from several market failures, stemming from such problems as governmental monopsony, artificial barriers to dual-use technology resulting from procurement regulations, capital and labor market rigidities, and artificially low returns on risky investments due to political constraints.[12] With respect to defense conversion in Russia, one must also consider potential market failures due to the overall transition from a centrally planned to a market economy. The most severe market failures stem from underdeveloped capital and financial markets, continued trade and currency restrictions, extremely limited labor mobility, and information problems. Although the existence of market failure does not necessarily imply that government intervention will have a positive effect on the conversion, it suggests that government intervention could be useful. The right government actions can ameliorate market failures and improve the overall situation. It is important to keep in mind, however, that even when market failures exist, the wrong government policies can exacerbate the situation. Thus, any government intervention in the defense conversion process must be well thought-out and focus on correcting identifiable market failures.

The second essential way in which defense conversion processes can vary is in the extent to which they rely on a direct as opposed to an indirect method of transferring capacity from the defense to the civilian sector. Conversion can be broadly viewed as a combination of two processes: a reduction in the capacity for defense production and an increase in civilian industrial capacity. As Bernstein notes, "The connection between the old military production enterprises and new civilian entities may not be as direct as would be implied by the term conversion."[13] Literal defense conversion, in which military production lines are physically altered so that they can produce commercial products, is a direct way of transferring capacity. Every instance of literal defense conversion involves a decrease of the defense base and a simultaneous increase in the civilian base within one enterprise. Conversion also occurs, however, when defense firms spin off divisions, which then begin producing commercial products, or when defense firms diversify into commercial production. These activities may or may not involve a direct transfer of resources. In addition, spin-offs or diversification activities can result from economic growth, rather than a direct transfer of assets, in which case commercial production increases without reducing defense capacity or production. Finally, macroeconomic defense conversion also occurs when defense firms close down and commercial firms are born. Human and capital assets leave the defense sector and flow into the civilian sector. There need not be any clear link between these events, but the overall effect is to promote defense conversion. To the extent that a given process of defense conversion relies on literal defense conversion, it is a *direct conversion process*. To the extent that it relies on spin-offs, diversification, or entry and exit, it is an *indirect conversion process*.

The U. S. government has found that the most successful approach to defense conversion is an economic and indirect one in which the declines in defense industrial capacity are not necessarily linked with increases in civilian production.[14] The American preference for economic over administrative conversion is natural, given that most defense production firms are privately owned. The belief that conversion is best achieved through an indirect, as opposed to a direct, transfer of productive capacity from the defense to the civilian industrial bases stems from experience. Nearly all attempts at literal conversion by American defense firms have been dismal failures. The few successful instances were actually diversification attempts, often involving the acquisition of another (commercial) firm.[15] Even in those cases, only a small fraction of the firm's defense-oriented assets were ever converted and used for commercial purposes. It should be stressed that even successful diversification activities were long and involved processes, showing profitable results only after five or ten years.

In general then, the U. S. approach to defense conversion has stressed economic, as opposed to administrative, conversion and indirect, as opposed to direct, conversion. In addition, government intervention has been limited to programs that help those who suffer most from the dislocations and programs that address particular market failures. In general, defense conversion aid can be targeted toward defense workers, defense firms, or communities severely impacted by the conversion process. To be consistent with the notion of economic conversion, any government intervention must be structured so as not to mandate that certain firms or workers do a certain thing but rather to provide incentives for the economic actor to make a certain decision. It is crucial that the ultimate decision be left up to the firm or the worker.

Government intervention that is designed to evoke particular responses from certain economic actors can be consistent with economic defense conversion. Indeed, special features of the defense industry often require governments to take specific actions to manipulate market forces so that they adequately reflect national security aims. For example, the government might want to ensure that there are two national tank producers and two submarine producers to prevent a monopolist in these industries from earning excessive profits from the government in times of national crisis, when demand is high. Although it may be more economical, because of the the existence of economies of scale, for one firm to produce one hundred tanks a year, as opposed to two firms producing fifty tanks a year, the government may decide to pay a higher per unit cost and continue procuring from two firms. In a sense, the government is paying a premium to maintain excess capacity and the potential for competition in times of high demand. Alternatively, the government might believe that dual-use technology serves national security interests and give grants to firms that use dual-use processes or produce dual-use products. The point is that the ultimate allocative decision, given the current and expected future demand for defense products, is delegated to the firm. Government influence over final results works indirectly, through the market. The government tries to induce firms to make certain decisions by providing them with the economic incentive to do so. If one of the aforementioned tank producers decides that it would be better off if it got out of the tank business and began producing minivans, the government would not force it to continue producing tanks. It might encourage the firm to do so by increasing the price it pays for a tank, but it does not order the firm to do anything. This process thus forces the government to evaluate the economic cost of various national security aims.

The Russian Defense Conversion Experience

The current process of Russian defense conversion began in 1988, when President Gorbachev suggested that the Soviet government needed to reduce military spending and encourage the increased production of consumer goods. Smart argues that the motivation for defense conversion at this stage was the belief that conversion would be the driving force behind an improvement in national economic performance:

> The fundamental motive behind all of Gorbachev's reforms was to revitalize the Soviet economy, and he understood that doing so meant slashing military spending. As his efforts to reshape the old system made things worse rather than better, however, his government's explanations began to stress the promise of military industries to supply the desperate consumer market. . . . Gorbachev's strategy to fulfill his conversion agenda was as simple as it was traditional: he hoped to apply the practices that had built Soviet military might to the rest of the economy.[16]

To implement this strategy, Gorbachev initiated many policies designed to transfer some of the best aspects of the defense sector into the civilian sector. For example, several military-industrial managers were placed in key governmental economic posts, many enterprises were transferred from civilian ministries to defense ministries, and many defense enterprises and design bureaus were ordered to work on civilian projects.

Although the discussion and political debate regarding defense conversion continued throughout the 1980s, by 1989, there was still no publicly stated national defense conversion program, no concrete blueprints for implementation, not even a guiding concept. [17] Firms were given production orders, but the logic behind and motivation for those mandates remained a mystery. Without such justification, managers had little interest in following the government's conversion directives and often ignored the central dictates. That resistance was based on several factors, including the general disdain for civilian production by defense workers, as well as the economic irrationality and infeasibility of the conversion mandates.

In January 1989, as Gorbachev's overall economic reform program was growing more market oriented, the government instituted a new system of self-financing and cost accounting for firms in the military-industrial complex. At the same time, it announced that the 1990 defense budget would be cut by 14 percent. As the economic crisis deepened, the government began cutting current year (1989) defense spending as well. Procurement orders fell dramatically, often without advance warning. [18] Although it was hoped that these changes would encourage firms to follow government orders to increase civilian production, this did not occur. The partial reforms left defense firms in a limbo between plan and market. The continued existence of price controls on final consumer goods made civilian production unattractive to the self-financing defense enterprises. They preferred to produce defense products or maintain idle capacity rather than incur the expenses associated with converting production capacity to increase the production of unprofitable consumer goods.

Throughout 1989 and 1990, in the face of declining defense orders, there were calls for a centralized and organized national defense conversion plan from defense industrialists and the military. Not only had Gorbachev's defense-sector policies of 1989 and 1990 failed to induce the intended increase in civilian production; they had also created a veritable crisis within the defense sector, as falling wages lowered worker morale and drove many skilled workers to leave the sector entirely. [19] The State Program of Conversion, drafted in 1989 and approved in December 1990, articulated an administrative, centrally controlled plan that set national conversion goals and allocated funds for retooling product lines. The defense ministries were to make the conversion decisions, and the firms were simply to do as they were told. In truth, the conversion program was more of a political statement than a concrete plan. Sherr argues that

> it provided for little conversion at all. Of R[rubles]45 billion allocated for civil MIC [military-industrial complex] production between 1991–95, only R9 billion was budgeted for the reshaping of existing weapons production. Whilst the share of civil MIC production was scheduled to rise—from 43 percent in 1989 to 65 percent in 1995—most of the increase was to come from expanding existing

civil capacity and from additional enterprise transfers. In absolute terms, weapons production was to remain constant.[20]

In most cases, the provisions for restructuring certain product lines were not based on consumer demand but on technological feasibility. This made the conversion plan especially unattractive to self-financing firms. As approval of the plan was delayed through 1990, and as the economic situation became increasingly chaotic, more and more firms realized the futility of waiting for the implementation of a government-directed, administrative defense conversion plan. By the time of the coup attempt in August 1991, few defense conversions had been accomplished according to the conversion plan,[21] although some firms were beginning to decrease defense activity and explore alternative opportunities.

Despite the dramatic political and economic changes that took place with the disintegration of the Soviet Union in 1991, one trend continued, namely, the decline in defense spending. It is estimated that Soviet, and now Russian, defense spending has declined by about 80 percent in real terms between 1989 and 1992, with a 68 percent real reduction occurring between 1991 and 1992 alone.[22] Because procurement spending has declined more than R&D spending, Russian defense producers are facing a catastrophic shock.

During the transition from Soviet to Russian rule, the declines in defense spending continued, but the defense conversion policy shifted dramatically. The Russian government under Yeltsin has shunned the notion of a top-down defense conversion strategy, preferring to concentrate on the overall economic reform and privatization program. To a great extent, individual defense firms have been left to deal with the details of defense conversion on their own. On a practical level, this represents little change from the conversion experience of the Gorbachev era, the main difference being that there is now a greater correlation between government policy and economic reality. Indeed, the 1992 law on defense conversion[23] explicitly states that "the main role in organizing the switch from military to civil production and the drawing up of conversion programs belongs to the defense enterprises" (Section 2, Article 4.1). In addition, the law stresses that participation in defense conversion programs is voluntary and should be based on the economic rationality of such a program. According to the new law, defense procurement is to be conducted through long-term contracts, which correspond to defense needs expressed in the national military doctrine. These long-term contracts should help firms rationally evaluate their conversion options. The law also provides for the establishment of a state conversion fund, which is to be funded through the national budget, and enterprise-level conversion funds, which are to be funded through enterprise profits. State conversion funds are to be awarded competitively on the basis of the extent to which the proposal helps to preserve the nation's scientific and technical expertise, promises to produce products that are up to world standards, employs dual-use technology, creates new jobs, and follows the logic of the international division of labor.

Although the provisions of the 1992 defense conversion law are encouraging, they have had little practical impact because the law specifies no mechanism for implementing them. In particular the nature of, source of funds for, and access to the conversion fund are not discussed, and the long-term defense procurement contracts have not materialized. Only fourteen conversion programs have been funded by the Russian government, and, according to Maley, "the money to fund the program has only begun to come in since the second half of 1993."[24] The failure of the law to provide any real support to converting defense firms is reflected in the presidential edict on defense industry issues of November 1993.[25] In this edict, Yeltsin stressed that the government must establish a commission to examine the conversion program of defense enterprises and ensure "continuous funding of enterprises' and organizations' conversion programs, approved in accordance with the established procedure, until they are completed." In addition, the edict requests that the Ministry of Defense submit a disarmament program for the period up to the year 2000, presumably to facilitate the negotiation of long-term contracts. The edict also authorizes the government to make advance payments to defense firms of up to 20 percent of the total amount of the contract. It is not possible at this time to evaluate the practical impact of this edict. The one thing that is clear is that defense conversion, and defense industry relations more generally, will remain an important item on the agenda of the Russian government.

Russian Defense Conversion in Perspective

The process of conversion under Gorbachev was an administrative and direct one that tried to link the decline in defense output with increases in commercial production through either literal conversion or a direct transfer of assets. This strategy proved unsuccessful for many reasons. First, the government never produced an organized or coherent defense conversion strategy; it hardly passed beyond the point of making broad proclamations and stating overall aims. Second, the government made poor decisions as it directed the process of literal conversion. The mandated plans were only loosely based on technological feasibility and were in no way sensitive to consumer demand for a given product. In addition, the government was hoping for rapid positive results and did not take into account that, even under ideal conditions, conversion would temporarily reduce the productivity of the enterprise, as capital was retooled and workers were retrained. Finally, many enterprise managers were opposed to conversion for various reasons and simply did not obey the conversion directives of the government. Administrative conversion can only work if the central directives are obeyed. Although the Ministry of Defense wanted to believe that it retained complete control over the firms in its domain and designed the conversion programs so as to maintain that control, its power was fictitious. Administrative, direct defense conversion was thus a dismal failure, and the Yeltsin government immediately distanced itself from that strategy when the Soviet government collapsed at the end of 1991.

To a great extent, the defense conversion strategy of the Yeltsin government has been a hands-off one, stressing indirect economic conversion. The government has severely cut production orders and left individual defense firms to decide how to deal with the economic implications of these cuts. The drastic cuts in defense spending, combined with a lack of central direction, have prompted one of three basic responses among managers of defense firms. Many managers are abandoning most if not all of their defense production and diversifying into civilian production. According to Bernstein, that diversification is being funded through enterprise funds (either credits or excess profits) as opposed to state conversion funds.[26] For those managers, the commercial market is viewed as more stable and more profitable in the long run. Other defense industrialists continue to lobby the government for a slowdown in defense conversion, pushing for state credits to aid defense firms and time to adjust to market reforms such as privatization, price liberalization, and so forth. Still other managers are delaying significant decisions until some of the environmental uncertainty is resolved or until they can convince the workforce that conversion is warranted.

If Russian spending on defense products continues to be maintained at current levels (approximately 5 percent of GNP), as opposed to the extraordinarily high levels of the cold war era (around 20 percent of GNP), then the government clearly needs to promote the first response among managers of defense firms. The success of economic reform depends on the ability of Russian enterprises in general, and Russian defense enterprises in particular, to improve efficiency and to redirect their activities into sectors of the economy where market demand is high. It should be stressed that government action, and in some cases government inaction, often makes the other options more attractive. Conversion and restructuring are difficult and often painful activities. As long as the government continues to make credits and subsidies available to defense firms on a nonsystematic basis and does not specify the future demand for military products, some general directors will continue to either lobby the government for credits and continued subsidies or simply wait for a resolution to the uncertainty, rather than undertake the extraordinary effort needed to begin commercial market activities.

Just as the administrative, direct conversion strategy proved difficult to implement when the government had less than perfect control over economic actors, an economic, indirect strategy may prove to be unsuccessful without some sort of government attention to the defense sector that at least establishes the "rules of the game." The ultimate logic behind the hands-off defense conversion strategy is that individual economic agents, driven by long-run economic interest, are in the best position to make allocative and investment decisions and that the government can do nothing to improve the decision-making process. The manager of a defense firm is thus left to decide whether the firm should continue producing defense products, diversify into some sort of commercial production, or simply sell its assets and go out of business because that manager is presumed to have sufficient information to evaluate the expected payoff from the various activities. It is also assumed either that the decision makers are risk neutral or that environmental uncertainty is small enough that it does not influence the decision. The fundamental argument—that individual firms are in the best position to make the allocative decisions—will not be questioned here. However, the government must seriously consider whether it can improve the conditions for decision making on the part of firms. The environment in which defense firms are currently operating is fraught with uncertainty, which makes rational decision making and business planning difficult. Although some of this uncertainty is due to forces outside governmental control, a significant amount of uncertainty can be directly attributed to action, or inaction, on the part of the Russian government.

To begin with, the process of defense conversion is imposing a much more serious shock on the Russian economy than on the U.S. economy. Although both the U.S. and the Russian governments have initiated significant cuts in defense spending, the relative magnitue of defense budget cuts is much greater in Russia. U.S. defense spending has already declined from a 1985 peak of $375.6 billion (constant 1993 dollars) to $267.6 billion in 1993. This reflects a 28.8 percent decline in real defense spending over eight years. The Department of Defense estimates that the defense budget will continue to decline and may be as low as $237 billion in 1997. If this trend continues, defense spending will have declined 36.8 percent over the twelve-year period from 1985 to 1997. In Russia it is estimated that defense spending has declined by about 80 percent in real terms between 1989 and 1992, with a 68 percent real reduction occurring between 1991 and 1992 alone. Because procurement spending has declined more than R&D spending, Russian defense producers are facing a catastrophic demand shock. The practical result is that the Russian defense industry will face greater relative declines in procurement orders than its U.S. counterpart. As much as 20 percent of the economy is in a state of flux due to the defense cuts, looking for new market opportunities. Nearly all defense producers need to diversify, if not totally convert. This creates a significant amount of uncertainty in the economic environment of defense firms, which renders decision making more difficult.

In addition to the uncertainty due to the magnitude of the defense conversion itself, additional uncertainty is created by the defense conversion being carried out in the context of an overall economic transition from a command to a market economy. This has several implications, one being that, as economic actors throughout the economy slowly become exposed to market forces, resources are being reallocated not only from the defense to the civilian sector as a whole but from one part of the civilian sector to another. For example, producers of industrial goods are trying to diversify and produce consumer goods, producers of unwanted consumer goods are entering the heretofore neglected service sector, and so on. This means that there are countless firms that might attempt to enter any particular market. Moreover, as industrial producers change their product lines, it is difficult to predict what sort of industrial inputs will be needed.

Despite this, the process of economic transition can also make conversion and diversification easier for Russian defense firms than it is for their U.S. counterparts. The economic development that occurred in Russia under communism left many consumer needs unsatisfied. If a defense firm can identify those market needs and has the capacity to satisfy them, it can be a profitable venture for the firm. A U.S. defense firm diversifying into commercial production is likely to face significant competition from more-efficient commercial producers from the moment of market entry. It does not have the luxury of time to learn the ways of doing business in the commercial sector, nor does it have time to adjust its organizational structure or adapt gradually to its new environment. It must immediately be as efficient as its competitors or face failure. In general, the organizational structure and culture that developed through years of doing business with the government put defense firms at a disadvantage relative to their commercial counterparts. As a result, the conversion attempts of defense firms tend to fail.

In Russia, defense firms do not face such a disadvantage vis-à-vis other potential competitors. Existing producers of commercial products also have irrational organizational structures, a legacy of the communist era. They also need to learn how to do business, how to advertise, how to market their products. Although diversification into domestic civilian markets is a risky activity, Russian defense firms should have a reasonable chance of success in such a conversion attempt. Russian defense firms attempting to enter highly competitive world markets for consumer goods, however, would face substantial problems. Their communist, defense-oriented organizational structure would put them at an immediate disadvantage vis-à-vis existing producers. Despite the attractiveness of the hard currency rewards that stem from foreign export, Russian firms would be wise to consider seriously the difficulties associated with world market competition. Even firms with stellar technological capability should consider production for export in conjunction with a foreign partner that could provide the necessary marketing expertise.

The aforementioned sources of uncertainty are largely outside the realm of government control. As long as the transition to a market economy and declines in defense spending continue, that uncertainty will exist. In addition, those sources of uncertainty impact the entire economy and do not put defense firms at a particular disadvantage vis-à-vis civilian enterprises. Other sources of uncertainty, however, are directly attributable to government action or inaction. Perhaps the greatest source of such uncertainty facing Russian defense firms is due to ownership transformation or, more precisely, the lack of it in the defense sector. As the mass privatization of civilian enterprises has proceeded rapidly in 1992 and 1993, many defense firms have been entirely prohibited from privatizing, including "enterprises or structural subdivisions of enterprises whose purpose relates to mobilization and which are not used in current production."[27] Most other defense firms can privatize but only with special governmental permission.

Of course, this special governmental permission is not easily obtained. The few defense enterprises that have been allowed to privatize have generally been special cases. Often, those firms that participated in collective ownership experiments during the Gorbachev era were able to take advantage of a series of temporary legal loopholes that allowed for various ownership transformations, ultimately leading to private ownership.[28] For firms that were not part of those experiments, privatization has been much more difficult. The 1992 law on defense conversion stipulates that the labor collective of firms undergoing *full* conversion may submit an application to privatize. Although the labor collective is allowed to participate in formulating the privatization plan, the plan must be approved by the Ministry of Industry. Thus, even defense firms that have fully converted and are no longer engaged in defense production are not automatically allowed to privatize. If the application is approved, however, the firm can privatize through the national privatization voucher auctions.

Until mid-1993, it was not clear what options would be available to firms undergoing only partial conversion In August 1993, the government announced that the management of partially converted defense enterprises could submit applications to privatize. The list of firms approved for privatization was apparently completed in December 1993 but, as of this writing, has not been released publicly. It is clear that the government would like to maintain a substantial ownership share in these enterprises; it is also clear that most partially converted defense firms want as little government ownership as possible. The privatization approval process for the partially converted defense firm is likely to consist of long and drawn-out negotiations. In the meantime, those firms remain wholly state owned, with all the disadvantages that entails.

This uncertainty regarding future ownership makes decisions related to conversion more complicated for Russian managers and diverts their attention from productive activities. In most cases, managers have a salient interest in the ultimate ownership structure of the firm. Until the ownership issue is resolved, they have a great incentive to devote time, energy, and resources toward the negotiations with the government over the privatization process. To the extent that foreign firms are hesitant to invest in state-owned Russian enterprises, and to the extent that Russian firms are hoping to use foreign investment for conversion, failure to resolve the ownership question leads to delays in the conversion process.[29]

Another aspect of Russian defense conversion that creates great uncertainty for Russian managers is the lack of a national defense strategy. In the course of the U.S. defense drawdown, the Department of Defense has continuously announced its priorities and long-run procurement needs. Although those change over time in response to world events, the government tries to give firms as much information as possible about the government's demand for defense products, so that those firms can plan their business strategy accordingly. Although the environment is changing rapidly in Russia and demand is declining, demand for defense products still does exist. There is still a need for some level of defense production. Some firms may decide that it is worthwhile to continue producing, and if the government gives them as much information as possible, those firms can better adapt to, and profitably exist in, the new environment.

Unfortunately for those firms, the government has yet to state its procurement priorities or give estimates as to the level of future procurement. The 1992 law on defense conversion states that exiting procurement contracts will be extended when necessary and that contracts for new military orders will be awarded on the basis of competitive contracts. However, it suggests neither on what basis proposals will be evaluated nor whether the structure of ownership will have anything to do with a firm being awarded a defense contract. Of particular concern is whether private firms will be able to do any defense work for the Russian government. In lieu of a real strategy, the government has been unexpectedly cutting defense orders and delaying payment on the orders it does maintain. With the severe inflation of the last few years, government payments for defense goods often do not allow firms to cover costs. As a result, many firms are desperately trying to get out of all their defense business. Although this disorganized governmental policy is certainly promoting defense conversion, it does not do so in an efficient way. If the government does not distinguish between valuable and valueless products in its nonpayment process, it may be driving some of the best and most-needed firms out of the market. To make good decisions related to restructuring and conversion, managers of defense firms need to have as much information as possible regarding the future relationship between the state and the defense sector.

To encourage rational economic defense conversion, the government must define the future relationship between the government and the defense industry. In particular, it must decide whether it prefers to maintain an arsenal structure, in which all defense products are built in state-owned enterprises, or to rely on a contractual procurement system. Alternatively, the government might decide that certain types of production should be state owned and others contracted out on a competitive basis. In any case, the structure of defense contracting needs to be publicly stated. Once the general relationship between the government and the defense sector has been determined, then the ownership question should be resolved as quickly and as systematically as possible. If the government decides to use an arsenal system to any extent, it may have to mandate that certain firms cannot privatize in order to preserve the defense base. The firms that fall into that category should be identified as quickly as possible. If any of those firms have commercial capacity, they should be spun off and privatized. To avoid costly and time-consuming negotiation processes, the government should establish a systematic privatization mechanism through which the remaining defense firms will be privatized. In addition, the government should determine its medium-term defense needs and articulate them to defense firms so that they can evaluate whether defense production will be a profitable activity.

In addition to environmental uncertainty, which renders decision making a difficult activity for Russian managers, there are certain market failures that are likely to inhibit the conversion process. As discussed earlier, well-thought-out government action can often help ameliorate the problems created by market failures. One of the most serious market failures in Russia during the economic transition stemmed from the lack of financial and credit markets. Currently, defense industry general directors have to rely on meager enterprise-level conversion funds or credits achieved on the basis of personal relationships with lenders. Government credits have generally been extended on the basis of political considerations to firms that use the funds to pay wages, rather than for conversion projects. A comprehensive defense conversion program could cost more than $150 billion.[30] There is no obvious source for such conversion funds. Arms exports might provide some resources, international lending organizations might provide credits for conversion, and international investors or even foreign governments might contribute funds for Russian defense conversion. Ultimately, however, the development of financial market institutions will provide a mechanism though which various sources of conversion funding will be matched with the most attractive projects.

Given that this development will take time, and that many crucial investments need to be made in the near future, a government conversion fund, such as that proposed in the 1992 defense conversion law and Yeltsin's 1993 defense industry edict, could play a useful role. The funds could be used to extend investment credits or provide grants to defense firms for conversion purposes. The government resources for conversion will certainly exceed the demand for such funds. As a result, the government should make it clear from the outset the amount of money available through the conversion fund and award the funds through a competitive process based on clearly stated criteria. The fund should not be used to help failing defense firms pay wages or to keep insolvent defense firms afloat. The government may need to help such firms, but that type of aid should come from another fund related to social welfare and should not be confused with investment in defense conversion. Money allocated for conversion purposes should be devoted to firms with good commercial prospects.

Another problem stems from the underdeveloped labor market. Labor markets play a crucial role in economic conversion by redirecting workers into activities in which their skills are most needed. Workers are released from employment in defense firms and are hired by firms in other industries. Loosely speaking, the firms that will benefit most from the labor of the worker will tend to pay the highest wages. If we assume that workers generally seek the highest wage available, then their labor will be efficiently allocated by the market. The ability of the market to do this depends on two things: the dissemination of employment information and labor mobility. Workers must know what jobs are available where and something about the wage offers associated with those jobs. Ideally, workers should have such information for the entire economy and be able (if not willing) to move to where the jobs are. In Russia, job information networks are only slowly beginning to develop. Employment exchange centers are springing up in major cities, but intercity job information is still difficult to come by. Perfect labor mobility is an unrealistic ideal in any country, as people are tied to their communities both economically and emotionally. Russia, however, has a serious labor mobility problem. Although the communist-era law requiring a residence permit of any individual moving to a new location was removed in 1993, acute housing shortages in the major cities continue to deter migration.

The lack of labor mobility exacerbates the problems created by the existence of company towns, particularly in the defense sector. As noted earlier, there are seventy-four Russian cities in which more than 80 percent of the workers are employed by defense sector enterprises. Many of those cities are dominated by one firm, which, in addition to providing employment for most of the population, provides many of the basic social and municipal services as well. For example, the city of Votkinsk, with a population of approximately 100,000, is dominated by the Votkinsk Factory Production Association, a conglomerate of factories that produces missiles. The factory is not simply an employer, however; it runs the local train station, produces consumer goods for the residents of Votkinsk, finances housing construction, provides child-care facilities, and contributes heavily to the development of medical facilities and public transportation services, as well as infrastructural maintenance for the entire city. Ritter stresses that "the dominance of the Votkinsk Factory Production Association over the social development of the city is underscored by the fact that the Votkinsk City Planning Commission has no department for economic development, that function being performed by the social planners of the Votkinsk Factory Production Association."[31] In the process of defense conversion, it is inevitable that certain firms will fail; perhaps their technology will be unsuitable for commercial production, or their managers will make the wrong diversification decisions. Regardless of the reason, they will not be financially soluble economic entities. If a firm in Moscow goes bankrupt, it is not a problem in that social and municipal services will not be significantly affected by the closure and there is enough economic activity in the area that workers have some hope of finding alternative employment.

The geographic concentration of the defense industry and the one-company town phenomenon create a social and political dilemma for the government. If the firm that supports a one-company town, such as the Votkinsk Factory Production Association, were to fail, a large number of people would be utterly devastated, with no one to provide basic social and municipal services, no alternative employment in the local area, and great difficulties involved in moving to another city. The regional and local impact of defense conversion in the United States is significant but nowhere near as severe as in Russia. Still, the U.S. government makes aid available to communities that are significantly impacted by defense conversion. Normally this aid is used for community development programs, which help the city attract new firms, investment, and jobs and help the community establish job-retraining programs and other employment services for the unemployed defense workers.

Given the extreme concentration of the defense industry, and the existence of closed cities devoted to military production in Russia, the government will need to consider more-drastic types of aid to communities. This may include granting private-enterprise development to affected communities, extending additional unemployment benefits to members of such communities, or keeping insolvent enterprises open with government funds until more housing is constructed in other cities and more commercial-sector jobs are created. The Polish government has instituted such a policy toward the coal industry. Employment in the industry will be reduced by about 50 percent over the next ten years, and several mines will be closed. Although those mines will continue to receive operational subsidies for the next few years, they have been told point-blank that they will be closed. If the Russian government deems it necessary to subsidize wages temporarily in certain defense firms for similar reasons, it must be equally honest about the firms' eventual closure, so that the citizens can plan accordingly. The government should not rush to support large number of firms in such a way, for it can be an inefficient way of providing social welfare. In cases where subsidies are introduced, the management of the firms should be tightly monitored, or even taken over by the government, to prevent the misuse of government funds. Any money allocated for such programs must be viewed as social welfare and should not be taken from a defense conversion investment fund.

Conclusion

Defense conversion is an crucial aspect of the overall economic transition from a centrally planned to a market economy, and the economic transition is essential to defense conversion. The Yeltsin government has expressed a commitment to an indirect economic approach to defense conversion. Economic conversion relies on economic actors such as firm managers and defense workers, ultimately driven by market forces, to allocate defense industry resources as they see fit. This chapter points out that many problems in the Russian economy might make it difficult for managers and workers to make these decisions well but does not imply that the chosen strategy is inappropriate. In fact, under current political and economic conditions, an administrative, direct conversion strategy, which requires a significant amount of government information gathering, control and financial support, would be impossible to implement. However, there are actions the government can take that would make the indirect economic conversion process work better. Government action on the defense conversion front need not conflict with the aim of economic, loosely linked conversion. Indeed, in many cases, a lack of government action interferes with achieving that aim. Given the status quo in Russia, with most of the defense firms still state owned, a lack of government action on various fronts can be viewed as an unintended form of intervention.

A decentralized, economic defense conversion strategy relies on the ability of economic actors to make good decisions and to take a long-run perspective. An economic conversion in which decision makers are motivated by short-term, speculative opportunities will not contribute to the overall conversion process. Although the Russian government cannot necessarily force managers to seek long-term, as opposed to short-term, payoffs, this chapter outlines ways in which it can create incentives for managers to do this, while maintaining the integrity of its economic conversion program. In particular, the government needs to state its medium-term procurement needs clearly, establish a clear set of procurement rules, work to systematically clarify the ownership structure of converting defense firms, establish a fund to support defense conversion, and distinguish defense conversion aid from social welfare. The economic transition will be difficult and involve a certain amount of failure. Civilian firms will fail, as will some defense firms. If a defense firm does not have good technology or good leadership, it should not be supported just because it was once a defense firm. At the same time, defense firms should not be disadvantaged because of their history. The main task of the government in defense conversion is to remain committed to the overall strategy of indirect economic defense conversion, while working to remove the environmental uncertainty that puts defense firms at a disadvantage vis-à-vis their civilian counterparts.

Notes

1. D. Bernstein and W. Perry, "Defense Conversion in Russia: A Strategic Imperative," *Stanford Journal of International Affairs*, Summer 1993.

2. Christopher Smart, "Amid the Ruins, Arms Makers Raise New Threats," *ORBIS*, Summer 1992.

3. B. Horrigan, "How Many People Work in the Soviet Defense Industry?" *Radio Free Europe/Radio Liberty* (hereafter, *RFE/RL*) *Research Report*, August 21, 1992.

4. Thierry Malleret, *Conversion of the Defense Industry in the Former Soviet Union* (New York: Institute for East-West Security Studies, 1992).

5. U.S. Congress, Office of Technology Assessment, *Defense Conversion: Redirecting R&D*, OTA-ITE-552 (Washington, D.C.: U.S. Government Printing Office, May 1993).

6. Malleret, *Conversion of the Defense Industry*.

7. J. Sherr, "Russia's Defence Industry—Conversion or Rescue?" *Jane's Intelligence Review*, July 1992.

8. M. Galeotti, "The Russian Arms Bazaar," *Jane's Intelligence Review*, November 1992.

9. P. Almquist, "Arms Producers Struggle to Survive as Defense Orders Shrink," *RFE/RL Research Report*, June 18, 1993.

10. M. McFaul and D. Bernstein, *Industrial Demilitarization, Privatization, Economic Reform, and Investment in Russia: Analysis and Recommendations* (Stanford: Center for International Security and Arms Control, 1993).

11. Malleret, *Conversion of the Defense Industry*, p. 28

12. For a detailed discussion of possible defense industry market failures, see J. Dertouzos and C. R. Neu, "Making Technology Reinvestment Work: Suggestions on Managing and evaluating ARPA's Technology Reinvestment Project," RAND, Santa Monica, Calif., June 1993.

13. D. Bernstein, "Conversion," in M. McFaul, ed., *Can the Russian Military-Industrial Complex Be Privatized? Evaluating the Experiment in Employee Ownership at the Saratov Aviation Plant* (Stanford: Center for International Security and Arms Control, 1993).

14. The U.S. defense conversion experience has been well documented and will not be repeated here. For more information, see J. Lynch, ed., *Economic Adjustment and Conversion of Defense Industries* (Boulder, Colo.: Westview Press, 1987).

15. R. DeGrasse, "Corporate Diversification and Conversion Experience," in Lynch, ed., *Economic Adjustment and Conversion of Defense Industries*.

16. Smart, "Amid the Ruins, Arms Makers Raise New Threats," pp. 351–52.

17. "Shortcomings in Current Conversion Effort Noted," *Foreign Broadcast Information*

Service–Soviet Union (hereafter, *FBIS-SOV*) *89-141*, July 25, 1989; from *Literaturnaya Gazeta*, July 12, 1989.

18. Ibid.

19. "More on Gorbachev Visit to Nizhni Tagil," *FBIS-SOV 90-084*, May 1, 1990; from *Sovetskaya Rossiya* April 28, 1990.

20. Sherr, "Russia's Defence Industry," p. 298.

21. "Economics of Defense Sector Conversion Viewed," *FBIS-SOV 91-120*, June 21, 1991.

22. Peter Almquist, "Arms Producers Struggle to Survive as Defense Orders Shrink," *RFE/RL Research Report* 2, no. 25 (June 18, 1993).

23. "Russian Federation Law on Conversion of the Defense Industry in the Russian Federation," *FBIS-SOV 92-083*, April 29, 1992.

24. "Mikhail Maley: Long Period Marking Time or Start of a Marathon? (Interview with Mikhail Maley, Chairman of the Security Council's Interdepartmental Commission for Scientific and Technical Questions of the Defense Industry, by Aleksandr Yegorov)," *FBIS-SOV 93-247*, December 23, 1993.

25. Edict No. 1850 of the Russian Federation president, "On the Stabilization of the Economic Status of Defense Industry Enterprises and Organizations and Measures to Guarantee the State Defense Order," *FBIS-SOV 93-219*, November 16, 1993.

26. Bernstein, "Conversion," in McFaul, ed., *Can the Russian Military-Industrial Complex Be Privatized?*

27. "Russian Federation Law," p. 29.

28. The privatization of Saratov Aviation Plant is an example of such a case. See McFaul, ed., *Can the Russian Military-Industrial Complex be Privatized?*

29. The law on defense conversion creates a mechanism through which commercial-oriented enterprises within large defense conglomerate firms can spin themselves off and privatize. The law states that "enterprises which belong to an association and are not legal persons in their own right, or . . . shops, sections, or other structural subdivisions of enterprises . . . may be designated as autonomous state enterprises with the rights of a legal person. The decision to designate a subdivision as an autonomous state enterprise is made on a vote at a general meeting of the subdivision's labor collective, by a majority of the total number of members of the collective." This could prove a useful mechanism for promoting defense conversion.

30. C. Hummel, "Russian Conversion Policy Encounters Opposition," *RFE/RL Research Report* 1, no. 32 (August 14, 1992).

31. W. Ritter, "Defense Conversion: The Votkinsk Machine-Building Plant," *Problems of Communism*, September–October 1991, p. 56.

PART FOUR

COMPARISONS AND EVALUATIONS

12

Employment and Unemployment after Communism

SIMON JOHNSON

Evidence from twelve countries in Eastern Europe and the former Soviet Union suggests that a significant increase in unemployment is an unavoidable consequence of economic reform. Initially, state enterprises try to maintain employment levels even in the face of steep output declines, preferring to reduce hours worked and to cut real wages. Over time they begin to fire workers, starting with those they consider least essential. In the first two years of serious economic reform, state industrial employment usually falls by 25–30 percent.

There are a large number of new employment opportunities in the private sector, but many of these are taken by people who voluntarily quit the state sector. Once fired, many former state workers have difficulty obtaining a new job. Rates of reemployment are particularly low for women and older people.

In almost every country in Eastern Europe, unemployment starts close to zero, rises 5–10 percentage points in the first year and a further 5–10 percentage points in the second year of serious reform. The same pattern is seen regardless of whether the government is trying to go fast or slow on economic reform. Unemployment rates in Eastern Europe are likely to remain at more than 15 percent in the foreseeable future, with a high proportion of the total—probably more than 50 percent—being long-term unemployed. The evidence available so far for the former Soviet Union suggests that serious reform has not yet begun in earnest but that when it does the unemployment outcomes will be similar to those in Eastern Europe.

Introduction

It has become painfully obvious that the transformation of post-communist economies involves a far-reaching change in the structure of employment. The evidence so far—based mostly on experience in Eastern Europe—indicates a pattern of net job destruction in the state sector and net job creation in the private sector. In large part the costs of economic transformation depend on the relative speeds with which old jobs disappear and new jobs appear and on the ability of different kinds of people to move between these jobs.

This chapter examines the details of unemployment and employment in the postcommunist countries of Eastern Europe and the former Soviet Union, primarily using official government statistics. These data are weak on several key points, however, particularly concerning the precise nature of employment reduction and the rate at which unemployed people find new jobs in the former Soviet Union. I therefore also report results from a study of unemployment and employment conducted by my own research team in Ukraine.

The four questions addressed and the most important answers provided in this chapter are as follows. First, how fast are jobs lost in the state sector? The evidence suggests that state enterprises are initially reluctant to fire workers but that nevertheless there is a gradual and steady reduction in state-sector employment. In all countries, after the first two years of serious economic reform, we find that employment in state industry has typically been reduced by around 25–30 percent.

Second, precisely who leaves state enterprises and under what circumstances? The facts indicate that the first people to leave are voluntary quits and various types of retirees. Layoffs grow in absolute and relative size over time, although the first people to be fired are white-collar and blue-collar workers seen by management as not essential to the production process.

Third, what happens to people who are fired from the state sector? The official data we report indicate that unemployed people find it hard to obtain a new job in Eastern Europe. This is surprising, given the rapid growth of the private sector, but several compelling pieces of evidence from Hungary and

Generous financial support was provided by Xerox Faculty Research Funds and the National Council for Soviet and East European Research. Helpful comments on an earlier version were provided by participants at the Second Workshop, World Bank Research Project, on "The Labour Market in Transitional Socialist Economies" in April 1993 and at the National Bureau for Economic Research Summer Workshop on Labor Economics in August 1993.

Poland indicate that the private sector hires people directly from the state sector rather than from the pool of unemployed.

Survey evidence from Ukraine, however, suggests that a high proportion of people who are fired in the former Soviet Union are quickly able to find a new job. The period of unemployment for these people is so short that they do not register as unemployed; it is as if they passed directly from the state sector to the private sector. Even in this upbeat interpretation of the evidence, however, rates of reemployment are lower for women, older people, and people with higher education. In addition, many of the new jobs pay low wages and represent a fall in people's standard of living. It is probably also true that the high growth rate of private-sector employment in 1992–93 in the former Soviet Union cannot be sustained.

Fourth, what are the outcomes in terms of the unemployment rate in each country? We found that in almost every country, irrespective of the precise reform path followed, the unemployment rate began at close to zero, showed an increase of up to 10 percentage points in the first year, after serious economic reform started, and climbed a further 5–10 percentage points in the second year.

The striking exception is the Czech Republic, in which unemployment has already peaked and is now at around 5 percent, a level which is low by international standards and extremely low in comparison with other countries in the region. This unusual performance is not yet fully understood but is probably due to a combination of good luck and good policy that is difficult to duplicate in other countries.

In summary, the evidence reviewed in this chapter indicates that there is a broadly similar labor market adjustment process under way in all the postcommunist countries of Eastern Europe and the former Soviet Union. Real economic reform requires and begins with a fall in state-sector employment. Because state industrial enterprises are reluctant to fire workers, initial employment reductions are due more to voluntary quits and retirements. Voluntary quits are hired directly by the private sector, although at wages that are usually not much higher than those in the state sector.

Over time state enterprises increasingly fire workers. In Eastern Europe, unemployed workers find it difficult to obtain a new job, and, on net, not many are hired by the private sector. In the former Soviet Union, rates of reemployment in the private sector are higher, but it is unlikely that they can be sustained. If they cannot, then the result will be the same as in Eastern Europe; owing to a combination of low inflow rates to unemployment and even lower outflow rates, the unemployment rate will grow and the proportion of long-term unemployed will increase.

I first review the available cross-country evidence on the four questions outlined above. Then I report more-detailed data on employment reductions and outflows from unemployment in Ukraine. I conclude with an assessment of the extent to which unemployment outcomes in the former Soviet Union are likely to resemble those in Eastern Europe.

Cross-Country Evidence

EMPLOYMENT REDUCTIONS

In all these countries, the overall macroeconomic context has been characterized by the elimination of excess demand, severe reductions in the production of military goods, and the complete disruption of the Council for Mutual Economic Assistance (Comecon) trading system. As a result, there have been sharp falls in industrial output throughout the region. State enterprises in postcommunist countries have proved reluctant to fire their workers and have done so only gradually. In all East European countries the rate of employment reduction in the first one to two years after reform has been less than the fall in state-sector output, in part because few large state enterprises have been forced to close and various forms of hidden subsidies have continued—such as tax breaks and special credits.

It appears, however, that serious economic reform requires that the budget constraint for state enterprises be hardened considerably. All attempts at reform in Eastern Europe and the Soviet Union without this condition have failed. As a result economic reform begins with serious pressure being put on state enterprises to improve their financial performance. The combination of adverse macroeconomic conditions and tighter budget constraints has therefore meant that state enterprises have released workers steadily, which has had a large cumulative effect.

For example, economic reform began in earnest in Poland with the Balcerowicz Plan, which was initiated at the beginning of 1990. At that time almost all industry was in the state sector. Employment in Polish industry fell from 3.979 million to 3.632 million (i.e., by 8.7 percent) in the course of 1990. Industrial employment declined further to reach 3.554 million by June 1991, a fall of 2.2 percent from December 1990 and a total cumulative fall of 11 percent (Coricelli and Revenga 1992, table 1). From that date, however, these aggregate numbers become increasingly unreliable because they do not allow us to distinguish the effect of growing private-sector industrial production.

More-reliable evidence in this regard is provided by a survey of seventy-five state firms in Poland that showed a total cumulative reduction in employment of 26.8 percent from September 1989 to June 1992. Employment rose 0.8 percent from September to December 1989—the quarter before economic reform really began. In the immediate aftermath of reform, employment fell 5 percent from December 1989 to June 1990 and a further 5 percent from June to December

1990. It then fell 6.6 percent from December 1990 to June 1991, 7.0 percent from June to December 1991, and 7.1 percent from December 1991 to June 1992 (Pinto, Belka, and Krajewski 1993, table 2).[1]

The output and sales declines in these firms, however, were initially much larger—around 20–30 percent by the middle of 1990. Differences in performance subsequently emerged, but even the group of firms that did best showed a continued fall in employment. In mid-1992 most managers said that their firms continued to have excess employment, although in all cases other than the worst-performing firms, the percent of excess labor was considered to be less than 10 percent (Pinto, Belka, and Krajewski 1993, table 14).

The former Soviet Union appears to be following the same path, although in most places it is still at the early stage in which output has fallen but state enterprises continue to hold onto labor. For example, in Kazakhstan there was a 10 percent fall in output in 1991 and a 14 percent fall in 1992 (European Bank for Reconstruction and Development 1993, 118). But state enterprises have preferred to reduce work hours, close temporarily, or cut real wages rather than fire people. With a workforce of 7.3 million, unemployment rose from 18,000 in December 1992 to 70,000 in March 1993. However, further firings may be imminent—the minister of labor predicted unemployment would reach 500,000 by the end of 1993, so unemployment could rise from 1 percent to 7 percent (Rutland and Isataev 1993, 8).

The same pattern was clearly exhibited in Russia during 1992. Physical output for a sample of firms drawn from a wide range of industrial activities fell by 14–15 percent from early 1991 to early 1992. Over the same period employment in these firms fell by only 3 percent. The firms with the worst output showed a decline of 35–50 percent in output from 1991 to 1992, yet their average employment contraction was only 15 percent (Commander, Liberman, and Yemtsov 1993a, 20; 1993b, 24).[2]

PATTERN OF JOB LOSSES

There is some evidence that the first round of employment reduction is accounted for by retirement, voluntary quits, and the firing of "noncore" workers. The proportion of unemployed who are laid off rises over time.

The change in retirement behavior has been noted in several countries. In Poland there was a sharp fall in the participation rate, from 65.3 percent in 1988 to 61.4 percent in 1992, along with a decline of one million in the total number of people in the labor force. Most of this decline was accounted for by an increase in early retirement (Hagemejer and Rybinski, 2). There was also an increase in people retiring because of a disability of some kind.

In Russia the previous rate of labor force participation was high for pensioners: 30–35 percent were still working in early 1980s (Commander, Liberman, and

Yemtsov 1993a, 10). Article 35 of the 1991 Russian Employment Law allows the Federal Employment Service to offer early retirement to people who are within two years of retiring (the retirement ages are fifty-five for women and sixty for men), and in 1992, fifty thousand people were offered early retirement (Marnie 1993, 41).

Much of the early employment reduction in the state sector is due to voluntary quits, most of whom presumably move directly to the private sector. In the last two quarters of 1992, voluntary quits accounted for more than 60 percent of all separations in Russia (Commander, McHale, and Yemtsov 1993, 7). In Hungary, more than 70 percent of the new hires in the private sector in 1992 came directly from the state sector, and only 11 percent were previously unemployed (Kollo 1993).

Survey evidence from Poland suggests that less than 13 percent of entrepreneurs were ever unemployed and that only 8 percent ever received unemployment benefits (Johnson 1993a). Most of these entrepreneurs worked in the state sector before 1990, and most of them voluntarily quit the state sector.

The evidence that noncore workers are fired first is more anecdotal. However, this was the strong conclusion of a World Bank study based on both official data and a survey of forty-one state firms, which argued that, while limited in 1992, net employment reductions were concentrated on the ancillary and clerical categories of staff (Commander, Liberman, and Yemtsov 1993b, 43). In the last two quarters of 1992, production workers accounted for 70 percent of the quits and 80 percent of the hires in state industry, while 50 percent of involuntary separations involved clerical workers (Commander, McHale, and Yemtsov 1993, 7).

The reluctance to fire workers in the face of massive output declines naturally implies a sharp fall in the number of hours worked. Evidence on this point is available for Romania, where total hours worked in industry fell 36 percent from 1989 to 1992 and hours worked per worker per year declined by more than 27 percent (Earle and Oprescu 1993, 10, table 2.2).

The proportion of mass layoffs rises over time. The proportion of unemployed in Poland who lost their jobs through "mass layoffs" was 4.3 percent in January 1990 but rose to 10.2 percent in June, 16.3 percent in December 1990, and 20.0 percent in June 1991 (Coricelli and Revenga 1992, table 1).

Mass layoffs may also have been discouraged or delayed by legislation. For example, Poland passed legislation in 1989 that allowed mass layoffs but that also required thirty to ninety days' advance notice and up to ninety days' severance pay for layoffs of 10 percent or more of employees (Coricelli and Revenga 1992). Similar legal requirements exist in Russia, where the Federal Employment Service and trade union organizations in principle have the right to order that mass layoffs be delayed for up to six months (Marnie 1993). Given these restrictions, it would not be surprising if firms tried to disguise mass layoffs by firing people more gradually and in small groups.

OUTFLOWS FROM UNEMPLOYMENT

Most people who are fired in these countries become unemployed and, once unemployed, have difficulty finding a new job. This statement would not be surprising for a Western market economy, but, given the sharp shift in employment from the state sector to the private sector in postcommunist countries, it was expected that the private sector would hire unemployed people. On the basis of Western experience, it was assumed that people would pass from state-sector employment to private-sector employment through an intermediate phase of unemployment.[3] Unfortunately, this assumption is not confirmed by the facts.

There has certainly been a rapid increase in private-sector employment in all postcommunist countries since 1990. In Hungary and Poland the private sector accounted for 8–10 percent of urban employment before 1990 and by 1992 had risen to 25–35 percent.[4] Total private-sector employment in Poland is even higher, in some estimates close to 50 percent, because agriculture is almost entirely private and labor-intensive. In the Czech Republic and other countries of Eastern Europe, the private sector started smaller and employed between 5–10 percent by the end of 1992 (Johnson 1994).

The important evidence, however, concerns what happens to unemployed people, in particular whether they will be reemployed somewhere—often summarized as their *transition probabilities*. Evidence on this issue is far from complete, but at least in Hungary the unemployed have a higher probability of being hired into the state sector than into the private sector (Kollo 1993, tables 2 and 5). Less than 8 percent of the new hires in the private sector come from unemployment. Furthermore, the net flow in Hungary is balanced from private employment to unemployment and back. There is *not* a net flow from unemployment to private employment.

In other words, the private sector hires most of its new workers from the state sector. When private-sector firms fire workers, these workers become unemployed, and this private-sector firing almost exactly balances the private-sector hiring from unemployment. Unemployed workers are more likely to get hired back into the state sector than to get hired into the private sector.

As a result, despite the sharp increase in private-sector employment in these countries, there has been relatively little hiring from the pool of unemployed. There are two measures of the rate of outflow from unemployment where the outflow is the fraction of unemployed people who will cease being unemployed in a particular month (see table 12.1). If this rate is lower, then the average time an unemployed person stays unemployed—the average duration of unemployment—will be higher.

Table 12.1   Unemployment Statistics

	Unemploy-ment Rate	Monthly Inflow Rate	Outflow Rates (total)	Outflow Rates (to job)	Percent Long-Term Unemployed [a]
			1992 Data		
Bulgaria	14.7	1.6	n.a.	1*	7.2
Czech Republic	3.2	0.6	25.8	18.0	15.0
Slovak Republic	11.6	1.1	9.8	4.8	25.5
Hungary [b]	10.3	0.6	7.0	2–3*	37.3
Poland	13.0	0.7	4.0	2.3	43.4
			1988 Data		
France	11.1	0.6	5.0	n.a.	45.0
Italy	8.6	0.2	3.0	n.a.	69.0
Spain	23.6	0.2	1.0	n.a.	62.0
United Kingdom	9.1	0.9	10.0	n.a.	45.0
United States	5.8	2.2	33.0	n.a.	7.0
Japan	2.6	0.5	20.0	n.a.	21.0

(n.a. = not available)

[a] Long-term unemployed are those without a job for more than twelve months, except in Bulgaria, where it is for more than nine months.

[b] Hungarian inflow and outflow data refer to unemployment benefit recipients. The inflow rate for total unemployment is 0.76.

SOURCES: The 1992 data are Organization for Economic Cooperation and Development (OECD) and national unemployment registers, as presented by Tito Boeri at the World Bank workshop "Labor Markets in Transitional Socialist Economies," Prague, April 16–17, 1993. Monthly inflow data are given in Boeri 1993, table 2. All data are the average of the first three quarters of 1992, except outflow rates for Hungary, which are only for the first five months of 1992. Monthly inflow rates are the ratio of average monthly inflows to average yearly labor force. Outflow rates are the proportion of unemployed who find a job each month. Outflow rates with an asterisk (*) were calculated from data on absolute outflows from unemployment to employment provided by Janos Kollo at the World Bank workshop "Labor Markets in Transitional Socialist Economies," Prague, April 16–17, 1993, combined with OECD data on registered unemployment in these countries.

The 1988 data are from Layard, Nickell and Jackman 1991, pp. 51 and 222. Monthly outflows (total) are calculated as the inverse of the average duration given by this source.

The first measure is of total outflow from unemployment (column 3, table 12.1), irrespective of where unemployed people go. This measure is flawed for our purposes because it includes people who withdraw from the labor force or who are placed in some kind of training program. Good cross-country data are available for this measure, however, so we provide them in order to compare Eastern Europe with Western economies. In terms of total outflow, the East European economies are much closer to Western Europe than to the United States or Japan. In common with France, Italy, Spain, and the United Kingdom, postcommunist Eastern Europe has a low monthly inflow rate and a low monthly outflow rate.

Viewed in terms of the overall outflow rate, Eastern Europe seems to be doing better than some West European economies. Rates of outflow to jobs, however, are lower than total outflow rates. Unemployment has become a partially "stagnant pool" in which there is a rising proportion of long-term unemployed.[5]

In Poland, for example, the number of unemployed who found a job using the services of employment offices each month was roughly constant during 1990–1992. As a result, the outflow rate to employment fell from 4 percent in the third quarter of 1990 to 2.3 percent on average in the first three quarters of 1992 (Hagemejer and Rybinski 1993, 7).

Part of the explanation for these low outflow rates may lie with the wage distribution in the private sector. The available evidence suggests that private-sector average wages are no higher than state-sector wages. In Hungary, wages and incomes are higher in the private sector but hourly earnings are equal. People in the private sector work three hours more a week compared with people in the state sector (Kollo 1993). In Poland, average private-sector wages at the beginning of 1993 appear to have been slightly lower than in the state sector (Johnson 1993a).[6] In addition, although the availability of nonwage benefits—ranging from cheap vacations to day care—has declined in the state sector, it is probably still greater than in the private sector.[7] Some people fired from the state sector may prefer to remain unemployed and seek a new state-sector job, rather than go to work in the private sector.

The most plausible interpretation of the available information on labor flows is that highly skilled people are hired directly from the state sector while less-skilled people who are fired from the state sector remain unemployed and may prefer to return to the state sector. Anecdotal evidence suggests that there is a good deal of turnover among the unskilled when they work in the private sector. We also know that, contrary to initial expectations of observers, state firms continue to hire new workers—up to 10 percent of their labor force a year—presumably to fill vacancies in essential production work left by voluntary quits.

Table 12.2   Registered Unemployment
(as percent of the labor force)

	End of Year					
	1987	*1988*	*1989*	*1990*	*1991*	*1992*
Albania	2.1	2.1	1.9	2.1	5.1	n.a.
Bulgaria	n.a.	n.a.	n.a.	1.5	10.4	15–16
Czech and Slovak Republic	n.a.	n.a.	n.a.	1.0	6.6	5
Hungary	n.a.	n.a.	0.3	2.5	8.0	12
Poland	0	0	0.1	6.1	11.8	14
Romania	n.a.	n.a.	1.6	2.0	2.9	10
Russian Federation	0	0	0	0	0.1	1.3
Slovenia	1.6	2.2	2.9	4.7	8.2	13.4
Tajikistan	0	0	0	0	0	13
Ukraine	0	0	0	0	0	1.2
Uzbekistan	0	0	0	0	0	1
Kazakhstan	0	0	0	0	n.a.	0.2

(n.a. = not available; all are probably zero, except Albania in 1992.)

SOURCES: All countries except Slovenia: European Bank for Reconstruction and Development (EBRD), *Annual Economic Review*, 1992. Figures for 1992 are estimates.

Slovenia: Cvikl, Kraft and Vodopivec 1993, table 3. Their numbers match those provided by the EBRD for 1990–92, but the EBRD does not give 1987–89 data.

Kazakhstan: Rutland and Isataev 1993, 8.

REGISTERED UNEMPLOYMENT

There are many reasons to regard registered unemployment in postcommunist countries as an inadequate measure of real unemployment. For instance, it is likely that some people are registered as unemployed even while they have some work. The Polish labor force survey of 1992 suggested that 30 percent of the registered unemployed actually had some work.[8]

However, the direction of the bias in official unemployment statistics is ambiguous. Official data on registered unemployment in Warsaw give a rate of 5 percent, but the 1992 labor force survey indicates that the true rate is 13 percent. In Russia, there is a significant difference between the number of unemployed people who look for a job using the official labor exchanges and those who are registered by those exchanges as actually unemployed. In addition, many people presumably look for and find work without consulting labor offices. In Poland, apparently only 20 percent of job vacancies are actually posted in labor offices.

Notwithstanding these reservations, we need to compare outcomes across countries in terms of the number of registered unemployed (see table 12.2).

Although the data are not complete and the numbers for the end of 1992 are only estimates, three points can be made.

First, in almost all countries there was no officially recorded unemployment before real economic reforms began. There was probably almost no real unemployment, with the exception of some unrecorded frictional unemployment (in Russia estimates of this vary from 0.6 to 2.7 percent) (Commander et al. 1993a).

A consideration of direct evidence on the policy changes and the effectiveness of reform policies suggests that the beginning of real reform dates from the moment unemployment begins to rise. Real reform appears to require effective pressure on state enterprises to reduce employment. This is because reform involves changes in the macroenvironment and the requirement that firms adjust their performance so as to at least break even or reduce their reliance on subsidies.

Thus Poland had little unemployment in 1989 under the influence of partial communist reform, but the unemployment rate rose sharply in 1990 when the more comprehensive Balcerowicz Plan was introduced (see table 12.2). In part the higher unemployment can be attributed to the collapse of trade within Comecon, including the loss of markets in the Soviet Union and the sharp increase in the price of imported energy. The real trade disruption, however, came at the beginning of 1991, and Poland in particular showed a sharp increase in unemployment before that. Similarly, Hungary showed a significant rise in unemployment when the pressure on state enterprises intensified in 1990.

Second, although unemployment emerged in all these countries at roughly the same time, there were significant differences. Among East European countries, unemployment rose much more sharply in Bulgaria during 1991 and in Romania during 1992. In both cases this can be attributed to the government becoming unwilling or unable to provide additional financing to state enterprises, thus forcing them to release labor (Beleva and Jackman 1993).[9]

There is a striking difference between countries from the former Soviet Union and Eastern Europe. Russia, Ukraine, and Uzbekistan show zero or almost zero unemployment through the end of 1991, and the low rates of unemployment at the end of 1992 suggest that reform had not had its full effect on state enterprises.

Even in Estonia, which introduced a new money and restrictive monetary policies in June 1992, unemployment had reached only 2.7 percent by mid-1993 (Hansson 1993, 5). Given that there is no reason to expect easier adjustment in the Baltics than in Eastern Europe, we would expect the unemployment rate to follow the same upward path seen further west if the Baltic states continue with their intention of implementing serious economic reform.

Third, several countries exhibit unusual performances (see table 12.2). Slovenia had significant unemployment in 1989 as a result of previously implemented reforms. In fact, unemployment had been a persistent problem in Yugoslavia during the 1970s and 1980s. Overall unemployment in Yugoslavia was 7.7 percent in 1970, 11.9 percent in 1980, and 16.4 percent in 1990 (Wyzan 1993, table 2).

Within Yugoslavia, Slovenia had low unemployment: 3.0 percent in 1970, 1.3 percent in 1980, and 5.2 percent in 1990. At the other extreme was Macedonia, with unemployment of 17.8 percent in 1970, 21.5 percent in 1980, and 23.0 percent in 1990. Recent Slovenian experience is interesting because, despite having an economy that appeared to be significantly different from the rest of Eastern Europe and a slightly higher starting unemployment rate, it has experienced a similar increase in unemployment.

In part the rise in Slovenian unemployment that began in 1990 can be attributed to the particular problems of Yugoslavia's breakup and civil war. But Yugoslavia's labor market conditions changed as they did in other East European countries; apparently, not more than one-fifth of the 38 percent fall in industrial production from June 1989 to June 1992 can be attributed to the collapse of the Yugoslav market. The remaining decline was due to the disruption of Comecon and policies adopted to combat inflation: state enterprises were required to become more nearly self-financing, and legal changes have reduced job security. In February 1991, the advance notification period for redundant workers was reduced from twenty-four to six months (Cvikl, Kraft, and Vodopivec 1993). All these elements indicate that Slovenia, like most postcommunist countries, is now in a new phase of real economic reform.

Albania showed an increase in unemployment earlier than one would have expected and a lower level for 1991 than seems plausible. Albanian real gross domestic product (GDP) fell by 10 percent in 1990 and by 30 percent in 1991, so these unemployment numbers may have been subject to some statistical manipulation in addition to the measurement problems experienced in other postcommunist countries.

The Tadzhik Republic had an extraordinary rise in unemployment in 1992, from 0 to 13 percent in one year, which is much higher than the reported numbers so far for other parts of the former Soviet Union. The primary reason for this performance is the civil war, which had a severe negative effect on the economy in the second half of 1992. Although there are no reliable unemployment figures, similar disruptions due to civil war have been reported for Georgia (Conway and Pant 1993) and Armenia.

The most interesting exception to the general pattern is that of former Czechoslovakia (referred to in table 12.2 as the Czech and Slovak Republic). Although unemployment rose in 1990 and 1991 as expected, it fell in 1992, ending at the remarkably low level of 5 percent. What can explain this performance?

Indications are that it is the Czech Republic rather than Slovakia that is an outlier in terms of its unemployment performance (see table 12.1). Czech unemployment peaked in the fourth quarter of 1991 at 221,700 and subsequently fell steadily, reaching 134,800 by the end of 1992. The overall unemployment rate of 3.2 percent in the first three quarters of 1992 was surprisingly low. The primary difference appears to lie not with inflow rates, which are the same as those of Hungary and close to those of Poland, but with much higher outflows from unemployment, particularly to jobs.

The Czech Republic was fortunate in that many of the sectoral shocks—particularly the breakup of Comecon, which affected all countries in the region—fell more in Slovakia because heavy industry had been concentrated there. In addition, relatively low interest rates in the Czech Republic may have helped stimulate the private sector. Rapid privatization and the substantial inflow of foreign investment were probably also helpful. There have also been some government schemes to provide jobs temporarily (Ham, Svejnar, and Terrell 1993, 32–38).

SUMMARY FINDINGS

I draw four conclusions from this survey of the available cross-country evidence. First, unemployment begins to rise when pressure is put on state enterprises. Since 1990 throughout this region, state enterprises have felt sufficient pressure to begin cutting employment, although their budget constraints may not have become completely "hard" because they have not been cut off from all forms of government support. The reductions in employment so far have been gradual but steady. The evidence suggests that a total employment reduction in state industrial enterprises of 25–30 percent can be expected in the first two to three years of real reform. Given this fact, it is reasonable to conclude that real reform has only just begun in the former Soviet Union.

Second, the initial employment reduction is accounted for primarily by retirements and voluntary quits. There is also a substantial reduction in hours worked. Over time the proportion of layoffs increases. Anecdotal evidence suggests that firms initially fire small groups of workers who are considered not essential to the production process but that over time they also fire larger groups of core workers. Nevertheless, monthly inflow rates to unemployment remain low.

Third, once people are unemployed they find it difficult to get a new job in Eastern Europe. Although the evidence is as yet far from complete, there is a strong suggestion that—with the exception of the Czech Republic—the new private sector does not hire much from the pool of unemployed. Thus, it is easier to find another job in the state sector, and state-sector hiring has continued at higher than expected levels, particularly to fill production jobs left vacant by voluntary quits. Even so the state sector hires far fewer than it fires, and this combination of conditions explains the low rates of outflow from unemployment to employment, rising unemployment, and the increasing share of long-term unemployed.

Fourth, as a result, unemployment displays the following characteristics. The unemployment rate begins to rise as soon as pressure is put on state enterprises. Typically, within one year the rate can rise from close to 0 to above 5 percent, and within two years it is above 10 percent. Unemployment rises sharply when the external trade system is disrupted, and it rises even faster in countries that have experienced severe internal disruption, such as a civil war. Unemployment appears to have peaked in only one country, the Czech Republic, which has special features that are not yet fully understood. For the other countries, unemployment appears likely to peak in the range of 15–20 percent with a relatively high percentage of long-term unemployed, probably more than 50 percent. In all likelihood unemployment in Eastern Europe will remain high for the foreseeable future.

Survey Evidence from Ukraine

The preceding discussion identified the outflow rate from unemployment to employment as a key issue in all postcommunist countries and showed that, according to official statistics, this rate is very low. Given the limitations of official statistics, it makes sense to verify this finding through independent surveys.[10]

This section reports on a survey in Ukraine that interviewed people who had been fired from state enterprises in an attempt to determine how many of them had found new jobs. This survey found higher rates of reemployment for fired people than one would expect on the basis of cross-country official statistics and suggests that so far unemployment in the former Soviet Union has differed somewhat from unemployment in Eastern Europe.

EMPLOYMENT REDUCTIONS IN UKRAINE

There was no unemployment in Ukraine at the end of 1991 and a recorded rate of only 1.2 percent at the end of 1992 (see table 12.2). Direct evidence on policies suggests that economic reform, in the sense of real pressure on state enterprises, only really began in 1992 and has remained less complete than in most parts of Eastern Europe and in Russia (Johnson and Ustenko 1993).

Our sample of thirteen firms was chosen from a list of state industrial enterprises operating in the city of Kiev. We divided the sample so that six firms were involved in military production of some kind and the other seven produced only consumer goods. In 1992 many military production firms continued to receive subsidies of some kind, but most civilian firms did not. We wanted to compare outcomes in terms of employment and what happened to fired people for the two sets of firms.

We charted the initial employment in all thirteen firms as well as whether they produced only military goods, only civilian goods, or some mix of goods

Table 12.3   Sample Composition

Enterprise Identification Number	Jurisdiction [a]	Type of Enterprise	Employment in December 1991
1	Moscow	Military	10,117
2	Kiev	Civilian	900
3	Kiev	Civilian	611
4	Kiev	Civilian	650
5	Moscow	Military/Civilian	7,080
6	Moscow	Military	6,560
7	Moscow	Military	20,700
8	Moscow	Civilian	714
9	Kiev	Military/Civilian	1,531
10	Moscow	Military	12,350
11	Moscow	Civilian	2,460
12	Moscow	Civilian	560
13	Kiev	Civilian	820
Total			65,053

[a] Indicates whether the firm was under all-union (Moscow) or republican (Kiev) control in mid-1991.

(see table 12.3). Interviews were conducted in December 1992. Most people with whom we spoke were fired after September 1992.[11] Total employment in all thirteen firms was 65,053 in December 1991, 64,869 in January 1992, and 56,446 in November 1992. The total reduction in employment in our sample was 13 percent from December 1991 to November 1992.[12]

Because of the size distribution of the firms in our sample, 73 percent of the employment reduction—6,280 of 8,607 jobs lost—was in three enterprises: numbers 5, 7, and 10, two of which are military and one of which is military/civilian (enterprises are identified by number in table 12.3). The percentage reduction in employment in almost all military and military/civilian enterprises, however, was less than in almost all civilian enterprises. The employment reduction in the seven civilian firms was across the board: −12 percent, −38 percent, −40 percent, −36 percent, −15 percent, −55 percent, and −32 percent. The employment reduction was greater than 20 percent in five civilian enterprises— the exceptions were number 2 with only a 12 percent fall and number 11 with a 15 percent fall. In contrast, two military enterprises had only a 1 percent reduction in employment, while the other two military enterprises had reductions of 19

Table 12.4   Average Changes in Employment

Type of Enterprise[a]	Employment December 1991	Change in Employment[c]	Percent Change[d]
Military	49,727	5,510	11%
Mixed (military/civilian)	8,611	1,299	15%
Civilian[b]	6,715	1,798	27%

[a] The type of enterprise is as defined in table 12.1 above. In our sample there are four military enterprises, two mixed enterprises (military and civilian production), and seven civilian enterprises.

[b] The figures for civilian enterprises assume that employment in enterprise number 13 was the same in December 1991 as in January 1992.

[c] Calculated as November 1992 employment–December 1991 employment.

[d] Calculated as change in employment/December 1991 employment.

percent and 14 percent, and the two military/civilian enterprises had reductions of 13 percent and 24 percent.

We then charted the different average employment reductions among the three types of enterprises (see table 12.4). Employment fell only 11 percent in pure military enterprises, while dropping 15 percent in mixed military/civilian enterprises.[13] The striking contrast is with civilian enterprises, which had a total employment reduction of 27 percent.

For further details on the composition of employment reduction, we need to look at its two main components: firings and retirements (see table 12.5; enterprises are identified by number). Of the two, firings are obviously an involuntary reduction in employment, but anecdotal evidence suggests that a large fraction of retirements also may be considered involuntary.[14]

The number of people fired as a percent of total involuntary job losses ranges between 29 percent and 80 percent, with an average of 61 percent. One of the two military enterprises that had a significant employment reduction (number 10) reported that only 29 percent of its involuntary reduction was accounted for by people who had been fired. Similarly, one of the two military/civilian enterprises (number 5) showed an unusually low ratio of fired people to total involuntary reduction—only 32 percent.

Interestingly, there were relatively few voluntary quits from enterprises in our sample. The total number of voluntary quits can be calculated as the total reduction in 1992 minus the total involuntary reduction—which gives 1,526, or 18 percent of the total employment reduction of 8,572(see table 12.5). However, of this amount, 1,111 people (73 percent) were accounted for by one enterprise

Table 12.5   Composition of Labor Force Reductions

Enterprise Number[a]	Total Reduction in 1992[b]	Number Fired[c]	Fired as % of December 1991[d]	Retirees and Invalids[e]	Total Involuntary Reduction[f]	Total %[g]	Fired/ Involuntary[h]
1 M	86	30	0.3%	20	50	0.5%	60%
2 C	87	49	5%	38	87	10%	56%
3 C	223	146	24%	77	223	36%	65%
4 C	218	138	21%	80	218	34%	63%
5 M/C	1,051	241	3%	516	757	11%	32%
6 M	30	21	0.3%	8	29	0.4%	72%
7 M	2,900	2,326	11%	574	2,900	14%	80%
8 C	245	167	23%	78	245	34%	68%
9 M/C	338	230	15%	108	338	22%	68%
10 M	2,511	400	3%	1,000	1,400	11%	29%
11 C	336	245	10%	91	336	14%	73%
12 C	287	202	36%	85	287	51%	70%
13 C	260	69	8%	107	176	21%	39%
Total	8,572	4,264	7%[i]	2,782	7,046	11%[i]	61%

[a] Military firms are identified by M, military/civilian firms are identified by M/C, and civilian firms are identified by C.

[b] The total reduction of employment during 1992 does not match in some cases with table 12.2 because firms reported numbers to mid-December. Unfortunately, the question we asked did not result in consistent information about the number of people who left the firms of their own free will. However, we do know that "about a thousand" left firm 10 for this reason and that eighty-four left firm 13 voluntarily. However, in our opinion these numbers are unusually high.

[c] This is the number of people who were dismissed.

[d] This is the number of people dismissed as a percentage of total employment in that firm in December 1991.

[e] This is the sum of retirees and people who retired on a disability pension.

[f] This is the sum of retirees and invalids plus the number fired.

[g] This is total involuntary reduction divided by employment in December 1992.

[h] This is the number fired expressed as a percentage of total involuntary reduction.

[i] Overall (total) number calculated as a percentage.

NOTE: The number of voluntary quits can be calculated as the total reductions minus the involuntary reductions. This number is zero for all enterprises except enterprise number 1, with 36 quits, number 5, with 294 quits, number 6, with 1 quit, number 10, with 1,111 quits, and number 13, with 84 quits. The difference between the number fired plus retired/invalid and the total reduction is due to several elements: death, call-up to the army, voluntary quits.

(number 10). For the other twelve enterprises, total voluntary quits were 415, which was only 0.2 percent of the total employment reduction of these enterprises (6,061) and of which 71 percent was accounted for by one enterprise (number 5).[15]

In summary, the employment reduction in 1992 in *civilian* firms has three main characteristics (see tables 12.4 and 12.5): First, it was large—the average employment reduction was 27 percent (see table 12.4). Second, the employment reduction was fairly evenly distributed across enterprises. Third, the share of fired people in the total involuntary reduction was high—65 percent for the seven civilian enterprises in our sample.

In contrast, military enterprises had a much lower average rate of employment reduction in 1992—11 percent for pure military enterprises and 12 percent for military and military/civilian combined (see table 12.4). Second, employment reduction was unevenly distributed across military and military/civilian enterprises. In two enterprises (numbers 1 and 6) hardly anyone was fired, and in two other enterprises (numbers 10 and 5) the number of people fired was less than 5 percent. In enterprises 7 and 9, however, the employment reduction was more in line with the reductions in civilian enterprises.

Military and military/civilian enterprises resembled civilian enterprises more closely: The average share of fired people in total involuntary employment reduction at military enterprises was 63 percent, which was very close to the number for civilian enterprises. There were, however, two outliers among the pure military enterprises—the share of fired people in total involuntary reduction was 80 percent in enterprise number 7 and only 29 percent in enterprise number 10. Furthermore, the other two pure military enterprises had less than a 1 percent involuntary employment reduction, so this aspect of their performance is not fully comparable.

In conclusion, in this sample of industrial enterprises in Kiev, there was a significant reduction of overall employment in 1992. The pattern is uneven, however, with a much larger reduction in civilian than in military enterprises. Enterprises producing both military and civilian goods appear to be an intermediate case.

How can we explain this, particularly when military enterprises are likely to have suffered a larger fall in output than civilian enterprises have?[16] The most likely reason is that those enterprises still producing military goods received enough in the way of subsidies to protect their workers either by minimizing the amount of involuntary unemployment reduction or by forcing people into retirement.

By late 1992, however, Ukrainian civilian industrial enterprises began firing workers. Some military enterprises also fired people. What happened to those people who became unemployed?

Table 12.6   Composition of Sample by Age and Education

| Age (years) | Total Number | EDUCATION LEVEL | |
		Higher	Secondary
20–25	82	7	75
	[23%]	(9%)	(91%)
26–30	91	65	26
	[26%]	(71%)	(29%)
31–35	55	39	16
	[16%]	(71%)	(29%)
36–40	32	11	21
	[9%]	(34%)	(66%)
41–50	79	47	32
	[23%]	(59%)	(41%)
Over 50	10	3	7
	[3%]	(30%)	(70%)
Total	349	172	177
	[100%]	[49%]	[51%]

NOTE: The numbers in brackets express the number they are below as a percentage of the total sample size (i.e., 349). The numbers in parentheses express the number they are below as a percentage of the row total.

OUTFLOWS FROM UNEMPLOYMENT

We contacted 491 people, of whom we were able to interview 349. Our sample of fired people was constructed so as to contain equal numbers of people with secondary education and people with higher education. We were particularly interested in comparing the outflow rates for people having different levels of education. But we also discovered some interesting data on the age structure of those unemployed who found new jobs.

In the age group twenty to twenty-five, 91 percent of our sample had only a secondary school education (see table 12.6). This is not surprising in that the average age for completing university or other higher education is about twenty-three in Ukraine.

In both the age groups twenty-six to thirty and thirty-one to thirty-five, 71 percent of our sample had some higher education. However, this percentage falls for subsequent groups: 34 percent of the thirty-six to forty age group had some higher education, 59 percent of the forty-one to fifty age group, and 30 percent of people over the age of fifty.[17]

A high percentage of job losers in our sample were young: 49 percent aged thirty or under and 74 percent forty or under (see table 12.7). There were almost

Table 12.7   The Subsequent Employment Status of
              People Who Had Been Fired

Age (years)	Total Number	CURRENT EMPLOYMENT STATUS [a]				
		State	Nonstate	Unem- ployed	Own Business	Business Plan [b]
20–25	81	15	52	14	30	18
	[23%]	(19%)	(64%)	(18%)	(38%)	(23%)
26–30	92	15	43	34	26	21
	[26%]	(16%)	(46%)	(37%)	(28%)	(23%)
31–35	55	17	33	5	21	15
	[16%]	(31%)	(60%)	(9%)	(38%)	(27%)
36–40	32	16	11	5	7	4
	[9%]	(50%)	(34%)	(16%)	(22%)	(13%)
41–50	79	43	9	27	6	6
	[23%]	(54%)	(11%)	(34%)	(8%)	(8%)
Over 50	10	2	0	8	0	2
	[3%]	(20%)	(0%)	(80%)	(0%)	(20%)
Total	349	108	148	93	90	66
	[100%]	[31%]	[42%]	[27%]	[26%]	[19%]

[a] Everyone is classified as either "state" for current employment in the state sector, "nonstate" for current employment in the nonstate sector, or "unemployed" for currently unemployed.

[b] People with business plans may have any current employment, including being currently self-employed.

NOTE: The numbers in brackets are the percent of the total sample (i.e., 349). The numbers in parentheses are the percent of the total number in that age group.

no people in our sample over fifty years of age, which is interesting given that the retirement age is sixty for men and fifty-five for women. (One strong implication of our survey is that few people over the age of forty have been fired in Kiev, although, as discussed earlier, a significant number of people retired in 1992.)

Younger job losers, however, are less likely to end up unemployed. Only 18 percent of the twenty to twenty-five age group became unemployed, 9 percent of the thirty-one to thirty-five age group, and 16 percent of the thirty-six to forty age group. In contrast, 34 percent of the forty-one to fifty age group became unemployed, and more than 80 percent of the over-fifty age group was without a job. The exception to this pattern was the twenty-six to thirty group, in which 37 percent were unemployed (discussed further below).[18]

There are also major differences between age groups in terms of where they ended up working. Younger people were both more likely to find a job and more likely to work in the nonstate sector. Of those finding work, 78 percent of the twenty to twenty-five age group, 74 percent of the twenty-six to thirty age group, and 66 percent of the thirty-one to thirty-five age group found work in the nonstate sector. In contrast, of those finding work in the nonstate sector were 41 percent of the thirty-six to forty age group, 17 percent of the forty-one to fifty age group, and no one older than fifty.

A much higher percentage of younger people either have their own business or plan to establish such a business (see table 12.7). Of the people aged thirty-five and under, 34 percent (77 out of 228) already had their own business. For people aged thirty-six and older, the figure is only 11 percent (13 out of 121). The same comparison also holds for those with plans for a new business. Of those aged thirty-five and under, 24 percent (54 out of 228) had a plan, while of those aged thirty-six and older, only 10 percent (12 out of 121) had a plan.[19]

Almost no one who worked in the state sector had any plans to start their own business, and the same was largely true of the unemployed, although seven unemployed people did say they wanted to start a trading business. In contrast, a relatively high proportion of people working in the nonstate sector wanted to start their own businesses, of which a surprisingly large percentage (42 percent) wanted to start production.[20]

The conclusion is that reemployment rates were higher for younger people; the key break point appears to be at thirty-five years of age—with the caveat that a relatively high percentage of people aged thirty-one to thirty-five found work in the state sector (see table 12.7). Similarly, the share of people aged twenty-six to thirty who were not reemployed was greater than both older and younger age groups, which suggests a problem for relatively young people who have just finished their higher education.

We turn now to examine how the outflow from unemployment depends depend on people's education level. The main results of our sample are broken down by education level (see table 12.8). Our results indicate that 29 percent of people with a secondary education found work in the state sector, as did 32 percent of people with a higher education. The difference is that a higher proportion of people with secondary education found work in the nonstate sector (48 percent versus 38 percent) and that a lower proportion were unemployed (23 percent versus 30 percent). The new jobs in the nonstate sector seem more suited to workers with only secondary school education.

Further, the new jobs were usually not in the same branch of industry; only 16 percent of people with a secondary education or higher reported that they now worked in the same sphere (see table 12.8). Anecdotal evidence suggests that many new nonstate jobs are in trading activities.

Conditional on being fired, 39 percent of women say they are unemployed,

Table 12.8   Employment Status by Education Level

Education Level	Total	CURRENT EMPLOYMENT STATUS				
		State Sector	Nonstate	Unem- ployed	Same Sphere	Same Specialty
Higher	171 [49%]	56 (32%)	64 (38%)	52 (30%)	27 (16%)	91 (53%)
Secondary School	178 [51%]	52 (29%)	84 (48%)	41 (23%)	29 (16%)	48 (27%)
Total	349 [100%]	108 [30%]	148 [42%]	93 [27%]	56 [16%]	139 [40%]

NOTE: The numbers in brackets are the percent of the total sample (i.e., 349). The numbers in parentheses are the percent of the row total.

while only 22 percent of women work in the nonstate sector, and a mere 10 percent say they have their own business (see table 12.9).[21] In contrast, only 12 percent of men are unemployed, 62 percent work in the state sector, and 34 percent have their own business.

We should mention one further relevant hypothesis, which is that, given the uneven pattern of employment reduction across types of firms, the characteristics of people fired may differ according to the type of enterprise in which they worked before. In fact, we find no evidence to support such a view. From all three types of enterprise—military, military/civilian, or civilian—the job losers appeared equally likely to become unemployed. (The shares are 27 percent, 27 percent, and 26 percent.) People who worked in civilian enterprises previously, however, seem slightly more likely to have secured jobs in the nonstate sector.

In summary, the overall rate of outflow from unemployment for this sample is high, much higher than one would expect from the evidence in Eastern Europe. Young people are much more able to find some form of reemployment. Once they have been fired, older people are more likely to be unemployed, less likely to work in the nonstate sector, and less likely to start their own business. Women are less likely than men to find a new job—particularly in the nonstate sector.

Conclusion

Cross-country statistical evidence identifies low outflow rates from unemployment as a key problem for Eastern Europe. Particularly disappointing have been the low rates of reemployment for unemployed people in the private sector. In comparison, our survey of Ukraine indicates high rates of reemployment in the private sector for people who are fired from state enterprises and who

Table 12.9   Employment Status by Sex

		CURRENT EMPLOYMENT STATUS			
Sex	*Total*	*State*	*Nonstate*	*Unem-ployed*	*Own Business*
Female	148 [53%]	57 (39%)	33 (22%)	58 (39%)	15 (10%)
Male	131 [47%]	34 (26%)	81 (62%)	16 (12%)	45 (34%)
Total	279 [100%]	91 (33%)	114 (41%)	74 (27%)	60 (22%)

NOTE: Data on the sex of respondents are available for all enterprises with the exception of numbers 2, 11, and 12. This gives a total subsample size of 279.

The numbers in brackets express the percentage of the sample they are below for which relevant data are available (i.e., 279). The numbers in parentheses express the percentage they are below the row total.

remain unemployed for only a short period. There are three possible explanations for this difference between Eastern Europe and the former Soviet Union.

First, because our study directly reaches people who have been fired, it avoids problems inherent in measuring only what happens to people who pass through the official unemployment system. If, as appears to be the case from our study, a high proportion of people find new jobs right away, they may be entirely missing from official statistics on flows into and out of unemployment. This would bias downward both inflow rates and outflow rates, with probably a more serious effect on outflow rates because the people who are missed have very short durations of unemployment.

Second, in the former Soviet Union during 1992 there was rapid growth in the private sector, which may have been a one-time adjustment as the private sector expanded into trade and small-scale services. If the same expansion that occurred in 1990 in Eastern Europe is repeated in the former Soviet Union, then the new jobs creation rate will slow in 1993 and 1994. This would reduce the number of fired people who can immediately find a job in the private sector and would increase the measured inflow rate to, and reduce the measured outflow rate from, unemployment.

Third, all our results should be cautiously interpreted and treated as the findings of a preliminary study with a limited sample, for the people surveyed were part of the first wave of firings in Ukraine and may have different characteristics from people who were fired subsequently. Although we do not have wage or other corroborating data, it is possible that many of the sampled people— particularly the young men with secondary educations—in Ukraine moved voluntarily into the nonstate sector and were then fired from their state jobs. This suggests that the reemployment rates for people who were truly fired are lower than those indicated by our study.

Unfortunately, even if only 27 percent of the people who were fired remain unemployed, the likely scale of job losses will generate large-scale unemployment in the former Soviet Union. Furthermore, the burden of unemployment so far has fallen unequally. Conditional on being fired, older people are less likely to be reemployed; if they are reemployed, their new job is more likely to be in the state sector. Anecdotal evidence and experience in other countries suggest we should be skeptical about whether those new state jobs will prove lasting. Furthermore, the extent of retirements in 1992—and anecdotal evidence—suggests that this is the most important form of involuntary loss of employment for older people.

Conditional on being fired, unemployment rates are also somewhat higher for people who have finished their higher education, although if these people find work, more than half of it is in their professional capacity. We interpret this as mixed news.

The worst news is for women. Once they are fired, our evidence suggests that women are much less likely to find another job. Furthermore, if they do find another job, it is more likely to be in the state sector. Also, at least in our sample, women are much less likely than men to start their own businesses.

Overall, our results show that job losses in the former Soviet Union are at least as substantial as those in Eastern Europe. Firms in the former Soviet Union are firing workers. For fired people over the age of forty, it is very difficult to find another job. Once fired, women may be more likely to withdraw from the labor force. One major difference from Western Europe is that young workers are better able to find new jobs in Ukraine.

Furthermore, although the emergence of a low-productivity, low-wage private sector in the former Soviet Union may generate enough new jobs to keep unemployment rates below East European levels, it will not by itself create acceptable living standards. The future of Russia and Ukraine probably involves a 10–15 percent unemployment rate, a high share of long-term unemployed, and a low standard of living for people who lost their jobs but are now reemployed. Being employed in the low-wage sector will be better than being unemployed, but for many people the difference may not be great.

Notes

1. A similar pattern is apparent in total Polish nonagricultural public-sector employment, defined to include both state enterprises and cooperatives. There was a cumulative

fall of 37.3 percent in this measure of employment between the end of 1988 and the end of 1992. The total change comprised a fall of 4 percent in 1989, 14 percent in 1990, 13 percent in 1991, and 13 percent in 1992 (Coricelli, Hagemejer, and Rybinski 1993).

2. In the first quarter of 1993, despite the continuing recession, industrial employment actually rose slightly (Commander, McHale, and Yemtsov 1993.)

3. For example, the model of Aghion and Blanchard (1993) applies standard Western labor market analysis to postcommunist conditions and includes this assumption.

4. One estimate is that the Polish private sector accounted for 38 percent of nonagricultural jobs (Frydman, Rapaczynski, and Earle 1993, 174).

5. For example, in Slovakia the long-term unemployed (out of work for twelve months or more) rose from 6.1 percent at the end of 1991 to 36.3 percent at the end of 1992. Even in the Czech Republic, which has relatively low unemployment and relatively high outflows from unemployment, the share of long-term unemployed in total unemployed rose from 3.9 percent to 17.1 percent in 1991–1992 (Boeri 1993).

6. Supportive evidence on this point is provided by a spring 1991 World Bank survey of private Polish manufacturing firms. The survey found that many private-sector jobs required unskilled labor, who earned 10 percent more than in the state sector, and there was a large private-sector wage premium—up to twice what could be earned in the state sector—only for skilled workers (Webster 1992, 22, para. 4.18). The rise in unemployment since spring 1991 may have pushed down unskilled wages in the private sector relative to wages in the state sector.

7. These average numbers mask the distribution of wages in the private sector. There is no clear dichotomy between good and bad jobs, but there is a marked distribution of wages from less than half what can be earned in the state sector to about double state-sector wages (Johnson 1993a).

8. The benefits for unemployed people were generous, at least initially, and this may have encouraged people who were not really in the labor force to register as being unemployed.

9. The Bulgarian program started in earnest in February 1991 (Beleva, Jackman, and Nenova-Amar 1993, 1). Reforms in Romania began in 1990 but became much more serious in 1991 and 1992 (Earle and Oprescu 1993, 10–16).

10. This section draws on joint ongoing work with Oleg Ustenko of Kiev State Economic University.

11. Table 12.3 also indicates whether an enterprise was under the jurisdiction of a central ministry in Moscow or a ministry in Kiev before the breakup of the Soviet Union. We looked for but did not find an independent effect of previous jurisdiction.

12. Anecdotal evidence suggests that employment reductions greatly accelerated in the second half of 1992, particularly the number of people who were fired.

We obtained a monthly breakdown of firings from only one enterprise (number 13), which showed that of the forty-nine people fired in 1992 (through November), only nine were fired through the end of June and twenty-two were fired in the last three months of the year. People retired at a steady rate during the first eight months of the year; of the 107 who went onto a pension in the whole of 1992, 17 went in the first quarter, 15 went in the second quarter, 19 in the third quarter, but 61 retired in the last quarter and of this total, 52 left in November.

13. The difference between results for military and civilian/military enterprises should not be overemphasized, particularly because we have only two mixed enterprises in our sample and it is difficult to be sure precisely how much civilian output is produced by a military enterprise.

14. It is hard to see why anyone would want to retire at the time of our survey: the average pension was around 4,800 rubles a month, and there was little variation about this mean.

15. It is possible that enterprises fired people who they thought or knew wanted to quit or who have already effectively quit by not coming to work. However, we have no reliable evidence on this point.

15. It is not possible to obtain information on the level of production in enterprises that produce military goods.

17. The fifty/fifty split in our sample on education levels means we probably oversampled the twenty-six to thirty-five age group to compensate for the high number of twenty- to twenty-five-year-olds who were fired with little or no higher education.

18. Many of these people just finished their higher education (see the discussion of table 12.9).

19. Some people said they were planning a new business although they already operated their own private business. This number should be interpreted as an indicator of people's expectations about the extent of new business opportunities in the private sector.

20. Of course, these numbers indicate only the preferences of actual and would-be entrepreneurs, not necessarily where the opportunities are.

21. Given the low level of living standards at present in Ukraine, it is unlikely that these women voluntarily withdrew from the labor force.

References

Aghion, Phillipe, and Olivier Jean Blanchard. "On the Speed of Transition in Eastern Europe." Mimeo, March 29, 1993.

Beleva, Iskra, and Richard Jackman. "The Labor Market in Bulgaria, II: Unemployment." Paper presented at the World Bank workshop "Labor Markets in Transitional Socialist Economies," Prague, April 16–17, 1993.

Beleva, Iskra, Richard Jackman, and Mariela Nenova-Amar. "The Labour Market in Bulgaria." Paper prepared for the World Bank Conference on Unemployment, Restructuring and the Labor Market in East Europe and Russia, Washington D.C., October 7 and 8, 1993.

Boeri, Tito. "Unemployment Dynamics and Labour Market Policies." Paper prepared for the World Bank Conference on Unemployment, Restructuring and the Labor Market in East Europe and Russia, Washington D.C., October 7 and 8, 1993.

Commander, Simon, Leonid Liberman, and Ruslan Yemtsov. "Wage and Employment Decisions in the Russian Economy: An Analysis of Developments in 1992." Mimeo, January 1993a.

———. "Unemployment and Labor Market Dynamics in Russia." Policy Research Working Paper Series, WPS1167, the World Bank, August 1993b.

Commander, Simon, John McHale, and Ruslan Yemtsov. "Russia." Paper prepared for the World Bank Conference on Unemployment, Restructuring and the Labor Market in East Europe and Russia, Washington, D.C., October 7 and 8, 1993.

Conway, Patrick, and Chandrashekar Pant. "Georgia: Defining National Independence within the Context of Economic Independence." Presented at the conference on First Steps toward Economic Independence, Stockholm School of Economics, August 23–24, 1993.

Coricelli, Fabrizio, and Ana Revenga. "Wages and Unemployment in Poland: Recent Developments and Policy Issues." Policy Research Working Paper Series, WPS821, the World Bank, January 1992.

Coricelli, Fabrizio, Krzysztof Hagemejer, and Krzysztof Rybinski. "Poland." Paper prepared for the World Bank Conference on Unemployment, Restructuring and the Labor Market in East Europe and Russia, Washington, D.C., October 7 and 8, 1993.

Cvikl, Milan, Evan Kraft, and Milan Vodopivec. "Costs and Benefits of Independence: Slovenia." Presented at the conference on First Steps toward Economic Independence, Stockholm School of Economics, August 23–24, 1993.

Earle, John S., and Gheorghe Oprescu. "Employment and Wage Determination, Unemployment and Labor Policies in Romania." Paper prepared for the World Bank Conference on Unemployment, Restructuring and the Labor Market in East Europe and Russia, Washington, D.C., October 7 and 8, 1993.

European Bank for Reconstruction and Development (EBRD). *Annual Economic Review 1992*. EBRD, February 1993.

Frydman, Roman, Andrzej Rapaczynski, John S. Earle, et al. *The Privatization Process in Central Europe*. London: Central European Press, 1993.

Hagemejer, Krzysztof, and Krzysztof Rybinski. "The Labor Market in Poland in 1990–92: Unemployment Trends." Mimeo. Presented at the World Bank workshop Labor Markets in Transitional Socialist Economies, Prague, April 16–17, 1993.

Ham, John, Jan Svejnar, and Katherine Terrell. "The Czech and Slovak Labor Markets during the Transition." Paper prepared for the World Bank Conference on Unemployment, Restructuring and the Labor Market in East Europe and Russia, Washington D.C., October 7 and 8, 1993.

Hansson, Ardo H. "Transforming an Economy while Building a Nation: The Case of Estonia." Presented at the conference on First Steps toward Economic Independence, Stockholm School of Economics, August 23–24, 1993.

Johnson, Simon. "Entrepreneurs and Employment in the Polish Private Sector." Paper prepared for the World Bank Conference on Unemployment, Restructuring and the Labor Market in East Europe and Russia, Washington D.C., October 7 and 8, 1993.

―――. "Private Business in Eastern Europe." In Olivier Blanchard, Kenneth Froot, and Jeffrey Sachs, eds. *The Transition in Eastern Europe*, NBER Conference Volume. Chicago: University of Chicago Press, 1994.

Johnson, Simon, and Oleg Ustenko. "The Road to Hyperinflation: Economic Independence in Ukraine, 1991–93." In *Proceedings of the Conference on First Steps toward Economic Independence*, Stockholm School of Economics, August 23–24, 1993.

Kollo, Janos. "Flows of Labour, Employment, and Wages in the Private Sector in Hungary." Paper presented at the World Bank workshop Labor Markets in Transitional Socialist Economies, Prague, April 16–17, 1993.

Layard, Richard, Stephen Nickell, and Richard Jackman. *Unemployment: Macroeconomic Performance and the Labour Market*. Oxford, Eng.: Oxford University Press, 1991.

Marnie, Sheila. "Who and Where Are the Russian Unemployed?" *Radio Free Europe/ Radio Liberty Research Report*. 2, no. 33 (August 20, 1993): 36–37.

Pinto, Brian, Marek Belka, and Stefan Krajewski. "Transforming State Enterprises in Poland: Evidence on Adjustment by Manufacturing Firms." *Brookings Papers on Economic Activity* 1 (1993): 213–70.

Rutland, Peter, and Timur Isateev. "Kazakhstan: First Steps towards Economic Independence." Paper presented at the conference on First Steps Toward Economic Independence, Stockholm School of Economics, August 23–24, 1993.

Webster, Leila. "Private Sector Manufacturing in Poland: A Survey of Firms." Industry and Energy Department Working Paper, Industry Series Paper no. 66, the World Bank, 1992.

Wyzan, Michael L. "Macedonia: An Economically Viable Nation?" Paper presented at the conference on First Steps toward Economic Independence, Stockholm School of Economics, August 23–24, 1993.

13

China's Nonconformist Reforms

JOHN MCMILLAN

How has China achieved its spectacular economic growth under reform, despite having no commercial law, no financial market, prices that are only partially freed, and no privatization? I argue that the fundamental reasons for China's success are not unique to China. China succeeded because it unleashed the forces of competition. China shows the power of incentives, but it also shows that, in a transition economy, workable incentives can take surprisingly nonstandard forms. Novel institutional forms evolved to solve the unprecedented problems of transition. Entry of new firms, albeit with an unusual ownership structure, produced a competitive, nonstate industrial sector. New state-imposed incentives induced the state-owned firms to improve their efficiency. The discipline on managers that comes from product-market competition helped compensate for the missing financial-market discipline. Reputational incentives substituted for formal legal enforcement of contracts.

WHAT ARE THE INDISPENSABLE COMPONENTS of economic reform? Underlying the reform policies enacted in Eastern Europe and the former Soviet Union is the view that a successful reform must quickly

- Free up prices
- Create a financial market
- Privatize state-owned firms
- Introduce laws of commerce

According to many Western advisers to reformist governments, these are among the prerequisites for successful market activity.[1]

The People's Republic of China has disregarded this prescription. China's financial system is in a mess. Finance remains dominated by state banks whose lending patterns make little economic sense. There is no financial market and no corporate control in the sense in which those terms are understood in the West. China has done almost no privatization. State-owned firms remain state controlled, and many continue to be propped up by subsidies. China did reform prices but so stealthily that many commentators failed to notice. China lacks the basic laws relevant to a market economy, and there is little prospect of the courts being able or willing to enforce any laws of contract.

According to our accumulated understanding of property rights, with no commercial law, no financial market, prices only partially freed, and no privatization, China should be stagnating. Unfortunately for conventional wisdom, it isn't.

China under reform has achieved spectacular economic growth and sustained it over a long period. China's 1993–1994 growth rate, at 13 percent, was the highest in the world. Per capita growth between 1980 and 1993 averaged almost 8 percent. Growth has brought improved living standards. Housing space per person, for example, more than doubled between 1978 and 1990, as did consumption of meat; ownership of consumer durables rose three- to fourfold. No major increase in inequality has accompanied this growth, so the improvements

This article, which draws on work done jointly with Barry Naughton, was written while I was visiting the Graduate School of Business, Stanford University, and the Institut d'Economie Industrielle, Université des Sciences Sociales de Toulouse. I thank the members of those institutions for their generous hospitality, the University of California Pacific Rim Research Program for support, and Charles Gitomer, Edward Lazear, Barry Naughton, and Susan Shirk for comments.

in living standards have been widely shared among the Chinese people. At the same time there has been a deep restructuring of the economy, away from the idiocies of central planning. Export volumes rose almost 13 percent per year between 1980 and 1993. A massive shift in employment has occurred: nonstate industrial firms now employ 100 million workers, about the same number who work in state-owned firms.[2]

The economic success is overshadowed by China's deplorable lack of progress in human rights and political freedoms. China is only slightly less authoritarian than it was before the economic reforms, and the people's hopes for liberalization have been cruelly dashed. Freedom of expression, of assembly, and of religion are all curtailed. Political prisoners, held in brutal conditions, probably number in the tens of thousands. Corruption is rampant, with no solution in sight. Even given these weighty caveats, however, raising the living standards of a billion poor people to two and a half times what they were before the reforms is a notable achievement.

In achieving rapid growth while making deep economic reforms, China's transition has been markedly different from that of the countries of Eastern Europe and the former Soviet Union, where reform, at least in its initial stages, has been accompanied by plummeting living standards. Can we learn anything from China about reform in general? Some argue that China is so different from the other reforming countries that there are no lessons to be drawn (Sachs and Woo 1994). I argue, on the contrary, that the fundamental reasons for China's success are not unique to China. The lessons are elementary: China succeeded because it unleashed the forces of competition. China shows the power of incentives; but it also shows that, in a transition economy, workable incentives can take surprisingly nonstandard forms.[3]

Bottom-up changes have driven China's reforms. Many crucial decisions were made at ground level, not in Beijing. Novel institutional forms evolved to solve some of the unprecedented problems of transition. The new economy has arisen as much from the initiatives of the Chinese people, who have built new firms and created new ways of doing business, as from changes imposed by the government.

The economy is still far from efficient: the imperfections in the financial system undoubtedly mean that some of the growth is based on misallocated investment. The government must eventually regularize China's financial and legal systems if an efficient market economy is to develop. (It should have begun doing so in the late 1980s.) But what China's success shows is that a transition economy does not have to set everything right all at once. It can get by, temporarily, with Band-Aid solutions: devices that may not exist in Western practice or in economics textbooks.

In any of the planned economies, the starting point for the transition is misaligned prices, unproductive firms, and unfilled market niches. Such an inefficient economy offers large scope for improvement. Introducing a few incentives and some competition into a highly distorted economy can have dramatic effects, as China illustrates. It is hard to predict, however, just which incentives will work in the peculiar circumstances of the transition economy. It follows that it is necessary to take an experimental approach and be willing to live for a while with unconventional institutions, if they work. These Band-Aid solutions may well not be discovered in a finance ministry, let alone in the World Bank or a Western university. They are more likely to be discovered by people whose livelihoods are on the line.

China's Reform Path

The key ingredients of China's reforms were

- The breakup of agricultural communes into (essentially) private farms
- Massive entry by new nonstate industrial firms
- New incentives for state-owned enterprises
- The introduction of a dual-price system

Agricultural reform achieved quick success. In the communes, the link between individual effort and reward had been tenuous. The reforms enacted from 1979 through the early 1980s gave each peasant family a long-term lease of a plot of land. The household must deliver a certain quota to the government each year; it may then sell to the government or in free markets anything produced beyond the quota. A household's income therefore depends directly on that household's efforts, which has resulted in big increases in the production of food. Agricultural output increased by 67 percent between 1978 and 1985. In part this was caused by an increase in inputs. But mainly it was due to the strengthened incentives; productivity increased by nearly 50 percent, compared with no increase in productivity over the previous two and a half decades (McMillan, Whalley, and Zhu 1989; Lin 1992).

Entry of new firms has been perhaps the most striking feature of China's transition. Although in the first few years of reform they were little noticed, the nonstate industrial firms grew remarkably quickly (their output grew by 25 percent each year in 1985–1991, according to Whiting [1994]) and, twelve years into the reforms, were producing half of industrial output. This entrepreneurial activity occurred despite the impediments of little law of contract, weak property rights, and underdeveloped capital markets. Scope for highly profitable entry existed because of the many market niches left unfilled by the state firms under the old planning system and because of the misaligned prices that planning had imposed.

The new nonstate firms have a novel organizational structure. Most are not private firms. To anyone schooled in Western—or, for that matter, Japanese—concepts of corporate control, these firms look strange. Mostly located in rural areas, they are run by village governments (and so are called township and village enterprises, or TVEs). Their ownership is vague, and there are no clear rights to residual returns. They have few of the usual instruments of corporate control: no stockholder controls and no threat of takeover (although there is some bank oversight). On a priori grounds, these firms simply should not work. But they not only function but function efficiently (Byrd and Lin 1990). The village-owned firms have been the main source of China's dynamism under reform.

Discussion of how the Eastern European countries should manage their transitions often implicitly equates the new private sector with privatized former state firms. The speed with which China's nonstate sector grew suggests, on the contrary, that the most promising source of a private sector is not privatization but entry.

China's state-owned industry, while shrinking relative to the rest of the economy because of the rapid growth of the nonstate sector, has itself achieved respectable productivity gains. This has been the result of liberalization measures that fall far short of privatization. Initially highly inefficient, these firms have increased their output under the reforms by over 7 percent annually. Most of this output increase is due to improved productivity, which has risen at an annual rate of over 4 percent.[4]

The productivity increase was a response to a range of incentives offered to the state firms (Groves et al. 1994a, 1994b; Jefferson and Rawski 1994). The government allowed firms to retain some of their profits according to a contractually specified formula. In some cases a firm now has to deliver a fixed amount of profit and can keep any extra profit, so the firm has full marginal incentives. The retained profits are used to fund worker bonuses, benefits such as housing and health care, and investment in new plant and equipment. Managers are now given monetary rewards explicitly based on their firm's performance. Managers obtained autonomy: the right to decide what to produce, how much to produce, and how to produce it was shifted from the state to the enterprise. Managers were permitted to pay workers bonuses and to hire some workers on fixed-term contracts. New methods of appointing managers were introduced. One extreme method, implemented occasionally, was to put managerial jobs up for auction, with bids being promises of future profits to be delivered, these promises being backed up by a bond posted by the manager. There was considerable managerial turnover (in a sample of state-owned firms, 90 percent changed their top manager during 1980–1989), and as a result better managers were appointed than the Communist Party officials who used to run these firms.[5] In addition to, and reinforcing, these incentives directly imposed by the state, the reforms faced the state-owned firms with greatly increased product-market competition, as discussed below, providing a further impetus to improving productivity.

Some state-owned firms are a perpetual drain on the state budget through the subsidies they receive (although, contrary to what is often asserted, the chronic loss makers are a minority among state-owned firms; a larger number of state-owned firms deliver more funds to the state, in remitted profits and taxes, than they receive in subsidies, as Morris and Liu [1993] show). The state-owned firms are still a long way from being efficient capitalist firms. Because of their strengthened incentives and improved organization, however, they are much less inefficient than they used to be and have contributed to China's overall growth under reform.

The Chinese government introduced price reform in an unconventional way. Before the reforms, state-owned enterprises were required to sell all their output to the state at state-fixed prices. Under the reforms, these firms were allowed to produce extra output, beyond the plan amounts, and to sell that extra output in free markets. The fraction of state-firm output sold on markets progressively rose so that, by 1989, on average, 38 percent of a state-owned firm's outputs were directly sold on markets; for some state firms market sales were 100 percent of output. Similarly, an increasingly large fraction of state firms' inputs were purchased on free markets, rather than being allocated by the state: in 1989, on average, 56 percent of a state-owned firm's inputs were procured through market purchases, and for some state firms, 100 percent of inputs were market procured. There was a dual-price system, with the market price usually being substantially above the official price.

From the viewpoint of economic incentives the key point about the dual-price system is that, at the margin, decisions are made in the face of market prices. The fact that the price received from the state is less than the price received from the market merely means that the firm is paying a lump sum tax. For a firm's decisions on how much to produce, what inputs to use, and what kind of investment to undertake, the state-imposed output quota is irrelevant as long as that quota is smaller than the total output. What matters for such decisions is the price that will be received for any extra output, which is the free-market price (Byrd 1987; McMillan and Naughton 1994a). Thus the dual-price system, although a gradual form of price reform, had an instantaneous impact in inducing firms' decision making to be market oriented.

Dual pricing forced state-owned firms to compete both with other state-owned firms and with nonstate firms. In order to sell in free markets, state-owned firms had to please their customers, which forced them to produce to a higher quality than when they had the government as guaranteed buyer.

The dual-price system was not ideal. It enabled illicit profits to be made by obtaining goods at the plan price and selling them at the market price. Buying low and selling high are normal market activities, but the dual-price system enabled certain well-connected people to buy at artificially low prices. Anger at such corrupt practices was one of the sparks that ignited Tiananmen. Dual pricing is a temporary expedient to smooth the reform process, and it should have been replaced by full market pricing as soon as was feasible: that is, by the late 1980s, rather than, as actually happened, in the early 1990s.[6]

Market Incentives in China

China's economic growth has taken place in a legal vacuum. As Clarke (1994) notes, "legal institutions remain essentially unreformed and ill-suited to the institutions of a market economy," and "property rights and contract rights are not well defined and reliably enforced." Even if the Chinese government were to write laws, Clarke argues, it is unlikely that China's courts would be capable of enforcing them. "The observance of court judgments for many institutions remains essentially voluntary." It is a deep and unresolved question whether China's growth has occurred *despite* the absence of the usual legal institutions or—the more intriguing possibility—*because* of that absence. Deals are made, however. People routinely and successfully consummate transactions, often across large distances and involving delayed returns.

Property rights in reform-era China arise from social custom. People honor agreements not because the law requires it but because they value their reputations (as analyzed by Tirole [1993], for example). Reputation and connections—the famous *guanxi*—serve as substitutes for formal laws. They are an imperfect substitute, however, as self-enforcing contracts have some limitations. Deals can be made only by people who know each other's reputation, either directly or through a third party. The economic circumstances may in some cases turn out to be such that it pays one of the parties to renege on a deal, and, anticipating this, the other party may refuse to agree to the deal. A fear of arbitrary expropriation by the government inhibits people from undertaking certain investments.[7] For these reasons, many potentially gainful transactions cannot be made when laws are absent. China will eventually have to develop laws of contract and a court system to enforce them if its economic success is to continue. But China's growth shows that reputational incentives can be a surprisingly effective basis for market activity.[8]

What makes China's firms productive, despite their unconventional organization? The taxonomy of sources of firm efficiency of Holmström and Tirole (1989)—capital-market discipline, labor-market discipline, internal discipline, and product-market discipline—can usefully be applied to China.

China's state and nonstate firms are largely insider controlled, and few of the usual capital-market disciplines operate on them. There are some substitute controls, though they are relatively weak. In the case of the nonstate firms, the smallness of the village (a few thousand people) means that the villagers can to some extent keep track of decisions being made in their own firms. Banks, which are state owned, provide some monitoring of village-owned firms. How much the bank is willing to lend a firm depends on the rating the bank gives it, which in turn depends on the firm's sales and profits. Political and social criteria and government interference also affect the bank's lending decisions, however, muting any disciplinary effect of the bank's rating practices on the firm. The absence of provisions for default on loans further undermines any discipline imposed by the banking system, and often the courts are unwilling to enforce loan contracts (Whiting 1994). In the case of state-owned firms, the industrial bureaus still maintain some active oversight, potentially substituting for capital-market controls (though this is not by itself an explanation for the state firms' improved performance, as historically such oversight notably failed to generate efficiency). There is a bankruptcy law, and firms are allowed or occasionally forced to go bankrupt.

Labor-market discipline puts some constraints on the decisions of managers in the state firms. The industrial bureaus demote managers whose firms are not performing up to potential and promotes those who do well (Groves et al. 1994b). In the nonstate sector also, managers' careers to some extent reflect their job performance (Whiting 1994). Because China's managerial labor market is thin, however, this labor market discipline is weak.

Some internal discipline exists in both state and nonstate firms. State-firm managers' pay reflects their firms' profits and sales, and a manager's pay is more sensitive to performance than is typically seen in the West. Managers are in some cases required to post a bond, which can be forfeited if the firm underperforms (Groves et al. 1994b). State-firm workers receive bonuses, which have grown to average about one-fifth of total pay, and there is some indirect evidence that bonuses are awarded differentially according to the individual worker's efforts (Groves et al. 1994a). State firms hire an increasing number of workers on fixed-term contracts, but it is still hard to fire most workers. In nonstate firms, it is possible to fire workers from outside the village but not local workers. The workers' pay is based on performance by means of bonuses and piece-rate payments. Managers have contracts that make their pay depend not only on the firm's sales and profit but also on social targets such as education and public order (Whiting 1994).

Product-market discipline operates on both state and nonstate firms. Nonstate firms operate in intensely competitive product markets. Entry into the industries in which they operate is easy, and any profits earned by one firm elicit a quick entry response by others (Byrd and Lin 1990). Village-owned firms sell much of their output outside their own province and increasingly sell on foreign markets. In response to a survey, many managers reported difficulties in marketing their products, complaining of "too much production of similar products" (Whiting

1994). State firms also must compete. The introduction of the dual-price system forced them to compete both with other state firms and with nonstate firms, and their profit-sharing contracts reward them for success in this competition (McMillan and Naughton 1992).

China's firms, then, operate under some forms of capital-market and labor-market discipline, which are, however, relatively ineffectual. They have some internal discipline, but this is limited by constraints on firing workers. The main discipline comes from the product market. Despite the virtual absence of mechanisms of corporate control, the strong competition to sell their products seems to have induced state firms to become much less inefficient than they used to be and nonstate firms to operate reasonably efficiently. Competition and ownership are alternative sources of incentives for managers. In the peculiar circumstances of the transition economy, competition seems to be enough to induce firms to be productive, despite state ownership or the fuzzily defined ownership of the village-owned firms. Competition matters more than ownership.

This conclusion is contrary to much of the thinking about economic reform. The big bang prescription for reform rests on the view that nothing short of a change of ownership, brought about by privatization, can improve the performance of state-owned firms. The significant improvement in the productivity of China's state-owned firms, resulting from the imposition of profit sharing and other incentives, contradicts this. The nonstate firms also subvert some presuppositions about the need for clearly defined ownership rights for firms to work well. If China had put Western advisers in charge of its reforms in 1978, it is inconceivable that they would have designed firms with the organizational structure that the village-owned firms developed for themselves.

China and Reform Practice

The most obvious and important difference between China and many of the countries of the former Soviet Union and Eastern Europe is in the form of government: China remains under communist control, whereas Russia and many of the Eastern European countries are democratic. Does this political difference rule out the possibility of economic lessons from China? Did China need its authoritarian government in order to follow the economic path that it did? Or could it have as successfully managed its evolutionary reforms if it had had a democratic government? It is impossible to prove that it could have (likewise, it is impossible to prove that it could not have). There are reasons to believe, however, that China's economics is, to some extent, separable from its politics and that it could have followed a similar economic path if it had been democratic.

China's economic reform policies were those not of a strong but of a weak government. The political impediments to economic reform in China were formidable, as Shirk (1993, 334) explains:

> Authoritarian communist regimes may look like strong states, but they rarely have the capacity to impose painful policies over the heads of bureaucrats. . . .
> The political challenge of economic reform was to build a constituency for reform from among the groups who would potentially benefit from it, namely, provincial officials, light industry, and agriculture, and to reorient the preferences of the groups with vested interests in the command economy [particularly heavy industry]. This task required artful strategy on the part of the political entrepreneurs at the top of the CCP.

Although many of the changes began at the top, not all did. The government's role has often been to permit change rather than to initiate it. Many of the reforms, in particular in agriculture, were initiated at ground level and only afterward ratified by the central government; like Gilbert and Sullivan's Duke of Plaza Toro, the Chinese government led from behind. There has been no overall plan: China's leaders had no clear idea of where they wanted China to go. Having discarded Marxism and Maoism, the Communist Party has little legitimacy; any legitimacy it has comes solely from its success in delivering economic growth. The government had little ability to commit itself to continuing reform. The commitment to reform came not from any inherent strength of the government but, as Fang (1994) argues, from the early and cumulative reform success.

Rather than destroying the old institutions and starting from scratch, China let its new economy grow around the old (Naughton 1994). China shows that introducing some competition and some elementary incentives into a highly distorted economy, while leaving the existing inefficient institutions in place, can generate huge improvements in efficiency.

A firm's success in the abnormal setting of the transition economy does not guarantee its continued success as the economy becomes more fully marketized. The improved performance of the state firms vindicates China's policy of not immediately privatizing them (which was, however, driven by political considerations, not economics, as Shirk [1993] documents). It does not provide a case for never privatizing them, however, or even for delaying privatization as much as has been done. Although competition and state-imposed incentives can, in the short run, improve state firms' performance,[9] in the long run privatization is the only way to ensure that firms are fully subject to market disciplines and to prevent politicians and bureaucrats from intervening in the firms' decisions in politically tempting but economically unproductive ways. It seems clear that China should have begun full-scale privatization, as well as the development of a capital market, by the late 1980s. Although little official privatization has been done as yet, managers of an increasing number of state-owned firms are obtaining ad hoc control, either through spontaneous privatization—the unofficial transfer of state assets to private hands (Nee and Su 1994)—or through joint ventures with foreign firms (Qian and Stiglitz 1994), and as a result the firms' behavior is becoming still more market oriented.

The village-owned firms, with their unconventional structure, have succeeded in the particular circumstances of the transition economy. They may in the future be crowded out by firms that have, by Western standards, more conventional organization. Some have already begun to change, converting themselves into a hybrid corporate form known as joint stock cooperatives, with employees holding shares in the firm (Qian 1994). Even if the village-owned firms' value turns out to be only for the transition, it has been a very high value.

Conclusion

China is different from most of the other reforming countries. Agriculture is a much smaller fraction of the economy in the former Soviet bloc countries than in China so cannot give as big a boost to reform as it did in China. The prospects for improvements in state-firm performance may (or may not) be less in other countries than in China. The village-owned firms' organizational form reflects particular features of China; in other countries the new start-up firms will take different forms.

China does not provide a model for the other reforming countries to emulate because of these differences and because many aspects of China's reforms could have been improved on. China does, however, cast doubt on some of the thinking underlying Eastern Europe's reforms. China is a counterexample to the view that, without a financial market, laws of commerce, and privatization, markets cannot work. Through experimentation, devices can be developed that serve as substitutes for these institutions during the transition to a full market economy.

The lessons from China are in generalities, not specifics. Perhaps the main lesson is that markets can flourish in an unpromising environment. Markets are more robust than sometimes thought. Market incentives can come in unfamiliar forms. The lesson for economists is do not take for granted anything we "know" about how economies work, for what we know about things like corporate control may well not be applicable to economies going through fundamental changes.

What the success of China's unconventional firms shows is that there are limits to what reformers can foresee. The transition cannot be planned because what will work cannot be anticipated. Reformers can design new institutions for the transition economy, and economic theory is useful in thinking through the issues of incentive system design and in analyzing why certain incentives work.[10]

But the reformers must be willing to accept novel solutions that do not conform to preconceived views. China's success reflects its reformers' openness to experimentation. No one could have predicted, at the outset of the reforms, the success under reform of either the state-owned firms or the village-owned firms. No one, therefore, could have prescribed China's reform path.

Notes

1. Macroeconomic stabilization is generally regarded as a key component of reform; some see it as the chief or even the sole component. I shall focus, however, on the microeconomic issues of property rights and incentives. Macroeconomic stability is obviously necessary for successful reform; but the many developing countries that have undergone stabilization programs without achieving economic growth show it is not enough by itself. What was wrong with the communist economies under planning was not so much macroeconomic instability as the absence of appropriate incentives for productive effort.

2. Vietnam has also achieved impressive growth by following a similar reform path to China's, though moving more quickly on financial-market development and price reform (see McMillan 1994).

3. Although China's incentives are not consistent with some versions of property rights theory, they are analyzable in terms of the modern theory of incentives, that is, agency theory. Agency theory underlies the discussion to follow and is used to analyze China's reforms by Groves, Hong, McMillan, and Naughton (1994a, 1994b) and Qian and Xu (1993) and some general issues of transition by Bolton and Roland (1992), Gates, Milgrom, and Roberts (1994), McAfee and McMillan (1994), Stiglitz (1991), and Tirole (1992).

4. State-firm productivity growth has been estimated, using various different data sets but obtaining similar productivity growth estimates, by Chen et al. (1988), Dollar (1990), Gordon and Li (1989), and Groves et al. (1994a, 1994c). One study, by Woo et al. (1993), claims productivity growth to be small, but this is hard to reconcile with the large increases in the state firms' output that have occurred.

5. In Russia's privatized firms, by contrast, little managerial turnover appears to be occurring, as Belyanova and Rozinsky (1994) show.

6. For a more detailed description of China's reform path than the simplified account given above, see Naughton (1994).

7. For some illuminating anecdotal accounts of how insecure property rights and inadequate contract enforcement in China make doing business difficult, see Lyons (1994).

8. Russia similarly lacks formal contract enforcement institutions. As in China, reputation-based incentives sometimes work to make contracts self-enforcing, as Greif and Kandel (1994) show, although in Russia the mafia is also used to enforce contracts.

9. In China's case, these short-run improvements have continued for a decade and a half.

10. As in the references in note 3 above, for example.

References

Belyanova, Elena, and Ivan Rozinsky. "Evolution of Commercial Banking in Russia and Its Implication in the Corporate Governance." Unpublished, Institute of World Economy and International Relations, Russian Academy of Science, April 1994.

Bolton, Patrick, and Gérard Roland. "Privatization in Central and Eastern Europe." *Economic Policy* (15 October 1992): 276–309.

Byrd, William A. "The Impact of the Two-Tier Plan/Market System in Chinese Industry." *Journal of Comparative Economics* 11 (1987): 295–308.

Byrd, W. A., and W. Li. *China's Rural Industry*. Oxford: Oxford University Press, 1990.

Chen, Kuan, Hongchan Wang, Yuzin Zheng, Gary H. Jefferson, and Thomas G. Rawski. "Productivity Change in Chinese Industry: 1953-1985." *Journal of Comparative Economics* 12 (1988): 570–91.

Clarke, Donald C. "The Creation of a Legal Structure for Market Institutions in China." In McMillan and Naughton (1994b).

Dollar, David. "Economic Reform and Allocative Efficiency in China's State-Owned Industry." *Economic Development and Cultural Change* 34 (1990): 89–105.

Fang, Xinghai. "Economic Transition: Government Commitment and Gradualism." In McMillan and Naughton (1994b).

Gates, Susan, Paul Milgrom, and John Roberts. "Complementarities in the Transition from Socialism: A Firm-Level Analysis." In McMillan and Naughton (1994b).

Gordon, Roger, and Wei Li. "The Change in Productivity of Chinese State Enterprises, 1983–1987: Initial Results." Unpublished, University of Michigan, 1989.

Greif, Avner, and Eugene Kandel. "Contract Enforcement Institutions: Historical Perpective and Current Status in Russia." In this volume.

Groves, Theodore, Yongmiao Hong, John McMillan, and Barry Naughton. "Autonomy and Incentives in Chinese State Enterprises." *Quarterly Journal of Economics* 109 (February 1994a): 183–209.

———. "China's Evolving Managerial Labor Market." Unpublished, UCSD, 1994b.

———. "Productivity Growth in China's State-Run Industry." In *China's State-Owned Enterprise Reforms*, ed. Dong Fureng, Cyril Lin, and Barry Naughton. London: Macmillan, 1994c.

Holmström, Bengt, and Jean Tirole. "The Theory of the Firm." In *Handbook of Industrial Organization*, ed. R. Schmaelensee and R. Willig. Amsterdam: North-Holland, 1989.

Jefferson, Gary H, and Thomas G. Rawski. "Enterprise Reform in Chinese Industry." *Journal of Economic Perspectives* 8 (Spring 1994): 47–70.

Lin, Justin Yifu. "Rural Reforms and Agricultural Growth in China." *American Economic Review* 82 (January 1992): 34–51.

Lyons, Thomas P. "Economic Reform in Fujian: Another View from the Villages." In

The Economic Transformation of South China, ed. Thomas P. Lyons and Victor Nee. Ithaca, N.Y.: East Asia Program, Cornell University, 1994.

McAfee, R. P., and J. McMillan. "Organizational Diseconomies of Scale." Unpublished, UCSD, 1994.

McMillan, John. "Vietnam's Grassroots Reforms." *International Economic Insights* 5 (March/April 1994): 33–35.

McMillan, John, and Barry Naughton. "How to Reform a Planned Economy: Lessons from China." *Oxford Review of Economic Policy* 8 (Spring 1992): 130–43.

———. "Evaluating the Dual-Track System." In *China's State-Owned Enterprise Reforms*, ed. Dong Fureng, Cyril Lin, and Barry Naughton. London: Macmillan, 1994a.

McMillan, John, and Barry Naughton, eds. *Reforming Asian Socialism: The Growth of Market Institutions*. Ann Arbor: University of Michigan Press, 1994b.

McMillan, John, John Whalley, and Lijing Zhu. "The Impact of China's Economic Reforms on Agricultural Productivity Growth." *Journal of Political Economy* 97 (August 1989): 781–807.

Morris, Derek, and Shaojia Guy Lui. "The Soft Budget Constraint in Chinese Industrial Enterprises in the 1980s." Unpublished, Oxford University, January 1993.

Naughton, Barry. *Growing out of the Plan: Chinese Economic Reform 1978–1993*. New York: Cambridge University Press, 1994.

Nee, Victor, and Sijin Su. "Local Corporatism and Informal Privatization in China's Market Transition." In McMillan and Naughton (1994b).

Qian, Yingyi. "Reforming Corporate Governance in China." Unpublished, Stanford University, April 1994.

Qian, Yingyi, and Joseph E. Stiglitz. "Institutional Innovations and the Role of Local Government in Transition Economies: The Case of Guangdong Province of China." In McMillan and Naughton (1994b).

Qian, Yingyi, and Chenggang Xu. "Why China's Economic Reforms Differ: The M-Form Hierarchy and Entry/Expansion of the Non-State Sector." *Economics of Transition* 1, no. 2 (June 1993): 135–70.

Sachs, Jeffrey, and Wing T. Woo. "Structural Factors in the Economic Reforms of China, Eastern Europe, and the Former Soviet Union." *Economic Policy* 18 (April 1994): 101–45.

Shirk, Susan L. *The Political Logic of Economic Reform in China*. Berkeley: University of California Press, 1993.

Stiglitz, Joseph E. "Theoretical Aspects of Privatization: Applications to Eastern Europe." Discussion Paper, Institute for Policy Reform, September 1991.

Tirole, Jean. "Privatization in Eastern Europe: Incentives and the Economics of Transition." In *NBER Macroeconomics Annual 1991*, ed. O. J. Blanchard and S. S. Fischer. Cambridge, Mass.: MIT Press, 1991.

———. "A Theory of Collective Reputations." Unpublished, Institut d'Economie Industrielle, Université des Sciences Sociales de Toulouse, 1993.

Whiting, Susan H. "Contract Incentives and Market Discipline in China's Rural Industrial Sector." In McMillan and Naughton (1994b).

Woo, W. T., W. Hau, Y. Jin, and G. Fan. "How Successful Has Chinese Enterprise Reform Been?" Unpublished, University of California, Davis, May 1993.

Contributors

ANNELISE ANDERSON is a senior research fellow at the Hoover Institution. She served as associate director of the Office of Management and Budget and as a member of the President's Commission on Privatization and the National Science Board. She has visited and consulted with policy makers in Czechoslovakia, Mongolia, Poland, Romania and Russia on banking, privatization, housing, crime and other issues. Her work has been translated and published in Russian. She has a Ph.D. from Columbia University.

PETER J. BOETTKE is an assistant professor of economics at New York University. He is the author of *The Political Economy of Soviet Socialism: The Formative Years, 1918–1928,* and *Why Perestroika Failed: The Politics and Economics of Socialist Transformation.* Boettke was a 1992–93 national fellow at the Hoover Institution.

JOHN COCHRANE, professor of economics and finance at the University of Chicago's Graduate School of Business, has also worked at the Council of Economic Advisers and the Department of Economics at Chicago. He received his Ph.D. in economics from the University of California at Berkeley. Primarily writing on macroeconomics, monetary economics, and finance, he has worked recently on health insurance and, together with Barry Ickes, has written several papers on macroeconomic aspects of reform in the former Soviet Union.

LARRY DIAMOND is senior research fellow at the Hoover Institution, coeditor of the *Journal of Democracy*, and codirector of the International Forum for Democratic Studies of the National Endowment for Democracy. He has written extensively on problems of democratic development around the world. Among his recent edited books are *Political Culture and Democracy in Developing Countries* and (with Marc F. Plattner) *Capitalism, Socialism, and Democracy Revisited* and *Nationalism, Ethnic Conflict, and Democracy*.

SUSAN GATES, a doctoral student at Stanford's Graduate School of Business, is writing her dissertation on restructuring and conversion in transitional economies. In the Russian Defense Conversion Project at the Center for International Security and Arms Control at Stanford, she is studying the problem of organizational decentralization in Russian defense enterprises. As a graduate student summer intern at the Rand Corporation, she worked on a project related to defense conversion and its impact on the California economy.

AVNER GREIF is an associate professor in the economics department at Stanford University. He has held visiting appointments at Tokyo and Tel Aviv Universities; fellowships at the Hoover Institution, the Center for Advanced Studies in the Behavioral Sciences at Stanford, and the Institute for Policy Reform in Washington; and three scholarships in the Institutional Reform and the Informal Sector Program at Maryland University. His main research concerns the role of institutions in the historical process of development.

BARRY W. ICKES, with a Ph.D. in economics from the University of California at Berkeley, has taught at Pennsylvania State University since 1983. He has also taught at Michigan, Pittsburgh, Rand, and the New Economic School in Moscow. He is a consultant to the World Bank and the Organization for Economic Cooperation and Development and has been a visiting scholar at the International Monetary Fund. With earlier research on economic organization under planning and on macroeconomic fluctuations in planned economies, he now focuses on the economics of transition.

SIMON JOHNSON is an assistant professor of economics at the Fuqua School of Business at Duke University and director of the Fuqua School of Business, Center for Manager Development, in Saint Petersburg. He is also a research associate at the Institute for Economic Analysis in Moscow. Professor Johnson has a Ph.D. from the Massachusetts Institute of Technology.

EUGENE KANDEL was born in Moscow and left the Soviet Union in 1977. He received his Ph.D. in economics from the University of Chicago's Graduate School of Business and is currently an assistant professor of organizations and markets at the University of Rochester's William E. Simon Graduate School of Business Administration. His research interests include industrial organization, organizational theory, and the economics of information, projects that he pursued while visiting Hebrew University's Department of Economics in 1993–94.

EDWARD P. LAZEAR, senior fellow at the Hoover Institution, is also a professor of human resource management and economics at Stanford University's Graduate School of Business, where he received the 1994 Distinguished Teaching Award. He was the 1993 Wicksell Lecturer in Stockholm and was previously the Brown Professor of Urban and Labor Economics at the University of Chicago's Graduate School of Business. He is the editor of the *Journal of Labor Economics* and is writing a textbook on personnel economics.

RONALD MCKINNON has taught at Stanford University, where he is now William E. Eberle Professor of International Economics, since receiving his Ph.D. from the University of Minnesota in 1961. His research has covered trade and financial liberalization to promote growth in developing countries, with extensive experience in Latin America and Asia. Recent work considers the problem of maintaining financial control in the transition from centrally planned to market economies in Eastern Europe and Asia, especially in China.

CHARLES MCLURE, senior fellow at the Hoover Institution, has advised many developing countries and international organizations. He chairs the Vice President's Working Group on Tax Reform in Kazakhstan. In Russia, Ukraine, and South Africa he has studied intergovernmental fiscal relations. Bolivia's president has asked him to design a cash-flow tax. His study of business taxation underlay Colombia's 1988 reforms. As deputy assistant secretary of the treasury, he developed recommendations to President Ronald Reagan underlying the 1986 Tax Reform Act.

JOHN MCMILLAN is professor of economics in the Graduate School of International Relations and Pacific Studies at the University of California at San Diego. A New Zealander, he previously taught at the University of Western Ontario, Canada. He has authored more than fifty articles on economic theory, applied macroeconomics, and international trade. His current research is on the reform of planned economies and the design of market institutions.

THOMAS GALE MOORE is a senior fellow at the Hoover Institution. He received his Ph.D. in economics from the University of Chicago. He has taught at the Carnegie Institute of Technology (now Carnegie Mellon University), Michigan State University, Stanford Business School, and the University of California at Los Angeles. He served on the staff of the President's Council of Economic

Advisers (1968–70) and was a member of the council (1985–89). His research and writing have been mainly on economic regulation and deregulation.

SHERWIN ROSEN is the Edwin and Betty Bergman Distinguished Service Professor of Economics at the University of Chicago and a senior research fellow at the Hoover Institution. He is a fellow of the American Academy of Arts and Sciences and the Econometric Society and an editor of the *Journal of Political Economy*. He has written on a variety of topics in labor economics and microeconomics.

Index